Taste of Home
Christmas

O9-BTO-742

TASTE OF HOME BOOKS • RDA ENTHUSIAST BRANDS, LLC • MILWAUKEE, WI

CHRISTMAS
STAR TWISTED
BREAD, 157

COVER PHOTOGRAPHER: Jim Wieland
COVER FOOD STYLIST: Lauren Knoelke
COVER SET STYLIST: Melissa Franco
PICTURED ON FRONT COVER: Gingerbread Buddies, page 196
PICTURED ON SPINE: Mediterranean Pastry Pinwheels, page 9
PICTURED ON BACK COVER: Crown Roast with Apricot Dressing,
page 89; Santa Deviled Eggs, page 37; Creamy Caramels, page
279; Citrus-Molasses Glazed Ham, page 109; Tropical Candy
Cane Freeze, page 15; Best-Ever Crescent Rolls, page 162
PICTURED ON TITLE PAGE: Garlic Herbed Beef Tenderloin,
page 93; Salted Peanut Rolls, page 272; Black Walnut Layer Cake,
page 218; Mocha Baked Alaskas, page 241; Appetizer Tortilla
Pinwheels, page 61; Easy Cocktail Party, page 52; Gift Mix Combo,
page 293; Peaches & Cream Waffle Dippers, page 80

© 2019 RDA Enthusiast Brands, LLC
1610 N. 2nd St., Suite 102
Milwaukee WI 53212-3906

INTERNATIONAL STANDARD BOOK NUMBER: 978-1-61765-764-1
LIBRARY OF CONGRESS CONTROL NUMBER: 2018939398

All rights reserved.

Taste of Home is a registered trademark
of RDA Enthusiast Brands, LLC.

Printed in China
1 3 5 7 9 10 8 6 4 2

641.5686
Tas

ORANGE POMEGRANATE SALAD
WITH HONEY, 143

CLASSIC CANDY CANE
BUTTER COOKIES, 185

TURKEY-STUFFED
ACORN SQUASH, 116

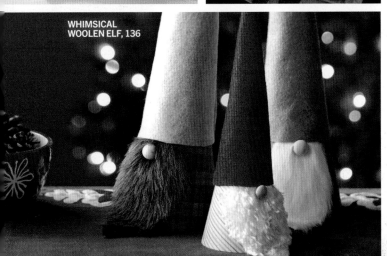

WHIMSICAL
WOOLEN ELF, 136

CHAPTER
CONTENTS

Holiday Helper

Look for these special **MAKE AHEAD** and **FAST FIX** icons that help you spend less time in the kitchen and more with family.

LIKE US
facebook.com/tasteofhome

TWEET US
twitter.com/tasteofhome

FOLLOW US
@ tasteofhome

PIN US
pinterest.com/taste_of_home

SHOP WITH US shoptasteofhome.com
SHARE A RECIPE tasteofhome.com/submit

MAKE YOUR HOLIDAY ONE TO REMEMBER

With all the recipes in this book, you have plenty of incredible options for your holiday party—whether it's a sit-down dinner, open house buffet or cocktail party. But once you've planned the menu, what else can you do to make sure your holiday celebration comes off without a hitch?

HOLIDAY HOSTING DO'S & DON'TS

Whether you're hosting the family feast or throwing a party for friends, if you spend more time stressing out than enjoying time with the people you love, it's time to take a different approach to planning. Here's a quick list of do's and don'ts to help you through your hosting duties.

DO plan a budget.
Even small, intimate get-togethers need a budget. Remember—the best parties aren't necessarily the most expensive. Before you shop, take inventory of the ingredients, decorations and dishes you already have; it'll save you time and money.

DON'T feel bad about asking guests to bring a dish.
If you have more spirit than cash, throwing a potluck party is always an option. Guests usually don't mind bringing food, especially if they have a must-have dish. But make sure you know what each guest plans to bring so you don't end up with all desserts!

DO get a head count.
Ask that guests RSVP, and follow up so you know how much room, food and other essential items you'll need. A firm head count actually makes it easier to fit in one or two unexpected guests.

DON'T underestimate cooking time.
Having more dishes to prepare than appliances to cook them in is a common problem. Read your recipes ahead of time and take into account not just cooking time but prep time and the tools needed for each dish.

DO make a grocery run a week before the party.
If your shopping is done early, you'll be able to cook, bake, decorate and set up without rushing. Picking up a few last-minute items is easier than a full-scale shopping trip the day before the party!

DON'T wait to clean your home until the day before.
Please. Just don't do it.

DO create ambiance.
Let your home create a holiday atmosphere. Christmas music sets the mood too, but it shouldn't be so loud that guests have to strain to talk.

DON'T do it all yourself.
Recruit help for the behind-the-scenes work. This is a great way to get preteens and older kids involved. 'Tis the season for helping one another, after all!

COMMON HOLIDAY COOKING MISTAKES...AND HOW TO FIX THEM

YOUR BAKED GOODS DON'T TURN OUT
The problem is usually the amount of flour. The amount of flour in a cup actually can vary dramatically. The best option is to use a kitchen scale to measure flour by weight. 1 cup of flour = 4.4 ounces or 125 grams.

YOU CHOSE A TRICKY NEW RECIPE
During the holidays, people often try new recipes outside their comfort zones. For the best results, read the recipe well in advance so you know the steps involved and can plan accordingly—no being caught off-guard by cookie dough that needs refrigeration before baking, or a cut of meat that needs hours of marinating.

YOU'RE COOKING WITH AN AUDIENCE
To avoid distraction, do any prep work you can before guests arrive. Organize your workspace and have the recipe and the equipment you need on hand. If time and space permit, have your ingredients measured and portioned out.

THE GRAVY IS LUMPY
Fix lumpy gravy by pouring it through a mesh strainer or pulsing it in a food processor.

THE MASHED POTATOES LOOK LIKE PASTE
Turn gluey potatoes into a gratin by spreading them in a thin layer in a baking dish. Top with butter, bread crumbs and cheese, and bake them until the top is crispy.

YOU BURNED THE SAUCE
Transfer the unburned portion into another pot, leaving the burnt layer behind, and continue cooking. If the smoky flavor is too strong, add stock and seasoning, tasting and adjusting as you go. This works for soup, too!

HOW MUCH FOOD? HOW MANY DRINKS?

Planning how much food to serve doesn't have to be daunting! Here's a quick guide to how many drinks and how much food to stock.

APPETIZERS

Each guest at a dinner party will have about six appetizers (12 if it's a cocktail party). Stock up on bulk items like nuts, pretzels and olives that can fill in any shortfall without drawing attention.

ENTREES AND SIDES

The list below estimates a serving size per person. Remember, the more options you offer, the smaller each portion will be.

Given a spread of tempting dishes, guests will take a little of each instead of a lot of just one.

- **Poultry, fish or meat:** 6 ounces
- **Grains:** 1.5 ounces as a side dish, 2 ounces as a main dish
- **Potatoes:** 5 ounces
- **Vegetables:** 4 ounces
- **Beans:** 2 ounces
- **Green salad:** 1 ounce
- **Bread:** 1-2 pieces

DRINKS

Several factors govern how many beverages you'll need, including the type of party, its duration and your guests. For a two-hour party:

- **Ice:** 1 pound per person
- **Nonalcoholic beverages:** One drink per person if alcohol is provided, three per person if alcohol isn't
- **Champagne:** 1.5 glasses per person for cocktails, three glasses per person at dinner
- **Wine:** One bottle of wine for every two adult guests
- **Spirits:** Three drinks per person (you'll get roughly 17 drinks per bottle)

DESSERTS

No matter how big the dinner, there's always room for dessert—especially at the holidays, when everyone looks forward to their favorite cakes or pies. Figure per guest:

- **Cake, tart or pastry:** 1 slice
- **Creamy desserts:** 4 ounces
- **Ice cream:** 5 ounces
- **Cookies:** 5-6 cookies—but these are the ultimate "just one more" treat, so err on the side of plenty. Also take the size of your cookies into account.

CRANBERRY COCKTAIL, HAM & CHEESE PUFFS AND
BACON-WRAPPED BLUE CHEESE SHRIMP, PAGE 32,
AND ONE-BITE TAMALES, PAGE 33

FESTIVE

APPETIZERS & BEVERAGES

VANILLA CITRUS CIDER

My mom used to make cider for the holidays, so I based my citrusy vanilla variation on her recipe. The longer the cider simmers, the stronger the flavors will be.

—Kristin Weglarz, Bremerton, WA

....

PREP: 10 min. • **COOK:** 70 min.
MAKES: 10 servings

- 8 cups apple cider or juice
- ¼ cup packed brown sugar
- ¼ cup thawed orange juice concentrate
- ⅛ tsp. salt
- 3 cinnamon sticks (3 in.)
- 1 tsp. whole cloves
- ¼ tsp. vanilla extract
  Apple slices, optional

1. In a large saucepan, combine the apple cider, brown sugar, orange juice concentrate and salt. Place cinnamon sticks and cloves on a double thickness of cheesecloth. Gather corners of cloth to enclose the seasonings; tie securely with a string. Add to pan.
2. Bring to a boil. Reduce heat; simmer, covered, for 1 hour to allow flavors to blend. Discard spice bag. Stir in vanilla. If desired, serve with orange slices.

❄ Holiday Helper

How to make vanilla extract
Use a sharp knife to slice down the middle of each of 6 vanilla beans, revealing the seeds. Do not scrape out the seeds.

Place the beans, with the seeds, in a tall jar with an airtight seal. Pour in 2 cups of vodka until the beans are covered by at least ½ in.

Seal the jar tightly. Let the beans soak for 6 weeks. Gently shake the jar once a week. After 6 weeks, open the jar. The extract is ready if it's deeply fragrant. Remove the beans and reseal the jar.

BAKED BRIE WITH MUSHROOMS

My sister craves this appetizer so much that I once made a batch and carried it on the plane when I flew to New Mexico to visit her. The combination of creamy Brie with earthy sauteed mushrooms is scrumptious.

—Melody Ansell, Portland, OR

....

PREP: 30 min. • **BAKE:** 15 min.
MAKES: 8 servings

- 1 Tbsp. butter
- 1 Tbsp. olive oil
- 1 lb. sliced fresh assorted mushrooms
- 2 small red onions, chopped
- ¼ tsp. salt
- ¼ tsp. pepper
- 5 garlic cloves, minced
- ⅔ cup port wine
- 1 round (8 oz.) Brie cheese
  Toasted French bread baguette slices

1. Preheat oven to 400°. In a large skillet, heat butter and oil over medium-high heat. Add mushrooms, onions, salt and pepper; cook until golden brown, 12-14 minutes, stirring occasionally. Add garlic; cook for 1 minute longer. Stir in wine. Bring to a boil; cook until liquid is almost evaporated.
2. Remove rind from the top of the cheese. Transfer to a 1½-qt. round baking dish. Top with mushroom mixture. Bake, uncovered, until cheese is melted, 15-20 minutes. Serve with baguette slices.
Test Kitchen tip: For assorted mushrooms, we recommend a mixture of white button, baby portobello, oyster and shiitake.

`MAKE AHEAD`
MEDITERRANEAN PASTRY PINWHEELS

These quick appetizers are irresistible on the plate, and the flavors of sun-dried tomatoes and pesto balance beautifully!

—Kristen Heigl, Staten Island, NY

....

PREP: 20 min. + freezing • **BAKE:** 15 min.
MAKES: 16 appetizers

- 1 sheet frozen puff pastry, thawed
- 1 pkg. (8 oz.) cream cheese, softened
- ¼ cup prepared pesto
- ¾ cup shredded provolone cheese
- ½ cup chopped oil-packed sun-dried tomatoes
- ½ cup chopped ripe olives
- ¼ tsp. pepper

1. Preheat oven to 400°. Unfold puff pastry; roll into a 10-in. square.
2. Beat cream cheese and pesto until smooth; stir in the remaining ingredients. Spread cheese mixture on pastry to within ½ in. of edges. Roll up jelly-roll style. Freeze 30 minutes. Cut crosswise into 16 slices.
3. Bake cut side down on a parchment paper-lined baking sheet until golden brown, 12-15 minutes.
Freeze option: Cover and freeze unbaked pastry slices on waxed paper-lined baking sheets until firm. Transfer to resealable plastic freezer bags; return to freezer. To use, preheat oven to 400°; bake pastries until golden brown, 15-20 minutes.

MAKE AHEAD

BUTTERNUT-GOUDA POT STICKERS

My family can't get enough butternut squash! I used pot sticker wraps to create these fun little appetizers.

—Carla Mendres, Winnipeg, MB

....

PREP: 45 min. • **COOK:** 15 min.
MAKES: about 4 dozen

- 1 small butternut squash (about 2½ lbs.)
- 1 Tbsp. butter
- 1 small sweet red pepper, finely chopped
- 1 small onion, finely chopped
- 2 cups shredded Gouda cheese
- ½ tsp. salt
- ½ tsp. minced fresh thyme or ⅛ tsp. dried thyme
- ½ tsp. pepper
- 1 pkg. (10 oz.) pot sticker or gyoza wrappers
- 3 Tbsp. canola oil, divided
- ¾ cup water, divided

1. Halve squash lengthwise; discard seeds. Place squash in a microwave-safe dish, cut side down; add ½ in. of water. Microwave, covered, on high until soft, 15-20 minutes; cool slightly. Scoop out pulp and mash.
2. In a skillet, heat butter over medium heat; saute pepper and onion until tender, 4-6 minutes. Add to squash; stir in cheese, salt, thyme and pepper.

3. Place 1 Tbsp. filling on each wrapper (keep the remaining wrappers covered with a damp towel). Moisten the edge of a wrapper with water; fold over to enclose filling, while pleating the front side to form a pouch. Stand pot sticker on a clean work surface to flatten bottom, curving ends slightly. Repeat until filling is gone.
4. In a large nonstick skillet, heat 1 Tbsp. oil over medium heat. Divide the pot stickers into three batches; working a batch at a time, place the pot stickers in pan; cook until the bottoms are lightly browned, 1-2 minutes. Add ¼ cup water (water may spatter); cook, covered, until filling is heated through, 3-4 minutes. Uncover; cook until bottoms are crisp and water is evaporated, 1-2 minutes.
Freeze option: Cover and freeze uncooked pot stickers on lightly floured baking sheets until firm. Transfer to resealable plastic freezer bags; return to freezer. To use, cook pot stickers as directed, increasing time as necessary to heat through.

FAST FIX

FESTIVE HOLIDAY PUNCH

This refreshing holiday punch has a gorgeous raspberry color and tangy flavor. To complete the magic, we use lime wedges to garnish the glasses.

—Tahnia Fox, Trenton, MI

....

TAKES: 5 min.
MAKES: 14 servings

- 1 bottle (64 oz.) cranberry-raspberry juice, chilled
- 1 can (12 oz.) frozen raspberry lemonade concentrate, thawed
- 1 bottle (2 liters) lemon-lime soda, chilled
  Fresh raspberries
  Ice cubes
  Lime wedges, optional

In a punch bowl, mix juice and lemonade concentrate. Stir in soda; top with fresh raspberries. Serve over ice. If desired, garnish glasses with lime wedges.

MAKE AHEAD

MUSHROOM, WALNUT & THYME CHEESECAKE

Cut thin wedges of this appetizer cheesecake to serve as a spread. With its buttery crust and savory filling, it always impresses guests.

—Erika Szymanski, Waitati, NZ

....

PREP: 35 min. + cooling
BAKE: 25 min. + chilling • **MAKES:** 24 servings

- 1 cup dry bread crumbs
- ¼ cup butter, melted
FILLING
- 1 Tbsp. butter
- ½ lb. baby portobello mushrooms, chopped
- 1 garlic clove, minced
- ⅓ cup chopped walnuts
- 1 Tbsp. minced fresh or 1 tsp. dried thyme
- 1 tsp. reduced-sodium soy sauce
- ¼ tsp. white pepper
- 2 pkg. (8 oz. each) cream cheese, softened
- ½ cup plain Greek yogurt
- 2 large eggs, lightly beaten
  Assorted crackers, baguette slices or sliced apples

1. Preheat oven to 325°. Mix bread crumbs and butter. Press onto bottom of a greased 9-in. springform pan. Place pan on baking sheet. Bake 15-17 minutes or until golden brown. Cool on a wire rack.
2. In a large skillet, heat the butter over medium-high heat. Add mushrooms; cook and stir until tender. Add garlic; cook 1 minute longer. Stir in walnuts; cook until toasted. Stir in the thyme, soy sauce and white pepper. Remove from heat and cool completely.
3. Beat cream cheese until smooth. Beat in yogurt. Add eggs; beat on low just until blended. Fold in mushroom mixture. Pour over the crust. Return pan to baking sheet.
4. Bake 25-30 minutes or until the center of the cheesecake is just set and the top appears dull. Cool 10 minutes on a wire rack. Loosen sides from pan with a knife. Cool 1 hour longer. Refrigerate overnight.
5. Remove the rim from the pan. Serve with crackers, baguette slices, or apples.

PIMIENTO CHEDDAR SPREAD

I was a theater major in college, and our director's mother always made sure we were well-fed. I was particularly fond of her pimento cheese sandwiches and I tried making a similar spread for crackers. It tastes just as good as I remember!
—Katrina Jameson, Brandon, MS

PREP: 15 min. + chilling • **MAKES:** 32 servings

- 1 pkg. (8 oz.) cream cheese, softened
- 2 jars (4 oz. each) diced pimientos, drained
- ¼ cup mayonnaise
- 2 Tbsp. finely chopped onion
- 4 cups shredded sharp cheddar cheese
  Saltines

In a large bowl, mix the cream cheese, pimientos, mayonnaise and onion until blended. Stir in the cheddar cheese. Refrigerate for at least 2 hours before serving. Serve with saltines.

❄ Holiday Helper

Pimientos are a mild, sweet red pepper; you can usually find them in the market sold in jars near the olives and other condiments. They are not the same thing as red bell peppers, but if you like, you can buy roasted red bell peppers—or roast your own!—and use them in place of pimientos in practically any recipe.

MAKE AHEAD
SPANAKOPITA BITES

Enjoy the taste of classic spanakopita without the hassle. This less-fussy version is cut into squares instead of triangle-shaped pockets.
—Barbara Smith, Chipley, FL

PREP: 20 min. + freezing • **BAKE:** 35 min.
MAKES: 10½ dozen

1	large egg, lightly beaten
1	pkg. (10 oz.) frozen chopped spinach, thawed and squeezed dry
2	cups crumbled feta cheese
1	cup 4% small-curd cottage cheese
¾	cup butter, melted
16	sheets phyllo dough (14x9-in.)

1. Preheat oven to 350°. In a large bowl, mix egg, spinach and cheeses. Brush a 15x10x1-in. baking pan with some butter.
2. Place one sheet of phyllo dough in the prepared pan; brush with butter. Layer with seven additional phyllo sheets, brushing each layer with butter. (Keep remaining phyllo covered with plastic wrap and a damp towel.) Spread with spinach mixture. Top with remaining phyllo dough, brushing each sheet with butter.
3. Freeze, covered, 30 minutes. Using a sharp knife, cut into 1-in. squares. Bake 35-45 minutes or until golden brown. Refrigerate leftovers.
Freeze option: Cover and freeze, unbaked, until ready to use. Cut and bake as directed.

MARINATED ALMOND-STUFFED OLIVES

Marinated stuffed olives go over so well with company that I try to keep a batch of them in the fridge at all times.

—Larissa Delk, Columbia, TN

PREP: 15 min. + marinating • **MAKES:** 8 cups

- 1 cup blanched almonds, toasted
- 3 cans (6 oz. each) pitted ripe olives, drained
- 3 jars (7 oz. each) pimiento-stuffed olives, undrained
- ½ cup white balsamic vinegar
- ½ cup dry red wine
- ½ cup canola oil
- 1 medium garlic clove, minced
- ½ tsp. sugar
- 1 tsp. dried oregano
- 1 tsp. pepper
- ½ tsp. dill weed
- ½ tsp. dried basil
- ½ tsp. dried parsley flakes

Insert an almond into each ripe olive; place in a large bowl. Add pimiento-stuffed olives with juice. In a small bowl, whisk vinegar, wine, oil, garlic, sugar and seasonings. Pour mixture over the olives. Refrigerate, covered, 8 hours or overnight, stirring occasionally. Transfer to a serving bowl.

❄ Holiday Helper

White balsamic vinegar differs from the traditional dark version in that the grape pressings (or "must") are blended with white wine vinegar and cooked at a low temperature to prevent the mixture from darkening. Dark balsamic vinegar is sweeter and white is milder, but the main motivation to opt for one over the other is aesthetic. Go for white balsamic when you don't want the color and syrupy cling of traditional dark balsamic vinegar.

MINI CRAB CAKES

Fresh crab is one of my all-time favorite foods. Whenever I get the opportunity to cook with it, I make this dish. These minis are amazing for appetizers; larger ones make a fantastic dinner paired with a simple salad.

—Ellen Riley, Murfreesboro, TN

PREP: 20 min. + chilling • **COOK:** 10 min./batch
MAKES: 16 appetizers

- ½ cup mayonnaise
- 1 Tbsp. dill pickle relish
- 1 tsp. prepared horseradish
- 1 tsp. Dijon mustard
- ½ tsp. hot pepper sauce
- ½ tsp. Worcestershire sauce

CRAB CAKES
- 1 large egg
- ¼ cup seasoned bread crumbs
- ¼ cup mayonnaise
- 1 green onion, chopped
- 1 Tbsp. minced fresh parsley
- 1 Tbsp. Dijon mustard
- ½ tsp. seafood seasoning
- ¼ tsp. hot pepper sauce
- 3 cups lump crabmeat, drained
- ¼ cup canola oil
- 16 dill pickle slices
   Minced chives

1. Mix the first six ingredients. Refrigerate, mixture, covered, until serving. For crab cakes, combine the egg, bread crumbs, mayonnaise, onion, parsley, mustard, seafood seasoning and pepper sauce. Fold in the crab. Refrigerate at least 30 minutes.
2. With floured hands, shape crab mixture into ½-in.-thick patties (2 Tbsp. of mixture each). In a large skillet, heat canola oil over medium heat. Add crab cakes in batches; cook until golden brown, 3-4 minutes on each side. Top each with a pickle slice and sauce. Sprinkle with chives.

GOAT CHEESE & ONION PASTRIES

Flaky puff pastry holds sweet caramelized onions and creamy goat cheese for this easy yet upscale appetizer. The recipe is a must on all of our entertaining menus.

—Heidi Ellis, Monument, CO

PREP: 30 min. • **BAKE:** 20 min. • **MAKES:** 1 dozen

- 6 bacon strips, chopped
- 2 large onions, finely chopped
- 3 shallots, thinly sliced
- ½ tsp. sugar
- ½ cup white wine
- 2 tsp. minced fresh or ½ tsp. dried thyme
- 2 garlic cloves, minced
- ¼ tsp. pepper
- 1 sheet frozen puff pastry, thawed
- 1 large egg white, beaten
- 1 log (4 oz.) fresh goat cheese, cut into 12 slices

1. Preheat oven to 400°. In a large skillet, cook bacon over medium heat until crisp, stirring occasionally. Remove with a slotted spoon; drain on paper towels. Discard the drippings, reserving 2 tsp. in pan. Add onions, shallots and sugar to drippings in pan; cook and stir until golden brown, 15-20 minutes.
2. Add wine, stirring to loosen browned bits from pan. Stir in thyme, garlic and pepper. Cook, uncovered, until liquid is evaporated, 2-3 minutes. Stir in bacon.
3. On a lightly floured surface, unfold puff pastry. Cut into three 9x3-in. rectangles. Transfer to a parchment paper-lined baking sheet. Brush dough with egg white; top with onion mixture and goat cheese. Bake until golden brown, 16-20 minutes. Cut each rectangle into four appetizers.

RICOTTA PUFFS

Ricotta cheese gives these pastry puffs a creamy, rich texture, while roasted red peppers add sweetness, Romano cheese adds tang and herbs lend their own spark.
—Maria Regakis, Saugus, MA

PREP: 20 min. • **BAKE:** 15 min.
MAKES: 1½ dozen

- 1   pkg. (17¼ oz.) frozen puff pastry, thawed
- ½   cup ricotta cheese
- ½   cup roasted sweet red peppers, drained and chopped
- 3   Tbsp. grated Romano or Parmesan cheese, divided
- 1   Tbsp. minced fresh parsley
- 1   tsp. dried oregano, crushed
- ½   tsp. pepper
- 1   tsp. 2% milk

1. Preheat oven to 400°. On a lightly floured surface, unfold puff pastry. Cut each sheet into nine squares. Mix ricotta cheese, red peppers, 2 Tbsp. Romano cheese, parsley, oregano and pepper.

2. Brush the edges of each pastry square with milk; place 2 rounded teaspoonfuls of cheese mixture in center of each square. Fold edges of pastry over the filling, forming a rectangle; seal edges with a fork. Cut slits in the pastry; brush with milk. Sprinkle with the remaining Romano cheese.

3. Place puffs 2 in. apart on lightly greased baking sheets. Bake until golden brown, 15-20 minutes. Remove to wire racks. Serve warm. Refrigerate leftovers.

FAST FIX

TROPICAL CANDY CANE FREEZE

When the Midwestern winter drags on and on, this frosty cold drink takes me away to a warm tropical beach! The recipe can easily be made family friendly by substituting water for the alcohol.
—Jennifer Stowell, Deep River, IA

TAKES: 10 min. • **MAKES:** 10 servings

- 1   can (10 oz.) frozen nonalcoholic pina colada mix
- 10   cups ice cubes, divided
- 1⅓   cups rum or 2 cups water, divided
- 1   can (10 oz.) frozen nonalcoholic strawberry daiquiri mix

In a covered blender, process pina colada mix, 5 cups ice and ⅔ cup rum (or 1 cup water) until blended. Repeat with the strawberry daiquiri mix and remaining ingredients. Slowly pour the prepared pina colada and prepared strawberry daiquiri by ¼ cupfuls into the center of 10 highball glasses, alternating layers. Serve immediately.

FAST FIX

WARM FETA CHEESE DIP

This super-easy baked dip is a mashup of some of our favorite ingredients. It goes well with a basket of crunchy tortilla chips or slices of French bread baguette.
—Ashley Lecker, Green Bay, WI

TAKES: 30 min. • **MAKES:** 2 cups

- 1   pkg. (8 oz.) cream cheese, softened
- 1½ cups crumbled feta cheese
- ½   cup chopped roasted sweet red peppers
- 3   Tbsp. minced fresh basil or 2 tsp. dried basil
     Sliced French bread baguette or tortilla chips

Preheat oven to 400°. Beat the cream cheese, feta cheese, peppers and basil until blended. Transfer to a greased 3-cup baking dish. Bake 25-30 minutes or until bubbly. Serve with baguette slices or chips. **Note:** To prepare in a slow cooker, mix ingredients as directed. Pour into a greased 1½-qt. slow cooker; cook, covered, on low 2-3 hours or until heated through.

❄ Reader Review

"I added this to a holiday appetizer night I hosted a few weeks ago, and everyone loved it. The feta cheese gives it a delicious salty kick and the cream cheese makes it so rich. It was super easy and I often have all of these ingredients on hand. I will definitely make this again!"

SHANNONDOBOS TASTEOFHOME.COM

BACON-WRAPPED SCALLOPS WITH PEAR SAUCE

I enjoy cooking for my parents, and they definitely enjoy my bacon-wrapped scallops. If you prefer, replace the pear preserves with preserves or jam of a different flavor.

—Ethan Hall, King, NC

PREP: 25 min. • COOK: 10 min.
MAKES: 1 dozen

- 12 bacon strips
- ¾ cup pear preserves
- 2 Tbsp. reduced-sodium soy sauce
- 1 Tbsp. brown sugar
- ¼ to ½ tsp. crushed red pepper flakes
- 12 sea scallops (about ¾ lb.)
- 1 tsp. olive oil
- ⅛ tsp. salt
- ⅛ tsp. pepper

1. Preheat oven to 375°. Place bacon in an ungreased 15x10x1-in. baking pan; bake 7-10 minutes or until partially cooked but not crisp. Remove to paper towels to drain; keep warm.
2. Meanwhile, in a small saucepan, combine the preserves, soy sauce, brown sugar and pepper flakes. Bring to a boil. Reduce heat; simmer, uncovered, for 3-5 minutes or until thickened.
3. Wrap a bacon strip around each scallop and secure with a toothpick. Sprinkle with salt and pepper. In a large skillet, cook in oil over medium-high heat for 5-7 minutes or until scallops are firm and opaque, turning once. Serve with pear sauce.

MAKE AHEAD
MULLED WINE

This mulled wine is soothing and satisfying with a delightful blend of spices warmed to perfection. Refrigerating overnight allows the flavors to blend, so don't omit this step!

—*Taste of Home* Test Kitchen

PREP: 15 min. • COOK: 30 min. + chilling
MAKES: 5 servings

- 1 bottle (750 milliliters) fruity red wine
- 1 cup brandy
- 1 cup sugar
- 1 medium orange, sliced
- 1 medium lemon, sliced
- ⅛ tsp. ground nutmeg
- 2 cinnamon sticks (3 in.)
- ½ tsp. whole allspice
- ½ tsp. aniseed
- ½ tsp. whole peppercorns
- 3 whole cloves
     Optional garnishes: orange slices, star anise and additional cinnamon sticks

1. In a large saucepan, combine the first six ingredients. Place the remaining spices on a double thickness of cheesecloth. Gather the corners of the cloth to enclose the spices; tie securely with string. Place in the saucepan.
2. Bring to a boil, stirring occasionally. Reduce heat; simmer gently, covered, for 20 minutes. Transfer to a covered container to cool slightly. Refrigerate, covered, overnight.
3. Strain mixture into a large saucepan, discarding fruit and spice bag; reheat. Serve warm. Garnish as desired.
Note: This recipe was tested with Rioja wine. Merlot would also work well.

LEMON-HERB SALMON TOASTS

Quick, light and tasty, these salmon toasts make irresistible finger food.
—Christie Wells, Lake Villa, IL

TAKES: 20 min. • **MAKES:** 2 dozen

- 1 pkg. (8 oz.) cream cheese, softened
- 4 green onions, chopped
- 2 Tbsp. snipped fresh dill or 2 tsp. dill weed
- ¾ tsp. sea salt
- ½ tsp. pepper
- ¼ tsp. cayenne pepper
- ¼ tsp. grated lemon zest
- 2 tsp. lemon juice
- 24 slices snack rye bread
- 8 oz. smoked salmon or lox
  Optional toppings: grated lemon zest, coarsely ground pepper and fresh dill sprigs

Preheat broiler. In a small bowl, beat the first eight ingredients. Place bread slices on baking sheets. Broil 4-5 in. from heat 1-2 minutes on each side or until lightly toasted. Spread with cream cheese mixture; top with lox. Top as desired.

CRANBERRY BOURBON

The subtle tang of cranberry and warm winter spices make this bourbon just right for holiday toasts—neat, on the rocks or in a cocktail.
—James Schend, Pleasant Prairie, WI

PREP: 10 min. + standing • **MAKES:** 20 servings

- 3 cups bourbon
- 1 cup dried cranberries
- 1 cinnamon stick (3 in.)
- 4 orange peel strips (3 in.)

In an airtight glass container, combine bourbon, cranberries, cinnamon stick and orange peel. Store in a cool, dry place for 2-4 weeks. Strain, discarding cranberries, cinnamon and orange peel. Return the bourbon to the glass container. Store in a cool, dry place.

❄ Holiday Helper

To prepare a Cranberry Manhattan:
Fill a shaker three-fourths full with ice. Add 2 oz. Cranberry Bourbon, ¾ oz. sweet vermouth and 2-3 dashes bitters; cover and shake until cold. Strain into a cocktail glass.

To prepare a Cranberry Old-Fashioned:
In a rocks glass, muddle an orange slice, cranberries and bitters. Add ice. Pour in 1½ oz. of Cranberry Bourbon, soda and juice to taste.

CALIENTE CHRISTMAS CHEESE CRISPS

To fire up the crowd, I pack these homemade crackers with bacon, pumpkin seeds and french-fried onion rings. For an extra kick, dunk them in picante sauce.

—Jeanne Holt, Mendota Heights, MN

PREP: 25 min. • BAKE: 15 min.
MAKES: 10 servings (3½ dozen)

- ¾ cup shredded extra sharp cheddar cheese
- ⅓ cup shredded pepper jack cheese
- ½ cup butter, softened
- ¼ tsp. garlic pepper blend
- ¼ tsp. ground cumin
- ⅛ tsp. salt
- 1 cup all-purpose flour
- ⅔ cup crispy brown rice cereal
- ¼ cup finely crumbled cooked bacon
- ¼ cup salted pumpkin seeds
- ¼ cup crumbled french-fried onions
  Pico de gallo or picante sauce, optional

1. Preheat oven to 350°. Beat the first six ingredients together until blended. Add flour; mix until a dough forms. Stir in the remaining ingredients (except optional sauce).
2. Shape dough into 1-in. balls. Place on ungreased baking sheets; flatten crackers with a lightly floured glass.
3. Bake until golden, 14-16 minutes. Remove to wire racks; cool completely. If desired, serve crisps with pico de gallo or picante sauce.
Note: For testing, we used Erewhon Crispy Brown Rice Cereal.

BAKED BABY POTATOES WITH OLIVE PESTO

These little cuties pack all the appeal of a baked potato into the perfect bite-sized appetizer. I top each one with a dollop of sour cream and coarsely ground pepper.

—Sarah Shaikh, Mumbai, IND

PREP: 35 min. • BAKE: 30 min.
MAKES: about 3 dozen

- 3 lbs. baby red potatoes (1¾ in. wide, about 36)
- 6 Tbsp. olive oil, divided
- 2 tsp. salt
- 1½ cups pimiento-stuffed olives
- ½ cup chopped onion
- ¼ cup pine nuts, toasted
- 2 garlic cloves, minced
- ½ cup sour cream
  Coarsely ground pepper, optional

1. Preheat oven to 400°. Place potatoes in a large bowl. Add 2 Tbsp. olive oil and salt; toss to coat. Transfer to a greased 15x10x1-in. baking pan. Bake until tender, 30-35 minutes.
2. Meanwhile, place olives, onion, pine nuts and garlic in a food processor; pulse until chopped. Gradually add the remaining oil; process to reach desired consistency.
3. When potatoes are cool enough to handle, cut thin slices off bottoms to allow potatoes to sit upright. Cut an X in the top of each potato; squeeze sides to open tops slightly. Place on a serving platter.
4. Spoon olive pesto onto potatoes; top with sour cream. If desired, sprinkle with pepper. Serve warm.
Test Kitchen tip: To toast nuts, bake in a shallow pan in a 350° oven 5-10 minutes or cook in a skillet over low heat until lightly browned, stirring occasionally.

STEAK & BLUE CHEESE BRUSCHETTA WITH ONION & ROASTED TOMATO JAM

Some of my favorite steakhouse flavors—ribeye, fresh tomato, sweet onion and blue cheese—inspired this bruschetta. It's hearty and delicious, and we make it for every party and holiday gathering.

—Debbie Reid, Clearwater, FL

PREP: 45 min. • GRILL: 10 min.
MAKES: 16 appetizers

    5   Tbsp. olive oil, divided
    1   large sweet onion, halved and thinly sliced
    1   cup grape tomatoes, halved
    ½   tsp. kosher salt, divided
    ¼   tsp. freshly ground pepper, divided
    6   oz. cream cheese, softened
    3   oz. crumbled blue cheese
    3   garlic cloves, minced
   16   slices French bread baguette (½ in. thick)
    2   beef ribeye steaks (¾ in. thick; 8 oz. each)
   1½   tsp. Montreal steak seasoning
    2   Tbsp. balsamic vinegar

1. Preheat oven to 400°. In large skillet, heat 2 Tbsp. oil over medium-high heat; saute onion until softened. Reduce heat to medium-low; cook until golden brown, 25-30 minutes, stirring occasionally.
2. Toss tomatoes with 1 Tbsp. oil, ¼ tsp. salt and ⅛ tsp. pepper; spread in a 15x10x1-in. pan. Roast until softened, 10-15 minutes. Stir tomatoes into the onion, mashing lightly. In small bowl, mix cream cheese, blue cheese, garlic and the remaining salt and pepper.
3. Brush bread slices with the remaining oil; grill, covered, over medium heat until lightly toasted, 1-2 minutes per side. Sprinkle steaks with steak seasoning. Grill, covered, over medium heat until meat reaches desired doneness (for medium-rare, a thermometer should read 135°; medium, 140°; medium-well, 145°), 3-5 minutes per side. Let stand 5 minutes before slicing.
4. To serve, spread toasts with the cheese mixture; top with sliced steak and the onion mixture. Drizzle with vinegar.

POMEGRANATE-GLAZED TURKEY MEATBALLS

A splash of pomegranate juice turns ordinary meatballs into something extraordinary. I love the sweet lightness of the glaze combined with the ground turkey, herbs and spices.

—Danielle D'Ambrosio, Brighton, MA

PREP: 30 min. • COOK: 10 min.
MAKES: 3 dozen

    1   large egg, beaten
    ½   cup soft bread crumbs
    ½   cup minced fresh parsley
    1   tsp. salt
    1   tsp. smoked paprika
    1   tsp. coarsely ground pepper
    ¼   tsp. garlic salt
   1¼   lbs. ground turkey
    3   cups plus 1 Tbsp. pomegranate juice, divided
    ½   cup sugar
    1   Tbsp. cornstarch

1. Preheat oven to 375°. In a large bowl, combine egg, bread crumbs, parsley, salt, paprika, pepper and garlic salt. Crumble turkey over the bread mixture and mix well. Shape into 1-in. balls.
2. Divide the meatballs between two ungreased 15x10x1-in. baking pans. Bake for 10-15 minutes or until a thermometer reads 165° and juices run clear.
3. Meanwhile, in a large skillet, combine 3 cups pomegranate juice and the sugar. Bring to a boil; cook until liquid is reduced to about 1 cup. Combine cornstarch and remaining juice; stir into skillet. Cook and stir for 1 minute or until thickened.
4. Gently stir in the meatballs and heat through. Serve in a slow cooker or chafing dish to keep warm.

FAST FIX

SANTA'S ORANGE-KISSED COCKTAIL

Refreshing but not overly sweet, this drink is a festive choice for Christmas get-togethers. Serve it during cocktail hour, at dinner or even for brunch in place of mimosas.

—Claire Beattie, Toronto, ON

TAKES: 5 min. • MAKES: 1 serving

        Ice cubes
- ¼   cup light rum
- ¼   cup unsweetened pineapple juice
- 1   Tbsp. lime juice
- 2   Tbsp. orange juice
- 1   tsp. grenadine syrup
- 3   Tbsp. lemon-lime soda

1. Fill a shaker three-fourths full with ice. Add rum, juices and grenadine syrup.
2. Cover and shake for 10-15 seconds or until condensation forms on the outside of the shaker. Strain into a chilled glass. Top with soda.

ROASTED RED PEPPER TAPENADE

When entertaining, I often rely on this recipe because it takes only 15 minutes to whip up and pop in the fridge. If you prefer, you can use walnuts or pecans instead of almonds.

—Donna Magliaro, Denville, NJ

PREP: 15 min. + chilling • MAKES: 2 cups

- 3   garlic cloves, peeled
- 2   cups roasted sweet red peppers, drained
- ½   cup blanched almonds
- ⅓   cup tomato paste
- 2   Tbsp. olive oil
- ¼   tsp. salt
- ¼   tsp. pepper
      Minced fresh basil
      Toasted baguette slices or water crackers

1. In a small saucepan, bring 2 cups water to a boil. Add garlic; cook, uncovered, just until tender, 6-8 minutes. Drain and pat dry. Place red peppers, almonds, tomato paste, oil, garlic, salt and pepper in a small food processor; process until blended. Transfer to a small bowl. Refrigerate at least 4 hours to allow the flavors to blend.
2. Sprinkle with basil. Serve with toasted baguette slices or water crackers.

ROSEMARY & THYME LEMON COCKTAIL

A bubbly drink means it's time to celebrate! Try dressing up the usual hard lemonade with sprigs of rosemary and thyme for a refreshingly different cocktail.
—Moffat Frazier, New York, NY

PREP: 5 min. + chilling • **MAKES:** 15 servings

- 5 fresh rosemary sprigs
- 5 fresh thyme sprigs
- 1 bottle (1¾ liters) lemonade

ADDITIONAL INGREDIENTS (PER SERVING)
- 1½ oz. vodka
  Ice cubes
- 2 oz. carbonated water, chilled

GARNISH
  Lemon slice, optional

1. In a 2-qt. pitcher, muddle rosemary and thyme; add lemonade. Cover and refrigerate overnight. Strain lemonade; discard herbs.
2. In a mixing glass or tumbler, combine ½ cup of lemonade and the vodka. Pour over ice in a highball glass; top with carbonated water. Garnish with a lemon slice if desired.

SPARKLING BERRY PUNCH

I often serve this refreshing nonalcoholic cranberry beverage at Christmastime, but it's a great choice for any special occasion. Add a few cranberries to each glass for extra flair.
—Kay Curtis, Guthrie, OK

TAKES: 10 min. • **MAKES:** about 2 qt.

- 6 cups cranberry juice, chilled
- 2 cans (12 oz. each) ginger ale, chilled
- ¼ tsp. almond extract
  Ice cubes

Combine all ingredients in a punch bowl or pitcher. Serve in a chilled glass over ice. Serve immediately.

CURRIED CRAB SPREAD

At holiday time, I always have cream cheese and crabmeat on hand. In case of drop-in guests, I can quickly mix up a spread by adding mango chutney and spices.
—Jennifer Phillips, Goffstown, NH

TAKES: 30 min. • **MAKES:** 24 servings

- 1 pkg. (8 oz.) cream cheese, softened
- 1 tsp. grated lemon zest
- ¾ tsp. curry powder
- ¼ tsp. salt
- 1 to 2 tsp. Sriracha Asian hot chili sauce, optional
- 1 can (6 oz.) lump crabmeat, drained
- 1 Tbsp. canola oil
- ½ cup panko (Japanese) bread crumbs
- ¾ cup mango chutney
- 1 Tbsp. minced fresh cilantro or chives
  Assorted crackers

1. In a small bowl, beat cream cheese, lemon zest, curry powder, salt and, if desired, chili sauce; gently fold in crab. Shape mixture into a disk; wrap in plastic. Refrigerate for 15 minutes.
2. Meanwhile, in a large skillet, heat oil over medium heat. Add bread crumbs; cook and stir 2-3 minutes or until golden brown. Transfer bread crumbs to a shallow bowl.
3. Unwrap disk and press all sides into bread crumbs; place on a serving plate. Spoon chutney over top; sprinkle with cilantro. Serve with crackers.

MARINATED OLIVE & CHEESE RING

We love to make Italian meals into full-on celebrations, and an antipasto always kicks off the party. This one is almost too pretty to eat…almost!

—Patricia Harmon, Baden, PA

PREP: 25 min. + chilling • **MAKES:** 16 servings

- 1 pkg. (8 oz.) cream cheese, cold
- 1 10-oz. block sharp white cheddar cheese, cut into ¼-in. slices
- ⅓ cup pimiento-stuffed olives
- ⅓ cup pitted Greek olives
- ¼ cup balsamic vinegar
- ¼ cup olive oil
- 1 Tbsp. minced fresh parsley
- 1 Tbsp. minced fresh basil or 1 tsp. dried basil
- 2 garlic cloves, minced
- 1 jar (2 oz.) pimiento strips, drained and chopped
   Toasted French bread baguette slices

1. Cut cream cheese lengthwise in half; cut each half into ¼-in. slices. On a serving plate, arrange cheeses upright in a ring, alternating cheddar and cream cheese slices. Place olives in center.

2. In a small bowl, whisk vinegar, oil, parsley, basil and garlic; drizzle over the cheeses and olives. Sprinkle with pimientos. Refrigerate, covered, 8 hours or overnight. Serve with baguette slices.

❄ Holiday Helper

This stylish appetizer is super adaptable. Any cheeses will work in place of the cream cheese and sharp cheddar—just keep the overall weight the same. For more variety, fold thin slices of deli cuts (such as salami and pepperoni) in half and tuck them between the cheese slices.

FAST FIX

CAMEMBERT & CRANBERRY PIZZAS

Appetizer pizza takes several steps up in elegance with creamy Camembert cheese. The bright red color and tangy flavor of the cranberries make this a welcome addition to any holiday party.

—Sue Sans, Buckeye, AZ

TAKES: 30 min. • MAKES: 2 dozen

1 tube (13.8 oz.) refrigerated pizza crust
1 can (14 oz.) whole-berry cranberry sauce
1 round (8 oz.) Camembert cheese, cut into ½-in. cubes
½ cup chopped pecans
Chopped fresh parsley, optional

1. Preheat oven to 425°. Unroll dough and press onto bottom and ½ in. up the sides of a greased 15x10-in. pan. Bake until golden brown, 6-8 minutes.
2. Place cranberry sauce in a bowl; stir to break into pieces. Spoon sauce over crust. Sprinkle with cheese and pecans. Bake until cheese is melted, 6-8 minutes. If desired, sprinkle with parsley. Cool on a wire rack 5 minutes. Cut into squares.

❄ Holiday Helper

Camembert is usually served at room temperature to allow it to soften, but for best results when using it in a recipe, refrigerate it and then use a sharp, clean knife and cut the cheese while it's cold. Cutting can be done early in the day. Just wrap the piecs of cheese tightly with plastic wrap or store in airtight containers and refrigerate.

FISH TACO BITES

These appetizers are even better than the full-size fish tacos I've had as an entree. Enjoy the creamy salsa drizzle not only on these bites but on other Mexican dishes, too.

—Carmell Childs, Clawson, UT

PREP: 30 min. • BAKE: 20 min.
MAKES: 3 dozen

½ cup salsa verde
4 oz. cream cheese, softened
2 Tbsp. lime juice, divided
2 Tbsp. minced fresh cilantro
1 tsp. honey
Dash salt
12 frozen breaded fish sticks
1 Tbsp. taco seasoning
36 tortilla chip scoops
1½ cups coleslaw mix
¾ cup cubed avocado
¾ cup chopped seeded tomato
Lime wedges and additional minced fresh cilantro

1. Preheat oven to 425°. In a blender, combine the salsa, cream cheese, 1 Tbsp. lime juice, cilantro, honey and salt. Cover and process until smooth; set aside.
2. Place fish sticks on a baking sheet. Bake for 10 minutes. Sprinkle with half of the taco seasoning. Turn fish sticks over; sprinkle with the remaining taco seasoning. Bake 7-9 minutes longer or until crisp.
3. Meanwhile, place tortilla chips on a serving platter. In a small bowl, combine the coleslaw mix, avocado, tomato, the remaining lime juice and ½ cup of the salsa mixture. Spoon into chips.
4. Cut each fish stick into three pieces. Place a piece in each chip; top with about ½ teaspoon salsa mixture. Garnish with lime wedges and additional cilantro.

HOT SAUSAGE & BEAN DIP

This is a spin-off of a Mexican dip I once had. The original was wicked good, but I was going through an I'm-so-over-Mexican-dip phase and decided to switch it up. If you take this one to a party you can be sure that no one else will bring anything like it!

—Mandy Rivers, Lexington, SC

PREP: 25 min. • BAKE: 20 min.
MAKES: 16 servings

1 lb. bulk hot Italian sausage
1 medium onion, finely chopped
4 garlic cloves, minced
½ cup dry white wine or chicken broth
½ tsp. dried oregano
¼ tsp. salt
¼ tsp. dried thyme
1 pkg. (8 oz.) cream cheese, softened
1 pkg. (6 oz.) fresh baby spinach, coarsely chopped
1 can (15 oz.) cannellini beans, rinsed and drained
1 cup chopped seeded tomatoes
1 cup shredded part-skim mozzarella cheese
½ cup shredded Parmesan cheese
Assorted crackers or toasted French bread baguette slices

1. Preheat oven to 375°. In a large skillet, cook sausage, onion and garlic over medium heat until sausage is no longer pink, breaking up sausage into crumbles; drain. Stir in wine, oregano, salt and thyme. Bring to a boil; cook until the liquid is almost evaporated.
2. Add cream cheese; stir until melted. Stir in spinach, beans and tomatoes; cook and stir until the spinach is wilted. Transfer to a greased 8-in. square baking dish; if using an ovenproof skillet, leave in the skillet. Sprinkle with cheeses.
3. Bake until bubbly, 20-25 minutes. Serve with crackers.

BRANDIED BLUE CHEESE SPREAD

Pour on the autumn spirit with a splash of brandy and three kinds of cheese. A topping of pumpkin seeds or pepitas make a crunchy contrast to the smooth spread.

—T.B. England, San Antonio, TX

....

PREP: 15 min. + chilling • **MAKES:** about 2 cups

    1   pkg. (8 oz.) cream cheese, softened
    1   pkg. (4 oz.) garlic-herb spreadable cheese
    ¾   cup crumbled blue cheese
    2   Tbsp. brandy
    1   shallot, finely chopped
    1   Tbsp. minced fresh parsley
    1   Tbsp. honey
    ⅛   tsp. salt
         Dash pepper
    ¼   cup salted pumpkin seeds or pepitas
         Assorted crackers

1. In a small bowl, mix the first nine ingredients until blended. Transfer to a serving dish; sprinkle with pumpkin seeds.
2. Refrigerate, covered, for 2 hours before serving. Serve with crackers.

FAST FIX

BRUSCHETTA WITH PROSCIUTTO

A crowd-pleaser any time of year, this savory appetizer is perfect for get-togethers.
—Debbie Manno, Fort Mill, SC

....

TAKES: 25 min. • **MAKES:** about 6½ dozen

    8   plum tomatoes, seeded and chopped
    1   cup chopped sweet onion
    ¼   cup grated Romano cheese
    ¼   cup minced fresh basil
    2   oz. thinly sliced prosciutto, finely chopped
    1   shallot, finely chopped
    3   garlic cloves, minced
    ⅓   cup olive oil
    ⅓   cup balsamic vinegar
    1   tsp. minced fresh rosemary
    ¼   tsp. pepper
    ⅛   tsp. hot pepper sauce, optional
    1   French bread baguette (10½ oz.),
         cut into ¼-in. slices

1. In a large bowl, combine the first seven ingredients. In another bowl, whisk the oil, vinegar, rosemary, pepper and pepper sauce if desired. Pour over the tomato mixture; toss to coat.
2. Place bread slices on an ungreased baking sheet. Broil 3-4 in. from the heat for 1-2 minutes or until golden brown. With a slotted spoon, top each slice with tomato mixture.

SPICED CRANBERRY-APPLE PUNCH

This festive and fruity punch is made with five kinds of juices plus cinnamon and allspice. It has a well-balanced flavor that's a delightful and surprising change of pace from the traditional holiday punch.
—Jennifer Stout, Blandon, PA

....

PREP: 10 min. • COOK: 4 hours
MAKES: 16 servings

- 4 cups apple juice
- 4 cups orange juice
- 2 cups cranberry juice
- 1 can (11.3 oz.) pineapple nectar
- ½ cup sugar
- 2 tsp. lemon juice
- 3 to 4 cinnamon sticks (3 in.)
- 8 whole allspice
- 8 to 10 orange slices
   Apple slices and fresh cranberries, optional

1. In a 5- or 6-qt. slow cooker, mix the first six ingredients. Place the cinnamon sticks and allspice on a double thickness of cheesecloth. Gather the corners of the cloth to enclose seasonings; tie securely with string. Place spice bag and orange slices in slow cooker. Cook, covered, on low for 4-5 hours to allow flavors to blend.
2. Discard spice bag and orange slices. If desired, top punch with apple slices and cranberries. Serve warm.

CURRIED MUSHROOM EMPANADAS

A rich mushroom filling spiced with mild curry and wrapped in flaky pastry cross Indian flavor with classic Mexican empanadas.
—Pat Cronin, Cotuit, MA

....

PREP: 20 min. + chilling • **BAKE:** 15 min./batch
MAKES: 3 dozen

- 1 cup butter, softened
- 1 pkg. (8 oz.) cream cheese, softened
- 3 cups all-purpose flour

FILLING

- 3 Tbsp. butter
- 3 Tbsp. olive oil
- 2 medium onions, finely chopped
- ½ lb. sliced fresh mushrooms, diced
- ½ lb. sliced baby portobello mushrooms, diced
- 2 Tbsp. all-purpose flour
- 2 tsp. curry powder
- ½ tsp. salt
- ⅛ tsp. pepper
- ½ cup half-and-half cream
  Mango chutney, optional

1. Cream butter and cream cheese until light and fluffy. Gradually beat in flour. Divide dough in half; flatten each into a disk. Wrap in plastic; refrigerate 1 hour or until easy to handle.

2. In a large skillet, heat butter and olive oil over medium-high heat. Add onions; saute until tender. Add mushrooms; saute until most of the liquid has evaporated, about 3 minutes. Reduce heat.

3. Combine flour, curry, salt and pepper; stir into skillet. Gradually add cream. Bring to a boil; cook and stir 1-2 minutes or until slightly thickened. Remove from heat.

4. On a lightly floured surface, roll dough to ⅛-in. thickness. Cut with a floured 3-in. round biscuit cutter. Place circles 2 in. apart on parchment paper-lined baking sheets. Place 1 Tbsp. filling on one side of each circle. Brush edges of pastry with water; fold circles in half. With a fork, press edges to seal; prick tops with a fork. Bake until golden brown, 12-15 minutes. Serve warm, with chutney if desired.

GINGERBREAD HOT COCOA

Are you in the Christmas spirit yet? If not, this special cocoa will do the trick. It's like drinking a chocolate gingerbread cookie!
—Erika Monroe-Williams, Scottsdale, AZ

TAKES: 15 min. • MAKES: 3 servings

- ¼ cup packed brown sugar
- ¼ cup baking cocoa
- 1 Tbsp. molasses
- 1½ tsp. ground cinnamon
- 1½ tsp. ground ginger
- ½ tsp. ground allspice
  Pinch salt
- 3 cups whole milk
- 1 tsp. vanilla extract
  Whipped cream

In a small saucepan, combine the first seven ingredients; gradually add milk. Cook and stir over medium heat until heated through. Remove from heat; stir in vanilla. Serve with whipped cream.

MUSHROOM & LEEK STRUDEL

This elegant hors d'oeuvre is almost effortless. Use fresh herbs if possible, and feel free to substitute whole wheat phyllo.
—Lisa Diehl, Edina, MN

PREP: 50 min. + cooling
BAKE: 20 min. + standing
MAKES: 2 strudels (12 slices each)

- 2 Tbsp. butter, divided
- 2 lbs. fresh mushrooms, finely chopped, divided
- 1 medium leek (white portion only), chopped, divided
- 2 garlic cloves, minced
- ¼ cup white wine
- ¼ cup heavy whipping cream
- 2 Tbsp. minced fresh parsley
- 1 Tbsp. minced fresh thyme or 1 tsp. dried thyme
- ½ tsp. salt
- ¼ tsp. pepper

ASSEMBLY
- 12 sheets phyllo dough (14x9 in.)
- ¾ cup butter, melted
- 4 Tbsp. grated Parmesan cheese, divided

1. In a large skillet, heat 1 Tbsp. butter over medium-high heat. Add half each of the mushrooms and leek. Cook and stir until mushrooms are lightly browned and leek is tender; remove from pan. Repeat with the remaining butter, mushrooms and leek, adding garlic during the last minute of cooking. Return all to pan.
2. Stir in wine and cream; cook 1-2 minutes or until the liquid is almost evaporated. Stir in herbs, salt and pepper. Remove from pan; cool completely.
3. Preheat oven to 375°. Place one sheet of phyllo dough on a work surface; brush with butter. Layer with five additional phyllo sheets, brushing each layer. (Keep the remaining phyllo covered with plastic wrap and a damp towel.)
4. Spoon half of the mushroom mixture down the center third of the phyllo dough to within 1 in. of ends. Sprinkle filling with 2 Tbsp. cheese. Fold up the short sides of the dough to enclose the filling. Roll up jelly-roll style, starting with a long side.
5. Transfer roll to a parchment paper-lined 15x10x1-in. baking pan, seam side down. Brush with additional butter. Repeat with the remaining ingredients. Bake for 18-22 minutes or until golden brown.
6. Let stand 10 minutes before slicing. Serve warm.

❄ *Reader Review*

"Excellent! I used some wild mushrooms I had dried and rehydrated them. I will make this again...for sure!"
DUBLINLAB TASTEOFHOME.COM

MEXICAN SHRIMP COCKTAIL

It's up to you how to enjoy this cocktail—eat it with a spoon as a chilled soup, or use tortilla chips or crackers for scooping.
—Erin Moreno, Arcadia, WI

PREP: 20 min. + chilling
MAKES: 12 servings (¾ cup each)

- 2 medium tomatoes, seeded and finely chopped
- 1 medium onion, finely chopped
- ½ cup chopped fresh cilantro
- 1 Tbsp. grated lime zest
- 1 tsp. salt
- 1 bottle (12½ oz.) mandarin natural flavor soda
- 1½ cups Clamato juice
- ¼ cup lime juice
- ¼ cup ketchup
- 1½ lbs. peeled and deveined cooked shrimp (100-150 per lb.)
- 2 avocados, finely chopped
  Tortilla chips

1. In a large bowl, combine the first five ingredients. Stir in soda, Clamato juice, lime juice and ketchup. Add shrimp. Refrigerate, covered, at least 2 hours.
2. Just before serving, add avocados. Serve with a slotted spoon and tortilla chips.

WHITE CHRISTMAS SANGRIA

This fruity sparkling sangria is alcohol-free, so everyone in your family can feel like a VIP.
—*Taste of Home* Test Kitchen

TAKES: 10 min. • **MAKES:** 21 servings (3¾ qt.)

- 6 cups white cranberry juice, chilled
- ¾ cup thawed lemonade concentrate
- 3 bottles (25.4 oz. each) sparkling grape juice
  Pomegranate seeds and sliced grapefruit, oranges and kiwi, optional

Combine cranberry juice and lemonade concentrate in a punch bowl; pour in sparkling grape juice. If desired, add pomegranate seeds and sliced fruit. Serve immediately.

GINGERED LEMON CHEESE BALLS

Roll your cheese balls in the gingersnap crumbs just before serving to keep the cookie bits crisp and crunchy—a nice contrast to the smooth, creamy spread underneath.
—Elizabeth Godecke, Chicago, IL

PREP: 15 min. + chilling
MAKES: 2 cheese balls (1½ cups each)

- 2 pkg. (8 oz. each) cream cheese, softened
- ½ cup butter, softened
- ⅓ cup sugar
- 3 Tbsp. light brown sugar
- 3 Tbsp. grated lemon zest
- 2 Tbsp. lemon juice
- 1 tsp. vanilla extract
- 10 gingersnap cookies, crushed
  Assorted sliced fresh fruit and graham crackers

1. In a large bowl, beat cream cheese, butter and sugars until smooth. Stir in lemon zest, juice and vanilla. Shape into two balls. Cover and refrigerate for at least 4 hours.

2. Just before serving, place the gingersnap crumbs in a shallow bowl. Roll cheese balls in crumbs. Serve with fruit and crackers.

MAPLE BRANDY PUNCH

Reminiscent of an old-fashioned brandy punch, this smooth, maple-infused beverage adds extra pizzazz to holiday dinner parties and other special occasions.
—*Taste of Home* Test Kitchen

PREP: 20 min. + cooling • MAKES: 20 servings

1⅓ cups maple syrup
2 cups apple brandy
2 cups Cognac
2 cups spiced rum
¼ cup lemon juice
2 tsp. bitters
2 bottles (1 liter each) carbonated
    water, chilled
    Ice cubes
    Thinly sliced apples and lemon twists

1. Place syrup in a small saucepan. Bring to a boil. Reduce heat; simmer, uncovered, for 5 minutes. Remove from heat and set aside to cool.
2. Combine the brandy, Cognac, rum, lemon juice and bitters in a punch bowl; stir in the maple reduction. Add the carbonated water. Serve over ice with apple slices and lemon twists.

TUSCAN TRUFFLES

For holiday potlucks, I make an appetizer truffle out of prosciutto, figs and toasted pine nuts. The creaminess comes from mascarpone and goat cheese.
—Roxanne Chan, Albany, CA

PREP: 25 min. + chilling • MAKES: 3 dozen

2 logs (4 oz. each) fresh goat cheese
1 carton (8 oz.) mascarpone cheese
6 Tbsp. grated Parmesan cheese
3 garlic cloves, minced
1½ tsp. olive oil
1½ tsp. white balsamic vinegar
¾ tsp. grated lemon zest
3 oz. (6 Tbsp.) chopped prosciutto
3 oz. (6 Tbsp.) finely chopped dried figs
3 Tbsp. minced fresh parsley
¼ tsp. pepper
1 cup pine nuts, toasted and chopped

Combine the first 11 ingredients until well blended. Shape into 36 balls; roll in pine nuts. Refrigerate, covered, until serving.
Note: To toast nuts, bake in a shallow pan in a 350° oven for 5-10 minutes or cook in a skillet over low heat until lightly browned, stirring occasionally.

❋ Holiday Helper

Also known as pignolia or pinon, the pine nut is the small seed from one of several pine tree varieties. They are small, elongated, ivory-colored nuts measuring about ⅜ in. long and having a soft texture and a buttery flavor. Frequently used in Italian dishes and sauces such as pesto, pine nuts are often toasted to enhance their flavor.

FAST FIX

CRANBERRY COCKTAIL

I adore the combination of flavors in this recipe. Thaw the lemonade so it's still slightly icy to make the cocktail cool and refreshing. For a no-alcohol option, swap peach juice and lemon-lime soda for the schnapps and vodka.

—Julie Danler, Bel Aire, KS

....

TAKES: 10 min. • **MAKES:** 4 servings

    Ice cubes
4   oz. vodka
4   oz. peach schnapps liqueur
4   oz. thawed lemonade concentrate
4   oz. cranberry-raspberry juice
16 maraschino cherries

1. Fill a shaker three-fourths full with ice cubes.
2. Add vodka, schnapps, lemonade concentrate and juice to shaker; cover and shake for 10-15 seconds or until condensation forms on outside of shaker. Strain into four cocktail glasses. Place a skewer with four cherries in each glass.

FAST FIX

HAM & CHEESE PUFFS

These marvelous little bites go over well with kids of all ages. They're also good with soups and many of the items you'd expect to find on a buffet table.

—Marvin Buffington, Burlington, IA

....

TAKES: 30 min. • **MAKES:** 2 dozen

1   pkg. (2½ oz.) thinly sliced deli ham, chopped
1   small onion, chopped
½   cup shredded Swiss cheese
1   large egg
1½ tsp. Dijon mustard
⅛   tsp. pepper
1   tube (8 oz.) refrigerated crescent rolls

1. Preheat oven to 375°. Combine the first six ingredients. Divide crescent dough into 24 portions. Press dough into greased mini muffin cups.
2. Spoon 1 tablespoon of the ham mixture into each cup. Bake until golden brown, 13-15 minutes.

BACON-WRAPPED BLUE CHEESE SHRIMP

Blue cheese, bacon and basil pack big flavor into a few bites. To save time, assemble the skewers the night before and then serve them hot from the broiler on the day of the meal.

—Vivi Taylor, Middleburg, FL

....

PREP: 30 min. • **COOK:** 10 min.
MAKES: 16 appetizers

¼   cup butter, melted
1   garlic clove, minced
1   tsp. hot pepper sauce
16 uncooked shrimp (16-20 per lb.), peeled and deveined
¼   tsp. salt
⅛   tsp. pepper
16 cubes blue cheese (½ in.)
16 fresh basil leaves
8   bacon strips, halved
¼   cup finely chopped celery
¼   cup crumbled blue cheese
1   Tbsp. minced fresh basil

1. Preheat broiler. Combine butter, garlic and pepper sauce. Cut a slit in each shrimp along the inside curve; flatten slightly. Sprinkle shrimp with salt and pepper. Press a cheese cube into slit. Wrap a basil leaf and bacon piece around each shrimp; secure with a toothpick.
2. Place shrimp on the greased rack of a broiler pan. Broil 6-8 in. from heat until the shrimp turn pink and the bacon is crisp, 5-6 minutes per side; basting occasionally with butter mixture.
3. Arrange the shrimp on a serving platter; sprinkle with celery, crumbled blue cheese and basil.

ONE-BITE TAMALES

These clever little meatballs deliver all the flavor and rich sauce of a traditional tamale in a bite-sized portion. They're a delightfully different addition to a holiday spread.

—Dolores Jaycox Gretna, LA

PREP: 40 min. • COOK: 3 hours 20 min.
MAKES: about 5½ dozen

1¼ cups cornmeal
½ cup all-purpose flour
5¾ cups V8 juice, divided
4 teaspoons chili powder, divided
4 teaspoons ground cumin, divided
2 teaspoons salt, divided
1 teaspoon garlic powder
½ to 1 teaspoon cayenne pepper
1 pound bulk spicy pork sausage
   Tortilla chip scoops

1. Preheat oven to 350°. Mix cornmeal, flour, ¾ cup of V8 juice, 2 teaspoons chili powder, 2 teaspoons cumin, 1 teaspoon salt, the garlic powder and cayenne. Add sausage; mix lightly but thoroughly. Shape into 1-in. balls.
2. Place meatballs on a greased rack in a 15x10-in. pan. Bake until cooked through, 20-25 minutes.
3. Meanwhile, in a 4-qt. slow cooker, mix the remaining V8 juice, chili powder, cumin and salt. Gently stir in meatballs. Cook, covered, on low until heated through, 3-4 hours. Serve with tortilla chip scoops.

MUFFIN TIN ADVENT CALENDAR

Every day brings a new surprise with this delightful homemade Advent calendar!

By hand or with a circle punch, cut 24 circles of scrapbook paper large enough to cover the openings in a 24-opening metal muffin tin. (You can make a more petite version using a mini-muffin tin, too!) Cut 24 smaller circles in a complementary color of paper. Use double-sided tape to secure the smaller circles on top of the larger circles. Add glitter glue around the edge of each smaller circle; let dry. Decorate as desired with holiday-themed stickers, and use adhesive scrapbook numbers (or cut-out numbers secured with glue) to label the circles 1 to 24.

To make the magnets, glue buttons to the tops of 24 small, round magnets. Place a piece of candy or a small toy in each cup, place a numbered circle over each opening, and use a button magnet to hold each circle in place over its cup. Remove the magnet to open one cup daily as you count down to Christmas.

FELIZ NAVIDAD
PARTY, PAGE 56

JOLLY

HOLIDAY PARTIES

CHRISTMAS TOY DRIVE

It's all about sharing the spirit of the season! Throw a toy collection party and ask each guest to bring a toy to be delivered to a selected charity. Then serve up a scrumptious lunch to spread the cheer even more. This is a great event for getting children involved, so they can know the joy of giving and sharing at the holiday season.

[MAKE AHEAD]

SWEET & SAVORY CHEESE PIE

Layer ruby red preserves on a savory appetizer spread as the crowning touch.

—Annette Whitmarsh, Lincoln, NE

PREP: 15 min. + chilling • **MAKES:** 32 servings

- 1 cup chopped pecans
- 1 pkg. (8 oz.) cream cheese, softened
- ½ cup mayonnaise
- 4 cups shredded sharp cheddar cheese
- 6 green onions, chopped
- ½ lb. bacon strips, cooked and crumbled
- 1 jar (10 oz.) seedless raspberry or strawberry preserves
  Sliced green onions, optional
  Assorted crackers

1. Spread pecans evenly over bottom of a greased 9-in. springform pan. In a large bowl, beat cream cheese and mayonnaise until smooth. Stir in cheddar cheese, green onions and bacon. Carefully spread over pecans. Refrigerate, covered, overnight.
2. Loosen sides from the pan with a knife; remove rim from pan. Spread preserves over top. If desired, top with sliced onions. Serve with crackers.

❄ Holiday Helper

When choosing crackers to accompany this rich and delicious cheese pie, opt for mild and understated. Steer clear of strong or sharp flavors like rye or cracked black pepper; the balance between the sweetness of the preserves and the tang of the cheddar is better served by a buttery, plain cracker.

SANTA DEVILED EGGS

I love creating special deviled eggs for parties. These little Santas are easy to make and everyone raves over them.

—Crystal Schlueter, Babbitt, MN

PREP: 40 min. • **MAKES:** 2 dozen

- 12 hard-boiled large eggs
  Hot water
- 2 tsp. red food coloring
- ½ cup mayonnaise
- 4½ tsp. Dijon mustard
- 1 Tbsp. sweet pickle relish
- ¼ tsp. paprika
- 1 Tbsp. horseradish sauce, optional
- 1 Tbsp. capers, drained
- 1 to 2 oz. thick sliced deli ham, cut into 24 pieces
- ½ roasted sweet red pepper strips, cut into 24 thin pieces
- ⅓ cup cream cheese, softened

1. Peel and cut eggs lengthwise in half. Remove yolks and place in a small bowl. Fill a mug ⅓ full with hot water. Stir in food coloring. Dip the narrow end of each egg white into the colored water and hold for 10-15 seconds. Drain egg whites on paper towels, cut side up.
2. Mash the yolks. Stir in mayonnaise, mustard, pickle relish, paprika and, if desired, horseradish sauce. Spoon or pipe yolk mixture into each egg white. Place capers for eyes, a ham piece for a nose and a pepper piece for a mouth.
3. Insert a #16 star pastry tip in a pastry bag or in a food-safe plastic bag with a small hole cut in one corner. Fill bag with cream cheese. Pipe eyebrows, mustache and beard on face; pipe pom-pom and trim on hat. Refrigerate, covered, until serving.

SLOW COOKER ITALIAN BEEF SANDWICHES

I have fond memories of my mother in the kitchen preparing her amazing beef dip sandwiches. They always made our house smell like an old-world Italian restaurant. As good as the aroma was, somehow the taste was even better. If you like, set out a jar of giardiniera to spoon on top.

—Kira Vosk, Milwaukee, WI

PREP: 1 hour • **COOK:** 7 hours
MAKES: 12 servings

- 4 Tbsp. olive oil, divided
- 1 boneless beef chuck eye or other boneless beef chuck roast (4 to 5 lbs.)
- 2¼ tsp. salt, divided
- 2¼ tsp. pepper, divided
- 2 small onions, coarsely chopped
- 9 garlic cloves, chopped
- ¾ cup dry red wine
- 4 cups beef stock
- 3 fresh thyme sprigs
- 4 tsp. Italian seasoning
- 1½ tsp. crushed red pepper flakes
- 4 medium green peppers, cut into ½-in. strips
- 1 tsp. garlic powder
- 12 crusty submarine buns or hoagie buns, split partway
- 12 slices provolone or part-skim mozzarella cheese
  Giardiniera, optional

1. In a 6-qt. stockpot, heat 3 Tbsp. oil over medium-high heat; brown roast on all sides. Sprinkle with 2 tsp. each salt and pepper. Transfer to a 6-qt. slow cooker.
2. Add onions to stockpot; cook and stir 2-3 minutes or lightly browned. Add garlic; cook 30 seconds longer. Add wine; cook 3-5 minutes, stirring to loosen browned bits from pan. Stir in stock, thyme, Italian seasoning and pepper flakes; transfer to the slow cooker. Cook, covered, on low for 7-9 hours or until the beef is tender.
3. About 30 minutes before serving, preheat oven to 350°. Place peppers in a 15x10x1-in. baking pan. Drizzle with the remaining oil. Sprinkle with garlic powder and the remaining salt and pepper; toss to coat. Roast 15-20 minutes or until softened, stirring halfway.
4. Remove roast; cool slightly. Strain cooking juices into a small saucepan, reserving strained mixture and removing thyme stems. Skim fat from juices; heat through and keep warm. Coarsely shred beef with two forks; stir in reserved strained mixture. If desired, moisten beef with some of the cooking juices.
5. To serve, preheat the broiler. Arrange buns on baking sheets, cut side up. Broil 3-4 in. from heat until lightly toasted. Remove from oven; top each bun with ⅔ cup of the beef mixture and 1 slice of cheese. Broil until the cheese is melted, about 30 seconds.
6. Top with green peppers and, if desired, giardiniera. Serve sandwiches with cooking juices for dipping.

BACON & BROCCOLI SALAD

You'll want to serve this family friendly side dish year-round. The broccoli gets a big flavor boost from bacon, toasted pecans, dried berries and a mayo dressing.

—Cindi Read, Hendersonville, TN

TAKES: 30 min.
MAKES: 16 servings

- 3 bunches broccoli, cut into florets (about 10 cups)
- 1 lb. bacon strips, cooked and crumbled
- 1 cup chopped pecans, toasted
- 1 cup dried blueberries
- 1 cup dried cherries
- ¼ cup finely chopped red onion

DRESSING
- 1 cup mayonnaise
- ¼ cup sugar
- ¼ cup cider vinegar

In a large bowl, combine the first six ingredients. For dressing, in a small bowl, whisk mayonnaise, sugar and vinegar. Pour over the broccoli mixture; toss to coat.

WALDORF ORANGE CINNAMON HOLIDAY MOLD

My family prefers this to traditional cranberry gelatin molds. The cinnamon zing really complements both ham and turkey.

—Nancy Heishman, Las Vegas, NV

PREP: 15 min. + chilling
MAKES: 12 servings

- 2 pkg. (3 oz. each) cherry gelatin
- ½ cup Red Hots
- ⅓ cup sugar
- 1½ cups water
- 1¾ cups orange juice
- ⅓ cup sour cream
- 1½ cups orange sections, chopped
- 1 medium apple, peeled and finely chopped
- ½ cup chopped pecans

Place gelatin in a large bowl. In a small saucepan, combine Red Hots, sugar and water. Cook and stir until the candies are dissolved and the mixture comes to a boil. Stir into the gelatin. Stir in orange juice and sour cream. Refrigerate 30-45 minutes or until thickened. Stir in orange, apple and pecans. Pour into a 6-cup ring mold coated with cooking spray. Refrigerate for 4 hours or until firm. Unmold onto a platter.

FOUR-LAYER CHOCOLATE DESSERT

With creamy layers in a big 13x9-in. pan, this simple dessert is tailor-made for a buffet table. Toasted slivered almonds on top are the perfect finishing touch.

—Linda Knoll, Jackson, MI

PREP: 20 min. • **BAKE:** 15 min. + chilling
MAKES: 15 servings

- 2 cups all-purpose flour
- ¾ cup cold butter
- 1 cup finely chopped pecans
- 1 pkg. (8 oz.) cream cheese, softened
- 1 cup confectioners' sugar
- 1 cup whipped topping
- 3 cups cold whole milk
- 2 pkg. (3.9 oz. each) instant chocolate pudding mix
- 2 cups heavy whipping cream, whipped
- ½ cup slivered almonds, toasted

1. Place flour in a bowl; cut in butter until crumbly. Stir in pecans. Press onto the bottom of an ungreased 13x9-in. baking dish. Bake at 350° for 15-20 minutes or until lightly browned. Cool on a wire rack.
2. Beat cream cheese and confectioners' sugar until smooth; fold in the whipped topping. Spread over the crust.
3. Whisk milk and pudding mixes for 2 minutes. Let stand for 2 minutes or until soft-set. Gently spread over cream cheese layer. Top with whipped cream; sprinkle with almonds. Refrigerate until cold.

KNIT MITTEN GARLAND

Evoke memories of winters past with this garland of mini mittens! Depending on the space you have to fill, use either real child-sized mittens or smaller, mitten-shaped pieces cut from an upcycled sweater, machine-knit material or thick fabric. Stitch brightly colored buttons onto the mittens with embroidery floss. To make the garland base, stretch a length of string or yarn across the edge of a shelf or mantelpiece, and use pushpins to secure it in place. Use miniature clothespins to attach the mittens to the string, spacing them evenly. It's as if they're hanging by the fire to dry after a day spent sledding!

CHRISTMAS MORNING BREAKFAST

Whether it's a family breakfast after the presents have all been opened or a celebratory brunch with a group of dear friends, this special day deserves a special breakfast. Take the time to sit down together at the table and savor the flavors of the season. Go sweet, savory or both—it's all delicious!

MAKE AHEAD

PEAR-STUFFED FRENCH TOAST WITH BRIE, CRANBERRIES & PECANS

This French toast is stuffed with fresh pears, dried cranberries, pecans, Brie and cream cheese. The elegant, rich and indulgent dish is surprisingly easy and gets prepped the night before—perfect for a special occasion!

—Lindsay Sprunk, Brooklyn, NY

PREP: 35 min. + chilling
BAKE: 35 min. + standing
MAKES: 10 servings

- 2 Tbsp. butter
- 4 medium pears, peeled and thinly sliced
- 3 Tbsp. packed brown sugar, divided
- 1 pkg. (8 oz.) cream cheese, softened
- ½ cup dried cranberries
- ⅓ cup chopped pecans, toasted
- 20 slices French bread (½ in. thick)
- 1 round (8 oz.) Brie cheese, rind removed and thinly sliced
- 3 large eggs
- 2 cups 2% milk
- 3 tsp. vanilla extract
- ½ tsp. ground cinnamon
- ¼ tsp. salt
  Maple syrup, optional

1. In a large skillet, heat butter over medium heat. Add pears and 2 Tbsp. brown sugar; cook and stir until the pears are tender, 4-6 minutes. In a bowl, mix cream cheese, cranberries and pecans.
2. Place half the bread slices in a greased 13x9-in. baking dish. Layer with the cream cheese mixture, pear mixture and Brie. Top with remaining bread slices. Whisk together the next five ingredients and the remaining brown sugar. Pour over bread. Refrigerate, covered, overnight.
3. Preheat oven to 375°. Remove from refrigerator and let stand while oven heats. Bake, uncovered, until top is golden brown, 35-40 minutes. Let stand 10 minutes before serving. If desired, serve with syrup.

CINNAMON APPLE CIDER MONKEY BREAD

I use cold-weather staples—cinnamon and apple cider—to turn plain cinnamon rolls into monkey bread. It's a hit with my boys, who love the sticky sweetness.

—Kelly Walsh, Aviston, IL

PREP: 20 min. • BAKE: 45 min. + standing
MAKES: 16 servings

- 5 envelopes (.74 oz. each) instant spiced cider mix
- 3 tubes (12.4 oz. each) refrigerated cinnamon rolls with icing
- 2 medium Granny Smith apples, peeled and chopped
- 1 cup chopped pecans or walnuts
- 6 Tbsp. butter, melted
- 2 tsp. ground cinnamon

1. Preheat oven to 350°. Combine cider mixes. Separate cinnamon rolls, setting aside icings; cut each roll into quarters. Add to cider mixture; toss to coat.
2. Arrange a third of the dough pieces in a well-greased 10-in. fluted tube pan; top with half of the apples and half of the pecans. Repeat layers once. Top with remaining dough.
3. Mix melted butter, cinnamon and one container of icing until blended. Drizzle over top of rolls. Bake until golden brown, 45-50 minutes. (If needed, cover the top loosely with foil during last 5 minutes to prevent overbrowning.)
4. Immediately invert monkey bread onto a serving plate; keep pan inverted for 10 minutes, allowing bread to release. Microwave the remaining icing, uncovered, until softened, about 10 seconds. Remove the pan and drizzle icing over monkey bread. Serve warm.

MAKE AHEAD
SPARKLING ORANGES

We were living in Texas when I found the recipe for this simple, elegant salad. I was thrilled—we had a surplus of fresh oranges! Since it's prepared ahead, there's no last-minute fuss.
—Janie Bush, Weskan, KS

PREP: 35 min. + chilling • **MAKES:** 8 servings

- ½ cup sugar
- ½ cup orange marmalade
- 1 cup white grape juice
- ½ cup lemon-lime soda
- 8 large oranges, peeled and sectioned
- 3 Tbsp. slivered almonds, toasted
- 3 Tbsp. sweetened shredded coconut, toasted

1. In a small saucepan over medium heat, combine sugar and marmalade; cook and stir until sugar is dissolved. Remove from heat. Stir in grape juice and soda. Pour over orange sections; toss to coat. Refrigerate, covered, overnight.
2. Using a slotted spoon, remove oranges to a serving dish. Sprinkle with almonds and coconut.
Note: To toast nuts and coconut, bake in separate shallow pans in a 350° oven for 5-10 minutes or until golden brown, stirring occasionally.

FAST FIX
EGGNOG PANCAKES

My family is delighted when they awake to a platter piled high with these featherlight flapjacks. Pancakes made from a mix just can't compare to these homemade treats.
—Marilyn Mueller, Fayetteville, AR

TAKES: 20 min. • **MAKES:** 12 pancakes

- 2 cups all-purpose flour
- 4 tsp. baking powder
- ½ tsp. salt
- ¼ tsp. ground nutmeg, optional
- 2 large eggs
- 1½ cups eggnog
- 2 Tbsp. butter, melted

1. Mix flour, baking powder, salt and, if desired, nutmeg. In another bowl, whisk together eggs, eggnog and butter; stir into the dry ingredients just until moistened.
2. Preheat griddle over medium heat and lightly grease. Pour batter by ¼ cupfuls onto griddle; cook until bubbles on top begin to pop and the bottoms are golden brown. Turn; cook until the second side is golden brown.
Note: This recipe was tested with commercially prepared eggnog.

FOUR-CHEESE BAKED EGGS

My husband normally prefers omelets for brunch, but he devoured his first helping of these eggs...then asked for more!
—Lisa Speer, Palm Beach, FL

PREP: 15 min. • **BAKE:** 25 min. + standing
MAKES: 12 servings

- 1 cup whole-milk ricotta cheese
- 3 oz. cream cheese, softened
- 7 large eggs
- 6 Tbsp. butter, melted
- ½ tsp. salt
- ¼ tsp. pepper
- 3 Tbsp. all-purpose flour
- ½ tsp. baking powder
- 3 cups grated Gruyere or Swiss cheese
- 2 Tbsp. minced chives or chopped green onions
- ¼ cup shredded Parmesan cheese

1. Preheat oven to 350°. Beat ricotta and cream cheese until smooth. Add eggs, butter, salt and pepper; beat until blended. In another bowl, whisk flour with baking powder; add to egg mixture. Stir in Gruyere and chives. Pour into a greased 13x9-in. baking dish. Sprinkle with Parmesan.
2. Bake, uncovered, until a knife inserted in center comes out clean, 25-30 minutes. Let stand 10 minutes before cutting.

RUSTIC CHRISTMAS TREE

Ask the kids to gather sticks and twigs from the yard to make this earthy decoration!

Start with a roughly 13x9-in. piece of barn wood or other rustic wood for the background; wipe it clean and brush it with a mixture of 1 part white acrylic craft paint to 1 part water to create an aged look. Use wood stain to stain a selection of star-shaped wooden cutouts. Set aside to dry.

Cut branches and twigs to length to form the shape of the tree. Start with a 7-in. piece for the widest part of the tree, then cut about 20 more pieces, each piece slightly shorter than the last. Cut two ¼-in. pieces for the trunk, and one 2-in. piece and four 1-in. pieces to make the tree topper.

Use a glue gun to glue the cut branches down on the painted background in the planned tree shape. Glue the stained stars along with snowflake-shaped novelty buttons to the tree and the background wherever desired.

If desired, add a sawtooth hanger to the back of the piece to mount it on a wall.

FAST FIX

CANADIAN BACON WITH APPLES

During the holidays, I'd rather spend my time with family and friends than in the kitchen, so I rely on easy recipes like this one. No one can resist Canadian bacon and apples coated with a brown sugar glaze.

—Paula Marchesi, Lenhartsville, PA

TAKES: 20 min. • **MAKES:** 6 servings

½ cup packed brown sugar
1 Tbsp. lemon juice
⅛ tsp. pepper
1 large unpeeled red apple
1 large unpeeled green apple
1 lb. sliced Canadian bacon

1. In a large skillet, mix brown sugar, lemon juice and pepper. Cook and stir over medium heat until sugar is dissolved. Cut each apple into 16 wedges; add to the brown sugar mixture. Cook over medium heat until apples are tender, 5-7 minutes, stirring occasionally. Remove the apples to a platter with a slotted spoon; keep warm.

2. Add bacon to skillet; cook over medium heat, turning once, until heated through, about 3 minutes. Transfer to platter. Pour the remaining brown sugar mixture over apples and bacon.

HOLIDAY OPEN HOUSE BUFFET

Open your door to family and friends with a casual yet festive Christmas party. Many neighborhoods organize a movable feast, with the party progressing from one open house to another throughout the day. A beautiful buffet of delicious food is sure to make all visitors feel welcome and make spirits bright!

PEPPER-STUFFED PORK TENDERLOIN

Spicy stuffing balances the delicate flavor of pork in this dish that looks great on the plate—and tastes even better!
—Margaret Allen, Abingdon, VA

PREP: 40 min. • BAKE: 45 min. + standing
MAKES: 8 servings

- 2 Tbsp. canola oil
- 3 small sweet red peppers, finely chopped
- 1 large onion, finely chopped
- 2 small celery ribs, finely chopped
- 1½ tsp. dried thyme
- ¾ tsp. garlic salt
- ¾ tsp. paprika
- ½ tsp. cayenne pepper
- 3 pork tenderloins (¾ lb. each)
- 4 tsp. lemon-pepper seasoning
- 4 tsp. fennel seed, crushed

1. Preheat oven to 325°. In a large skillet, heat oil over medium-high heat. Add the red peppers, onion and celery; saute until tender, 3-4 minutes. Add thyme, garlic salt, paprika and cayenne; saute for 1 minute longer. Remove from heat; set aside.
2. Cut a lengthwise slit down the center of each tenderloin to within ½ in. of bottom. Open tenderloins so they lie flat; cover with plastic wrap. With a meat mallet, flatten pork to ½-in. thickness. Remove plastic wrap; fill tenderloins with vegetable stuffing mixture. Close the tenderloins. Tie at 2-in. intervals with kitchen string; secure ends with toothpicks.
3. Place on a rack in a shallow baking pan coated with cooking spray. Combine lemon-pepper seasoning and fennel; rub over the tenderloins.
4. Bake until a thermometer inserted into pork reads 145°, 45-55 minutes. Remove tenderloins from oven; let stand 5 minutes. Discard the toothpicks and string. Cut each tenderloin into eight slices.

APRICOT HAM BALLS

My family always requests these flavorful ham balls for our annual open house. I usually have to double the recipe to make sure I have enough for the guests!
—Loretta Walker, Great Falls, MT

PREP: 20 min. • BAKE: 45 min.
MAKES: 2 dozen

- 3 large eggs
- 1¾ cups apricot nectar, divided
- 1 cup dry bread crumbs
- ¼ cup chopped onion
- 1½ lbs. ground fully cooked ham
- 1 lb. bulk pork sausage
- 1 cup packed brown sugar
- ¼ cup vinegar
- 2 Tbsp. all-purpose flour
- 1 tsp. ground mustard
- ½ tsp. ground allspice
- ½ tsp. Worcestershire sauce

1. Preheat oven to 325°. Whisk eggs with ¾ cup apricot nectar. Stir in bread crumbs and onion. Add ham and sausage; mix lightly but thoroughly. Shape into 2-in. balls. Place in an ungreased 13x9-in. baking dish.
2. In a second bowl, mix the remaining ingredients and nectar. Pour over the ham balls. Bake, uncovered, until the meat is no longer pink, 45-50 minutes.

GINGER-APRICOT TOSSED SALAD

This is a nice change from ordinary salad and is elegant enough for company. The sweetnesss of the dressing complements the crisp greens and crunchy green beans.
—Trisha Kruse, Eagle, ID

PREP: 25 min. • COOK: 10 min.
MAKES: 6 servings (¾ cup salad dressing)

- 1 can (16 oz.) apricot halves, drained
- ¼ cup rice vinegar
- 1 tsp. sugar
- ½ tsp. minced fresh gingerroot
- 1 garlic clove, minced
- ¼ tsp. salt
- ¼ tsp. pepper
- 1½ lbs. fresh green beans, trimmed and cut into 2-in. pieces
- 5 cups torn mixed salad greens
- 1 medium mango, peeled and cubed
- 3 Tbsp. coarsely chopped dry roasted peanuts

1. Process the first seven ingredients in a blender until smooth. Fill a 6-qt. stockpot two-thirds full with water and bring to a boil. Add green beans; cook, uncovered, until crisp-tender, 8-10 minutes.
2. Remove beans and immediately drop into ice water. Drain and pat dry. Combine salad greens, mango and beans. Sprinkle with peanuts. Serve with dressing.

HASH BROWN BROCCOLI BAKE

Here's a perfect dish for a potluck or holiday buffet. It goes well with fish, poultry, pork or beef. Cheddar cheese can be substituted for Swiss. I double the recipe to serve a crowd.
—Jeanette Volker, Walton, NE

PREP: 25 min. • **BAKE:** 50 min.
MAKES: 14 servings

- 4 Tbsp. butter, divided
- 2 Tbsp. all-purpose flour
- 1 tsp. salt
- ⅛ tsp. ground nutmeg
- ⅛ tsp. pepper
- 2 cups 2% milk
- 1 pkg. (8 oz.) cream cheese, cubed
- 2 cups shredded Swiss cheese
- 6 cups frozen shredded hash brown potatoes (about 20 oz.), thawed
- 1 pkg. (16 oz.) frozen chopped broccoli, thawed
- ½ cup dry bread crumbs

1. Preheat the oven to 350°. In a large saucepan, melt 2 Tbsp. butter. Stir in the flour, salt, nutmeg and pepper until smooth; gradually add the milk. Bring to a boil; cook and stir until thickened, about 2 minutes. Remove from heat. Add the cheeses; stir until melted. Stir in potatoes.
2. Spoon half of the potato mixture into a greased 2-qt. baking dish. Top with broccoli and the remaining potato mixture. Bake, covered, 35 minutes.
3. Melt the remaining butter; toss with bread crumbs. Sprinkle over casserole. Bake, covered, until heated through and topping is golden, 15-20 minutes.

SNOWFLAKE DOORMAT

Use spray paint and masking tape to turn an inexpensive coir mat into a welcoming decoration at your door.

Cover your work surface with a drop cloth, and place a plain coir doormat in the center of the work surface, right side up. There should be several inches of protected surface all the way around the mat. Use various widths of masking tape to create snowflakes. Spray-paint across the entire top of the mat using smooth, continuous motions. To ensure even coverage, begin each pass a few inches to one side of the mat, spray across the mat and end a few inches on the other side of mat. Apply additional coats of paint as needed to achieve the desired color saturation, waiting a few minutes between coats. After applying the final coat, wait several minutes before removing tape. Let the mat dry completely before use.

MAKE AHEAD
MAKE-AHEAD MARINATED SHRIMP

Dress up your holiday buffet table with this tasty shrimp recipe. You'll have time to enjoy your party because this appetizer is that easy.

—Phyllis Schmalz, Kansas City, KS

PREP: 15 min. + marinating • **MAKES:** 6 cups

- ¾ cup water
- ½ cup red wine vinegar
- ¼ cup olive oil
- ¾ tsp. salt
- ¾ tsp. minced fresh oregano or ¼ tsp. dried oregano
- ¾ tsp. minced fresh thyme or ¼ tsp. dried thyme
- 1 garlic clove, minced
- ¼ tsp. pepper
- 1½ lbs. peeled and deveined cooked shrimp (16-20 per lb.)
- 1 can (14 oz.) water-packed artichoke hearts, rinsed, drained and halved
- ½ lb. small fresh mushrooms, halved

In a large bowl, combine the first eight ingredients. Add shrimp, artichokes and mushrooms; turn to coat. Cover and refrigerate 8 hours or overnight, turning occasionally.

❄ Reader Review

"This shrimp recipe is so easy and so good. I got rave reviews and several requests for the recipe."

YANKEE CAT TASTEOFHOME.COM

NAPOLEON CREMES

For our annual holiday party, I set out a buffet with lots of food and candies, including these lovely layered treats. They're so creamy, and with that green layer of pistachio pudding peeking out, they're very merry!

—Gloria Jesswein, Niles, MI

PREP: 15 min. + chilling • **MAKES:** 4 dozen

- 2 cups finely crushed graham cracker crumbs
- 1 cup sweetened shredded coconut
- ¼ cup granulated sugar
- ¼ cup baking cocoa
- ½ cup plus 2 Tbsp. butter, melted
- 1 tsp. vanilla extract

FILLING
- ½ cup butter, softened
- 2 cups confectioners' sugar
- 1 pkg. (3.4 oz.) instant pistachio or lemon pudding mix
- 3 Tbsp. whole milk

TOPPING
- 1 cup semisweet chocolate chips
- 3 Tbsp. butter

1. Combine graham cracker crumbs, coconut, sugar and cocoa. Stir in melted butter and vanilla. Press onto the bottom of a greased 9-in. square baking dish. Refrigerate for 30 minutes.

2. For the filling, beat softened butter until smooth. Add confectioners' sugar, pudding mix and milk; beat until fluffy. Spread over crust. Refrigerate until firm, 1½-2 hours.

3. For the topping, microwave chocolate chips and butter on high, stirring every 30 seconds, until melted and smooth. Cool. Spread over the pudding layer. Refrigerate until set. Cut into bars.

MAKE & TAKE YULETIDE FAVORITES

Christmastime is the party season, with celebrations and get-togethers held at churches, clubs, offices and the homes of friends and family. For a holiday potluck gathering, we all want dishes that are warm, comforting, and yes—we confess— that will also wow the crowd!

APPETIZER TOMATO CHEESE BREAD

I found this recipe in a dairy cookbook, and it has become a family favorite. We milk 180 cows and have a large garden, so we welcome dishes that use dairy and fresh vegetables. My husband and our two children are meat-and-potato eaters, but there are no complaints when I make this bread!

—Penney Kester, Springville, NY

PREP: 20 min. • **BAKE:** 25 min. + standing
MAKES: 12 servings

- 2 Tbsp. butter
- 1 medium onion, minced
- 1 cup shredded cheddar cheese
- ½ cup sour cream
- ¼ cup mayonnaise
- ¾ tsp. salt
- ¼ tsp. pepper
- ¼ tsp. dried oregano
    Pinch rubbed sage
- 2 cups biscuit/baking mix
- ⅔ cup whole milk
- 3 medium tomatoes, cut into ¼-in. slices
    Paprika

1. Preheat oven to 400°. In a small skillet, heat butter over medium heat. Add onion and cook until tender. Remove from the heat. Stir in cheddar cheese, sour cream, mayonnaise and seasonings; set aside.
2. In a bowl, combine the baking mix and milk to form a soft dough. Turn the dough onto a well-floured surface; knead lightly 10-12 times. Pat into a greased 13x9-in. baking dish, pushing dough up the sides of the dish to form a shallow rim. Arrange tomato slices over the top. Spread with topping; sprinkle with paprika.
3. Bake for 25 minutes. Let stand for 10 minutes before cutting.

SLOW-COOKED TURKEY WITH BERRY COMPOTE

This delicious dish delivers yummy turkey flavor without heating up the house, and the berries make the perfect chutney. For a browner turkey, just broil for a few minutes before serving.

—Margaret Bracher, Robertsdale, AL

PREP: 35 min. + standing
COOK: 3 hours
MAKES: 12 servings (3¼ cups compote)

- 1 tsp. salt
- ½ tsp. garlic powder
- ½ tsp. dried thyme
- ½ tsp. pepper
- 2 boneless turkey breast halves (2 lbs. each)
- ⅓ cup water

COMPOTE
- 2 medium apples, peeled and finely chopped
- 2 cups fresh raspberries
- 2 cups fresh blueberries
- 1 cup white grape juice
- ¼ tsp. crushed red pepper flakes
- ¼ tsp. ground ginger

1. Mix the salt, garlic powder, thyme and pepper; rub over turkey breasts. Place in a 5- or 6-qt. slow cooker. Pour water around the turkey. Cook, covered, on low 3-4 hours (a thermometer inserted in turkey should read at least 165°).
2. Remove turkey from slow cooker and tent with foil. Let turkey stand 10 minutes before slicing.
3. Meanwhile, in a large saucepan, combine the compote ingredients. Bring to a boil. Reduce heat to medium; cook, uncovered, stirring occasionally, until slightly thickened and apples are tender, 15-20 minutes. Serve turkey with compote.

HOLIDAY WINE BOTTLE LABELS

Whether you're giving wine as a hostess gift or setting up a buffet, make a label that matches the occasion.

For the base, cut a 10x4-in. strip of scrapbook paper or card stock; the strip should fit around a wine bottle. Cut smaller pieces of scrapbook paper to layer on the base. Run double-sided tape from corner to corner on the back of the smaller pieces and adhere them to the base. (If you used card stock for your base, form it around the bottle before applying the tape so that the seal will hold.) Layer paper until you're happy with your design.

Center a length of ribbon on the label, lined up so that the ends are of even lengths and each long enough to wrap once around the bottle. Run double-sided tape on the back of the ribbon where it touches the label and adhere it to the label. Use the ends of the ribbon to tie the label on the bottle.

Decorate the label further with scrapbook stickers, personal photos, ribbons or tulle. Add a tag with twine or double-sided tape. Or use a hole punch to make a hole in one of your layers, and tie on the tag with thread or twine.

MAKE AHEAD
MAKE-AHEAD MEATBALLS

My husband and I have company often. Keeping a supply of these frozen meatballs on hand means I can prepare a satisfying meal, even on short notice. The versatile meatball mix makes about 12 dozen meatballs, which I freeze in batches for future use.
—Ruth Andrewson, Leavenworth, WA

PREP: 30 min. • **COOK:** 10 min.
MAKES: 5 batches
(about 30 meatballs per batch)

- 4   large eggs, lightly beaten
- 2   cups dry bread crumbs
- ½   cup finely chopped onion
- 1   Tbsp. salt
- 2   tsp. Worcestershire sauce
- ½   tsp. white pepper
- 4   lbs. lean ground beef (90% lean)

1. In a large bowl, combine the first six ingredients. Crumble beef over mixture and mix well. Shape into 1-in. balls, about 12 dozen.
2. Place meatballs on greased racks in shallow baking pans. Bake at 400° for 10-15 minutes or until no longer pink, turning often; drain. Cool.
Freeze option: Freeze cooled meatballs in freezer containers. To use, partially thaw in refrigerator overnight. Reheat on a greased 15x10x1-in. baking pan in a preheated 350° oven until heated through.

CRANBERRY BBQ PULLED PORK

Cranberry sauce adds a yummy twist to traditional pulled pork. My family can't get enough of it! The pork cooks to tender perfection in the slow cooker, which also makes this dish conveniently portable.
—Carrie Wiegand, Mount Pleasant, IA

PREP: 20 min. • **COOK:** 9 hours
MAKES: 14 servings

- 1   boneless pork shoulder roast (4 to 6 lbs.)
- ⅓   cup cranberry juice
- 1   tsp. salt

SAUCE
- 1   can (14 oz.) whole-berry cranberry sauce
- 1   cup ketchup
- ⅓   cup cranberry juice
- 3   Tbsp. brown sugar
- 4½ tsp. chili powder
- 2   tsp. garlic powder
- 1   tsp. onion powder
- ½   tsp. salt
- ¼   tsp. ground chipotle pepper
- ½   tsp. liquid smoke, optional
- 14 hamburger buns, split

1. Cut roast in half. Place in a 4-qt. slow cooker. Add cranberry juice and salt. Cover and cook on low for 8-10 hours or until meat is tender.
2. Remove roast and set aside. In a small saucepan, combine the cranberry sauce, ketchup, cranberry juice, brown sugar, seasonings and liquid smoke if desired. Cook and stir over medium heat for 5 minutes or until slightly thickened.
3. Skim fat from cooking juices; set aside ½ cup juices. Discard remaining juices. When cool enough to handle, shred pork with two forks and return to slow cooker.
4. Stir in the sauce mixture and reserved cooking juices. Cover and cook on low for 1 hour or until heated through. Serve on buns.

DOUBLE CHOCOLATE ORANGE BROWNIES

I have to give my husband credit for this idea—we love chocolate and orange together, so he suggested I come up with this recipe. Now I'm always asked to bake these brownies for family gatherings.

—Elinor Townsend, North Grafton, MA

PREP: 15 min. • BAKE: 30 min. + cooling
MAKES: 2 dozen

- ¾ cup butter, cubed
- 4 oz. unsweetened chocolate, chopped
- 3 large eggs
- 2 cups sugar
- 1 tsp. orange extract
- 1 cup all-purpose flour
- 1 cup semisweet chocolate chips
  Confectioners' sugar

1. Preheat oven to 350°. In a microwave, melt the butter and chocolate together; stir until smooth. Cool slightly. In a large bowl, beat eggs and sugar. Stir in the chocolate mixture. Beat in orange extract. Gradually add flour to chocolate mixture.
2. Pour batter into a greased 13x9-in. baking dish. Sprinkle with chocolate chips. Bake for 30-35 minutes or until a toothpick inserted in the center comes out clean (do not overbake).
3. Cool completely on a wire rack. Cut into squares. Just before serving, sprinkle with confectioners' sugar.

MAKE AHEAD
GINGERSNAP PUMPKIN CAKE

One year, on the first day that really felt like fall, we were getting together with friends. I had to make this pumpkin cake! It was the perfect way to welcome the season.
—Koni Brewer, Woodway, TX

PREP: 20 min. • BAKE: 50 min. + cooling
MAKES: 12 servings

- 1 can (15 oz.) solid-pack pumpkin
- 2 cups sugar
- 4 large eggs
- 1 cup canola oil
- 2 cups all-purpose flour
- 2 tsp. baking soda
- 2 tsp. pumpkin pie spice
- ½ tsp. salt

ICING
- 4 oz. cream cheese, softened
- ¼ cup butter, softened
- ½ tsp. vanilla extract
- 1¾ cups confectioners' sugar
- 5 gingersnap cookies, crushed

1. Preheat oven to 350°. Grease and flour a 10-in. fluted tube pan; set aside.
2. In a large bowl, beat pumpkin, sugar, eggs and oil until well blended. In another bowl, whisk flour, baking soda, pie spice and salt; gradually beat dry ingredients into the pumpkin mixture.
3. Transfer batter to the prepared pan. Bake 50-55 minutes or until a toothpick inserted in center comes out clean. Cool in the pan 10 minutes before removing to a wire rack to cool completely.
4. In a small bowl, beat cream cheese, butter and vanilla until blended. Gradually beat in confectioners' sugar until smooth. Frost cake; sprinkle with crushed cookies.
Freeze option: Wrap cooled, unfrosted cake in plastic wrap, then cover securely in foil; freeze. To use, thaw cake before unwrapping. Make frosting; frost and decorate as directed.

≈► CELEBRATE ◄≈

EASY
COCKTAIL PARTY

It's the most wonderful time of the year—and
the busiest. Shopping, baking, sending cards,
running errands, wrapping presents...even
the most jovial of merrymakers can feel a little
tapped out. Put the spark back in the season
with an impromptu, at-home happy hour!
This selection of beverages and easy-but-
impressive savory small bites will have you
and your guests bubbling with joy.

FAST FIX
CRANBERRY POMEGRANATE MARGARITAS

I came up with this beverage to serve at holiday celebrations as a festive twist on the traditional margarita. It's light and refreshing, and it looks absolutely beautiful with sugar crystals in place of salt on the glass rims.
—Mindie Hilton, Susanville, CA

TAKES: 5 min.
MAKES: 12 servings

4½ cups diet lemon-lime soda, chilled
1½ cups tequila
1½ cups cranberry juice, chilled
1½ cups pomegranate juice, chilled
       Pomegranate seeds and frozen cranberries, optional

In a pitcher, combine soda, tequila and juices. Serve in chilled glasses. Garnish with pomegranate and cranberries if desired.

FAST FIX
BUTTERSCOTCH MARTINIS

The rich flavors of butterscotch and chocolate pair beautifully for a nightcap that will satisfy any sweet tooth.
—Clara Coulson Minney, Washington Court House, OH

TAKES: 10 min. • MAKES: 2 servings

    Ice cubes
2   oz. clear creme de cacao
2   oz. creme de cacao
1½ oz. vodka
1½ oz. butterscotch schnapps liqueur
6   semisweet chocolate chips

1. Fill a shaker three-fourths full with ice cubes. Add the creme de cacao, vodka and schnapps.
2. Cover and shake for 10-15 seconds or until condensation forms on the outside of the shaker. Divide chocolate chips between two chilled cocktail glasses; strain butterscotch mixture over chips.

MAKE AHEAD
BOURBON SLUSH

This slush is definitely a favorite at our harvest parties. Have fun experimenting with different types and flavors of tea. We like black tea, green tea and orange spice.
—Darcene Sigler, Louisville, OH

PREP: 10 min. + freezing
MAKES: 24 servings

7   cups water
1½ cups sugar
1   can (12 oz.) frozen orange juice concentrate
1   can (12 oz.) frozen lemonade concentrate
2   cups strong brewed tea, cooled
2   cups bourbon
3   liters lemon-lime soda, chilled

1. In a Dutch oven, combine water and sugar; bring to a boil, stirring to dissolve the sugar. Remove from heat.
2. Stir in the orange juice and lemonade concentrates, tea and bourbon. Transfer to freezer containers; freeze for 12 hours or overnight.
3. To serve, place about ½ cup bourbon mixture in each glass; top with ½ cup soda.

BUBBLY CHAMPAGNE PUNCH

This elegant punch was served at my wedding—we ladle it up at special events to this day!
—Anita Geoghagan, Woodstock, GA

PREP: 10 min. + freezing
MAKES: 16 servings

3   orange slices, halved
     Fresh or frozen cranberries
2½ cups unsweetened pineapple juice
1½ cups ginger ale
2   bottles (750 milliliters each) brut champagne, chilled
1   bottle (375 milliliters) sweet white wine, chilled
1   can (12 oz.) frozen lemonade concentrate, thawed

1. Line the bottom of a 6-cup ring mold with orange slices and cranberries. Combine pineapple juice and ginger ale; pour over the fruit. Freeze until solid.
2. Just before serving, unmold the ice ring into a punch bowl. Gently stir in remaining ingredients.

SIPPING PRETTY

Add these colorful ice cubes to drinks to make them extra special. Just fill an ice cube tray with water, pop in fresh herbs, citrus or berries, and let it freeze!

BERRIES
Strawberries • Blueberries • Raspberries

HERBS
Basil • Mint

CITRUS
Lemon • Lime • Orange

BLUE CHEESE-STUFFED SHRIMP

Cooked shrimp become something even more extraordinary when stuffed with blue cheese.
—Amy Dollimount, Glace Bay, NS

PREP: 20 min. + chilling • **MAKES:** 2 dozen

- 3 oz. cream cheese, softened
- ⅔ cup minced fresh parsley, divided
- ¼ cup crumbled blue cheese
- 1 tsp. chopped shallot
- ½ tsp. Creole mustard
- 24 cooked jumbo shrimp, peeled and deveined

1. Beat cream cheese until smooth. Beat in ⅓ cup of parsley, blue cheese, shallot and mustard. Refrigerate for at least 1 hour.
2. Starting with the tail end of each shrimp, make a deep slit along the deveining line to within ¼-½ in. of the bottom. Stuff with cream cheese mixture; press remaining parsley onto cream cheese mixture.

MAPLE JALAPENOS

Craving something sweet with a little bit of heat? Try these creamy, sweet, hot and savory treats. One bite, and you won't be able to stop!
—Nicole Larson, American Fork, UT

PREP: 45 min. • **BAKE:** 20 min.
MAKES: 50 appetizers

- 25 jalapeno peppers
- 1 pkg. (8 oz.) cream cheese, softened
- 1 cup crumbled feta cheese
- ½ cup maple syrup
- ½ lb. bacon strips, cooked and crumbled
- ¼ cup packed brown sugar

1. Cut jalapenos in half lengthwise and remove seeds. In a small bowl, beat the cream cheese, feta cheese and syrup until smooth. Spoon into pepper halves.
2. Place in two greased 15x10x1-in. baking pans. Top with bacon and sprinkle with brown sugar. Bake at 350° for 20 minutes for spicy flavor, 30 minutes for medium and 40 minutes for mild.
Note: Wear disposable gloves when cutting hot peppers; the oils can burn skin.

FAST FIX

POMEGRANATE PISTACHIO CROSTINI

Bright red pomegranate seeds, green pistachios and chocolate, of course…that's how you make crostini for the holidays!
—Elisabeth Larsen, Pleasant Grove, UT

TAKES: 30 min. • **MAKES:** 3 dozen

- 36 slices French bread baguette (¼ in. thick)
- 1 Tbsp. butter, melted
- 4 oz. cream cheese, softened
- 2 Tbsp. orange juice
- 1 Tbsp. honey
- 1 cup pomegranate seeds
- ½ cup finely chopped pistachios
- 2 oz. dark chocolate candy bar, grated

1. Preheat oven to 400°. Arrange bread slices on an ungreased baking sheet; brush tops with butter. Bake until lightly toasted, 4-6 minutes. Remove from pan to a wire rack to cool.
2. Beat cream cheese, orange juice and honey until blended; spread over toasts. Top with the remaining ingredients.

FAST FIX

FESTIVE DIP

This colorful dish is great for all parties and festivities. My daughter loves helping to prepare it!
—Donna Kollar, Austintown, OH

TAKES: 10 min. • **MAKES:** 4 cups

- 1 can (15½ oz.) black-eyed peas, rinsed and drained
- 1 medium sweet red pepper, finely chopped
- 1 medium green pepper, finely chopped
- ⅓ cup finely chopped onion
- 1 jalapeno pepper, seeded and chopped
- ½ cup Italian salad dressing
  Corn chips

In a large bowl, combine the first five ingredients. Drizzle with salad dressing; toss to coat. Serve with corn chips.
Note: Wear disposable gloves when cutting hot peppers; the oils can burn exposed skin. Avoid touching your face.

LITTLE HOLIDAY CAKES

My college friend shared this cupcake recipe that has pie crust on the bottom, raspberry jam in the middle and cake on top. They're just right for a buffet or potluck.
—Dana Beckstrom, Salt Lake City, UT

....

PREP: 20 min. • BAKE: 15 min. + cooling
MAKES: 2 dozen

Pastry for double-crust pie (9 in.)
½ cup seedless raspberry jam
1   pkg. red velvet cake mix (regular size)
1   can (16 oz.) vanilla frosting
Red and green sprinkles

1. Preheat oven to 350°. Roll pastry to ⅛-in. thickness. Cut twenty-four 2½-in. circles. Press onto the bottom and ½ in. up the sides of greased muffin cups. Top each with 1 tsp. jam; set aside.
2. Prepare cake mix batter according to package directions for cupcakes. Fill prepared muffin cups three-fourths full.
3. Bake for 14-16 minutes or until a toothpick inserted in the center comes out clean. Cool for 10 minutes before removing from pans to wire racks to cool completely. Frost with vanilla frosting and decorate with sprinkles.

Pastry for double-crust pie (9 in.):
Combine 2½ cups all-purpose flour and ½ tsp. salt; cut in 1 cup cold butter until crumbly. Gradually add ⅓-⅔ cup of ice water, tossing with a fork until dough holds together when pressed. Divide dough in half. Shape each into a disk; wrap in plastic. Refrigerate 1 hour or overnight.

FAST FIX
CONTEST-WINNING MOCHA FONDUE

At our friends' 25th anniversary celebration, we had fun concocting this chocolate fondue. With fresh fruit and cubes of pound cake as dippers, all of your guests will want to dive into dessert!
—Karen Boehner, Glen Elder, KS

....

TAKES: 20 min. • MAKES: 10 servings

2   cups semisweet chocolate chips
¼   cup butter, cubed
1   cup heavy whipping cream
3   Tbsp. strong brewed coffee
⅛   tsp. salt
2   large egg yolks, lightly beaten
Cubed pound cake, sliced bananas and fresh strawberries and pineapple chunks

1. In a heavy saucepan, combine the first five ingredients; cook and stir over medium heat until chips are melted. Remove from heat. In a small bowl, whisk a small amount of the hot mixture into egg yolks; return all to pan, whisking constantly. Cook and stir until a thermometer reads 160°.
2. Transfer to a fondue pot and keep warm. Serve with cake and fruit.

❄ Holiday Helper

Let your imagination run wild when serving fondue! Cake, cookies and fruit make good dippers—brownies are extra decadent! This fondue is mocha, but you can dress it up with any chocolate-compatible flavor, including Amaretto, Chambord, Frangelico and other flavored liqueurs.

FELIZ NAVIDAD

For many families, Christmas traditions kick off with a big batch of tamales—bundles of masa (corn dough) stuffed with meat and other savory or sweet fillings and steamed in corn-husk wrappers. This year, serve them alongside a zesty lineup of stuffed peppers, pinto beans, rice and sangria for a fiesta like none other. *Deliciosa!*

HOMEMADE GUACAMOLE

This easy recipe comes together fast, making it a satisfying go-to appetizer for entertaining.
—Joan Hallford, North Richland Hills, TX

TAKES: 10 min. • **MAKES:** 2 cups

- 3 medium ripe avocados, peeled and cubed
- 1 garlic clove, minced
- ¼ to ½ tsp. salt
- 2 medium tomatoes, seeded and chopped, optional
- 1 small onion, finely chopped
- ¼ cup mayonnaise, optional
- 1 to 2 Tbsp. lime juice
- 1 Tbsp. minced fresh cilantro

Mash avocados with garlic and salt. Stir in the remaining ingredients as desired.

TOPSY-TURVY SANGRIA

I got this recipe for sangria from a friend a few years ago. It's perfect for relaxed get-togethers. It's even better if you make it the night before and let the flavors steep. But watch out—it goes down easy!
—Tracy Field, Bremerton, WA

TAKES: 10 min.
MAKES: 10 servings

- 1 bottle (750 milliliters) merlot
- 1 cup sugar
- 1 cup orange liqueur
- ½ to 1 cup brandy
- 3 cups cold lemon-lime soda
- 1 cup sliced fresh strawberries
- 1 medium orange, sliced
- 1 medium lemon, sliced
- 1 medium peach, sliced
  Ice cubes

In a pitcher, stir first four ingredients until sugar is dissolved. Stir in soda and fruit. Serve over ice.

SOUTHWESTERN RICE

I created this colorful side after enjoying a rice dish like it at a restaurant and wanting my own. Sometimes I add cubes of grilled chicken breast to make it a meal in itself.
—Michelle Dennis, Clarks Hill, IN

TAKES: 30 min. • **MAKES:** 8 servings

- 1 Tbsp. olive oil
- 1 medium green pepper, diced
- 1 medium onion, chopped
- 2 garlic cloves, minced
- 1 cup uncooked long grain rice
- ½ tsp. ground cumin
- ⅛ tsp. ground turmeric
- 1 can (14½ oz.) reduced-sodium chicken broth
- 2 cups frozen corn (about 10 oz.), thawed
- 1 can (15 oz.) black beans, rinsed and drained
- 1 can (10 oz.) diced tomatoes and green chilies, undrained

1. In a large nonstick skillet, heat oil over medium-high heat; saute pepper and onion 3 minutes. Add garlic; cook and stir for 1 minute.
2. Stir in rice, spices and broth; bring to a boil. Reduce heat; simmer, covered, until the rice is tender, about 15 minutes. Stir in the remaining ingredients; cook, covered, until heated through.

❄ Holiday Helper

Turmeric, used to add color and flavor in many Asian cuisines (especially Indian curries), is part of the ginger family. The deep orange-yellow powder has a warm, peppery flavor and an earthy aroma; it's what makes yellow mustard yellow. Turmeric is said to have a wide range of health benefits, including anti-inflammatory properties and the ability to reduce migraines and whiten teeth.

CHILE RELLENO SQUARES

A friend I worked with shared this recipe several years ago. It's easy to prepare and complements any Mexican or Spanish meal.
—Fran Carll, Long Beach, CA

PREP: 10 min. • **BAKE:** 25 min.
MAKES: 16 servings

- 3 cups shredded Monterey Jack cheese
- 1½ cups shredded cheddar cheese
- 2 cans (4 oz. each) chopped green chilies, drained
- 2 large eggs
- 2 Tbsp. whole milk
- 1 Tbsp. all-purpose flour

1. Preheat oven to 375°. Sprinkle half of each of the cheeses onto bottom of a greased 8-in. square baking dish. Layer with chilies and remaining cheeses.
2. Whisk together eggs, milk and flour; pour over top. Bake 25-30 minutes, uncovered, until set. Cool 15 minutes before cutting.

FRIED ICE CREAM

Refrigerated pie crust sprinkled with cinnamon sugar makes short work of this eye-catching, mouthwatering treat. Keep a batch of these scoops in your freezer for impromptu entertaining all year long!
—*Taste of Home* Test Kitchen

PREP: 30 min. + freezing • MAKES: 8 servings

- 1 sheet refrigerated pie pastry
- 1½ tsp. sugar
- 1 tsp. ground cinnamon
- 1 qt. vanilla ice cream
  Oil for deep-fat frying
- ½ cup honey

1. Preheat oven to 400°. Unroll pastry onto an ungreased baking sheet. Mix sugar and cinnamon; sprinkle over pastry. Prick thoroughly with a fork. Bake until golden brown, 10-12 minutes. Cool completely on a wire rack.

2. Place pastry in a large resealable plastic bag; crush to form coarse crumbs. Transfer to a shallow bowl. Using a ½-cup ice cream scoop, drop a scoop of ice cream into crumbs; roll quickly to coat and shape into a ball. Transfer to a waxed paper-lined baking sheet; place in freezer. Repeat seven times; freeze until firm, 1-2 hours.

3. To serve, heat oil to 375° in an electric skillet or deep-fat fryer. Fry ice cream balls until golden, 8-10 seconds. Drain on paper towels. Serve immediately in chilled dishes. Drizzle with honey.

CHICKEN TAMALES

I love making tamales. They're fairly time-consuming but worth the effort. I usually make them for Christmas, but my family wants them more often, so I freeze a big batch.
—Cindy Pruitt, Grove, OK

PREP: 2½ hours + soaking • COOK: 50 min.
MAKES: 20 tamales

- 24 dried corn husks
- 1 broiler/fryer chicken (3 to 4 lbs.), cut up
- 1 medium onion, quartered
- 2 tsp. salt
- 1 garlic clove, crushed
- 3 qt. water

DOUGH
- 1 cup shortening
- 3 cups masa harina

FILLING
- 6 Tbsp. canola oil
- 6 Tbsp. all-purpose flour
- ¾ cup chili powder
- ½ tsp. salt
- ¼ tsp. garlic powder
- ¼ tsp. pepper
- 2 cans (2¼ oz. each) sliced ripe olives, drained
  Hot water

1. Cover corn husks with cold water; soak until softened, at least 2 hours.

2. Place chicken, onion, salt and garlic in a 6-qt. stockpot. Pour in water; bring to a boil. Reduce heat; simmer, covered, until chicken is tender, 45-60 minutes. Remove chicken from broth. When cool enough to handle, remove bones and skin; discard. Shred chicken. Strain cooking juices; skim fat. Reserve 6 cups stock.

3. For dough, beat shortening until light and fluffy, about 1 minute. Beat in small amounts of masa harina alternately with small amounts of reserved stock, using no more than 2 cups stock. Drop a small amount of dough into a cup of cold water; dough should float. If not, continue beating, rechecking every 1-2 minutes.

4. For filling, heat oil in a Dutch oven; stir in flour until blended. Cook and stir over medium heat until lightly browned, 7-9 minutes. Stir in seasonings, chicken and remaining stock; bring to a boil. Reduce heat; simmer, uncovered, stirring occasionally, until thickened, about 45 minutes.

5. Drain corn husks and pat dry; tear four husks to make 20 strips for tying tamales. (To prevent husks from drying out, cover with plastic wrap and a damp towel until ready to use.) On wide end of each remaining husk, spread 3 Tbsp. dough to within ½ in. of side edges; top each with 2 Tbsp. chicken filling and 2 tsp. olives. Fold the long sides of the husk over filling, overlapping slightly. Fold over narrow end of husk; tie with a strip of husk to secure.

6. Place a large steamer basket in the stockpot over water; place tamales upright in steamer. Bring to a boil; steam, covered, adding hot water as needed, until dough peels away from husk, about 45 minutes.

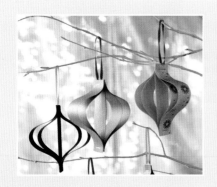

RETRO PAPER ORNAMENTS

This child-friendly craft is simple to create, but the result is surprisingly sophisticated. Gathering as many 12-in. squares of double-sided card stock as you'd like (one sheet makes four ornaments). For each ornament, cut one 4x1-in. strip, two 5x1-in. strips and two 6x1-in. strips. Stack the strips with the shortest in the center, two medium-length strips on either side and the two longest strips on the outside. Position the stack so that they are flush at one end. Cut a 6-in. length of narrow ribbon. Fold the ribbon in half; place the open ends between layers of paper at the flush end. Staple all the layers at the flush end. Hold the stapled end with one hand; use your other hand to pinch the opposite ends of the longest strips. Push the pinched ends up toward the stapled end, capturing the medium-length strips as you go. Continue pushing up until all ends meet at the end of the shortest strip, then staple the ends in place.

WHITE ELEPHANT PARTY

We've all heard the saying that one person's trash is another's treasure, but at a white elephant party, the lines between trash and treasure blur completely. And while your guests are swapping, stealing and showing off their kitschy treasures (see party rules, page 63), serve up a big helping of scrumptious appetizers, sides, mains and desserts—all in pale hues appropriate to the party theme.

APPETIZER TORTILLA PINWHEELS

A friend gave me this recipe, and whenever I serve these pretty appetizers, people ask me for the recipe, too! Besides being attractive and tasty, they can be made ahead of time and sliced just before serving, leaving you time for other last-minute party preparations.

—Pat Waymire, Yellow Springs, OH

PREP: 20 min. + chilling
MAKES: about 4 dozen

- 1 pkg. (8 oz.) cream cheese, softened
- 1 cup shredded cheddar cheese
- 1 cup sour cream
- 1 can (4¼ oz.) chopped ripe olives
- 1 can (4 oz.) chopped green chilies, well drained
- ½ cup chopped green onions
  Garlic powder to taste
  Seasoned salt to taste
- 5 flour tortillas (10 in.)
  Salsa, optional

1. Beat cream cheese, cheese and sour cream until blended. Stir in olives, green chilies, green onions and seasonings.
2. Spread cream cheese mixtures over tortillas; roll up tightly. Wrap each roll in plastic, twisting ends to seal; refrigerate for several hours.
3. Unwrap. Cut into ½- to ¾-in. slices, using a serrated knife. If desired, serve with salsa.

COUNTRY WHITE BREAD

Any time is the right time for a comforting slice of homemade bread. These loaves are especially nice since the crust stays so tender. This recipe is my husband Nick's favorite. He makes most of the bread at our house.

—Joanne Shew Chuk, St. Benedict, SK

PREP: 20 min. + rising • BAKE: 25 min. + cooling
MAKES: 2 loaves (16 slices each)

- 2 pkg. (¼ oz. each) active dry yeast
- 2 cups warm water (110° to 115°)
- ½ cup sugar
- 2 tsp. salt
- 2 large eggs
- ¼ cup canola oil
- 6½ to 7 cups all-purpose flour

1. In a large bowl, dissolve the yeast in warm water. Add sugar, salt, eggs, oil and 3 cups flour; beat on medium speed until smooth. Stir in enough remaining flour to form a soft dough.
2. Turn dough onto a floured surface; knead until smooth and elastic, 6-8 minutes. Place in a greased bowl, turning once to grease the top. Cover and let rise in a warm place until doubled, about 1 hour.
3. Punch down dough. Divide in half and shape into loaves. Place into two greased 9x5-in. loaf pans. Cover with clean kitchen towels; let rise in a warm place until dough has doubled, about 1 hour. Preheat the oven to 375°.
4. Bake until golden brown, 25-30 minutes. Remove from pans to wire racks to cool.

SLOW-COOKED WHITE BEAN CHILI

My friend Caroline and I came up with this delicious slow-cooked chicken chili. It's unusual because it calls for Alfredo sauce.

—Cindi Mitchell, St. Marys, KS

PREP: 15 min. • COOK: 3 hours
MAKES: 12 servings

- 3 cans (15½ oz. each) great northern beans, rinsed and drained
- 3 cups cubed cooked chicken breast
- 1 jar (15 oz.) Alfredo sauce
- 2 cups chicken broth
- 1½ cups frozen gold and white corn (about 8 oz.), thawed
- 1 cup shredded Monterey Jack cheese
- 1 cup shredded pepper jack cheese
- 1 cup sour cream
- 1 small sweet yellow pepper, chopped
- 1 small onion, chopped
- 1 to 2 cans (4 oz. each) chopped green chilies
- 3 garlic cloves, minced
- 3 tsp. ground cumin
- 1½ tsp. white pepper
- 1 to 1½ tsp. cayenne pepper
  Salsa verde, optional
  Chopped fresh cilantro, optional

In a 5- or 6-qt. slow cooker, combine all ingredients except salsa and cilantro. Cook, covered, on low until vegetables are tender and flavors are blended, 3-4 hours, stirring once. If desired, serve with salsa and cilantro.

❄ Holiday Helper

If you want to shave calories off the Appetizer Toritilla Pinwheels (above), swap out the cream cheese for Neufchatel. Neufchatel cheese is a soft unripened cheese that originates in France. The American version is similar to cream cheese, and is made from pasteurized milk and cream. American Neufchatel is a bit lower in calories than cream cheese and has slightly more moisture. It can be used in place of regular cream cheese in recipes for dips and spreads, but it may impact the texture of cooked products calling for cream cheese.

WHITE CHEDDAR MAC & CHEESE

My macaroni and cheese is simple and has lots of flavor from the ground chipotle. I like to use conchiglie pasta; its shape allows more melted cheese to pool inside. Yum!
—Colleen Delawder, Herndon, VA

TAKES: 25 min. • **MAKES:** 8 servings

- 1 pkg. (16 oz.) small pasta shells
- ½ cup butter, cubed
- ½ cup all-purpose flour
- ½ tsp. onion powder
- ½ tsp. ground chipotle pepper
- ½ tsp. pepper
- ¼ tsp. salt
- 4 cups 2% milk
- 2 cups shredded sharp white cheddar cheese
- 2 cups shredded Manchego or additional white cheddar cheese (about 8 oz.)

1. In a 6-qt. stockpot, cook pasta according to package directions. Drain; return to pot.
2. Meanwhile, in a large saucepan, melt butter over medium heat. Stir in flour and seasonings until smooth; gradually whisk in milk. Bring to a boil, stirring constantly; cook and stir until thickened, 6-8 minutes. Remove from heat; stir in cheeses until melted. Add to pasta; toss to coat.

❄ Reader Review

"Good recipe. We had it with grilled chicken and a salad. My child who doesn't care for mac & cheese ate it. Good enough amount to make everyone in this house happy."

ROBBRD TASTEOFHOME.COM

SNOW-TOPPED WHITE CHOCOLATE MACADAMIA COOKIES

Just like snowflakes, these fluffy cookies will melt in your mouth and disappear before they touch the cookie tray.
—*Taste of Home* Test Kitchen

PREP: 35 min. • **BAKE:** 15 min./batch + cooling
MAKES: about 3 dozen

- 1 tube (16½ oz.) refrigerated sugar cookie dough
- ⅓ cup all-purpose flour
- ½ tsp. vanilla extract
- ¾ cup white baking chips
- ½ cup finely chopped macadamia nuts, toasted

GLAZE

- 1½ cups confectioners' sugar
- 3 Tbsp. 2% milk
- ½ tsp. lemon extract
- 1½ cups sweetened shredded coconut

1. Preheat oven to 350°. Place cookie dough in a large bowl; let stand at room temperature 5-10 minutes to soften.
2. Add flour and vanilla to dough; beat until blended (dough will be slightly crumbly). Stir in baking chips and nuts. Shape level tablespoonfuls of dough into balls; place 2 in. apart on parchment paper-lined baking sheets.
3. Bake until bottoms are lightly browned, 12-14 minutes. Remove to wire racks to cool completely.
4. For glaze, mix confectioners' sugar, milk and extract until smooth. Dip tops of cookies in glaze. Sprinkle with coconut, patting gently to adhere. Let stand until set.
Note: To toast nuts, bake in a shallow pan in a 350° oven for 5-10 minutes or cook in a skillet over low heat until lightly browned, stirring occasionally.

LAYERED CANDY CANE DESSERT

This fabulous dessert has the magical flavor of candy canes plus the bonus of an Oreo cookie crust. And it looks like a winter wonderland.
—Dawn Kreuser, Green Bay, WI

PREP: 25 min. + chilling • **MAKES:** 24 servings

- 1 pkg. (14.3 oz.) Oreo cookies
- 6 Tbsp. butter, melted
- 1 pkg. (8 oz.) cream cheese, softened
- ¼ cup sugar
- 2 Tbsp. 2% milk
- 1 carton (12 oz.) frozen whipped topping, thawed, divided
- ¾ cup crushed candy canes (about 7 regular size), divided
- 2 pkg. (3.3 oz. each) instant white chocolate pudding mix
- 2¾ cups cold 2% milk

1. Pulse cookies in a food processor until fine crumbs form. Add melted butter; pulse just until combined. Press onto bottom of a 13x9-in. dish. Refrigerate while preparing the filling.
2. Beat cream cheese, sugar and milk until smooth. Fold in 1 cup whipped topping and ½ cup crushed candies. Spread over crust.
3. Whisk pudding mix and milk 2 minutes; spread over cream cheese layer. Spread remaining whipped topping over the top. Refrigerate, covered, 4 hours. Sprinkle with remaining candies just before serving.

HOW TO PLAY WHITE ELEPHANT

This wildly fun gift exchange has many varieties of play. Here's the most widely used version.
1. Place gifts in a central spot. Every guest brings a wrapped gift with a cost of under $10 (it can also be something they already own).
2. Place numbered slips of paper—one for each participant—in a basket. Each guest draws a number. Guest 1 goes first, selects a gift and opens it.
3. Guest 2 either selects a gift from the pile and opens it, or steals Guest 1's gift. If 2 steals, 1 picks another gift from the pile and opens it.
4. Guest 3 can select a gift from the pile or steal a gift from Guest 1 or 2. The guest whose gift is stolen will always choose a replacement gift, either from the pile or from another guest. (They can't steal their own gift back in the same turn, though!) After a maximum of three swaps, the turn ends.
5. Continue until the last guest has either selected from the pile or stolen a gift from another guest. The exchange then ends when a guest decides to keep their gift instead of stealing one.

BRUNCH HASH &
EGG BAKE, PAGE 66

JOYFUL

MORNING
MEALS

MAPLE MORNING GRANOLA

Salty and sweet ingredients combine for an easy, wholesome breakfast or snack. Hosting a kids' party? Pack the granola into treat bags and present them as take-home favors.
—Elizabeth Godecke, Chicago, IL

PREP: 15 min. • BAKE: 35 min. + cooling
MAKES: 5 cups

- 3 cups old-fashioned oats
- ⅔ cup chopped pecans
- ⅓ cup salted pumpkin seeds or pepitas
- ½ cup maple syrup
- 4 tsp. butter, melted
- 1½ tsp. ground cinnamon
- ¼ tsp. salt
- ¼ tsp. ground nutmeg
- ½ cup dried apples, chopped
- ½ cup dried cranberries
  Plain yogurt

1. Preheat oven to 325°. In a large bowl, combine oats, pecans and pumpkin seeds. In a small bowl, mix maple syrup, butter, cinnamon, salt and nutmeg. Pour over the oat mixture and toss to coat.
2. Transfer to a 15x10x1-in. baking pan coated with cooking spray. Bake until golden brown, 35-40 minutes, stirring occasionally. Cool completely on a wire rack. Stir in dried fruits; serve with yogurt. Store granola in an airtight container.

❄ Holiday Helper

Quick-cooking and old-fashioned oats are largely interchangeable; the main difference is that quick-cooking oats are cut into smaller pieces before being rolled. The old-fashioned oats in this recipe are larger, providing a more substantial, heartier texture.

BRUNCH HASH & EGG BAKE

When my kids were growing up, I was cooking for eight. I couldn't conveniently fry eggs for eight, so I devised this recipe. Mild and salty feta cheese is my favorite for the dish, but shredded cheddar or Parmesan work, too.
—Lily Julow, Lawrenceville, GA

PREP: 45 min. • BAKE: 15 min.
MAKES: 8 servings

- 2 lbs. Yukon Gold potatoes, ed and cut into ¾-in. pieces
- 1 lb. bulk Italian sausage
- 1 large onion, finely chopped
- ¼ cup olive oil
- ¼ tsp. salt
- ¼ tsp. pepper
- 8 large eggs
- 1 cup crumbled feta cheese
  Minced fresh parsley

1. Preheat oven to 375°. Place potatoes in a large saucepan; add water to cover. Bring to a boil. Reduce heat; cook, uncovered, until almost tender, 6-8 minutes. Drain.
2. Meanwhile, in an ovenproof 12-in. skillet, cook and crumble sausage with chopped onion over medium heat until no longer pink, 6-8 minutes. Remove from pan with a slotted spoon; wipe skillet clean.
3. In the same pan, heat oil over medium-high heat. Add potatoes; sprinkle with salt and pepper. Cook until golden brown, 10-15 minutes, turning occasionally. Stir in sausage mixture. Remove from heat.
4. With the back of a spoon, make eight wells in the potato mixture. Break one egg into each well. Sprinkle with cheese.
5. Bake until the egg whites are set and yolks begin to thicken but are not hard, 12-15 minutes. Sprinkle with parsley.

CHRISTMAS MORNING FRENCH TOAST

Dress up French toast for the holidays with a nutty cream cheese filling and a citrusy sauce. No syrup needed!

—Janet Caico, Fleming Island, FL

PREP: 25 min. • **BAKE:** 5 min./batch
MAKES: 12 servings

- 1 pkg. (8 oz.) cream cheese, softened
- ½ cup crushed pineapple, drained
- 1 jar (12 oz.) orange marmalade, divided
- ½ cup chopped pecans, toasted
- 12 slices French bread (1½ in. thick)
- 5 large eggs
- 2 tsp. brown sugar
- 1 tsp. ground cinnamon
- ½ tsp. vanilla extract
- ⅛ tsp. ground nutmeg
- 1½ cups heavy whipping cream, divided
- ¼ cup orange juice
  Confectioners' sugar

1. In a small bowl, beat cream cheese, pineapple and ¼ cup of the marmalade until light and fluffy. Stir in pecans. Cut a pocket in the side of each bread slice; fill with cream cheese mixture.

2. In a shallow bowl, whisk eggs, brown sugar, cinnamon, vanilla, nutmeg and 1 cup of cream. Dip both sides of the filled bread slices into the egg mixture.

3. Cook on a greased hot griddle until golden brown, 2-3 minutes on each side.

4. Meanwhile, in a small saucepan, combine orange juice and the remaining marmalade. Cook and stir over medium heat until smooth. Add the remaining cream; heat through. Dust French toast with confectioners' sugar and serve with the orange sauce.

SLOW-COOKED BIG BREAKFAST

We make this during the holidays or on mornings when we know we're going to have a busy day. You can set this to cook overnight on low for an early breakfast, or for three hours on high for a leisurely brunch.

—Delisha Paris, Elizabeth Cty, NC

PREP: 30 min. • COOK: 3 hours + standing
MAKES: 12 servings

- 1 lb. bulk pork sausage
- 2 lbs. potatoes (about 4 medium), peeled and cut into ½-in. cubes
- ¼ cup water
- 1 large onion, finely chopped
- 1 medium sweet red pepper, chopped
- 2 cups fresh spinach
- 1 cup chopped fresh mushrooms
- 1 lb. cubed deli ham
- 1 cup shredded cheddar cheese
- 12 large eggs
- ½ cup 2% milk
- 1 tsp. garlic powder
- 1 tsp. pepper
- ½ tsp. salt

1. In a large skillet, cook and crumble the sausage over medium heat until it is no longer pink, 5-7 minutes; drain.

2. Meanwhile, place potatoes and water in a large microwave-safe dish. Microwave, covered, on high until potatoes are tender, 6 minutes, stirring halfway. Drain and add to sausage.

3. Stir in onion, sweet red pepper, spinach, mushrooms, ham and cheese. Transfer to a greased 6-qt. slow cooker.

4. Whisk together remaining ingredients until blended; pour over sausage mixture. Cook, covered, on low until the eggs are set, 3-4 hours. Let stand, uncovered, for 10 minutes before serving.

CRANBERRY ORANGE PANCAKES

If you need something special to serve on Christmas morning, these fluffy pancakes are drop-dead gorgeous, ready in just minutes and brimming with sweet, tart and tangy flavor. Seconds, anyone?

—Nancy Zimmerman, Cape May Court House, NJ

PREP: 20 min. • COOK: 5 min./batch
MAKES: 12 pancakes (1¼ cups syrup)

SYRUP
- 1 cup fresh or frozen cranberries
- ⅔ cup orange juice
- ½ cup sugar
- 3 Tbsp. maple syrup

PANCAKES
- 2 cups biscuit/baking mix
- 2 Tbsp. sugar
- 2 tsp. baking powder
- 2 large eggs
- 1 large egg yolk
- 1 cup evaporated milk
- 2 Tbsp. orange juice
- 1 tsp. grated orange zest
- ½ cup chopped fresh or frozen cranberries
  Orange peel strips, optional

1. In a small saucepan, bring the cranberries, orange juice and sugar to a boil. Reduce heat; simmer, uncovered, for 5 minutes. Cool slightly. With a slotted spoon, remove ¼ cup of the cranberries; set aside.

2. In a blender, process the cranberry mixture until smooth. Transfer to a small bowl; stir in maple syrup and the reserved cranberries. Keep warm.

3. In a large bowl, combine the biscuit mix, sugar and baking powder. In another bowl, whisk together the eggs, egg yolk, milk, orange juice and orange zest. Stir into the dry ingredients just until blended. Fold in the chopped cranberries.

4. Drop batter by ¼ cupfuls onto a greased hot griddle; turn when bubbles form on top. Cook until second side is golden brown. Serve with syrup. Garnish with orange peel strips if desired.

MAKE AHEAD

STUFFING & SAUSAGE STRATA

We're big fans of stuffing at our house, so we use it in this sausage strata. If you have leftover turkey, use it as a substitute for the sausage.

—Elizabeth Ray, Corona, CA

PREP: 20 min. + chilling
BAKE: 1 hour + standing • MAKES: 12 servings

- 1 lb. Italian turkey sausage links, casings removed
- ½ cup sliced fresh mushrooms, optional
- 6 cups cooked stuffing
- 2 cups shredded sharp cheddar cheese
- 10 large eggs
- 3 cups 2% milk
- 1 tsp. salt

1. In a large skillet, cook the sausage and sliced mushrooms over medium heat for 6-8 minutes or until meat is no longer pink, breaking into crumbles; drain.

2. In a greased 13x9-in. baking dish, layer half each of the stuffing, cheddar cheese and sausage mixture. Repeat layers. In a large bowl, whisk eggs, milk and salt until blended. Pour over layers. Refrigerate, covered, overnight.

3. Preheat oven to 325°. Remove strata from the refrigerator while the oven heats. Bake, uncovered, for 1-1¼ hours or until a knife inserted in the center comes out clean. Let stand 10 minutes before serving.

[MAKE AHEAD]

BRIE & PROSCIUTTO TART

Feel free to experiment with this versatile tart. Substitute ham or Canadian bacon for prosciutto, Swiss chard for spinach and your favorite kind of creamy cheese for Brie.
—Amy Tong, Anaheim, CA

PREP: 30 min. + cooling • **BAKE:** 30 min.
MAKES: 12 servings

- ½ cup finely chopped pecans
- 1½ cups all-purpose flour
- 2 tsp. sugar
- ½ cup cold butter, cubed
- 1 large egg yolk
- 1 Tbsp. water
- 1 tsp. Dijon mustard

FILLING

- 3 shallots, thinly sliced
- 1 Tbsp. olive oil
- 2 cups fresh baby spinach
- 4 thin slices prosciutto or deli ham
- 3 large eggs
- ⅔ cup 2% milk
- ¼ tsp. salt
- ⅛ tsp. pepper
- ⅛ tsp. ground nutmeg
- ⅛ tsp. crushed red pepper flakes
- 4 oz. Brie cheese, rind removed and cubed
- ¼ tsp. minced fresh thyme

1. Preheat oven to 350°. In a food processor, process pecans until finely chopped. Add flour and sugar; cover and pulse until blended. Add butter; cover and pulse until mixture resembles coarse crumbs. In a small bowl, whisk egg yolk, water and mustard. While processing, gradually add egg yolk mixture until the dough forms a ball.

2. Press onto the bottom and up the sides of an ungreased 14x4-in. fluted tart pan with removable bottom. Bake for 18-22 minutes or until crust is lightly browned. Cool on a wire rack.

3. In a large skillet, saute shallots in oil until tender. Add spinach; cook for 1-2 minutes longer or until wilted. Remove from skillet and set aside to cool.

4. In the same skillet, cook prosciutto over medium heat until slightly crisp. Remove to paper towels; drain. In a large bowl, whisk eggs, milk and seasonings. Spoon spinach mixture into the crust; pour the egg mixture over top. Top with prosciutto and cheese.

5. Bake 30-35 minutes or until a knife inserted in the center comes out clean. Sprinkle with thyme. Serve warm.

Freeze option: Before topping with thyme, securely wrap and freeze cooled tart in plastic wrap and foil. To use, partially thaw in refrigerator overnight. Remove from refrigerator 30 minutes before baking. Preheat oven to 350°. Unwrap quiche; reheat in oven until heated through and a thermometer inserted in center reads 165°. Sprinkle with thyme.

Note: You may use an ungreased 9-in. round fluted tart pan with removable bottom instead of the 14x4-in. pan. Bake as directed.

❄ Holiday Helper

"I use lots of nuts in my cooking and baking, and I would get upset when I ran out at a crucial time. Now I buy large bags of walnuts, pecans and other nuts from wholesale stores, pour them into freezer bags, label them and store them in the freezer. When fixing a recipe, I just pour out the amount of nuts called for and put the rest back in the freezer." —Doris Russell, Fallston, MD

CHOCOLATE CHUNK PANCAKES WITH RASPBERRY SAUCE

Chocolate and raspberries are two of my favorite ingredients, so I pack both into pancakes. I make these for my sister, who adores chocolate, too.
—Katherine Nelson, Centerville, UT

PREP: 20 min. • **COOK:** 5 min./batch
MAKES: 12 pancakes (1½ cups sauce)

- 1 pkg. (10 oz.) frozen sweetened raspberries, thawed
- ¼ cup orange juice
- 3 Tbsp. lemon juice
- 2 Tbsp. sugar

PANCAKES

- 1½ cups all-purpose flour
- 3 Tbsp. sugar
- 1 tsp. baking powder
- ½ tsp. baking soda
- ¼ tsp. salt
- 2 large eggs
- 1 cup 2% milk
- ¾ cup vanilla yogurt
- ¼ cup butter, melted
- ½ cup semisweet chocolate chunks or chips

1. Place raspberries, orange juice, lemon juice and sugar in a blender; cover and process until pureed. Press through a fine-mesh strainer into a bowl; discard the seeds.

2. In a large bowl, whisk flour, sugar, baking powder, baking soda and salt. In another bowl, whisk eggs, milk, yogurt and the melted butter until blended. Add to the dry ingredients, stirring just until moistened. Fold in chocolate chunks.

3. Lightly grease a griddle; heat over medium heat. Pour batter by ¼ cupfuls onto griddle. Cook until bubbles on top begin to pop and bottoms are golden brown. Turn; cook until second side is golden brown. Serve with raspberry sauce.

MAKE AHEAD

DOUBLE-CRUSTED SAUSAGE EGG CASSEROLE

This breakfast has become a Christmas tradition in our house. I love being able to assemble the casserole the night before. Then I pop it into the oven to bake while we open gifts in the morning.

—Lynne German, Woodland Hill, CA

PREP: 25 min. + chilling • **BAKE:** 35 min.
MAKES: 12 servings

- 2 lbs. bulk pork sausage
- 4 cups shredded Monterey Jack cheese
- 2 cans (8 oz. each) refrigerated crescent rolls
- 7 large eggs
- ¼ cup 2% milk
- ¼ tsp. salt
- ¼ tsp. pepper
- ¼ cup grated Parmesan cheese

1. In a large skillet, cook sausage over medium heat 8-10 minutes or until no longer pink, breaking into crumbles; drain. Stir in Monterey Jack cheese.
2. Unroll one tube of crescent dough into one long rectangle; press the perforations to seal. Press onto bottom of a greased 13x9-in. baking dish. Top dough with the sausage mixture.
3. Separate 1 egg; reserve the egg white for brushing top. In a small bowl, whisk egg yolk, milk, salt, pepper and remaining eggs until blended; pour over sausage mixture. Sprinkle with Parmesan cheese.
4. On a lightly floured surface, unroll the remaining crescent dough and roll into a 13x9-in. rectangle; cut crosswise into 13 strips. Twist each strip and place over the filling; brush with the reserved egg white. Refrigerate, covered, overnight.
5. Remove from refrigerator 30 minutes before baking. Preheat oven to 350°. Bake 35-40 minutes or until golden brown. Let stand 5-10 minutes before serving.

MAKE AHEAD

ORANGE BREAKFAST SOUFFLE WITH DRIED CHERRIES

Our family often took this sweet souffle to a local park as part of our Father's Day picnic brunch because it travels well.

—Sharon Ricci, Mendon, NY

PREP: 20 min. + chilling
BAKE: 45 min. + standing • MAKES: 9 servings

- ½ cup orange juice
- ¾ cup dried cherries, divided
- 6 large eggs
- 2 cups 2% milk
- ¼ cup sugar
- 1 Tbsp. grated orange zest
- 2 tsp. vanilla extract
- 1 tsp. ground cinnamon
- ¼ tsp. salt
- 8 cups cubed brioche or egg bread
- 1½ cups cubed Havarti cheese
- 1 cup maple syrup
  Confectioners' sugar

1. Pour orange juice over ½ cup of the cherries in a small bowl; let stand for 15 minutes. In a large bowl, whisk eggs, milk, sugar, orange zest, vanilla, cinnamon and salt until blended. Stir in the cherry mixture. Gently stir in bread cubes; transfer to a greased 8-in. square baking dish. Sprinkle with cheese. Refrigerate, covered, several hours or overnight.
2. Preheat oven to 350°. Remove souffle from refrigerator while oven heats. Bake for 45-55 minutes or until puffed, golden and a knife inserted in the center comes out clean. Let stand 10 minutes before cutting.
3. In a small saucepan, combine maple syrup and remaining cherries; heat through. Serve with souffle; dust with confectioners' sugar.

ROASTED TOMATO QUICHE

This comes together fast enough that I don't have to wake up early to get it on the table.

—Elisabeth Larsen, Pleasant Grove, UT

PREP: 45 min. • BAKE: 40 min. + standing
MAKES: 6 servings

- 1 sheet refrigerated pie pastry
- 1 cup grape tomatoes
- 1 Tbsp. olive oil
- ⅛ tsp. plus ½ tsp. salt, divided
- ⅛ tsp. plus ¼ tsp. pepper, divided
- ½ lb. bulk Italian sausage
- 1 small onion, chopped
- 1 pkg. (6 oz.) fresh baby spinach, chopped
- 1 cup shredded part-skim mozzarella cheese
- 3 large eggs
- 1 cup half-and-half cream
- ½ tsp. garlic powder

1. Unroll pastry into a 9-in. pie plate; flute edges. Line unpricked pastry with a double thickness of heavy-duty foil. Fill with dried beans, uncooked rice or pie weights.
2. Bake at 450° for 8 minutes. Remove foil and weights; bake 5 minutes longer. Cool on a wire rack.
3. Place tomatoes in a 15x10x1-in. baking pan. Drizzle with oil; sprinkle with ⅛ tsp. each salt and pepper. Bake until skins blister, 8-10 minutes.
4. In a large skillet, cook the sausage and onion over medium heat until sausage is no longer pink; drain. Remove sausage. In the same skillet, cook spinach until wilted, 4-5 minutes.
5. Combine sausage, tomatoes, spinach and cheese; transfer to crust. Whisk eggs, cream, garlic powder and remaining salt and pepper; pour over the top.
6. Bake at 375° until a knife inserted in center comes out clean, 40-45 minutes. If needed, cover edges with foil during the last 15 minutes to prevent overbrowning. Let stand 10 minutes before serving.
Note: Let pie weights cool before storing. Beans and rice may be reused for pie weights, but not for cooking.

MAKE AHEAD

BAKED BLUEBERRY-MASCARPONE FRENCH TOAST

When I want something special to serve my guests for brunch, I turn to this recipe. It never fails.

—Patricia Quinn, Omaha, NE

PREP: 15 min. + chilling
BAKE: 1 hour + standing • **MAKES:** 10 servings

- 8 slices French bread (½ in. thick), cubed (about 4 cups)
- 2 cups fresh or frozen blueberries
- 2 cartons (8 oz. each) mascarpone cheese
- ½ cup confectioners' sugar
- 10 slices French bread (1 in. thick)
- 8 large eggs
- 2 cups half-and-half cream
- 1 cup whole milk
- ⅓ cup granulated sugar
- 1 tsp. vanilla extract
   Additional confectioners' sugar
- 1 cup sliced almonds, toasted
   Additional fresh blueberries, optional

1. In a greased 13x9-in. baking dish, layer bread cubes and blueberries. In a small bowl, beat mascarpone cheese and confectioners' sugar until smooth; drop by tablespoonfuls over blueberries. Top with bread slices. In a large bowl, whisk eggs, cream, milk, granulated sugar and vanilla; pour over bread cubes. Refrigerate, covered, overnight.
2. Preheat oven to 350°. Remove French toast from refrigerator while oven heats. Bake, covered, for 30 minutes. Bake, uncovered, 30-40 minutes longer or until puffed and golden and a knife inserted in the center comes out clean.
3. Let stand 10 minutes before serving. Dust with additional confectioners' sugar; sprinkle with almonds. If desired, serve with additional blueberries.
Note: To toast nuts, bake in a shallow pan in a 350° oven for 5-10 minutes or cook in a skillet over low heat until lightly browned, stirring occasionally.

CHOCOLATE CREPES WITH RASPBERRY SAUCE

Everyone at the table will feel special eating this scrumptious treat. Seemingly rich and decadent, these crepes are actually low in fat.

—Rebecca Baird, Salt Lake City, UT

PREP: 25 min. + chilling • **COOK:** 20 min.
MAKES: 8 servings

- 1 cup fat-free milk
- ½ cup fat-free evaporated milk
- 2 large egg whites
- 1 large egg
- 1 cup all-purpose flour
- ¼ cup plus ⅓ cup sugar, divided
- ¼ cup baking cocoa
- ½ tsp. salt
- 4½ tsp. cornstarch
- 1 cup water
- 4½ cups fresh or frozen raspberries, thawed, divided
   Reduced-fat whipped cream in a can
- 1 tsp. confectioners' sugar

1. In a small bowl, combine the milk, evaporated milk, egg whites and egg. Combine the flour, ¼ cup of the sugar, the cocoa and salt; add to milk mixture and mix well. Cover and refrigerate for 1 hour.
2. In a small saucepan, combine the cornstarch and remaining sugar; set aside. Place water and 3½ cups raspberries in a blender; cover and process for 2-3 minutes or until pureed.
3. Strain puree into the cornstarch mixture and discard seeds. Bring to a boil; cook and stir 2 minutes or until thickened. Transfer to a small bowl; refrigerate until chilled.
4. Coat an 8-in. nonstick skillet with cooking spray; heat over medium heat. Stir the crepe batter; pour a scant 3 Tbsp. into center of skillet. Lift and tilt the pan to coat bottom evenly. Cook until top appears dry; turn and cook 15-20 seconds longer. Remove to a wire rack.
5. Repeat with the remaining batter, coating skillet with cooking spray as needed. When cool, stack crepes with waxed paper or paper towels in between.

6. Spread each crepe with 2 Tbsp. sauce. Fold each crepe into quarters; place two crepes on each of eight plates. Top with the remaining sauce and 1 Tbsp. whipped cream. Garnish with remaining raspberries and sprinkle with confectioners' sugar.

❄ *Reader Review*

"A decadent breakfast that's perfect if you have guests! Who doesn't want to eat dessert first?"

GINA.KAPFHAMER TASTEOFHOME.COM

FAST FIX

APPLE-HONEY DUTCH BABY

I love to make this treat on Sunday mornings. It's so impressive when it's served warm right out of the oven. . .and the honey and apple filling is wonderful!

—Kathy Fleming, Lisle, IL

TAKES: 30 min. • **MAKES:** 4 servings

- 3 large eggs
- ¾ cup 2% milk
- ¾ cup all-purpose flour
- 1 Tbsp. sugar
- 2 Tbsp. butter

TOPPING
- 1 Tbsp. butter
- 2 large apples, sliced
- ½ cup honey
- 2 to 3 tsp. lemon juice
- ½ tsp. ground cardamom
- 1 tsp. cornstarch
- 2 tsp. cold water

1. Preheat oven to 400°. In a large bowl, whisk together the first four ingredients until smooth. Place the butter in a 10-in. ovenproof skillet; heat in oven until melted, 2-3 minutes.
2. Tilt pan to coat bottom and sides with melted butter. Pour batter into hot skillet. Bake until puffed and edges are lightly browned, 16-20 minutes
3. Meanwhile, for the topping, in a large saucepan, heat butter over medium heat; saute apples until lightly browned. Stir in honey, lemon juice and cardamom. Mix cornstarch and water until smooth; stir into apple mixture. Bring to a boil; cook and stir until thickened, 1-2 minutes. Spoon into pancake; serve immediately.

LOADED TATER TOT BAKE

I keep frozen Tater Tots on hand for meals like this yummy casserole. It's a super brunch, breakfast or side dish for kids of all ages.
—Nancy Heishman, Las Vegas, NV

PREP: 15 min. • **BAKE:** 35 min.
MAKES: 6 servings

- 1 Tbsp. canola oil
- 1 medium onion, finely chopped
- 6 oz. Canadian bacon, cut into ½-in. strips
- 4 cups frozen Tater Tots, thawed
- 6 large eggs, lightly beaten
- ½ cup reduced-fat sour cream
- ½ cup half-and-half cream
- 1 Tbsp. dried parsley flakes
- ¾ tsp. garlic powder
- ½ tsp. pepper
- 1½ cups shredded cheddar cheese

1. Preheat oven to 350°. In a large skillet, heat oil over medium heat. Add onion; cook and stir 2-3 minutes or until tender. Add Canadian bacon; cook 1-2 minutes or until lightly browned, stirring occasionally. Remove from heat.
2. Line bottom of a greased 11x7-in. baking dish with Tater Tots; top with Canadian bacon mixture. In a large bowl, whisk eggs, sour cream, cream and seasonings until blended. Stir in cheese; pour over top. Bake, uncovered, 35-40 minutes or until golden brown.
Shepherd's Inn Breakfast Pie: Substitute 1½ pounds bulk pork sausage, cooked and drained, for the onion and Canadian bacon. Substitute ¾ cup milk for the sour cream and cream; omit pepper. Assemble and bake as directed. Top with 2 chopped fresh tomatoes.

PUMPKIN SPICE OATMEAL

There's nothing like a warm cup of oatmeal in the morning, and my spiced version works in a slow cooker so you can have it ready when you wake up. Store leftovers in the fridge.
—Jordan Mason, Brookville, PA

PREP: 10 min. • **COOK:** 5 hours
MAKES: 6 servings

- 1 can (15 oz.) solid-pack pumpkin
- 1 cup steel-cut oats
- 3 Tbsp. brown sugar
- 1½ tsp. pumpkin pie spice
- 1 tsp. ground cinnamon
- ¾ tsp. salt
- 3 cups water
- 1½ cups 2% milk
  Optional toppings: toasted chopped pecans, ground cinnamon, and additional brown sugar and milk

In a large bowl, combine the first six ingredients; stir in water and milk. Transfer mixture to a greased 3-qt. slow cooker. Cook, covered, on low 5-6 hours or until oats are tender, stirring once. Serve with toppings as desired.

GINGERBREAD BELGIAN WAFFLES

I combine the sweet and spicy taste of gingerbread with tart cream cheese icing in this breakfast treat. It's a heavenly way to start the day.

—Jannine Fisk, Malden, MA

PREP: 25 min. • **COOK:** 5 min./batch
MAKES: 6 waffles (1½ cups icing)

- ½ cup butter, softened
- 2 oz. cream cheese, softened
- ½ tsp. vanilla extract
- ⅛ tsp. salt
- 1½ cups confectioners' sugar
- 2 Tbsp. 2% milk

WAFFLES

- 2 cups all-purpose flour
- ¼ cup packed brown sugar
- 3 tsp. baking powder
- 1½ tsp. ground ginger
- 1 tsp. baking soda
- 1 tsp. ground cinnamon
- ½ tsp. salt
- ¼ tsp. ground nutmeg
- 4 large eggs, separated
- 2 cups buttermilk
- ½ cup butter, melted
- ½ cup molasses
- 2 tsp. vanilla extract

1. Beat the first four ingredients until smooth; gradually beat in confectioners' sugar, then milk. Cover and set aside.
2. Preheat Belgian waffle maker. Whisk together the first eight waffle ingredients. In another bowl, whisk together egg yolks, buttermilk, melted butter, molasses and vanilla. Add to the dry ingredients; stir just until moistened.
3. In a clean bowl, beat the egg whites until stiff but not dry. Gently fold into batter. Bake waffles according to manufacturers' directions. Drizzle with icing.

BRUNCH PUFF WITH SAUSAGE GRAVY

When company stays overnight, I make this puff with sausage gravy as a hearty breakfast treat. It's meaty, cheesy and delightful with a fresh fruit salad.

—Danielle Cochran, Grayling, MI

PREP: 25 min. • **BAKE:** 20 min.
MAKES: 9 servings

- 7 large eggs, divided use
- ¼ cup 2% milk
- ¼ tsp. salt
- ¼ tsp. plus ⅛ tsp. pepper, divided
- 1 Tbsp. butter
- 1 Tbsp. water
- 1 pkg. (17.3 oz.) frozen puff pastry, thawed
- 8 oz. sliced deli ham (¼ in. thick)
- 1 cup shredded cheddar cheese

SAUSAGE GRAVY

- ¾ lb. bulk pork sausage
- 1 envelope country gravy mix

1. Preheat oven to 400°. In a small bowl, whisk 6 eggs, milk, salt and ¼ tsp. pepper until blended.
2. In a large nonstick skillet coated with cooking spray, heat butter over medium heat. Pour in egg mixture; cook and stir just until eggs are thickened and no liquid egg remains. Remove from heat.
3. In a small bowl, whisk remaining egg with water. On a lightly floured surface, unfold one sheet of puff pastry and roll to a 10-in. square. Transfer to a parchment paper-lined baking sheet. Arrange ham over pastry to within 1 in. of edges; top with scrambled eggs. Sprinkle with cheese.
4. Brush beaten egg mixture over edges of pastry. Roll remaining puff pastry to a 10-in. square; place over filling. Press edges with a fork to seal; cut slits in top. Brush top with additional egg mixture; sprinkle with remaining pepper. Bake 20-25 minutes or until golden brown.
5. In a large skillet, cook sausage over medium heat 6-8 minutes or until no longer pink, breaking into crumbles. Remove with a slotted spoon; drain on paper towels. Discard drippings; wipe skillet clean.
6. In same pan, prepare the gravy mix according to package directions. Stir in sausage. Serve with pastry.

HASH BROWN PANCAKES WITH SMOKED SALMON & DILL CREAM

On weekends when I was growing up, pancakes, salmon and bagels were our brunch staples. Here, I've combined these elements, using whipped cream instead of cream cheese.
—Arlene Erlbach, Morton Grove, IL

PREP: 15 min. • **COOK:** 20 min.
MAKES: 4 servings

- ⅓ cup heavy whipping cream
- 1⅛ tsp. dill weed, divided
- 4 cups frozen shredded hash brown potatoes, thawed
- 2 large eggs, beaten
- 2 Tbsp. minced chives
- ¼ tsp. salt
- 1 pkg. (3 to 4 oz.) smoked salmon or lox

1. Beat heavy whipping cream and 1 tsp. dill on high until stiff peaks form. Cover and refrigerate.

2. Preheat griddle over medium heat. Stir together potatoes, eggs, chives and salt until well combined. Grease griddle. Drop the potato mixture by heaping ½ cupfuls onto griddle; flatten to ½-in. thick. Cook until the bottoms are golden brown, about 10 minutes. Turn; cook until second side is golden brown. Keep warm.

3. To serve, place smoked salmon slices on pancakes. Top with whipped cream; sprinkle with remaining dill.

❄ Holiday Helper

Preheat the griddle to get an even crust on potato pancakes. To preheat a cast iron, set your stovetop between medium-low and medium heat; the griddle is at temperature when water sizzles on the surface.

MUSHROOM & ASPARAGUS EGGS BENEDICT

This recipe is easy, but it looks as if you spent hours! I serve it with broiled grapefruit topped with brown sugar and ginger for breakfast, and with a green salad tossed with tomatoes and balsamic vinaigrette for brunch.

—Nadine Mesch, Mount Healthy, OH

PREP: 25 min. • COOK: 25 min.
MAKES: 4 servings

- 12 fresh asparagus spears
- 3 tsp. olive oil, divided
- 1 shallot, finely chopped
- 2 Tbsp. butter, divided
- 2⅔ cups sliced baby portobello mushrooms
- 2½ cups sliced fresh shiitake mushrooms
- 1 garlic clove, minced
- ¼ cup sherry
- ½ cup heavy whipping cream
- ½ tsp. salt
- 1 Tbsp. minced fresh basil
- 1 Tbsp. white vinegar
- 4 large eggs
- 4 slices French bread (¾ in. thick), toasted
- ¼ tsp. pepper
- 2 tsp. balsamic vinegar

1. In a large skillet, saute asparagus in 1 tsp. oil in a large skillet until crisp-tender; remove and keep warm.
2. Saute shallot in remaining oil and 1 Tbsp. butter in the same skillet until tender. Add mushrooms and garlic; cook 4 minutes more. Add sherry; stir to loosen browned bits from pan. Stir in cream and salt. Bring to a boil. Cook and stir for 1-2 minutes or until slightly thickened. Stir in basil.
3. Meanwhile, place 2-3 in. of water in a large skillet with high sides; add white vinegar. Bring to a boil; reduce heat and simmer gently. Break cold eggs, one at a time, into a custard cup or saucer. Holding the cup close to the surface of the water, slip each egg into water.
4. Cook, uncovered, until the egg whites are completely set and the yolks are still soft, about 4 minutes. With a slotted spoon, lift eggs out of the water.
5. Spread the remaining butter over toast slices. Top each with asparagus, a poached egg and mushroom mixture. Sprinkle with pepper and drizzle with balsamic vinegar. Serve immediately.

APPLE-CRANBERRY BREAKFAST RISOTTO

Cranberries and apples are tart enough to balance the sweetness in this hearty dish. It's fun for an after-presents breakfast on Christmas morning.

—Betsy King, Duluth, MN

PREP: 15 min. • COOK: 3 hours
MAKES: 10 servings

- ¼ cup butter, cubed
- 1½ cups uncooked arborio rice
- 2 medium apples, peeled and chopped
- ⅓ cup packed brown sugar
- ¼ tsp. kosher salt
- 1½ tsp. ground cinnamon
- ⅛ tsp. ground nutmeg
- ⅛ tsp. ground cloves
- 3 cups 2% milk
- 2 cups unsweetened apple juice
- 1 cup dried cranberries

1. Heat butter in a 4-qt. slow cooker on high heat until melted. Add rice; stir to coat. Add apples, brown sugar, salt and spices. Stir in milk and apple juice.
2. Cook, covered, on low until the rice is tender, 3-4 hours, stirring halfway. Stir in the cranberries during the last 15 minutes of cooking.

❄ Holiday Helper

Arborio, a medium-grain rice, gives risotto its creamy texture. If you can't find arborio, look for a rice with a high starch content, such as brown rice or white sushi rice, or go for pearled barley, farro or Israeli (pearl) couscous.

PEACHES & CREAM WAFFLE DIPPERS

I've prepared these for many brunches. Peaches are my personal favorite, but you can use strawberries or blueberries if you prefer. People of all ages enjoy dunking these crispy waffle strips!

—Bonnie Geavaras-Bootz, Scottsdale, AZ

PREP: 30 min. • BAKE: 5 min./batch
MAKES: 6 servings (2 cups sauce)

- 1 cup all-purpose flour
- 1 Tbsp. sugar
- 1 tsp. baking powder
- ¼ tsp. salt
- 2 large eggs, separated
- 1 cup 2% milk
- 2 Tbsp. butter, melted
- ¼ tsp. vanilla extract
- 1¼ cups chopped frozen peaches, thawed, divided
- 2 cups sweetened whipped cream or whipped topping
- ¾ cup peach yogurt
  Toasted pecans and ground cinnamon, optional

1. In a large bowl, whisk flour, sugar, baking powder and salt. In another bowl, whisk egg yolks, milk, butter and vanilla until blended. Add to dry ingredients; stir just until moistened. Stir in 1 cup peaches.
2. In a small bowl, beat egg whites until stiff but not dry. Fold into the batter. Bake in a preheated waffle iron according to manufacturer's directions until golden brown. Cut the waffles into 1-in. strips.
3. In a small bowl, fold the whipped cream into the yogurt. Serve with waffles. Sprinkle with the remaining peaches and, if desired, pecans and cinnamon.

CORNFLAKE-COATED CRISPY BACON

I've loved my aunt's crispy coated bacon ever since I was a child. Now I share the super simple side dish with my own children. We enjoy a big panful every Christmas morning, and on many other days throughout the year.

—Brenda Severson, Norman, OK

PREP: 20 min. • BAKE: 25 min.
MAKES: 9 servings

½	cup evaporated milk
2	Tbsp. ketchup
1	Tbsp. Worcestershire sauce
	Dash pepper
18	bacon strips (1 lb.)
3	cups crushed cornflakes

Preheat oven to 375°. In a large bowl, combine milk, ketchup, Worcestershire sauce and pepper. Add bacon strips, turning to coat. Dip strips in crushed corn flakes, patting to help coating adhere. Place bacon on two racks in ungreased 15x10x1-in. baking pans. Bake for 25-30 minutes or until golden and crisp, rotating pans halfway through baking.

❄ Reader Review

"My husband was skeptical when he saw that I was coating his bacon with cornflake crumbs, but when I set it out for breakfast he was really impressed! There was a bit of a battle for the last piece."

REDCOTTAGECHRONICLES TASTEOFHOME.COM

HASH BROWN NESTS WITH PORTOBELLOS & EGGS

Hash browns make a fabulous crust for individual egg quiches. They look fancy but are actually easy to make. These little nests have been a hit at holiday brunches and other special occasions.

—Kate Meyer, Brentwood, TN

PREP: 30 min. • BAKE: 15 min.
MAKES: 12 servings

- 2 Tbsp. butter
- ½ lb. sliced baby portobello mushrooms, chopped
- ¼ cup chopped shallots
- 1 garlic clove, minced
- ½ tsp. salt
- ¼ tsp. pepper
    Dash cayenne pepper
- 2 Tbsp. sour cream
- 1 Tbsp. minced fresh basil or 1 tsp. dried basil
- 4 cups frozen shredded hash brown potatoes (about 1 lb.), thawed
- 7 large eggs, lightly beaten
- ¼ cup shredded Swiss cheese
- 2 bacon strips, cooked and crumbled

1. Preheat oven to 400°. In a large skillet, heat butter over medium-high heat; saute mushrooms and shallots until tender. Add garlic and seasonings; cook and stir 1 minute. Remove from heat; stir in sour cream and basil.
2. Press about ¼ cup potatoes into bottom and up sides of greased muffin cups. Fill each with about 2 Tbsp. of the beaten eggs. Top with the mushroom mixture, cheese and bacon.
3. Bake until eggs are set, 15-18 minutes.

FAST FIX
CHORIZO & GRITS BREAKFAST BOWLS

Growing up, I bonded with my dad over chorizo and eggs. My approach combines them with grits and black beans. Add a spoonful of pico de gallo for more fresh flavor.

—Jenn Tidwell, Fair Oaks, CA

TAKES: 30 min. • MAKES: 6 servings

- 2 tsp. olive oil
- 1 pkg. (12 oz.) fully cooked chorizo chicken sausages or flavor of choice, sliced
- 1 large zucchini, chopped
- 3 cups water
- ¾ cup quick-cooking grits
- 1 can (15 oz.) black beans, rinsed and drained
- ½ cup shredded cheddar cheese
- 6 large eggs
    Pico de gallo and chopped fresh cilantro, optional

1. In a large nonstick skillet, heat oil over medium heat. Add sausage; cook and stir 2-3 minutes or until lightly browned. Add zucchini; cook and stir 4-5 minutes longer or until tender. Remove from pan and keep warm.
2. Meanwhile, in a large saucepan, bring water to a boil. Slowly stir in grits. Reduce heat to medium-low; cook, covered, about 5 minutes or until thickened, stirring occasionally. Stir in beans and cheese until blended. Remove from heat.
3. Wipe skillet clean; coat with cooking spray and place over medium heat. In batches, break eggs, one at a time, into pan. Immediately reduce heat to low; cook until whites are completely set and yolks begin to thicken but are not hard, about 5 minutes.
4. To serve, divide grits mixture among six bowls. Top with chorizo mixture, eggs and, if desired, pico de gallo and cilantro.

FAST FIX

PUMPKIN-CHOCOLATE CHIP PANCAKES

Who can resist a sky-high stack of golden, fluffy pancakes? Pumpkin and chocolate chips take them over the top!

—Elizabeth Godecke, Chicago, IL

TAKES: 30 min. • MAKES: 15 pancakes

- 2⅓ cups pancake mix
- ½ tsp. ground cinnamon
- ¼ tsp. ground nutmeg
- ¼ tsp. ground cloves
- 2 large eggs
- 1¼ cups buttermilk
- ⅓ cup canned pumpkin
- ¼ cup butter, melted
- 1 Tbsp. honey
- ½ cup miniature semisweet chocolate chips
  Additional miniature semisweet chocolate chips and honey

1. In a large bowl, combine pancake mix, cinnamon, nutmeg and cloves. In a small bowl, whisk eggs, buttermilk, pumpkin, melted butter and honey; stir into the dry ingredients just until moistened. Fold in chocolate chips.

2. Lightly grease a griddle; heat over medium heat. Pour batter by ¼ cupfuls onto griddle. Cook until bubbles on top begin to pop and bottoms are golden brown. Turn; cook until second side is golden brown. Serve with additional chocolate chips and honey.

WESTERN OMELET CASSEROLE

When I'm hosting brunch, I make omelets the easy way. From youngest to oldest, my whole family's on board.

—Kathleen Murphy, Littleton, CO

PREP: 15 min. • COOK: 6 hours + standing
MAKES: 8 servings

- 1 pkg. (30 oz.) frozen shredded hash brown potatoes, thawed
- 1 lb. cubed fully cooked ham or 1 lb. bulk pork sausage, cooked and drained
- 1 medium onion, chopped
- 1 medium green pepper, chopped
- 1½ cups shredded cheddar cheese
- 12 large eggs
- 1 cup 2% milk
- 1 tsp. salt
- 1 tsp. pepper

1. In a greased 5- or 6-qt. slow cooker, layer half of each of the following: potatoes, ham, onion, green pepper and cheese. Repeat layers.

2. Whisk together remaining ingredients; pour over top. Cook, covered, on low until set, 6-7 hours. Turn off the slow cooker. Remove insert; let stand, uncovered, 15-30 minutes before serving.

COUNTRY SAUSAGE & EGG ROLLS

These savory rolls are always a great choice. They're nice enough to serve guests and make an excellent on-the-go breakfast, too.

—Lisa Speer, Palm Beach, FL

PREP: 50 min. • BAKE: 30 min.
MAKES: 12 servings

- 1 lb. bulk pork sausage
- 1 cup chopped sweet onion
- 1 garlic clove, minced
- ½ tsp. pepper, divided
- 8 large eggs
- 3 Tbsp. whole milk
- ¼ tsp. salt
- 1 Tbsp. butter
- ¾ cup shredded sharp cheddar cheese
- 3 green onions, chopped
- 15 sheets phyllo dough (14x9 in.)
- ⅓ cup butter, melted

1. In a large skillet, cook sausage, sweet onion, garlic and ¼ tsp. of the pepper over medium heat 6-8 minutes or until the meat is no longer pink, breaking into crumbles; drain. Remove and keep warm.

2. In a small bowl, whisk eggs, milk, salt and the remaining pepper. In same skillet, melt butter over medium-high heat. Pour in the egg mixture; cook and stir until almost set. Stir in cheese, green onions and sausage mixture. Remove from heat.

3. Preheat oven to 350°. Place one sheet of phyllo dough on a work surface; brush with melted butter. Layer with four additional phyllo sheets, brushing with butter after each layer. (Keep remaining phyllo covered with plastic wrap and a damp towel to prevent it from drying out.) Repeat, making three stacks.

4. Cut each stack in half lengthwise and in half crosswise, forming four 7x4½-in. rectangles. Spoon ¼ cup of the egg mixture along a long side of each rectangle; roll up.

5. Place the rolls on an ungreased baking sheet, seam side down. With a sharp knife, make four shallow slashes across each roll; brush with butter. Bake 30-35 minutes or until golden brown.

SANTA BELT NAPKIN RINGS

Bright red napkins that resemble Santa's suit—how jolly! Just cinch them up with belt napkin rings made of black ribbon and gold-sparkle card stock. For each ring, punch or cut a square from the card stock. Using a pencil, mark two slits in the center that are as long as the width of your ribbon. Use a craft knife to cut the slits, then thread the ribbon through the slits and tie it around a napkin.

GARLIC HERBED
BEEF TENDERLOIN, PAGE 93

CHRISTMAS

DINNER
MENUS

CROWN ROAST WITH APRICOT DRESSING

I'd been making crown roasts for years but was only satisfied with the results when I combined recipes to come up with this guest-pleasing version. It's beautifully roasted with an apricot glaze and a nicely browned dressing.

—Isabell Cooper, Cambridge, NS

PREP: 20 min. • **BAKE:** 2½ hours + standing
MAKES: 12 servings

- 1 pork crown roast (12 ribs and about 8 lbs.)
- ½ tsp. seasoned salt
- ⅓ cup apricot preserves
- **APRICOT DRESSING**
- ¼ cup butter, cubed
- 1 cup sliced fresh mushrooms
- 1 medium onion, finely chopped
- 1 celery rib, finely chopped
- 1 cup chopped dried apricots
- ½ tsp. dried savory
- ½ tsp. dried thyme
- ¼ tsp. salt
- ¼ tsp. pepper
- 3 cups soft bread crumbs

1. Preheat oven to 350°. Place roast on a rack in a shallow roasting pan. Sprinkle with seasoned salt. Bake, uncovered, for 1 hour.
2. Brush sides of roast with preserves. Bake until a thermometer reads 145°, 1½-2 hours longer. Transfer roast to a serving platter. Let stand 20 minutes before carving.
3. For dressing, in a large skillet, heat butter over medium-high heat. Add mushrooms, onion and celery; cook and stir 6-8 minutes or until tender. Stir in the apricots and seasonings. Add bread crumbs; toss to coat. Transfer to a greased 8-in. square baking dish. Bake for 15-20 minutes or until lightly browned. Carve roast between ribs; serve with dressing.
Note: For presentation purposes, if desired, spoon dressing into center of roast.

Apple-Cranberry Stuffed Crown Roast:
For dressing, melt ½ cup butter in a large skillet. Add 1 chopped large onion and 1 chopped celery rib; saute until tender. Transfer to a large bowl; stir in 2 chopped, peeled medium apples, ½ cup dried cranberries, ½ tsp. dried thyme, ½ tsp. salt and ½ tsp. pepper. Add 8 cups soft whole grain bread crumbs; toss to coat. Stir in ½ cup chicken broth. Proceed as directed.

AU GRATIN TURNIPS

My father's favorite food was turnips, either cooked or raw. This dish always reminds me of his many second helpings of turnips at the dinner table.

—Janie Colle, Hutchinson, KS

PREP: 30 min. • **BAKE:** 20 min.
MAKES: 12 servings

- 3 lbs. medium turnips (about 6), peeled and cubed
- ½ cup butter, cubed
- 4 green onions, chopped, divided
- ⅓ cup all-purpose flour
- ¾ tsp. salt
- ¼ tsp. pepper
- 3 cups half-and-half cream
- 2 cups shredded cheddar cheese, divided

1. Preheat oven to 350°. Place turnips in a 6-qt. stockpot; add water to cover. Bring to a boil. Cook, uncovered, 12-15 minutes or until tender. Drain and return to pan.
2. In a large saucepan, melt butter over medium heat. Add half of the green onions. Cook and stir 2-3 minutes or until tender. Stir in flour, salt and pepper until blended; gradually whisk in cream. Bring to a boil, stirring constantly; cook and stir for 2-3 minutes or until thickened. Stir in ¾ cup cheese until melted. Pour sauce over turnips; toss to coat. Transfer to a greased 3-qt. baking dish. Top with remaining cheese. Bake, uncovered, 20-25 minutes or until bubbly and cheese is melted. Sprinkle with the remaining onions.

RUM-RAISIN SWEET POTATOES

We've traded in baked potatoes for these sweet potatoes with a spicy twist. The Chinese five-spice powder gives an added kick.

—Pamela Weatherford, San Antonio, TX

PREP: 20 min. • **COOK:** 1 hour + cooling
MAKES: 16 servings

- 8 large sweet potatoes (about 6½ lbs.)
- 1 cup raisins
- ⅔ cup dark rum
- 1 cup half-and-half cream
- ½ cup butter, cubed
- 3 Tbsp. brown sugar
- 1 Tbsp. Chinese five-spice powder
- 1¼ tsp. salt
- ½ tsp. pepper
- ½ cup chopped walnuts, toasted

1. Place potatoes in a stockpot; add water to cover. Bring to a boil. Reduce heat; cook, uncovered, 40-45 minutes or until tender. Meanwhile, in a microwave-safe bowl, combine raisins and rum. Microwave, uncovered, on high for 30 seconds; set aside. In a small saucepan, heat cream and butter until butter is melted. Drain potatoes. When cool enough to handle, peel potatoes; return to pan.
2. Mash potatoes, gradually adding brown sugar, five-spice powder, salt, pepper and butter mixture. Stir in raisin mixture. If necessary, warm potatoes over low heat, stirring occasionally. Transfer to a serving bowl. Sprinkle with walnuts.

MUSHROOM PASTRY TARTS

Putting anything on a puff pastry crust makes for a special treat, but these mushrooms are so good that combining the two creates an unforgettable dish.

—Susan Scarborough, Fernandina Beach, FL

....

PREP: 50 min. • BAKE: 15 min. • MAKES: 1 dozen

<table>
<tr><td>¼</td><td>cup chopped walnuts or hazelnuts</td></tr>
<tr><td>3</td><td>Tbsp. olive oil, divided</td></tr>
<tr><td>2</td><td>medium sweet onions, thinly sliced</td></tr>
<tr><td>1</td><td>garlic clove, minced</td></tr>
<tr><td>1</td><td>tsp. brown sugar</td></tr>
<tr><td>½</td><td>tsp. sea salt</td></tr>
<tr><td>¼</td><td>tsp. coarsely ground pepper</td></tr>
<tr><td>⅓</td><td>cup dry red wine</td></tr>
<tr><td>10</td><td>oz. sliced fresh shiitake mushrooms</td></tr>
<tr><td>½</td><td>lb. sliced baby portobello mushrooms</td></tr>
<tr><td>2</td><td>tsp. minced fresh thyme, divided</td></tr>
<tr><td>1</td><td>sheet frozen puff pastry, thawed</td></tr>
<tr><td>1</td><td>pkg. (4 oz.) fresh goat cheese</td></tr>
</table>

1. In a small dry skillet, toast walnuts over low heat for 5-7 minutes or until lightly browned, stirring occasionally. Remove and set aside.

2. In a large skillet, heat 2 Tbsp. oil over medium heat. Add onions; cook and stir 6-8 minutes or until softened. Reduce heat to medium-low; cook 20-22 minutes or until deep golden brown, stirring occasionally. Add garlic, brown sugar, salt and pepper; cook 1 minute longer. Transfer to a small bowl.

3. Add red wine to pan, stirring to loosen any browned bits. Bring to a boil. Cook and stir 1 minute; pour over onions. In same skillet, heat remaining oil over medium-high heat. Add mushrooms and 1 tsp. of the thyme; cook and stir 8-10 minutes or until liquid is almost absorbed. Stir in onions. Remove from heat; cover and set aside.

4. Preheat oven to 400°. Unfold puff pastry. On a lightly floured surface, roll pastry into a 12-in. square. Cut into two 12x6-in. rectangles. Transfer to baking sheet. Using a sharp knife, score ½ in. from edges of each pastry (do not cut through). Using a fork, poke holes in pastry. Bake 10-12 minutes or until puffed and lightly browned. Remove from oven. Press down center with a spoon if necessary. Reduce oven setting to 350°.

5. Spoon the mushroom mixture over pastry. Sprinkle with walnuts; top with cheese. Sprinkle with remaining thyme. Bake 5 minutes longer or until cheese is melted. Cut each tart into six pieces.

CHERRY-COCONUT CHOCOLATE TORTE

I love chocolate-covered cherries and old-fashioned Cherry Mash candy bars. This wonderful torte reminds me of these favorites. It will satisfy your sweet tooth!

—Dian Hicks Carlson, Omaha, NE

....

PREP: 30 min. • BAKE: 20 min. + chilling
MAKES: 12 servings

<table>
<tr><td>1</td><td>cup sugar</td></tr>
<tr><td>2</td><td>large eggs</td></tr>
<tr><td>½</td><td>tsp. vanilla extract</td></tr>
<tr><td>½</td><td>cup butter, melted</td></tr>
<tr><td>½</td><td>cup all-purpose flour</td></tr>
<tr><td>⅓</td><td>cup baking cocoa</td></tr>
<tr><td>¼</td><td>tsp. salt</td></tr>
<tr><td>¼</td><td>tsp. baking powder</td></tr>
</table>

CHERRY LAYER

<table>
<tr><td>4</td><td>jars (10 oz. each) maraschino cherries</td></tr>
<tr><td>4</td><td>cups confectioners' sugar</td></tr>
<tr><td>¼</td><td>cup butter, softened</td></tr>
</table>

COCONUT LAYER

<table>
<tr><td>1</td><td>pkg. (14 oz.) sweetened shredded coconut</td></tr>
<tr><td>¼</td><td>cup sweetened condensed milk</td></tr>
</table>

CHOCOLATE GANACHE

<table>
<tr><td>12</td><td>oz. semisweet chocolate, chopped</td></tr>
<tr><td>1</td><td>cup heavy whipping cream</td></tr>
<tr><td>1</td><td>cup chopped walnuts, toasted</td></tr>
</table>

1. Preheat oven to 350°. In a large bowl, beat sugar, eggs and vanilla until blended. Beat in the melted butter. In a small bowl, whisk flour, cocoa, salt and baking powder; gradually add to the batter and mix well.

2. Spread mixture into a greased 9-in. springform pan. Bake for 18-20 minutes or until a toothpick inserted in the center comes out clean. Cool completely in pan on a wire rack.

3. Drain cherries, reserving ½ cup juice. Arrange cherries evenly around the top edge of the brownie; place the remaining cherries over top. In a large bowl, beat confectioners' sugar, butter and reserved cherry juice until creamy. Spread evenly over the cherries.

4. In a large bowl, combine coconut and milk. Sprinkle over the cherry layer, carefully smoothing down near edges and pressing gently to form an even layer.

5. Place chocolate in a large bowl. In a small saucepan, bring cream just to a boil. Pour over chocolate. Let stand 5 minutes; whisk until smooth. Pour over the coconut layer. Refrigerate until set. Loosen sides of pan with a knife. Remove rim from pan. Sprinkle with walnuts.

Note: To toast nuts, bake in a shallow pan in a 350° oven for 5-10 minutes or cook in a skillet over low heat until lightly browned, stirring occasionally.

EGGNOG CREAM PUFFS

If you want to receive rave reviews and recipe requests, combine two Christmas classics: eggnog and cream puffs. When it comes to Santa, this recipe goes on the "nice" list!
—Kristen Heigl, Staten Island, NY

PREP: 40 min. • BAKE: 30 min. + cooling
MAKES: about 2 dozen

- 1 cup water
- ½ cup butter, cubed
- ⅛ tsp. salt
- 1 cup all-purpose flour
- ¾ tsp. ground nutmeg
- 4 large eggs

WHIPPED CREAM
- 1½ cups heavy whipping cream
- 1½ cups confectioners' sugar
- ¼ cup eggnog
- 1 tsp. vanilla extract
- ⅛ tsp. ground nutmeg
   Additional confectioners' sugar

1. Preheat oven to 400°. In a large saucepan, bring water, butter and salt to a rolling boil. Add flour and nutmeg all at once and stir until blended. Cook over medium heat, stirring vigorously until mixture pulls away from sides of pan. Remove from heat; let stand 5 minutes.
2. Add eggs, one at a time, beating well after each addition until smooth. Continue beating until mixture is smooth and shiny. Drop dough by rounded tablespoonfuls 1 in. apart onto greased baking sheets. Bake 30-35 minutes or until puffed, very firm and golden brown. Pierce the sides of each puff with tip of a knife. Cool on wire racks. Cut top third off each puff.
3. In a large bowl, beat cream until it begins to thicken. Add confectioners' sugar, eggnog, vanilla and nutmeg; beat until soft peaks form. Fill cream puffs with whipped cream; replace tops. Dust with additional confectioners' sugar. Serve immediately.

MUSICAL CANDLES

Enjoy carols by candlelight by decorating pillar candles with paper or cardstock with a musical pattern. Measure the candle's circumference and height, add ½ in. to the circumference and cut a piece of paper to those dimensions. With a sponge brush, apply a coat of decoupage glue to the back of the paper; wrap the paper around the candle, overlapping at the seam. Gently roll the candle on a flat surface to remove any air bubbles, and let dry. If desired, add a coat of decoupage glue to the outside of the paper to seal it, and attach ribbons or other embellishments to the candle—making sure they're not too close to the wick!

GARLIC HERBED BEEF TENDERLOIN

You don't need much seasoning to add flavor to this tender beef roast. The mild blend of rosemary, basil and garlic does the trick.

—Ruth Andrewson, Leavenworth, WA

PREP: 5 min. • BAKE: 40 min. + standing
MAKES: 12 servings

- 1 beef tenderloin roast (3 lbs.)
- 2 tsp. olive oil
- 2 garlic cloves, minced
- 1½ tsp. dried basil
- 1½ tsp. dried rosemary, crushed
- 1 tsp. salt
- 1 tsp. pepper

1. Preheat oven to 425°. Tie tenderloin at 2-in. intervals with kitchen string. Combine oil and garlic; brush over meat. Combine the basil, rosemary, salt and pepper; sprinkle evenly over meat. Place on a rack in a shallow roasting pan.
2. Bake, uncovered, for 40-50 minutes or until meat reaches desired doneness (for medium-rare, a thermometer should read 135°; medium, 140°; medium-well, 145°). Let stand for 10 minutes before slicing.

FAST FIX
GORGONZOLA PEAR TARTLETS

Whether you serve these simple tartlets as an appetizer or dessert, they're too good to pass up. I leave the peel on the pear to add texture.

—Susan Hein, Burlington, WI

TAKES: 30 min. • MAKES: 2½ dozen

- 1 large pear, finely chopped
- 1 cup crumbled Gorgonzola cheese
- ½ cup finely chopped hazelnuts, toasted
- 2 pkg. (1.9 oz. each) frozen miniature phyllo tart shells

1. In a small bowl, combine the pear, cheese and hazelnuts. Spoon into the tart shells. Place on ungreased baking sheets.
2. Bake at 350° for 10-12 minutes or until shells are lightly browned. Serve warm.

FAST FIX
THYME-ROASTED CARROTS

Cutting carrots lengthwise gives a simple side dish a special look. If you like, garnish with sprigs of fresh thyme or parsley.

—Deirdre Cox, KS City, MO

TAKES: 30 min.
MAKES: about 12 servings (2 carrot halves each)

- 3 lbs. medium carrots, halved lengthwise
- 2 Tbsp. minced fresh thyme or 2 tsp. dried thyme
- 2 Tbsp. canola oil
- 1 Tbsp. honey
- 1 tsp. salt

Preheat oven to 400°. Divide carrots between two greased 15x10x1-in. baking pans. In a small bowl, mix thyme, oil, honey and salt; brush over carrots. Roast for 20-25 minutes or until tender.

FAST FIX
GARLIC-MASHED RUTABAGAS & POTATOES

My family absolutely loves garlic mashed potatoes. When I snuck in some rutabagas, they were just as enthusiastic.

—Rosemary Tatum, Sterlington, LA

TAKES: 30 min. • MAKES: 8 servings

- 4 medium potatoes, peeled and cubed (about 4 cups)
- 2 medium rutabagas, peeled and cubed (about 5 cups)
- 2 garlic cloves, peeled
- 2 Tbsp. butter
- 1 tsp. salt
- ¼ tsp. pepper
- ¼ to ⅓ cup warm buttermilk

1. Place potatoes, rutabagas and garlic in a Dutch oven; add water to cover. Bring to a boil. Reduce heat; cook, uncovered, 15-20 minutes or until tender.
2. Drain; return to pan. Mash potatoes, gradually adding butter, salt, pepper and enough buttermilk to reach desired consistency.

PARMESAN BOWLS MADE EASY

1. Spread shredded Parmesan evenly in heated skillet; add seasonings or nuts to melted cheese if desired.

2. Cook over medium heat 1-2 minutes until edges are lightly brown; lift out of pan with spatula.

3. Form hot cheese disk over bottom of an inverted glass or ramekin; allow to cool.

CAESAR SALAD IN PARMESAN BOWLS

Edible salad bowls look impressive but are a cinch to make. It can be your little secret!
—Melissa Wilkes, St. Augustine, FL

PREP: 20 min. • COOK: 15 min.
MAKES: 8 servings

- 2 cups shredded Parmesan cheese
- ½ tsp. coarsely ground pepper
- 2 romaine hearts, cut into bite-size pieces (about 6 cups)
- 1 cup grape tomatoes, halved
- ¾ cup Caesar salad croutons, slightly crushed
- ¼ cup creamy Caesar salad dressing

1. In a small bowl, toss cheese with pepper. Heat a small nonstick skillet over medium heat. Evenly sprinkle ¼ cup of the cheese mixture into pan to form a 6-in. circle; cook, uncovered, until bubbly and edges are golden brown, about 1-2 minutes. Remove skillet from heat; let stand 15 seconds.
2. Using a spatula, carefully remove cheese and immediately drape over an inverted 4-oz. ramekin; press cheese gently to form a bowl. Cool completely. Repeat with the remaining cheese, making eight bowls.
3. In a large bowl, combine the romaine, tomatoes and croutons. Just before serving, drizzle with dressing and toss to coat. Serve in Parmesan bowls.

RASPBERRY SWIRLED CHEESECAKE PIE

My dad always said my cheesecake pie was his favorite dessert. He is gone now but I remember his smile every time I make it.
—Peggy Griffin, ELBA, NE

PREP: 15 min. • BAKE: 35 min. + chilling
MAKES: 8 servings

- 1 pkg. (8 oz.) cream cheese, softened
- ½ cup sugar
- 2 large eggs, lightly beaten
- 1 graham cracker crust (9 in.)
- 1 can (21 oz.) raspberry pie filling, divided

1. Preheat oven to 350°. In a large bowl, beat cream cheese and sugar until smooth. Add eggs; beat on low speed just until blended. Pour batter into crust. Drop ½ cup pie filling by tablespoonfuls over batter. Cut through the batter with a knife to swirl.
2. Bake 35-45 minutes or until the center is set. Transfer remaining raspberry filling to a covered container; refrigerate until serving.
3. Cool 1 hour on a wire rack. Refrigerate at least 2 hours, covering when completely cooled. Serve with the reserved filling.

LEMON HERB GAME HENS

My mom made game hens for my dad once a week. When my sister and I were little, we would try to sneak some of the chicken from his plate. For this dish, use whatever herbs you have on hand. If you have some in the garden, even better!
—Meagan Meyer, Irving, TX

PREP: 20 min. • **COOK:** 1¼ hours
MAKES: 6 servings

- 6 Cornish game hens (20 to 24 oz. each)
- 3 medium lemons
- 1 whole garlic bulb, separated into 18 cloves
- ¾ cup olive oil
- 1 tsp. onion powder
- 1 tsp. garlic powder
- 1 tsp. salt
- 1 tsp. pepper
- 1 cup coarsely chopped fresh basil
- 1 Tbsp. minced fresh rosemary
- 1 Tbsp. minced fresh thyme

1. Preheat oven to 375°. Place hens in a roasting pan. Cut 1½ lemons into six wedges. Rub a lemon wedge over each hen; place wedges in roasting pan. Peel and cut garlic cloves in half. Rub cut side of a garlic half over each hen; place in cavity with five additional garlic halves. Rub 2 Tbsp. oil over each hen; sprinkle with onion powder, garlic powder, salt and pepper.
2. In a small bowl, mix the basil, rosemary and thyme. Sprinkle half of the herb mixture over the hens; place the remaining herb mixture in cavities. Cut the remaining lemons into 12 slices; place over hens. Roast 1¼-1½ hours or until a thermometer inserted in the thickest part of the thigh reads 170°.

BOURBON-INFUSED FINGERLING POTATOES

These saucy potatoes turn out so full of flavor from the combination of bourbon, Worcestershire sauce and garlic. What an easy way to do something different with potatoes!
—JoAnn Mathias, Hoschton, GA

PREP: 15 min. • **COOK:** 30 min.
MAKES: 10 servings

- 2 lbs. assorted fingerling or other small potatoes
- 5 Tbsp. butter, divided
- 2 medium red onions, finely chopped
- 2 medium green peppers, finely chopped
- ½ cup bourbon
- ¼ cup reduced-sodium soy sauce
- 2 Tbsp. brown sugar
- 2 Tbsp. canola oil
- 2 Tbsp. Worcestershire sauce
- 2 garlic cloves, minced
- ½ tsp. salt
- ½ tsp. pepper

1. Place potatoes in a large saucepan; add water to cover. Bring to a boil. Reduce heat; cook, uncovered, 10-15 minutes or until tender. Drain.
2. In a 12-in. skillet, heat 2 Tbsp. butter over medium-high heat; add onions and green peppers. Cook and stir until tender; remove from pan.
3. In same pan, heat remaining butter over medium-high heat; add potatoes. Using a fork or potato masher, flatten potatoes slightly. Cook 3-4 minutes on each side or until lightly browned. Return onion mixture to pan.
4. In a small bowl, whisk the remaining ingredients until blended; add to the pan. Bring to a boil; cook 1-2 minutes or until the liquid is absorbed.

SPICED ORANGE-CRANBERRY CHUTNEY

The aroma of simmering chutney signals the start of the holidays and sets the mood for my seasonal baking. Try it as an appetizer along with cream cheese and graham crackers.
—Pat Stevens, Granbury, TX

PREP: 15 min. • **COOK:** 55 min. + chilling
MAKES: 8 cups

- 2¼ cups packed brown sugar
- 1½ cups cranberry juice
- ½ cup cider vinegar
- ½ tsp. ground ginger
- ¼ tsp. ground allspice
- 3 pkg. (12 oz. each) fresh cranberries
- 2 Tbsp. grated orange peel
- 2 medium oranges, peeled and sectioned
- 1 medium tart apple, peeled and coarsely chopped
- ½ cup dried currants
- ½ cup coarsely chopped dried apricots

In a 6-qt. stockpot, combine the first five ingredients. Cook, uncovered, over medium heat until the brown sugar is dissolved. Stir in the cranberries, orange peel, oranges, apple, currants and apricots. Bring to a boil. Reduce heat; simmer, uncovered, 50-60 minutes or until thickened; stir occasionally. Serve chilled.

NUTTY PUMPKIN BISQUE

Hearty and comforting pumpkin soup is the perfect starter to a holiday meal. The addition of toasted pecans and pumpkin seeds creates a wonderful depth of flavor. This soup can be served immediately or made a day in advance and then reheated.

—Lauri Knox, Pine, CO

PREP: 15 min. • **COOK:** 20 min.
MAKES: 4 servings

- 2 Tbsp. butter
- 1 medium onion, chopped
- 2 garlic cloves, minced
- 3 cups chicken stock
- 1 can (15 oz.) solid-pack pumpkin
- ½ cup sherry or chicken stock
- 2 tsp. brown sugar
- ½ tsp. dried thyme
- ½ tsp. ground cumin
- ½ tsp. dried rosemary, crushed
- ¼ tsp. salt
- 1 cup heavy whipping cream
- ¾ cup chopped pecans, toasted
- ½ cup salted pumpkin seeds or pepitas, toasted
  Optional toppings: sour cream, fresh rosemary sprigs, additional toasted chopped pecans and pumpkin seeds

1. In a 6-qt. stockpot, heat butter over medium-high heat. Add the onion; cook and stir 2-3 minutes or until tender. Add garlic; cook 1 minute longer. Stir in the stock, pumpkin, sherry, brown sugar and seasonings; bring to a boil. Reduce heat; simmer, uncovered, 10 minutes or until slightly thickened.
2. Stir in the cream, pecans and seeds. Remove from heat; cool slightly. Process in batches in a blender until smooth. Return all to pan; heat through. If desired, serve with optional toppings.

CRUNCHY SPINACH CASSEROLE

Our holidays would not be the same without this family tradition. My mother made it every Thanksgiving; now I make it every Christmas and Thanksgiving. We always triple the recipe because the kids can't get enough.

—Sharon Scaletta, Johnstown, PA

PREP: 15 min. • **BAKE:** 35 min.
MAKES: 4 servings

- ½ cup butter, divided
- 2 celery ribs, finely chopped
- 1 small onion, finely chopped
- 2 pkg. (10 oz. each) frozen chopped spinach, thawed and squeezed dry
- 1 can (10¾ oz.) condensed cream of mushroom soup, undiluted
- 2 cups cubed bread (½ in.)

1. Preheat oven to 350°. In a large skillet, heat ¼ cup butter over medium heat. Add celery and onion; cook and stir 4-5 minutes or until tender. Stir in spinach and soup.
2. Transfer to a 1½-qt. round baking dish. In a small saucepan, melt the remaining butter over medium heat. Stir in bread cubes. Sprinkle over top. Bake 35-40 minutes or until bubbly and the bread cubes are golden brown.

FAST FIX
COMPANY MASHED CARROTS

Although I call these company carrots, I'll often serve them on a weeknight to my family. No matter who's eating it, the fast, easy dish is always a favorite.

—Cynthia Hanus-Beard, Tamarac, FL

TAKES: 30 min. • **MAKES:** 6 servings

- 2 lbs. carrots, sliced
- ½ cup butter, cubed
- 2 Tbsp. sugar
- 1 Tbsp. orange liqueur
- ½ tsp. salt
- ½ tsp. pepper
- ¼ tsp. ground nutmeg

1. Place carrots in a Dutch oven; add water to cover. Bring to a boil. Cook, covered, 15-20 minutes or until very tender. Drain carrots; return to pan.
2. Mash carrots with remaining ingredients by hand or puree in a food processor until blended.

CARAMEL APPLE PIE WITH STREUSEL TOPPING

I developed this recipe through the years to get it exactly where we want it. I've entered several pie contests with it and placed first each time!

—Laurel Dalzell, Manteca, CA

PREP: 50 min. + chilling • BAKE: 35 min.
MAKES: 12 servings

1⅔ cups all-purpose flour
2 tsp. sugar
¾ tsp. salt
¾ cup cold butter, cubed
4 to 5 Tbsp. ice water

FILLING
9 medium Golden Delicious or Braeburn apples (about 3 lbs.), peeled and cut into ¾-in. chunks
½ cup butter, cubed
½ cup packed brown sugar
2 Tbsp. all-purpose flour
1 Tbsp. pumpkin pie spice

TOPPING
1 cup all-purpose flour
½ cup packed brown sugar
¼ tsp. salt
½ cup cold butter, cubed
½ cup finely chopped walnuts
1 large egg
2 Tbsp. water

1. In a large bowl, mix flour, sugar and salt; cut in butter until crumbly. Gradually add water, tossing with a fork until the dough holds together when pressed. If desired, separate one-fourth of the dough for decorative cutouts; shape both portions into disks and wrap in plastic. Refrigerate 1 hour or overnight.
2. Meanwhile, preheat oven to 450°. In a Dutch oven, combine filling ingredients. Cook over medium heat 10-15 minutes or until the apples are almost tender, stirring occasionally; remove from heat.
3. On a lightly floured surface, roll larger portion of dough to a ⅛-in.-thick circle; transfer to a 9-in. deep-dish pie plate. Trim pastry to ½ in. beyond rim of plate; flute edge. Line the unpricked pastry with a double thickness of foil. Fill with pie weights, dried beans or uncooked rice.
4. Bake for 8 minutes. Remove foil and weights; bake 5 minutes longer. Cool on a wire rack. Reduce oven setting to 375°.
5. For topping, in a small bowl, combine flour, brown sugar and salt; cut in butter until crumbly. Stir in walnuts. If desired, make cutouts with the remaining dough.
6. Spoon filling into crust; sprinkle with topping. Arrange cutouts over pie. In a small bowl, whisk egg and water; brush over cutouts. Bake pie 35-45 minutes or until golden brown and filling is bubbly. Cool on a wire rack.
Note: Let pie weights cool before storing. Beans and rice may be reused for pie weights, but not for cooking.

ORNAMENT CENTERPIECE
Put your cupcake stand to good use and create a lovely table setting! Set globe ornaments in the cupcake holders, then surround them with your choice of festive holiday foliage.

WHITE SEAFOOD LASAGNA

We make lasagna with shrimp and scallops as part of our traditional Italian Feast of the Seven Fishes. Every bite delivers a tasty jewel from the sea.

—Joe Colamonico, North Charleston, SC

PREP: 1 hour • BAKE: 40 min. + standing
MAKES: 12 servings

- 9 uncooked lasagna noodles
- 1 Tbsp. butter
- 1 lb. uncooked shrimp (31 to 40 per lb.), peeled and deveined
- 1 lb. bay scallops
- 5 garlic cloves, minced
- ¼ cup white wine
- 1 Tbsp. lemon juice
- 1 lb. fresh crabmeat

CHEESE SAUCE
- ¼ cup butter, cubed
- ¼ cup all-purpose flour
- 3 cups 2% milk
- 1 cup shredded part-skim mozzarella cheese
- ½ cup grated Parmesan cheese
- ½ tsp. salt
- ¼ tsp. pepper
  Dash ground nutmeg

RICOTTA MIXTURE
- 1 carton (15 oz.) part-skim ricotta cheese
- 1 pkg. (10 oz.) frozen chopped spinach, thawed and squeezed dry
- 1 cup shredded part-skim mozzarella cheese
- ½ cup grated Parmesan cheese
- ½ cup seasoned bread crumbs
- 1 large egg, lightly beaten

TOPPING
- 1 cup shredded part-skim mozzarella cheese
- ¼ cup grated Parmesan cheese
  Minced fresh parsley

1. Preheat oven to 350°. Cook lasagna noodles according to the package directions; drain.
2. Meanwhile, in a large skillet, heat butter over medium heat. Add the shrimp and scallops in batches; cook 2-4 minutes or until the shrimp turn pink and the scallops are firm and opaque. Remove from pan.
3. Add garlic to same pan; cook 1 minute. Add wine and lemon juice, stirring to loosen browned bits from pan. Bring to a boil; cook 1-2 minutes or until liquid is reduced by half. Add crab; heat through. Stir in the shrimp and scallops.
4. For the cheese sauce, melt butter over medium heat in a large saucepan. Stir in flour until smooth; gradually whisk in milk. Bring to a boil, stirring constantly; cook and stir 1-2 minutes or until thickened. Remove from heat; stir in the remaining cheese sauce ingredients. In a large bowl, combine the ricotta mixture ingredients; stir in 1 cup of the cheese sauce.
5. Spread ½ cup of the cheese sauce into a greased 13x9-in. baking dish. Layer with three noodles, half the ricotta mixture, half the seafood mixture and ⅔ cup of the cheese sauce. Repeat layers. Top with the remaining noodles and cheese sauce. Sprinkle with the remaining mozzarella cheese and Parmesan cheese.
6. Bake, uncovered, 40-50 minutes or until bubbly and the top is golden brown. Let stand 10 minutes before serving. Sprinkle with parsley.

FAST FIX
INSALATA CAPRESE

A classic Caprese salad has colors that resemble the Italian flag. For extra zing, I add a splash of balsamic vinegar.

—Joe Colamonico, North Charleston, SC

TAKES: 25 min. • MAKES: 8 servings

- 2½ lbs. plum tomatoes (about 10), cut into 1-in. pieces
- 1 carton (8 oz.) fresh mozzarella cheese pearls
- ½ cup pitted ripe olives
- 3 Tbsp. olive oil
- ¼ cup thinly sliced fresh basil
- 2 tsp. minced fresh oregano
- ½ tsp. salt
- ¼ tsp. pepper
  Balsamic vinegar, optional

In a large bowl, mix tomatoes, cheese and olives. Drizzle with oil. Sprinkle with basil, oregano, salt and pepper; toss to coat. Let stand 10 minutes before serving. If desired, drizzle with vinegar.

❄ Reader Review

"This is so good that I threw away the seafood lasagna recipe I had been using for the past 25 years!"

DARJUR TASTEOFHOME.COM

CALABRIAN HOLIDAY SOUP

My family is from the Italian region of Calabria; our version of Italian wedding soup has been handed down through the generations. We serve this soup with the Christmas meal as well as at weddings.

—Gwen Keefer, Sylvania, OH

PREP: 15 min. • COOK: 3 hours
MAKES: 14 servings (3½ qt.)

- 1 broiler/fryer chicken (4 to 5 lbs.)
- 3 tsp. salt, divided
- 1 tsp. dried oregano
- 1 tsp. dried basil
- 2½ tsp. pepper, divided
- 1 lb. lean ground beef (90% lean)
- 3 cups uncooked instant rice
- 1 pkg. (10 oz.) frozen chopped spinach, thawed and squeezed dry
- 3 large eggs, beaten

1. Place chicken in a 6-qt. stockpot; add water to cover. Slowly bring to a boil. Reduce heat; simmer, covered, 2-3 hours. Meanwhile, in a large bowl, mix 1½ tsp. salt, oregano, basil and 1 tsp. pepper. Add ground beef; mix lightly but thoroughly. Shape into ½-in. balls.

2. Remove carcass from stockpot; cool. Return broth to a simmer; add meatballs. Cook, uncovered, 8-10 minutes or until the meatballs are cooked through.

3. Remove chicken from carcass; shred meat with two forks and return to pot. Discard bones and skin. Bring broth to a boil; stir in rice and spinach. Reduce heat; simmer, covered, 5 minutes. Drizzle beaten eggs into soup, stirring constantly. Stir in the remaining salt and pepper.

FAST FIX
RUSTIC TUSCAN PEPPER BRUSCHETTA

If you love sweet peppers, pair them with fresh mint for a cold kitchen appetizer. Marinate for up to one hour before assembling.

—Noelle Myers, Grand Forks, ND

TAKES: 30 min. • MAKES: 4 dozen

- 2 Tbsp. olive oil
- 2 Tbsp. balsamic vinegar
- 1 Tbsp. honey
- 1 Tbsp. minced fresh mint
- 1 each medium sweet yellow, orange and red pepper, cut into thin 1-in. strips
- 6 oz. fresh goat cheese
- ⅔ cup whipped cream cheese
- 48 assorted crackers

1. In a large bowl, whisk oil, vinegar, honey and mint. Add peppers; toss to coat. Let stand 15 minutes.

2. Meanwhile, in a small bowl, beat the goat cheese and cream cheese. Spread 1 rounded teaspoonful on each cracker. Drain the peppers well. Arrange peppers on cheese-topped crackers.

FAST FIX
PEPPER PARMESAN BEANS

A colorful mixture of peppers and green beans gets the Italian treatment with basil and Parmesan cheese in this delightful vegetable dish.

—Marian Platt, Sequim, WA

TAKES: 15 min. • MAKES: 8 servings

- 1 large sweet red pepper, diced
- 1 small green pepper, diced
- ¼ cup chopped onion
- 1 garlic clove, minced
- ¼ cup olive oil
- 1½ lbs. fresh green beans, cut into 2-in. pieces
- 1 Tbsp. minced fresh basil or 1 tsp. dried basil
- 1 tsp. salt
- ⅓ to ½ cup shredded Parmesan cheese

In a large skillet, saute the peppers, onion and garlic in oil until the vegetables are tender, about 3 minutes. Add the beans, basil and salt; toss to coat. Cover and cook over medium-low heat for 7-8 minutes or until beans are crisp-tender. Stir in cheese; serve immediately.

SPUMONI TORTE

I made up this recipe to end a big Italian Christmas Eve dinner. I thought it would be nice and light after a heavy meal.
—Lynne Ogg, Cedar, MN

PREP: 30 min. • **BAKE:** 25 min. + cooling
MAKES: 16 servings

- 2 pkg. white cake mix (regular size)
- 1 tsp. almond extract

FILLING
- 2¼ cups heavy whipping cream
- 1 cup confectioners' sugar, divided
- ½ cup 2% milk
- 1 pkg. (3.4 oz.) instant pistachio pudding mix
- 6 Tbsp. cream cheese, softened, divided
- ¼ cup baking cocoa
- 1 cup chopped maraschino cherries
- ½ tsp. almond extract

1. Preheat oven to 350°. Line bottoms of three greased 9-in. round baking pans with parchment paper; grease paper. Prepare cake mix batter according to package directions, adding almond extract before mixing batter. Transfer to prepared pans. Bake 25-30 minutes or until a toothpick inserted in center comes out clean. Cool as package directs.

2. In a small bowl, beat cream until it begins to thicken. Add ⅔ cup confectioners' sugar; beat until soft peaks form. Place 1½ cups whipped cream in each of three bowls. In another bowl, whisk milk and pudding mix for 2 minutes. Let stand for 2 minutes or until soft-set. Fold pudding into one bowl of whipped cream. In second bowl of whipped cream, beat in 3 Tbsp. cream cheese, cocoa and the remaining confectioners' sugar. In third bowl, beat in maraschino cherries, almond extract and the remaining cream cheese.

3. Place one cake layer on a serving plate; spread with pistachio filling. Top with a second cake layer; spread with maraschino filling. Top with the remaining cake layer; spread with chocolate filling. Refrigerate until serving.

CHRISTMAS CENTERPIECE

Bowl over your party guests with these table trims! Fill a clear bowl-shaped glass vase nearly full with cold water. Submerge arborvitae leaves (or festive greenery like pine or holly boughs); float cranberries on top. Snip the stem from a spider mum or other flower and place the bloom on the cranberries. If you don't have a fishbowl or a bowl-shaped vase, check your local craft store. For a dramatic effect, use multiple bowls of different heights and sizes, or place one or two on cake stands or a platter.

STOVETOP ROOT VEGETABLE BEEF STEW

To me, the definition of cozy is a pot of tender beef simmering with sweet potatoes and parsnips. It doesn't get better than that.

—Beth Rossos, Estacada, OR

PREP: 30 min. • COOK: 1¾ hours
MAKES: 8 servings (2 qt.)

- ⅔ cup all-purpose flour
- 1½ tsp. salt, divided
- 1¼ tsp. pepper, divided
- 2 lbs. beef stew meat
- 4 Tbsp. olive oil
- ⅔ cup Burgundy wine
- 3 cups water
- 1 can (14½ oz.) stewed tomatoes
- 2 garlic cloves, minced
- 2 tsp. beef base
- ¼ tsp. dried thyme
- ¼ tsp. ground cinnamon
- ¼ tsp. crushed red pepper flakes
- 1 large sweet potato (about 1 lb.), peeled and coarsely chopped
- 2 medium carrots, coarsely chopped
- 1 medium onion, chopped
- 1 medium parsnip, peeled and coarsely chopped
  Sliced green onions

1. In a shallow bowl, mix flour and 1 tsp. each salt and pepper. Add beef, a few pieces at a time, and toss to coat; shake off excess.

2. In a Dutch oven, heat 2 Tbsp. oil over medium heat. Brown beef in batches, adding additional oil as necessary. Remove beef with a slotted spoon. Add wine, stirring to loosen browned bits from the pan.

3. Return beef to pan. Add water, tomatoes, garlic, beef base, thyme, cinnamon, pepper flakes and the remaining salt and pepper; bring to a boil. Reduce heat; simmer, covered, for 1¼ hours, stirring halfway through cooking.

4. Stir in sweet potato, carrots, onion and parsnip. Cook, covered, 30-45 minutes longer or until the beef and vegetables are tender. Sprinkle with green onions.

MAKE AHEAD

SESAME HERB PULL-APART BREAD

The beauty of this bread is that all the prep work is done a day ahead. The savory herbs make it irresistible.

—Mary Shivers, Ada, OK

PREP: 15 min. + chilling
BAKE: 30 min. + cooling • MAKES: 24 servings

- 3 Tbsp. minced fresh chives
- 3 Tbsp. minced fresh parsley
- 1 tsp. each dried basil, oregano and thyme
- 3 Tbsp. sesame seeds
- 24 frozen bread dough dinner rolls
- ¼ cup butter, melted

1. In a small bowl, mix chives and parsley. In another bowl, mix basil, oregano and thyme. In a greased 10-in. fluted tube pan, sprinkle 1 Tbsp. sesame seeds, 2 Tbsp. fresh herbs and 1 tsp. dried herbs.

2. Arrange eight dinner rolls over herbs. Sprinkle with 1 Tbsp. sesame seeds, 2 Tbsp. of the fresh herbs and 1 tsp. of the dried herbs. Drizzle with one-third of the butter. Repeat layers. Arrange remaining rolls over top; drizzle with remaining butter. Refrigerate, covered, 12-24 hours.

3. Remove from refrigerator 30 minutes before baking. Preheat oven to 350°. Bake, uncovered, 20 minutes. Cover loosely with foil; bake until golden brown, 10-15 minutes longer. Cool in pan 10 minutes before inverting onto a serving plate. Serve warm.

CLASSIC APPLE CRANBERRY CRISP

For a little old-fashioned goodness, treat your clan to this divine dish that bakes up warm and bubbly. It's great on its own or served with a scoop of ice cream.

—Billie Moss, Walnut Creek, CA

PREP: 10 min. • **BAKE:** 25 min.
MAKES: 4 servings

      3 cups chopped peeled tart apples
    1½ cups fresh or frozen cranberries, thawed
     ¾ cup packed brown sugar, divided
      1 Tbsp. lemon juice
     ½ tsp. ground cinnamon
     ½ cup all-purpose flour
     ⅓ cup cold butter, cubed
          Vanilla ice cream, optional

1. Preheat oven to 375°. In a large bowl, combine apples, cranberries, ¼ cup brown sugar, lemon juice and cinnamon. Pour into a greased 8-in. square baking dish. In a small bowl, mix flour and the remaining brown sugar. Cut in butter until crumbly. Sprinkle over fruit.
2. Bake, uncovered, 25-30 minutes or until the topping is golden brown and the filling is bubbly. If desired, serve with ice cream.

RISOTTO WITH CHICKEN & MUSHROOMS

Portobello mushrooms add an earthy flavor to this creamy classic, while shredded rotisserie chicken makes it a snap to prepare. You'll savor every bite.

—Charlene Chambers, Ormond Beach, FL

PREP: 15 min. • **COOK:** 50 min.
MAKES: 4 servings

      1 carton (32 oz.) chicken broth
      1 to 1½ cups water
      4 Tbsp. unsalted butter, divided
      2 Tbsp. olive oil
     ½ lb. sliced baby portobello mushrooms
      1 small onion, finely chopped
    1½ cups uncooked arborio rice
     ½ cup dry white wine or chicken broth
      1 Tbsp. lemon juice
      2 cups shredded rotisserie chicken
      3 Tbsp. grated Parmesan cheese
      2 Tbsp. minced fresh parsley
     ½ tsp. salt
     ¼ tsp. pepper

1. In a large saucepan, bring broth and water to a simmer; keep hot. In another large saucepan, heat 2 Tbsp. butter and the oil over medium heat. Add mushrooms and onion; cook and stir 6-8 minutes or until tender. Add rice; cook and stir for 2-3 minutes or until the rice is coated.
2. Stir in wine and lemon juice. Reduce heat to maintain a simmer; cook and stir until wine mixture is absorbed. Add hot broth mixture, ½ cup at a time. After each addition, cook and stir until the broth has been absorbed. Continue until the rice is tender but firm to the bite and the risotto is creamy.
3. Stir in chicken, cheese, parsley, salt, pepper and the remaining butter; heat through. Serve immediately.

BLEACHED PINECONE CENTERPIECE

Showcase nature's beauty all winter long with this idea! Place pinecones—either store-bought, or ones you've collected—in a large bucket. (If you opt for purchased pinecones, choose unscented ones without any coating.) Make a mixture of 2 parts bleach to 1 part water and pour enough into the bucket to cover the pinecones completely. Place a plate on top of them to keep them from floating. Keep the pinecones in the bleach mixture at least 24 hours.

Wearing rubber gloves, carefully remove pinecones from bleach mixture and place them on baking sheets lined with paper towels. (The pinecones will have closed up and some may not appear bleached.) Let them dry and reopen indoors, or place them outside in sunlight to speed drying. Drying may take 1-3 days.

Arrange a piece of natural burlap on a platter. Set a wide, clear cylindrical vase on top. Place a narrower clear glass vase inside the wider one. Set a pillar candle inside the smaller vase. Arrange pinecones inside the wide vase and around it on the platter. Tuck evergreen sprigs around pinecones on the platter as desired.

CITRUS-MOLASSES GLAZED HAM

We are always searching for new ways to utilize Florida citrus, which is plentiful in our own backyard during the holidays!
—Charlene Chambers, Ormond Beach, FL

PREP: 15 min. • **BAKE:** 2 hours
MAKES: 12 servings

- 1 fully cooked bone-in ham (7 to 9 lbs.)
GLAZE
- ½ cup grapefruit juice
- ½ cup orange juice
- ¼ cup molasses
- 3 Tbsp. honey
- 1 Tbsp. packed brown sugar
- 1 Tbsp. Dijon mustard
- 3 tsp. coarsely ground pepper

1. Preheat oven to 325°. Place ham on a rack in a shallow roasting pan. Using a sharp knife, score the surface of the ham with ¼-in.-deep cuts in a diamond pattern. Cover and bake until a thermometer reads 130°, 1¾-2¼ hours.
2. Meanwhile, in a large saucepan, combine grapefruit and orange juices. Bring to a boil; cook 6-8 minutes or until reduced by half. Stir in the remaining ingredients; return to a boil. Reduce heat; simmer, uncovered, 12-15 minutes or until thickened.
3. Remove ham from oven. Brush with ⅓ cup of the glaze. Bake, uncovered, basting occasionally with the remaining glaze, until a thermometer reads 140°, 15-20 minutes longer.

❄ Holiday Helper

If you have any of this ham left over, cut it into cubes and freeze it. Ham makes a great addition to everything from scrambled eggs to soup to mac and cheese, and having it cubed and ready to go is a great time-saver.

MAKE AHEAD
ICEBOX POTATO ROLLS

These meltaway rolls are a favorite with our large family. Make the dough in advance and bake when you're ready.
—Barb Linnerud, Boiling Springs, SC

PREP: 1 hour + rising • **BAKE:** 15 min.
MAKES: about 2½ dozen

- 1¼ lbs. potatoes, peeled and cubed
- ¾ cup sugar
- 2 tsp. salt
- 1 pkg. (¼ oz.) active dry yeast
- 5½ to 6 cups bread flour
- 1 cup 2% milk
- ½ cup water
- ½ cup shortening
- 3 large eggs
- ⅓ cup butter, melted

1. Place potatoes in a saucepan; add water to cover. Bring to a boil. Reduce heat; cook, uncovered, 10-15 minutes or until tender. Drain; return to pan. Mash potatoes (you should have about 2 cups). Cool slightly.
2. In a large bowl, mix sugar, salt, yeast and 2 cups flour. In a small saucepan, heat milk, water and shortening to 120°-130°. Add to dry ingredients; beat on medium speed 2 minutes. Add eggs and potatoes; beat on high 2 minutes. Stir in enough remaining flour to form a soft dough (dough will be very sticky).
3. Do not knead. Place dough in a large greased bowl. Cover with greased plastic wrap; refrigerate overnight.
4. Punch down dough. Using a Tablespoon dipped in melted butter, drop three spoonfuls of dough into a greased muffin cup. Repeat, re-dipping spoon in butter.
5. Cover dough with greased plastic wrap;

---

set in warm place until almost doubled, about 45 minutes. Preheat oven to 375°.
6. Brush tops with remaining melted butter. Bake 12-15 minutes or until golden brown. Cool in pans 5 minutes. Remove to wire racks; serve warm.
Note: The dough can be made up to 3 days before baking. Prepare dough as directed, then refrigerate for 1-3 days, punching down every 24 hours. Shape and bake rolls as directed.

MAKE AHEAD
OVERNIGHT LAYERED LETTUCE SALAD

This classic is a family favorite from a church cookbook I've had for 40 years. The bacon adds a fabulous crunch.
—Mary Brehm, Cape Coral, FL

PREP: 20 min. + chilling
MAKES: 16 servings

- 1 medium head iceberg lettuce, torn
- 1 medium green pepper, chopped
- 1 small sweet red pepper, chopped
- 1 medium onion, sliced and separated into rings
- 2 cups frozen peas (about 10 oz.)
- 1 cup mayonnaise
- 2 Tbsp. sugar
- 1 cup shredded cheddar cheese
- 12 bacon strips, cooked and crumbled
- ¾ cup dried cranberries

1. In a 4-qt. or 13x9-in. glass dish, layer the first five ingredients. In a small bowl, mix mayonnaise and sugar; spoon over salad, spreading to cover.
2. Sprinkle top with cheese, bacon and cranberries. Refrigerate, covered, overnight.

TWICE-BAKED CHEDDAR POTATO CASSEROLE

Bacon, cheddar and sour cream turn ordinary potatoes into an extraordinary casserole. It's one of our family's beloved standards for the holidays.

—Kyle Cox, Scottsdale, AZ

PREP: 70 min. • BAKE: 15 min.
MAKES: 12 servings

- 8 medium baking potatoes (about 8 oz. each)
- ½ cup butter, cubed
- ⅔ cup sour cream
- ⅔ cup 2% milk
- 1 tsp. salt
- ¾ tsp. pepper
- 10 bacon strips, cooked and crumbled, divided
- 2 cups shredded cheddar cheese, divided
- 4 green onions, chopped, divided

1. Preheat oven to 425°. Scrub potatoes; pierce several times with a fork. Bake 45-60 minutes or until tender. Remove from oven; reduce oven setting to 350°.
2. When potatoes are cool enough to handle, cut each potato lengthwise in half. Scoop out pulp and place in a large bowl; discard shells. Mash pulp with butter; stir in sour cream, milk, salt and pepper.
3. Reserve ¼ cup crumbled bacon for the topping. Gently fold the remaining bacon, 1 cup of cheese and half the green onions into the potato mixture (do not overmix).
4. Transfer to a greased 11x7-in. baking dish. Top with the remaining cheese and green onions; sprinkle with the reserved bacon. Bake 15-20 minutes or until heated through and cheese is melted.

BACON & FONTINA STUFFED MUSHROOMS

What's better than lots of bacon and cheese in a mushroom cap? Yum!

—Tammy Rex, New Tripoli, PA

PREP: 30 min. • BAKE: 10 min. • MAKES: 2 dozen

4 oz. cream cheese, softened
1 cup shredded fontina cheese
8 bacon strips, cooked and crumbled
4 green onions, chopped
¼ cup chopped oil-packed sun-dried tomatoes
3 Tbsp. minced fresh parsley
24 large fresh mushrooms, stems removed
1 Tbsp. olive oil

1. Preheat oven to 425°. In a small bowl, mix the first six ingredients until blended. Arrange mushroom caps in a greased 15x10x1-in. baking pan, stem side up. Spoon about 1 Tbsp. filling into each.
2. Drizzle tops with oil. Bake, uncovered, 9-11 minutes or until golden brown and mushrooms are tender.

CITRUS CANDLE

Freshen up your holiday table! Cut a citrus fruit in half and remove the flesh. Wash and dry the shell; rub the outside with olive oil. Melt candle wax in a double boiler; add a few drops of essential oil. Place a candle wick in the center of the shell. Pour melted wax around the wick.

FROZEN GRASSHOPPER TORTE

I first made this minty cool torte for a ladies' meeting at our church. I'm still making it, and the compliments keep coming.

—Elma Penner, Oak Bluff, MB

PREP: 25 min. + freezing • MAKES: 12 servings

4 cups crushed Oreo cookies (about 40 cookies)
¼ cup butter, melted
1 pint (2 cups) vanilla ice cream, softened if necessary
2 cups heavy whipping cream
1 jar (7 oz.) marshmallow creme
¼ cup 2% milk
¼ to ½ tsp. peppermint extract
3 drops green food coloring, optional

1. In a large bowl, combine the crushed cookies and melted butter; toss until coated. Reserve ¼ cup of the cookie mixture for topping. Press the remaining mixture onto bottom of a 9-in. springform pan or 13x9-in. dish. Freeze 10 minutes. Spread ice cream over the crust. Freeze, covered, until firm.
2. In a bowl, beat the cream until soft peaks form. In a large bowl, mix the marshmallow creme, milk, extract and, if desired, food coloring until blended. Fold in the whipped cream.
3. Spread over ice cream. Sprinkle with the reserved cookie mixture. Freeze, covered, until firm.

SPATCHCOCKED HERB-
ROASTED TURKEY, PAGE 120

VERY

MERRY
ENTREES

CRANBERRY-GORGONZOLA CHICKEN BREASTS

Ordinary chicken becomes extraordinary when stuffed with tart cranberries and creamy Gorgonzola cheese. I like to serve these with a lemon wedge and side of couscous or veggies. If you want to make them ahead of time, just prepare as directed and then cover and refrigerate until you're ready to bake.
—Kara Firstenberger, Cardiff, CA

PREP: 30 min. • BAKE: 35 min.
MAKES: 6 servings

- 6 boneless skinless chicken breast halves (6 oz. each)
- 1 cup crumbled Gorgonzola cheese
- ½ cup dried cranberries
- ⅔ cup chopped walnuts
- ⅓ cup packed fresh parsley sprigs
- ⅔ cup dry bread crumbs
- ½ tsp. salt
- ½ tsp. pepper
- 2 large eggs, beaten
- 1 Tbsp. Dijon mustard
- ½ cup all-purpose flour

1. Flatten chicken to ¼-in. thickness. In a small bowl, combine the cheese and cranberries. Spoon ¼ cup cheese mixture down the center of each chicken breast. Roll up and secure with toothpicks.
2. Place walnuts and parsley in a food processor; cover and process until ground. Transfer to a shallow bowl; stir in the bread crumbs, salt and pepper. In another shallow bowl, combine eggs and mustard. Place flour in a third shallow bowl. Coat chicken with flour, then dip in egg mixture and coat with walnut mixture.
3. Place seam side down in a greased 15x10x1-in. baking pan. Bake at 350° for 35-40 minutes or until a thermometer reads 170°. Discard toothpicks.

ITALIAN HERB-CRUSTED PORK LOIN

I like to change things up during the holidays by roasting pork loin with my favorite herbs and veggies. This dish is a showpiece that really dazzles my family.
—Kim Palmer, Kingston, GA

PREP: 15 min. + chilling
BAKE: 50 min. + standing • MAKES: 8 servings

- 3 Tbsp. olive oil
- 5 garlic cloves, minced
- 1 tsp. salt
- 1 tsp. each dried basil, thyme and rosemary, crushed
- ½ tsp. Italian seasoning
- ½ tsp. pepper
- 1 boneless pork loin roast (3 to 4 lbs.)
- 8 medium carrots, halved lengthwise
- 2 medium onions, quartered

1. In a small bowl, mix oil, garlic and seasonings; rub over the roast. Arrange carrots and onions on the bottom of a 13x9-in. baking pan. Place the roast over the vegetables, fat side up. Refrigerate, covered, for 1 hour.
2. Preheat oven to 475°. Roast the pork for 20 minutes.
3. Reduce oven setting to 425°. Roast the pork 30-40 minutes longer or until a thermometer reads 145° and vegetables are tender. Remove roast from oven; tent with foil. Let stand 20 minutes before slicing and serving.

SPINACH & CHICKEN PHYLLO PIE

For a brunch showstopper, we make chicken pie with phyllo and spinach. Even our kids go for it. It's so good served with a minty fruit salad on the side.

—Katie Ferrier, Houston, TX

PREP: 35 min. • **BAKE:** 35 min.
MAKES: 8 servings

- 2   lbs. ground chicken
- 1   large onion, chopped
- 1   tsp. pepper
- 1   tsp. dried oregano
- ¾ tsp. salt
- ½ tsp. ground nutmeg
- ¼ tsp. crushed red pepper flakes
- 3   pkg. (10 oz. each) frozen chopped spinach, thawed and squeezed dry
- 4   large eggs, lightly beaten
- 3   cups crumbled feta cheese
- 20 sheets phyllo dough (14x9-in. size)
     Cooking spray

1. Preheat oven to 375°. In a large skillet, cook chicken and onion over medium-high heat for 7-9 minutes or until chicken is no longer pink, breaking up chicken into crumbles; drain. Stir in seasonings. Add spinach; cook and stir until the liquid has evaporated. Transfer to a large bowl; cool slightly. Stir in beaten eggs and cheese.

2. Layer 10 sheets of phyllo dough in a greased 13x9-in. baking dish, spritzing each sheet with cooking spray. (Keep the remaining phyllo covered with plastic wrap and a damp towel to prevent it from drying out.) Spread spinach mixture over phyllo. Top with the remaining sheets of phyllo, spritzing each with cooking spray. Cut into eight rectangles.

3. Bake, uncovered, for 35-40 minutes or until golden brown. If necessary, recut rectangles before serving.

TURKEY-STUFFED ACORN SQUASH

We stuff acorn squash with holiday leftovers like turkey, dressing and cranberry sauce. Make as much or as little as you need to use everything up!

—Cindy Romberg, Mississauga, ON

PREP: 10 min. • BAKE: 55 min.
MAKES: 4 servings

- 2 medium acorn squash (about 1½ lbs. each)
- 1 small onion, finely chopped
- 2 cups cubed cooked turkey
- 2 cups cooked stuffing
- ½ cup whole-berry cranberry sauce
- ⅓ cup white wine or chicken broth
- ½ tsp. salt

1. Preheat oven to 350°. Cut each squash lengthwise in half; remove and discard seeds. Using a sharp knife, cut a thin slice from the bottom of each half to allow them to lie flat. Place in a shallow roasting pan, hollow side down; add ¼ in. of hot water. Bake, uncovered, 30 minutes.

2. Meanwhile, place the onion in a large microwave-safe bowl; microwave, covered, on high for 1-2 minutes or until tender. Stir in the turkey, stuffing, cranberry sauce and wine or broth.

3. Carefully remove the squash from the roasting pan; drain water. Return squash to pan, hollow side up; sprinkle with salt. Spoon turkey mixture into the squash cavities. Bake, uncovered, 25-30 minutes longer or until heated through and the squash is easily pierced with a fork.

PRIME RIB WITH FRESH HERB SAUCE

Nothing says special occasion like a perfectly seasoned prime rib. Savory, succulent and tender…it's the perfect choice when you want to share something truly divine.

—Tonya Burkhard, Palm Coast, FL

PREP: 40 min. • BAKE: 3¼ hours + standing
MAKES: 10 servings (1½ cups sauce)

1 bone-in beef rib roast (6 to 8 lbs.)
1 tsp. kosher salt
1 tsp. freshly ground pepper
3 cups water
2 small onions, halved
7 garlic cloves, crushed
5 fresh sage sprigs
5 fresh thyme sprigs
2 bay leaves

SAUCE
2 Tbsp. butter
2 shallots, thinly sliced
4 garlic cloves, thinly sliced
5 fresh sage sprigs
5 fresh thyme sprigs
2 bay leaves
1 Tbsp. all-purpose flour
2 Tbsp. cracked black pepper
¼ tsp. kosher salt
1½ to 2½ cups beef stock, divided
½ cup dry red wine or beef stock
½ tsp. red wine vinegar
 Fresh thyme sprigs, optional

1. Preheat oven to 450°. Place roast in a shallow roasting pan, fat side up; rub with salt and pepper. Add 1 cup water, onions, garlic and herbs to roasting pan. Roast for 15 minutes.

2. Reduce the oven setting to 325°. Roast 3-3½ hours longer or until meat reaches desired doneness (for medium-rare, a thermometer should read 135°; medium, 140°; medium-well, 145°), adding 1 cup water every hour.

3. For sauce, in a large saucepan, heat butter over medium-high heat. Add shallots; cook and stir 5-6 minutes or until tender. Add garlic and herbs; cook 1 minute longer. Stir in flour, pepper and salt until blended. Gradually stir in 1½ cups of stock. Remove from heat.

4. Remove roast to a serving platter; tent with foil. Let stand for 15 minutes before carving. Meanwhile, strain any pan juices into a measuring cup; discard onions and herbs. Skim fat from juices. If necessary, add additional stock to the pan juices to measure 1 cup. Add to shallot mixture.

5. Place roasting pan over two burners; add wine. Bring to a boil; cook 2-3 minutes, stirring to loosen browned bits from pan. Add to the sauce. Bring to a boil, stirring occasionally; cook until mixture is reduced to about 1½ cups, 10-15 minutes.

6. Stir in vinegar; strain, discarding shallots and herbs. Serve with roast and, if desired, garnish with thyme.

❄ Holiday Helper

Typically, a ribeye roast is the cut of beef used when preparing a prime rib dinner. Because the rib area gets the least exercise, these cuts are the most tender. Choose a ribeye or rib roast that feels firm to the touch and is a bright red color and well marbled. Marbling is a good indicator of tenderness.

GORGONZOLA BEEF WELLINGTONS

Your guests will certainly be impressed when you serve these Wellingtons. This is one of those dishes that makes it look like you worked all day, but it's surprisingly easy to prepare.
—Joyce Moynihan, Lakeville, MN

PREP: 40 min. + chilling • **BAKE:** 25 min.
MAKES: 8 servings

- 8 beef tenderloin steaks (6 to 8 oz. each)
- ½ tsp. plus ⅛ tsp. salt, divided
- ½ tsp. plus ⅛ tsp. pepper, divided
- 4 Tbsp. butter, divided
- 1 lb. fresh mushrooms, thinly sliced
- 2 shallots, finely chopped
- 6 garlic cloves, minced
- 1 pkg. (17.3 oz.) frozen puff pastry, thawed
- 1 cup crumbled Gorgonzola cheese
- 2 large eggs, beaten
- 4 cups reduced-sodium beef broth
- ½ cup Madeira wine or additional reduced-sodium beef broth
- 2 Tbsp. tomato paste
- 1 tsp. dried thyme

1. Sprinkle steaks with ½ tsp. each salt and pepper. In a large skillet, brown steaks in 2 Tbsp. butter in batches. Remove from the skillet; cool slightly and refrigerate until chilled.

2. In the same skillet, saute mushrooms and shallots in the remaining butter until tender. Add the garlic and the remaining salt and pepper; cook 1 minute longer.

3. On a lightly floured surface, roll each puff pastry sheet into a 14-in. square. Cut into four 6½-in. squares (use scraps to make decorative cutouts if desired).

4. Place 2 Tbsp. cheese in the center of each square; top with 3 Tbsp. mushroom mixture and a steak. Lightly brush pastry edges with the beaten egg. Bring opposite corners of the pastry over the steak; pinch seams to seal tightly.

5. Place seam side down in a greased 15x10x1-in. baking pan. Cut four small slits in the top of the pastry. Arrange cutouts over tops if desired. Brush with egg. Bake at 425° for 25-30 minutes or until the pastry is golden brown and meat reaches desired doneness (for medium-rare, a thermometer should read 135°; medium, 140°; medium-well 145°).

6. Meanwhile, in a large saucepan, combine broth and wine. Bring to a boil; cook until liquid is reduced by half, about 30 minutes. Stir in tomato paste and thyme. Serve with beef Wellingtons.

MAKE AHEAD
SAUSAGE & SWISS LASAGNA

Rustic and comforting, this rich and cheesy lasagna is a great way to get kids to eat their greens—it's such a tasty casserole, they'll never know the Swiss chard is there!
—Candace Morehouse, Show Low, AZ

PREP: 45 min. • **BAKE:** 55 min. + standing
MAKES: 6 servings

- 1 lb. bulk Italian sausage
- 1¾ cups sliced fresh mushrooms
- 2 garlic cloves, minced
- 1 bunch Swiss chard (about 10 oz.)
- 3 Tbsp. butter
- ¼ cup all-purpose flour
- 3 cups 2% milk
- 1 cup shredded Gruyere or Swiss cheese, divided
- 1 Tbsp. minced fresh parsley or 1 tsp. dried parsley flakes
- 1 Tbsp. minced fresh oregano or 1 tsp. dried oregano
- 1 tsp. grated lemon zest
- ½ tsp. salt
- ⅛ tsp. pepper
- 6 no-cook lasagna noodles

1. Preheat oven to 350°. In a large skillet, cook sausage, mushrooms and garlic over medium heat for 8-10 minutes or until sausage is no longer pink and mushrooms are tender, breaking up the sausage into crumbles. Remove from pan with a slotted spoon. Remove drippings.

2. Remove stems from the Swiss chard; coarsely chop leaves. In the same skillet, heat butter over medium heat. Stir in flour until smooth; gradually whisk in milk. Bring to a boil, stirring constantly; cook and stir 1-2 minutes or until thickened. Add ¾ cup of cheese, the parsley, oregano, lemon zest, salt and pepper; stir until cheese is melted. Stir in Swiss chard leaves.

3. Spread one-fourth of the cheese sauce into a greased 8-in. square baking dish. Layer with each of the following: two noodles, one-third of the meat mixture and one-fourth of the cheese sauce. Repeat layers twice. Sprinkle with the remaining cheese.

4. Bake, covered, 45 minutes. Bake, uncovered, 8-10 minutes longer or until cheese is melted. Let stand 10 minutes before serving.

Freeze option: Cool unbaked lasagna; cover and freeze. To use, partially thaw in the refrigerator overnight. Remove from refrigerator 30 minutes before baking. Preheat oven to 350°. Cover lasagna with foil; bake as directed, increasing covered time to 55-60 minutes or until heated through and a thermometer inserted in center reads 165°. Uncover; bake 10-12 minutes longer or until bubbly.

SPATCHCOCKED HERB-ROASTED TURKEY

This moist and tender turkey cooks up with even browning and crispy skin in half the time of a whole turkey.

—Matthew Hass, Franklin, WI

PREP: 15 min. + chilling
BAKE: 1¼ hours + standing
MAKES: 16 servings

1 turkey (12 to 14 lbs.)
3 Tbsp. kosher salt
2 tsp. coarsely ground pepper
1 Tbsp. minced fresh rosemary
1 Tbsp. minced fresh thyme
1 Tbsp. minced fresh sage

1. Place turkey breast side down, tail facing you on a work surface. Using kitchen shears, cut along each side of the backbone; remove and save for gravy. Turn turkey breast side up; flatten by pressing down firmly on the breastbone until it cracks. Using a knife, remove wing tips by cutting through the joints; save for gravy.
2. Mix the remaining ingredients; rub onto all sides of the turkey. Transfer to a rack in a foil-lined rimmed baking pan. Refrigerate, uncovered, overnight.
3. Preheat oven to 450°. Remove turkey from refrigerator while oven heats. Roast until a thermometer inserted in thickest part of thigh reads 170°-175°, 1¼-1½ hours. Remove turkey from oven; let stand for 15 minutes before carving.

❄ Holiday Helper

When you set the turkey in the refrigerator to chill overnight, don't cover it with plastic or foil. Instead, allow it to air out. The more the skin is exposed to the air in the fridge, the crisper it will be after roasting.

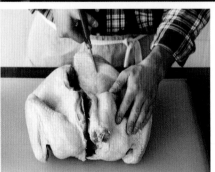

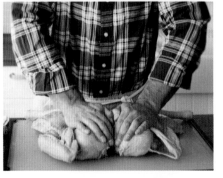

ROAST GOOSE WITH SWEET GLAZE

While goose is a traditional Christmas entree, some people do not care for the all-dark-meat bird. My recipe will change their minds in one bite. The sweet citrus glaze complements the rich, juicy meat perfectly.

—Colleen Sturma, Milwaukee, WI

PREP: 15 min. • **BAKE:** 2¾ hours + standing
MAKES: 10 servings

- 1 domestic goose (10 to 12 lbs.)
- 1 tsp. salt
- 2 small navel oranges, quartered
- 1 small onion, quartered
- 2 garlic cloves
- ¾ cup orange marmalade
- 3 Tbsp. Dijon mustard
- 2 Tbsp. reduced-sodium soy sauce
- 1 Tbsp. brown sugar
- ½ tsp. pepper

1. Preheat oven to 350°. Sprinkle goose and inside cavity with salt. Prick skin well with a fork. Place the oranges, onion and garlic in cavity. Tuck wings under goose; tie drumsticks together. Place breast side up on a rack in a roasting pan.
2. Bake, uncovered, for 2¾-3¼ hours or until a thermometer reads 180°. Cover loosely with foil if goose browns too quickly. If necessary, drain fat from the pan as it accumulates.
3. In a small saucepan, combine the marmalade, mustard, soy sauce, brown sugar and pepper. Cook and stir over medium heat until heated through. During the last 15 minutes of cooking, baste some of the glaze over goose.
4. Place the goose on a serving platter; cover and let stand for 15 minutes before carving. Just before serving, brush with the remaining glaze.

FAST FIX
CONFETTI PASTA

Our Christmas Eve tradition is to make linguine with red and green peppers and shrimp. We serve it with a salad and garlic bread.
—Ellen Fiore, Montvale, NJ

TAKES: 25 min. • **MAKES:** 8 servings

- 1 pkg. (16 oz.) linguine
- 1 cup chopped sweet red pepper
- 1 cup chopped green pepper
- ⅓ cup chopped onion
- 3 garlic cloves, peeled and thinly sliced
- ¼ tsp. salt
- ¼ tsp. dried oregano
- ⅛ tsp. crushed red pepper flakes
- ⅛ tsp. pepper
- ¼ cup olive oil
- 2 lbs. peeled and deveined cooked shrimp (61-70 per lb.)
- ½ cup shredded Parmesan cheese

1. Cook linguine according to package directions. Meanwhile, in a Dutch oven, saute the peppers, onion, garlic and seasonings in oil until the vegetables are tender.
2. Add shrimp; cook and stir 2-3 minutes longer or until heated through. Drain the linguine; toss with shrimp mixture. Sprinkle with cheese.

SPECIAL MUSHROOM LASAGNA

This rich, cheesy recipe proves that casseroles can be both convenient and classy. If you want to take it even further, stir in fresh crabmeat.
—Amanda Blair, Lebanon, OR

PREP: 2 hours • **BAKE:** 55 min. + standing
MAKES: 12 servings

- 6 Tbsp. butter, divided
- 3½ lbs. sliced baby portobello mushrooms
- 1 large onion, thinly sliced
- 1 cup marsala wine
- 8 garlic cloves, minced, divided
- 2 Tbsp. dried minced onion
- 12 uncooked lasagna noodles
- 5 Tbsp. all-purpose flour
- 1 tsp. onion powder
- ½ tsp. white pepper
- ½ tsp. ground nutmeg
- ¼ tsp. cayenne pepper
- 3 cups whole milk
- 1 pkg. (8 oz.) cream cheese, softened
- ½ cup minced chives
- 1 jar (2 oz.) diced pimientos, drained
- 1 Tbsp. lemon juice
- ½ tsp. grated lemon zest
- ½ tsp. salt
- 2 cups grated Parmesan cheese
- 6 oz. fresh crabmeat, optional

CRUMB TOPPING
- 1 French bread demi-baguette (about 4 oz.)
- ½ cup grated Parmesan cheese
- 2 Tbsp. butter, melted
- ½ cup minced chives

1. In a Dutch oven, melt 2 Tbsp. butter over medium heat. Add mushrooms and onion; saute until tender. Add wine, four minced garlic cloves and the minced onion; bring to a boil. Cook until liquid is absorbed, about 30 minutes.

2. Meanwhile, cook the lasagna noodles according to package directions. In a large saucepan over medium heat, melt the remaining butter. Stir in the next five ingredients and the remaining garlic until blended; gradually add milk. Bring to a boil; cook and stir until thickened, 1-2 minutes. Stir in next six ingredients until blended. Remove from heat.

3. Preheat oven to 350°. Drain lasagna noodles. Spread 1 cup cream cheese sauce in a greased 13x9-in. baking pan. Layer with three noodles, 1 cup sauce, a third of the mushroom mixture and ⅔ cup Parmesan cheese. Repeat layers, adding crabmeat, if desired, between mushrooms and Parmesan. Layer with three more noodles, 1 cup sauce, the remaining mushroom mixture and the remaining Parmesan cheese. Top with the remaining noodles and sauce.

4. For the crumb topping, pulse baguette, cheese and butter in a food processor until finely chopped. Stir in chives. Sprinkle over lasagna. Bake, covered, about 50 minutes. Uncover; bake until bubbly, 5-10 minutes longer. Let stand 10 minutes before cutting.

❄ Reader Review

"We love the complex flavors in this fantastic vegetable lasagna!"

NICOLE TASTEOFHOME.COM

SEAFOOD-STUFFED SALMON FILLETS

You can get stuffed salmon from a big-box store, but my fillets are loaded up at home with crab, cream cheese and savory herbs. We love them.

—Mary Cokenour, Monticello, UT

PREP: 25 min. • **BAKE:** 20 min.
MAKES: 12 servings

- 1½ cups cooked long grain rice
- 1 pkg. (8 oz.) imitation crabmeat
- 2 Tbsp. cream cheese, softened
- 2 Tbsp. butter, melted
- 2 garlic cloves, minced
- ½ tsp. each dried basil, marjoram, oregano, thyme and rosemary, crushed
- ½ tsp. celery seed, crushed
- 12 salmon fillets (8 oz. each and 1½ in. thick)
- 3 Tbsp. olive oil
- 2 tsp. dill weed
- 1½ tsp. salt

1. Preheat oven to 400°. In a large bowl, combine rice, crab, cream cheese, butter, garlic, basil, marjoram, oregano, thyme, rosemary and celery seed.

2. Cut a pocket horizontally in each fillet to within ½ in. of opposite side. Fill with stuffing mixture; secure with toothpicks. Place salmon on two greased 15x10x1-in. baking pans. Brush with oil; sprinkle with dill and salt.

3. Bake for 18-22 minutes or until fish just begins to flake easily with a fork. Discard toothpicks before serving.

STUFFED TURKEY WITH MOJO SAUCE

This recipe combines fresh ingredients and wonderful spices. It's a southwestern turkey recipe with a healthier twist because it uses chicken sausage instead of chorizo.
—Melissa Lauer, San Antonio, TX

PREP: 30 min. • COOK: 5 hours + standing
MAKES: 8 servings (about 1 cup sauce)

- 1 medium green pepper, finely chopped
- 1 medium onion, finely chopped
- 2 garlic cloves, minced
- 2 tsp. ground coriander
- 1 tsp. ground cumin
- ⅛ tsp. cayenne pepper
- 1 lb. uncooked chicken sausage links, casings removed
- 1 fresh boneless turkey breast (4 lbs.)
- ¼ tsp. salt
- ¼ tsp. pepper

MOJO SAUCE
- 1 cup orange juice
- ½ cup fresh cilantro leaves
- ¼ cup minced fresh oregano or 4 tsp. dried oregano
- ¼ cup lime juice
- 4 garlic cloves, minced
- 1 tsp. ground cumin
- ½ tsp. pepper
- ¼ tsp. salt
- ⅛ tsp. cayenne pepper
- 1 cup olive oil

1. In a bowl, combine first six ingredients. Crumble sausage over the mixture and mix well.

2. With skin side down, pound turkey breast with a meat mallet to ½-in. thickness. Sprinkle with salt and pepper. Spread sausage mixture over turkey to within 1 in. of edges. Roll up jelly-roll style, starting with a short side; tie at 1½-in. to 2-in. intervals with kitchen string. Place in a 5-qt. oval slow cooker.

3. In a blender, combine the first nine sauce ingredients; cover and process until blended. While processing, gradually add oil in a steady stream. Pour over turkey.

4. Cover and cook on low for 5 hours or until a thermometer inserted in center reads 165°. Remove from slow cooker; cover and let stand for 10 minutes before slicing. Discard string.

5. Meanwhile, skim fat from cooking juices; transfer juices to a small saucepan. Bring to a boil; cook until liquid is reduced by half. Serve with turkey.

Bake option: Place turkey roll in a 13x9-in. baking dish. Pour sauce over top. Bake, uncovered, at 400° for 70-80 minutes or until a thermometer inserted in center of stuffing reads 165°. (Cover loosely with foil during the last 20 minutes if turkey browns too quickly.) Remove from oven; cover and let stand for 10 minutes before slicing. Discard string. Skim fat from cooking juices; serve juices with turkey.

MAKE AHEAD
SPINACH-BASIL LASAGNA

My husband and I like to use classic ingredients in new ways. I came up with this lasagna one day and haven't made another type since. We love it!
—Charlotte Gehle, Brownstown, MI

PREP: 20 min. • BAKE: 45 min.
MAKES: 9 servings

- 1 large egg, lightly beaten
- 2 cups reduced-fat ricotta cheese
- 4 oz. crumbled feta cheese
- ¼ cup grated Parmesan cheese
- ¼ cup chopped fresh basil
- 2 garlic cloves, minced
- ¼ tsp. pepper
- 1 jar (24 oz.) pasta sauce
- 9 no-cook lasagna noodles
- 3 cups fresh baby spinach
- 2 cups shredded part-skim mozzarella cheese

1. Preheat oven to 350°. Mix the first seven ingredients.

2. Spread ½ cup of pasta sauce into a greased 13x9-in. baking dish. Layer with three lasagna noodles, ¾ cup of the ricotta mixture, 1 cup spinach, ½ cup mozzarella cheese and ⅔ cup sauce. Repeat layers twice. Sprinkle with the remaining mozzarella cheese.

3. Bake, covered, 35 minutes. Uncover; bake until heated through and cheese is melted, 10-15 minutes. Let stand 5 minutes before serving.

Freeze option: Cover and freeze unbaked lasagna. To use, partially thaw in the refrigerator overnight. Remove from refrigerator 30 minutes before baking. Preheat oven to 350°. Bake lasagna as directed, increasing time as necessary to heat through and for a thermometer inserted in center to read 165°.

BALL ORNAMENT WREATH

Upcycle your old ornaments into this striking salute to the merriest season! Start with a 14-in. foam wreath form. Use aluminum floral wire to make a hanging hook, and insert it deep into the back of the form. Tightly wrap the form in wide ribbon, covering it completely; secure the ribbon ends with glue. Remove the metal tops from shatterproof ball ornaments and glue the ornaments, tops down, to the form. Start with larger balls, then add different sizes for a layered look. Fill any gaps with miniature ornaments. Let glue dry before hanging the wreath.

SMOKED MOZZARELLA FLATBREAD PIZZA

Top a refrigerated crust with portobello mushrooms, smoked mozzarella and prosciutto for a hearty starter. You could also cut the pizza into larger pieces and serve it as an entree.
—Edwina Gadsby, Hayden, ID

PREP: 25 min. • **BAKE:** 15 min.
MAKES: 24 servings

- 2 Tbsp. butter, divided
- 2 Tbsp. olive oil, divided
- ⅔ cup sliced red onion
- ½ lb. sliced baby portobello mushrooms
- 1 garlic clove, minced
- 2 tsp. minced fresh rosemary or ½ tsp. dried rosemary, crushed
- 1 tube (13.8 oz.) refrigerated pizza crust
- 1½ cups shredded smoked mozzarella cheese
- 2 oz. sliced prosciutto or deli ham, finely chopped

1. Preheat oven to 400°. In a large skillet, heat 1 Tbsp. butter and 1 Tbsp. oil over medium-high heat. Add onion; cook and stir 2-3 minutes or until softened. Reduce heat to medium-low; cook 8-10 minutes or until golden brown, stirring occasionally. Remove from pan.
2. In same skillet, heat the remaining butter and oil over medium-high heat. Add the mushrooms; cook and stir 2-3 minutes or until tender. Add garlic and rosemary; cook 1-2 minutes longer or until the liquid has evaporated.
3. Unroll and press dough onto bottom of a greased 15x10x1-in. baking pan. Using your fingertips, press several dimples into the dough. Sprinkle with ½ cup cheese; top with the onion, mushroom mixture and prosciutto. Sprinkle with remaining cheese. Bake 15-18 minutes or until golden brown and cheese is melted.

FAST FIX
SEARED SCALLOPS WITH CITRUS HERB SAUCE

Be sure to pat the scallops with a paper towel to remove any excess moisture before cooking them. This helps create perfectly browned and flavorful scallops.
—April M. Lane, Greeneville, TN

TAKES: 20 min. • **MAKES:** 2 servings

- ¾ lb. sea scallops
- ¼ tsp. salt
- ¼ tsp. pepper
- ⅛ tsp. paprika
- 3 Tbsp. butter, divided
- 1 garlic clove, minced
- 2 Tbsp. dry sherry or chicken broth
- 1 Tbsp. lemon juice
- ⅛ tsp. minced fresh oregano
- ⅛ tsp. minced fresh tarragon

1. Pat scallops dry with paper towels; sprinkle with salt, pepper and paprika. In a large skillet, heat 2 Tbsp. butter over medium-high heat. Add scallops; sear for 1-2 minutes on each side or until golden brown and firm. Remove from the skillet; keep warm.
2. Wipe skillet clean if necessary. Saute garlic in remaining butter until tender; stir in the sherry. Cook until the liquid is almost evaporated; stir in remaining ingredients. Serve with scallops.

HALIBUT WITH CITRUS-OLIVE SAUCE

This poached halibut is one of my favorite fish entrees. The lovely sweet-and-salty sauce has incredible flavor, texture and color.

—Gloria Bradley, Naperville, IL

PREP: 30 min. • COOK: 15 min.
MAKES: 4 servings

2½ cups orange juice, divided
⅓ cup white wine
2 Tbsp. lime juice
2 Tbsp. chopped shallot
¼ cup butter, cut into four pieces
2 Tbsp. chopped sweet red pepper
1 Tbsp. chopped pitted green olives
1 Tbsp. chopped Greek olives
3 garlic cloves, minced
1 tsp. dried oregano
4 halibut fillets (6 oz. each)

1. In a small saucepan, bring 1½ cups orange juice, wine, lime juice and shallot to a boil; cook until liquid is reduced to ½ cup, about 15 minutes. Reduce heat to low; gradually whisk in butter until butter is melted. Remove from heat; stir in red pepper and olives. Keep warm.
2. In a large skillet, bring garlic, oregano and the remaining orange juice to a boil. Reduce heat; add the fillets and steam, uncovered, for 8-10 minutes or until fish flakes easily with a fork. Serve with sauce.

ROASTED VEGGIE STRUDEL

Roasted Brussels sprouts and potatoes go so well with bacon and Brie in my shortcut strudel. I leave the potato skin on for extra flavor and texture.

—Carole Holt, Mendota Heights, MN

PREP: 40 min. + cooling
BAKE: 20 min. • MAKES: 4 servings

2 cups Brussels sprouts, quartered
1 small Yukon Gold potato, cut into ½-in. cubes
1 Tbsp. olive oil
½ tsp. garlic pepper blend
¼ tsp. salt
⅓ cup julienned oil-packed sun-dried tomatoes
2 green onions, chopped
1 tube (8 oz.) refrigerated crescent rolls
4 oz. Brie cheese, cut into ½-in. cubes
5 bacon strips, cooked and crumbled
1 large egg
3 Tbsp. pine nuts

1. Preheat oven to 425°. Toss the first five ingredients; spread in a greased 15x10x1-in. pan. Roast until tender, about 15 minutes, stirring once.
2. Drain tomatoes, reserving 1 Tbsp. of the oil for egg wash. Add tomatoes and green onions to the roasted vegetables; cool. Reduce oven setting to 350°.
3. On a lightly floured surface, unroll the crescent dough into one long rectangle; pinch to seal the perforations. Roll dough into a 14x9-in. rectangle; transfer to a large baking sheet. Stir cheese and bacon into vegetables; spoon lengthwise down the center third of rectangle. On each long side, cut 1-in. strips at an angle to within ½ in. of the filling. Fold one strip from each side over the filling, pinching ends to join; repeat. Seal the ends of the braid.
4. Whisk together egg and the reserved oil; brush over strudel. Sprinkle with pine nuts. Bake until golden brown, 20-25 minutes.

NEW ORLEANS-STYLE SPICY SHRIMP

We have family members who attended college in New Orleans. This shrimp captures their favorite flavors from the Big Easy, with just the right touch of spices and heat.

—Susan Seymour, Valatie, NY

PREP: 15 min. • **BAKE:** 20 min.
MAKES: 12 servings

- 3 medium lemons, sliced
- ⅔ cup butter, cubed
- ½ cup ketchup
- ¼ cup Worcestershire sauce
- 2 Tbsp. seafood seasoning
- 2 Tbsp. chili garlic sauce
- 2 Tbsp. Louisiana-style hot sauce
- 1 Tbsp. Italian salad dressing mix
- 4 lbs. uncooked shell-on shrimp (31-40 per lb.)
- 2 bay leaves
  French bread

1. Preheat oven to 350°. In a microwave-safe bowl, combine first eight ingredients. Microwave, covered, on high 2-3 minutes or until butter is melted; stir until blended.
2. Divide the shrimp and bay leaves between two ungreased 13x9-in. baking dishes. Add half of the lemon mixture to each dish; toss to combine.
3. Bake, uncovered, 20-25 minutes or until shrimp turn pink, stirring halfway. Remove bay leaves. Serve with bread.

SWEET POTATO TORTELLINI WITH HAZELNUT SAUCE

Using wonton wrappers instead of fresh pasta dough makes homemade tortellini easier to prepare. For more formal dinners, this is an impressive vegetarian entree.
—Charlene Chambers, Ormond Beach, FL

PREP: 1 hour • **COOK:** 10 min./batch
MAKES: 8 servings

3	large sweet potatoes (about 2½ lbs.), peeled and cubed
¼	cup olive oil, divided
1½	tsp. herbes de Provence
¾	tsp. salt, divided
½	tsp. pepper, divided
2	shallots, chopped
2	garlic cloves, minced
1	cup whole-milk ricotta cheese
1	Tbsp. hazelnut liqueur
¼	tsp. ground nutmeg
72	wonton wrappers
3	qt. water
¾	cup unsalted butter, cubed
3	Tbsp. minced fresh sage
½	cup dried cherries, chopped
¼	cup chopped hazelnuts, toasted
1	cup shaved Asiago cheese

1. Preheat oven to 400°. Place sweet potatoes in a greased 15x10x1-in. baking pan; toss with 2 Tbsp. olive oil, herbes de Provence, ½ tsp. salt and ¼ tsp. pepper. Roast 25-30 minutes or until tender, stirring once. Cool slightly.

2. In a small skillet, heat remaining oil over medium-high heat. Add shallots and garlic; cook and stir until tender. Transfer to a food processor. Add sweet potatoes, ricotta cheese, liqueur, nutmeg and the remaining salt and pepper; process until blended.

3. Place 1 Tbsp. filling in the center of each wonton wrapper. (Cover remaining wrappers with a damp paper towel until ready to use.) Moisten wrapper edges with water. Fold one corner diagonally over the filling to form a triangle; press edges to seal. Pull opposite corners together, forming a boat; moisten with water and pinch to seal.

4. In a Dutch oven, bring water to a boil. Reduce heat to a gentle boil. Cook tortellini in batches 30-60 seconds or until they float. Remove with a slotted spoon; keep warm.

5. In a small, heavy saucepan, melt butter over medium heat. Add sage; heat for 5-7 minutes or until butter is golden brown, stirring constantly. Remove from heat; stir in cherries and hazelnuts. Serve with tortellini. Top with cheese.

Freeze option: Freeze uncooked tortellini on waxed paper-lined baking sheets until firm. Transfer to resealable plastic freezer bags; return to freezer. To use, cook the tortellini as directed, increasing time to 1½-2 minutes or until they float. Serve as directed.

To make ahead: The sweet potato puree can be made and refrigerated the day before filling the wontons.

MEDITERRANEAN RACK OF LAMB

It's elegant. It's special. And it will have your guests thinking you went all out. They don't have to know how simple it really is!

—Susan Nilsson, Sterling, VA

PREP: 10 min. • BAKE: 30 min.
MAKES: 4 servings

- 2 racks of lamb (1½ lbs. each)
- ¼ cup grated lemon zest
- ¼ cup minced fresh oregano or 4 tsp. dried oregano
- 6 garlic cloves, minced
- 1 Tbsp. olive oil
- ¼ tsp. salt
- ¼ tsp. pepper
  Fresh oregano and lemon slices, optional

1. Preheat oven to 375°. Place lamb in a shallow roasting pan. In a small bowl, combine the lemon zest, oregano, garlic, oil, salt and pepper. Rub over the lamb.
2. Bake 30-40 minutes or until the meat reaches desired doneness (for medium-rare, a thermometer should read 135°; medium, 140°; medium-well, 145°). Let stand 5 minutes before cutting. If desired, serve with fresh oregano and lemon slices.

SWEDISH MEATBALLS ALFREDO

I'm a big fan of this potluck-perfect dish. It only takes a few hours, unlike many other slow cooker recipes. Plus, it's easy. I'm all for the easy!

—Carole Bess White, Portland, OR

PREP: 10 min. • COOK: 2 hours
MAKES: 10 servings

- 2 jars (15 oz. each) roasted garlic Alfredo sauce
- 2 cups heavy whipping cream
- 2 cups sour cream
- ¾ tsp. hot pepper sauce
- ½ tsp. garlic powder
- ½ tsp. dill weed
- ⅛ tsp. pepper
- 1 pkg. (32 oz.) frozen fully cooked Swedish meatballs, thawed
  Paprika
  Hot cooked egg noodles

1. In a 5-qt. slow cooker, combine the first seven ingredients. Stir in the meatballs. Cook, covered, on low 2-3 hours or until meatballs are heated through.
2. Sprinkle with paprika. Serve with cooked egg noodles.

STENCILED PEACE SIGN

Stand this welcoming sign of the season by your front door! Start with a new or recycled wood plank; wipe it clean with a damp cloth and let dry. Using a bristle brush, apply 2 coats of yellow latex paint, then 2-3 coats of red latex paint. Use broad strokes, follow the wood grain, and let the paint dry after each application. Let the plank dry completely, and tape letter stencils in place. With a foam brush, dab antique-white latex paint into the stencils; let it dry and add a second coat. When completely dry, remove the stencils. Lightly sand the corners and edges of the sign, following the grain and applying more or less pressure as needed to reveal the undercoat. Sand lightly over the letters. If your plank has knots, sand those areas more vigorously.

MAKE AHEAD
OVEN-BAKED BRISKET

Texans like brisket cooked on the smoker, but this recipe offers convenient prep in the oven. Sometimes I make extra sauce to serve on the side. Round out the meal with potato salad and slaw.

—Katie Ferrier, Houston, TX

PREP: 15 min. + marinating • BAKE: 4¼ hours
MAKES: 8 servings

- 1 fresh beef brisket (4 to 5 lbs.)
- 2 Tbsp. Worcestershire sauce
- 2 Tbsp. soy sauce
- 1 Tbsp. onion salt
- 1 Tbsp. liquid smoke
- 2 tsp. salt
- 2 tsp. pepper
  Dash hot pepper sauce

SAUCE
- ½ cup ketchup
- 3 Tbsp. brown sugar
- 1 Tbsp. lemon juice
- 1 Tbsp. soy sauce
- 1 tsp. ground mustard
- 3 drops hot pepper sauce
  Dash ground nutmeg

1. Place the brisket, fat side down, in a 13x9-in. baking dish. In a small bowl, mix the Worcestershire, soy sauce, onion salt, liquid smoke, salt, pepper and hot pepper sauce; pour over brisket. Turn brisket fat side up; refrigerate, covered, overnight.
2. Remove brisket from the refrigerator. Preheat oven to 300°. Bake, covered, for 4 hours. In a small bowl, combine sauce ingredients. Spread over brisket. Bake, uncovered, 15-30 minutes longer or until tender. Cut diagonally across the grain into thin slices.
Note: This is a fresh beef brisket, not corned beef.

WINTER
BEET SALAD,
PAGE 147

YULETIDE

SIDE
DISHES

ROASTED SQUASH, CARROTS & WALNUTS

After the turkey's done, I dial up the oven temp and roast veggies for this yummy side.
—Lily Julow, Lawrenceville, GA

PREP: 15 min. • **BAKE:** 35 min.
MAKES: 8 servings

- 2 lbs. carrots (about 12 medium), peeled
- 1 medium butternut squash (3 lbs.), peeled and cubed
- ¼ cup packed brown sugar
- ¼ cup olive oil
- 2 tsp. kosher salt
- ½ tsp. ground cinnamon
- ¼ tsp. ground nutmeg
- 1 cup chopped walnuts

1. Preheat oven to 400°. Cut carrots in half lengthwise, then in half crosswise.
2. In a large bowl, toss squash and carrots with brown sugar, oil, salt, cinnamon and nutmeg. Transfer mixture to two greased, foil-lined 15x10x1-in. baking pans. Roast for 30 minutes, stirring occasionally.
3. Sprinkle walnuts over vegetables. Roast 5-10 minutes longer or until the vegetables are tender.

MOM'S APPLE CORNBREAD STUFFING

My speedy recipe is the end-all be-all stuffing in our family. We never have leftovers.
—Marie Forte, Raritan, NJ

PREP: 15 min. • **BAKE:** 35 min.
MAKES: 16 servings

- 6 large Granny Smith apples, peeled and chopped
- 1 pkg. (14 oz.) crushed cornbread stuffing
- ½ cup butter, melted
- 1 can (14½ oz.) chicken broth

1. Preheat oven to 350°. Combine apples, stuffing and butter. Add broth; mix well.
2. Transfer mixture to a greased 13x9-in. baking dish. Bake until golden brown, 35-40 minutes.

MAKE AHEAD
BAKED TWO-CHEESE & BACON GRITS

When I combine grits with bacon and cheese, everyone asks for a second helping.
—Melissa Rogers, Tuscaloosa, AL

PREP: 25 min. • **BAKE:** 40 min. + standing
MAKES: 12 servings

- 6 thick-sliced bacon strips, chopped
- 3 cups water
- 3 cups chicken stock
- 1 tsp. garlic powder
- ½ tsp. pepper
- 2 cups quick-cooking grits
- 12 oz. process cheese (Velveeta), cubed (about 2⅓ cups)
- ½ cup butter, cubed
- ½ cup 2% milk
- 4 large eggs, lightly beaten
- 2 cups shredded white cheddar cheese

1. Preheat the oven to 350°. In a large saucepan, cook bacon over medium heat until crisp, stirring occasionally. Remove pan from heat. Remove bacon with a slotted spoon; drain on paper towels.
2. Add water, stock, garlic powder and pepper to bacon drippings; bring to a boil. Slowly stir in grits. Reduce heat to medium-low; cook, covered, 5-7 minutes or until thickened, stirring occasionally. Remove from heat.
3. Add process cheese and butter; stir until melted. Stir in milk. Slowly stir in the beaten eggs until blended. Transfer to a greased 13x9-in. baking dish. Sprinkle with bacon and shredded cheese. Bake, uncovered, 40-45 minutes or until edges are golden brown and cheese is melted. Let stand for 10 minutes before serving.
Freeze option: Cool unbaked casserole; cover and freeze. To use, partially thaw in refrigerator overnight. Remove casserole from refrigerator 30 minutes before baking. Preheat oven to 350°. Bake the grits as directed, increasing time to 50-60 minutes or until heated through and a thermometer inserted in center reads 165°.

WHIMSICAL WOOLEN ELF

These fuzzy friends bring elfin magic to any holiday display. Turn scraps of colorful felt into decorations as warm and comforting as the holiday itself. Use coordinating colors to create a cluster of elves for your mantel.

For the body, wrap a 12-in. square of patterned scrapbook paper around the lower half of a 7- to 10-in.-tall papier-mâché cone. Trim as needed, and use a glue gun to secure the paper at the seam.

Cut a raindrop shape out of a sheet of decorative fur; this is your elf's beard. Trim to a size proportionate to the cone. Use hot glue to secure the beard in place, pointed end down, and overhanging the bottom of the cone.

For the hat, wrap a craft felt sheet around the upper half of the cone, slightly overlapping the beard. Use hot glue to secure the hat along its back edge. Trim excess felt as needed. Glue or sew a bell to the tip of the hat.

As a finishing touch, glue a wooden bead to the center of the beard, below the hat rim, for the nose. Repeat to make as many elves as you want!

FAST FIX

GRAPEFRUIT & FENNEL SALAD WITH MINT VINAIGRETTE

My dad has a red grapefruit tree and shares his crop with me. I toss the grapefruit with onion, fennel, honey and mint for a fresh, fabulous salad.

—Catherine Wilkinson, Dewey, AZ

....

TAKES: 15 min. • **MAKES:** 4 servings

- 1 medium red grapefruit
- 1 medium fennel bulb, halved and thinly sliced
- ¼ cup thinly sliced red onion

VINAIGRETTE
- 3 Tbsp. fresh mint leaves
- 2 Tbsp. sherry vinegar
- 1½ tsp. honey
- ⅛ tsp. salt
- ⅛ tsp. coarsely ground pepper
- 2 Tbsp. olive oil

1. Cut a thin slice from the top and bottom of the grapefruit; stand grapefruit upright on a cutting board. With a knife, cut off peel and outer membrane from grapefruit. Cut along the membrane of each segment to remove fruit. Arrange fennel, grapefruit and onion on a serving platter.
2. Place mint, vinegar, honey, salt and pepper in a small food processor; cover and process until mint is finely chopped. While processing, gradually add oil in a steady stream. Drizzle over salad.

❄ Holiday Helper

Fennel is an aromatic herb and a member of the carrot family. It has a large pale green bulb, celery-like stems and feathery leaves. Uncooked fennel has a mild licorice flavor and crunchy texture. The leaves have milder flavor and can be used in soups and salads or as a garnish.

POMEGRANATE-CRANBERRY SALAD

Juicy pomegranate seeds give cranberry gelatin a refreshing twist. For the crowning touch, serve the salad with whipped topping and a sprinkling of pecans.

—Lorie Mckinney, Marion, NC

....

PREP: 15 min. + chilling • **MAKES:** 8 servings

- 1 pkg. (.3 oz.) sugar-free cranberry gelatin
- 1 cup boiling water
- ½ cup cold water
- 1⅔ cups pomegranate seeds
- 1 can (14 oz.) whole-berry cranberry sauce
- 1 can (8 oz.) unsweetened crushed pineapple, drained
- ¾ cup chopped pecans
  Frozen whipped topping, thawed, optional
  Additional chopped pecans, optional

In a large bowl, dissolve gelatin in boiling water. Add cold water; stir. Add the pomegranate seeds, cranberry sauce, pineapple and pecans. Pour into a 1½-qt. serving bowl. Refrigerate for 4-5 hours or until firm. If desired, top with whipped topping and additional pecans.

CHERRY & FONTINA STUFFED PORTOBELLOS

I developed this hearty appetizer for my mushroom-lovin' kids. They're grown now, with families of their own, but they still lobby for these when they come home.
—Wendy Rusch, Cameron, WI

PREP: 30 min. • BAKE: 15 min.
MAKES: 12 servings

- 6 large portobello mushrooms
- ½ cup butter, cubed
- 1 medium onion, chopped
- 1 cup pecan halves, toasted
- 1 pkg. (5 oz.) dried tart cherries, coarsely chopped
- ½ tsp. poultry seasoning
- ½ tsp. dried thyme
- 7 oz. (about 4½ cups) seasoned stuffing cubes
- 1½ to 2 cups chicken broth
- 1½ cups shredded fontina cheese, divided

1. Preheat oven to 375°. Wipe mushroom caps clean with a damp paper towel; remove stems and gills and discard. Place caps on a foil-lined 15x10-in. baking pan.
2. In a large skillet, melt butter over medium heat until it begins to brown and smell nutty. Add onion; saute until translucent, stirring occasionally. Stir in pecans, cherries and seasonings; cook and stir for 3 minutes. Remove from heat.
3. Combine the onion mixture and stuffing cubes, tossing to coat evenly. Add 1½ cups broth to the onion-stuffing mixture, stirring until well mixed. Add the remaining broth as needed. Stir in 1 cup cheese.
4. Fill mushroom caps with stuffing until mounded, about 1 cup each. Sprinkle with the remaining cheese. Bake until the mushrooms are heated through and the cheese is melted, 15-20 minutes.
Note: To toast nuts, bake in a shallow pan in a 350° oven for 5-10 minutes or cook in a skillet over low heat until lightly browned, stirring occasionally.

FAST FIX

BRUSSELS SPROUTS IN ROSEMARY CREAM SAUCE

Brussels sprouts in an herb cream sauce? You've never had them like this—and you may never want them any other way!
—Liz Koschoreck, Berea, KY

TAKES: 30 min. • **MAKES:** 6 servings

- 1 lb. fresh Brussels sprouts (about 4 cups)
- ¼ cup butter, cubed
- 1 Tbsp. all-purpose flour
- 1 cup heavy whipping cream
- 1 Tbsp. coarsely chopped fresh rosemary
- 2 garlic cloves, minced
- ¾ tsp. salt
- ¼ cup shredded Parmigiano-Reggiano cheese
  Freshly ground pepper

1. Trim Brussels sprout stems; using a paring knife, cut an X in the bottom of each. Place sprouts in a large saucepan; add water to cover. Bring to a boil. Reduce heat; simmer, covered, 6-8 minutes or until almost tender. Drain.

2. Meanwhile, in a large saucepan, melt butter over medium heat. Stir in flour until smooth; gradually whisk in cream. Bring to a boil, stirring constantly; cook and stir for 1-2 minutes or until thickened. Stir in rosemary and garlic. Add Brussels sprouts and salt; heat through, stirring to combine. Sprinkle with cheese and pepper.

CRUNCHY HONEY-GLAZED BUTTERNUT SQUASH

I'm now required to bring this to every family gathering during the holidays because it's so awesome! This year, why not start a new tradition with your family?
—Sarah Farmer, Waukesha, WI

PREP: 20 min. • **BAKE:** 45 min.
MAKES: 10 servings

- ½ cup honey
- 1 tsp. dried thyme, divided
- 1 large butternut squash (about 5 lbs.), peeled, halved, seeded and thinly sliced
- 3 Tbsp. water
- ¼ cup plus 2 Tbsp. olive oil, divided
- 1½ tsp. salt, divided
- 1½ tsp. pepper, divided
- ½ cup panko (Japanese) bread crumbs

1. Preheat oven to 375°. In a large saucepan, heat honey and ½ tsp. thyme, stirring occasionally, over low heat until fragrant, 3-4 minutes.
2. Meanwhile, in a large microwave-safe dish, combine the squash and water; microwave, covered, on high until squash is tender, 6-8 minutes. Drain. Add ¼ cup olive oil, 1 tsp. salt and 1 tsp. pepper; toss to coat.
3. On a flat surface, stack the squash slices. Arrange stacks on their sides in a greased 9-in. square baking dish. (To make stacking easier, set baking dish on its end; fill with squash stacks. When dish is full, return it to its original position.) Drizzle 3 Tbsp. honey mixture over squash.
4. Bake 45-50 minutes or until squash is tender. In a small skillet, heat remaining oil over medium heat. Add bread crumbs; toss with remaining thyme and remaining salt and pepper. Cook and stir until golden brown, about 5 minutes. Sprinkle over the baked squash; if desired, drizzle with additional honey mixture.

ITALIAN ARTICHOKE-GREEN BEAN CASSEROLE

My mother and I made changes to a recipe from a cookbook to create this casserole. We increased the vegetables significantly, and it receives rave reviews at get-togethers. It's definitely not your average green bean casserole. See for yourself!
—Denise Klibert, Shreveport, LA

PREP: 25 min. • **BAKE:** 25 min.
MAKES: 10 servings

- 6 cups cut fresh green beans (about 1½ lbs.)
- ⅓ cup olive oil
- 1 medium onion, chopped
- 2 garlic cloves, minced
- 3 cans (14 oz. each) water-packed artichoke hearts, drained and chopped
- ½ cup minced fresh parsley
  Pinch cayenne pepper
  Pinch pepper
- 1 cup seasoned bread crumbs
- 1 cup grated Parmesan cheese, divided

1. Preheat the oven to 350°. In a large saucepan, bring 6 cups water to a boil. Add green beans; cook, uncovered, 3-4 minutes or just until crisp-tender. Drain and set aside.
2. In a 6-qt. stockpot, heat oil over medium heat. Add onion; cook and stir 3-4 minutes or until tender. Add garlic; cook 1 minute longer. Add green beans, artichoke hearts, parsley, cayenne and pepper. Stir in bread crumbs and ¾ cup of the cheese.
3. Transfer mixture to a greased 11x7-in. baking dish. Sprinkle with the remaining cheese. Bake for 25-30 minutes or until lightly browned.

TWICE-BAKED RUTABAGAS

Mix it up for dinner by substituting your go-to spuds dish with rutabagas. This recipe boasts bacon, cheese and whipping cream—even the skeptics won't be able to resist a bite!
—Lisa L. Bynum, Brandon, MS

PREP: 30 min. • **BAKE:** 20 min.
MAKES: 8 servings

- 4 small rutabagas, peeled and cut into 1-in. cubes
- 3 Tbsp. water
- 8 cooked bacon strips, chopped
- 1 cup heavy whipping cream
- ¼ cup butter, cubed
- 2 tsp. garlic powder
- ½ tsp. salt
- ¼ tsp. pepper
- 2 cups shredded cheddar cheese, divided
- 3 green onions, sliced, divided

1. Preheat oven to 350°. In a microwave-safe bowl, combine the rutabagas and water. Microwave, covered, on high for 16-20 minutes or until tender, stirring halfway. Mash rutabagas; add bacon, cream, butter, garlic powder, salt and pepper. Stir in 1 cup cheese and ¼ cup green onions.
2. Spoon the mixture into eight greased 6-ounce ramekins or custard cups, then sprinkle with the remaining cheese. Place the ramekins on a baking sheet. Bake for 18-22 minutes or until bubbly and cheese is melted. Sprinkle with the remaining green onions.

❄ Holiday Helper

When shopping for rutabagas, select those that are smooth-skinned, unblemished, heavy and firm, and preferably no larger than 4 in. in diameter. Store, unwashed, in a plastic bag in your refrigerator's crisper drawer for up to 1 week.

FESTIVE THREE-GRAIN SALAD

Wholesome ingredients, easy prep and a festive appearance make this colorful side dish one of my holiday staples. I assemble it the night before and store it in the refrigerator.
—Teri Kreyche, Tustin, CA

PREP: 15 min. • **COOK:** 1 hour + cooling
MAKES: 8 servings

- ¾ cup uncooked wheat berries
- 5 cups water
- ½ cup uncooked medium pearl barley
- ⅓ cup uncooked long grain brown rice
- 1 medium apple, chopped
- ½ cup pomegranate seeds, dried cherries or dried cranberries
- 4 green onions, chopped
- ¼ cup finely chopped carrot
- ¼ cup finely chopped celery
- ¼ cup minced fresh parsley

DRESSING
- ⅓ cup cider vinegar
- 3 Tbsp. finely chopped red onion
- 3 Tbsp. canola oil
- 2 to 3 Tbsp. sugar
- 1 Tbsp. Worcestershire sauce
- 2 garlic cloves, minced
- ½ tsp. salt
- ¼ tsp. pepper

1. In a large saucepan, combine wheat berries and water; bring to a boil. Reduce heat; simmer, covered, 10 minutes. Stir in barley; simmer, covered, 5 minutes. Stir in rice; simmer, covered, 40-45 minutes or until grains are tender. Drain; transfer to a large bowl. Cool to room temperature.
2. Add apple, pomegranate seeds, green onions, carrot, celery and parsley to the wheat berry mixture; toss to combine.
3. In a small bowl, whisk the dressing ingredients until blended. Pour over the salad; toss to coat. Serve immediately or refrigerate and serve cold.

CRANBERRY RICOTTA GNOCCHI WITH BROWN BUTTER SAUCE

To make light, airy gnocchi, work quickly and handle the dough as little as possible. You'll be pleased with the resulting pillowy dumplings.
—Sally Sibthorpe, Shelby Township, MI

PREP: 30 min. + standing • **COOK:** 5 min.
MAKES: 8 servings

- ¾ cup dried cranberries, divided
- 2 cups ricotta cheese
- 1 cup all-purpose flour
- ½ cup grated Parmesan cheese
- 1 large egg, lightly beaten
- ¾ tsp. salt, divided
- 4 qt. water
- ¾ cup butter, cubed
- 2 Tbsp. minced fresh sage
- ½ cup chopped walnuts, toasted
- ⅛ tsp. white pepper

1. Finely chop ¼ cup cranberries. In a large bowl, combine the ricotta, flour, Parmesan cheese, egg, ½ tsp. salt and chopped cranberries; mix until blended. On a clean, lightly floured surface, knead 10-12 times, forming a soft dough. Cover and let rest for 10 minutes.
2. Divide dough into four portions. On a floured surface, roll each portion into a ¾-in.-thick rope; cut into ¾-in. pieces. Press and roll each piece with a lightly floured fork.
3. In a Dutch oven, bring water to a boil. Cook gnocchi in batches 30-60 seconds or until they float. Remove with a slotted spoon; keep warm.
4. In a large heavy saucepan, cook butter over medium heat for 5 minutes. Add sage; cook 3-5 minutes longer or until the butter is golden brown, stirring occasionally. Stir in the walnuts, white pepper, remaining cranberries and salt. Add the gnocchi; stir gently to coat. Serve immediately.

CRANBERRY-APPLE RED CABBAGE

When I was looking for something new to go with pork, I started playing with flavors and came up with this colorful slow-cooked dish. I think my German grandmother would be impressed!
—Ann Sheehy, Lawrence, MA

PREP: 15 min. • **COOK:** 3 hours
MAKES: 8 servings

- 1 medium head red cabbage, coarsely chopped (8 cups)
- 1 can (14 oz.) whole-berry cranberry sauce
- 2 medium Granny Smith apples, peeled and coarsely chopped
- 1 large white onion, chopped
- ½ cup cider vinegar
- ¼ cup sweet vermouth or white wine, optional
- 1 tsp. kosher salt
- ¾ tsp. caraway seeds
- ½ tsp. coarsely ground pepper

Combine all ingredients; transfer to a 5-qt. slow cooker. Cook, covered, on low until the cabbage is tender, 3-4 hours. Serve with a slotted spoon.

CAPE COD CORN PUDDING

A family member passed along this recipe for corn baked with cheddar and ricotta. Don't skip the fresh basil—it adds a hint of sweet flavor reminiscent of mint and anise.
—Melinda Messer, Benson, NC

PREP: 20 min. • **BAKE:** 30 min. + standing
MAKES: 8 servings

- ¼ cup butter, cubed
- 5 cups frozen corn (about 24 oz.)
- 1 medium onion, finely chopped
- 4 large eggs, lightly beaten
- 2 cups whole milk
- 1 cup whole-milk ricotta cheese
- ½ cup cornmeal
- 1 Tbsp. sugar
- 1 tsp. salt
- ¾ tsp. pepper
- 1½ cups shredded cheddar cheese, divided
- 2 Tbsp. chopped fresh basil, optional

1. Preheat oven to 375°. In a 6-qt. stockpot, heat butter over medium-high heat. Add corn and onion; cook and stir 6-8 minutes or until corn is crisp-tender. Remove from the heat.
2. In a large bowl, whisk eggs, milk, ricotta cheese, cornmeal, sugar, salt and pepper. Stir in ¾ cup cheddar cheese, corn mixture and, if desired, basil.
3. Transfer to a greased 11x7-in. baking dish. Sprinkle with the remaining cheddar. Bake, uncovered, 30-35 minutes or until set. Let stand for 10 minutes before serving.

FAST FIX
PORTOBELLO GNOCCHI SALAD

Pan-sauteing gnocchi eliminates the need to boil it and creates a wonderful, crispy coating. The baby bellas lend an earthiness to this Italian-influenced salad.
—Fran Fehling, Staten Island, NY

TAKES: 25 min. • **MAKES:** 14 servings

- 1 pkg. (16 oz.) potato gnocchi
- 2 Tbsp. plus ⅓ cup olive oil, divided
- ½ lb. sliced baby portobello mushrooms
- 3 tsp. lemon juice
- 3 large plum tomatoes, seeded and chopped
- 1 can (15 oz.) garbanzo beans or chickpeas, rinsed and drained
- 1 pkg. (5 oz.) fresh baby arugula or fresh baby spinach, coarsely chopped
- ½ cup pitted Greek olives, cut in half
- ⅓ cup minced fresh parsley
- 2 Tbsp. capers, drained and chopped
- 2 tsp. grated lemon zest
- ½ tsp. salt
- ¼ tsp. coarsely ground pepper
- ½ cup crumbled feta cheese
- ¼ cup chopped walnuts, toasted

1. In large nonstick skillet over medium-high heat, cook the gnocchi in 1 Tbsp. oil for 6-8 minutes or until lightly browned, turning once. Remove from the skillet; cool slightly.
2. In the same skillet, saute mushrooms in 1 Tbsp. oil until tender. Place mushrooms and gnocchi in a serving bowl. Add lemon juice and remaining oil; gently toss to coat.
3. Add the tomatoes, chickpeas, arugula, olives, parsley, capers, lemon zest, salt and pepper; toss to combine. Garnish with cheese and walnuts.
Note: Look for potato gnocchi in the pasta or frozen foods section.

ROASTED BALSAMIC SWEET POTATOES

By the end of summer, I'm done with the usual potato salad. This warm, spicy side kicks off the cozy winter season in my home.
—Karen Vande Slunt, Watertown, WI

PREP: 30 min. • **COOK:** 30 min.
MAKES: 12 servings

- 6 medium sweet potatoes, cubed
- 1 tsp. olive oil
- ½ tsp. salt
- ½ tsp. pepper
- 1 lb. bacon strips, chopped
- 4 celery ribs, chopped
- 1 medium onion, thinly sliced
- 3 garlic cloves, minced
- 1 cup beef stock
- ⅔ cup balsamic vinegar
- 4 tsp. paprika
- ¾ tsp. ground cumin, optional
- 6 green onions, chopped
  Minced fresh parsley, optional

1. Preheat oven to 375°. Place sweet potatoes in a 15x10-in. pan; drizzle with oil and sprinkle with salt and pepper. Turn to coat. Bake until tender, 30-35 minutes.
2. Meanwhile, in a large skillet, cook bacon over medium-low heat until crisp; drain. Discard all but 4 tsp. of the drippings.
3. Cook celery and onion in drippings over medium heat until tender, 6-8 minutes. Stir in garlic; cook 1 minute. Add beef stock and balsamic vinegar; simmer until the liquid is reduced by half, 5-8 minutes. Add paprika and, if desired, cumin; cook 1 minute longer.
4. Pour the balsamic mixture over sweet potatoes; add bacon. Toss to coat. Top with green onions and, if desired, minced fresh parsley; serve immediately.

FAST FIX

ORANGE POMEGRANATE SALAD WITH HONEY

I discovered this fragrant salad in a cooking class. Orange flower water (or orange blossom water), perks up the orange segments, but can be hard to find. Don't worry—orange juice adds a nice zip, too!

—Carol Richardson Marty, Lynwood, WA

TAKES: 15 min. • **MAKES:** 6 servings

- 5 medium oranges or 10 clementines
- ½ cup pomegranate seeds
- 2 Tbsp. honey
- 1 to 2 tsp. orange flower water or orange juice

1. Cut a thin slice from the top and bottom of each orange; stand orange upright on a cutting board. With a knife, cut off peel and outer membrane from oranges. Cut crosswise into ½-in. slices.
2. Arrange orange slices on a serving platter; sprinkle with pomegranate seeds. In a small bowl, mix honey and orange flower water; drizzle over the fruit.

FAST FIX

SMOKY CAULIFLOWER BITES

These healthy little treats work well as a side or a fun appetizer. Roasting the cauliflower adds deep flavor and an irresistible crunch.

—Courtney Stultz, Weir, KS

TAKES: 20 min. • **MAKES:** 4 servings

- 3 Tbsp. olive oil
- ¾ tsp. sea salt
- 1 tsp. paprika
- ½ tsp. ground cumin
- ¼ tsp. ground turmeric
- ⅛ tsp. chili powder
- 1 medium head cauliflower, broken into florets

Preheat oven to 450°. Mix the first six ingredients. Add cauliflower florets; toss to coat. Transfer to a 15x10x1-in. baking pan. Roast until tender, 15-20 minutes, stirring halfway.

HERBED APPLE-CRANBERRY BREAD DRESSING

Not all stuffings are created equal. My version of the classic side dish features apples for a sweet crunch and cranberries for just a hint of tartness.

—Aysha Schurman, Ammon, ID

PREP: 30 min. • **BAKE:** 45 min.
MAKES: 16 servings

- 1 cup butter, cubed
- 3 medium red onions, chopped (about 2⅔ cups)
- 2 to 3 celery ribs, chopped (about 1⅓ cups)
- 5 cups dry bread crumbs
- 3 medium tart apples, chopped (about 2⅔ cups)
- 1⅓ cups dried cranberries
- 1⅓ cups minced chives
- 1 cup chicken broth
- 1 cup unsweetened applesauce
- ⅔ cup orange juice
- ¼ cup minced fresh cilantro
- ¼ cup minced fresh parsley
- 4 tsp. minced fresh rosemary
- 4 garlic cloves, minced
- 1½ tsp. salt
- 1 tsp. pepper

1. Preheat oven to 325°. In a 6-qt. stockpot, heat butter over medium-high heat. Add the onions and celery; cook and stir for 6-8 minutes or until onions are tender. Stir in the remaining ingredients. Transfer to a greased 13x9-in. baking dish.
2. Bake, covered, 30 minutes. Uncover; bake 15-20 minutes longer or until lightly browned.

TRA VIGNE GREEN BEANS

The name of this recipe, *tra vigne,* is Italian and translates to "among the vines." I was inspired by a restaurant of the same name in the Napa Valley. To me, the flavors in this dish represent the essence of its title.

—Jenn Tidwell, Fair Oaks, CA

PREP: 15 min. • **COOK:** 25 min.
MAKES: 9 servings

- 2 lbs. fresh green beans, trimmed
- 12 bacon strips, chopped
- 2 shallots, minced
- 4 garlic cloves, minced
- ½ tsp. salt
- ½ tsp. pepper
- 2 cups white grape juice
- ¼ cup white wine vinegar
- ½ cup minced chives

1. In a large saucepan, bring 4 cups water to a boil. Add green beans; cover and cook for 5 minutes. Drain and immediately place green beans in ice water. Drain and pat dry.
2. Meanwhile, in a large skillet, cook bacon over medium heat until crisp. Remove to paper towels with a slotted spoon; drain, reserving 1 Tbsp. of drippings.
3. In the same skillet, saute shallots in the bacon drippings until tender. Add garlic, salt and pepper; cook 1 minute longer. Stir in juice and vinegar. Bring to a boil; cook until the liquid is reduced by half.
4. Add green beans and bacon; cook until heated through. Sprinkle with chives.

NANNY'S PARMESAN MASHED POTATOES

My grandsons rave over these creamy potatoes loaded with Parmesan. That's all the endorsement I need! Sometimes I use red or golden potatoes and leave the skins on.

—Kallee Krong-Mccreery, Escondido, CA

PREP: 20 min. • **COOK:** 20 min.
MAKES: 12 servings

- 5 lbs. potatoes, peeled and cut into 1-in. pieces
- ¾ cup butter, softened
- ¾ cup sour cream
- ½ cup grated Parmesan cheese
- 1¼ tsp. garlic salt
- 1 tsp. salt
- ½ tsp. pepper
- ¾ to 1 cup 2% milk, warmed
- 2 Tbsp. minced fresh parsley

1. Place potatoes in a 6-qt. stockpot; add water to cover. Bring to a boil. Reduce heat; cook, uncovered, 10-15 minutes or until tender. Drain potatoes; return to pot and stir over low heat 1 minute to dry.
2. Coarsely mash potatoes, gradually adding butter, sour cream, cheese, seasonings and enough milk to reach desired consistency. Stir in parsley.

❄ Holiday Helper

Keep these tips in mind for making perfect mashed potatoes this season:

• Cut all of the potatoes to roughly the same size. If the pieces vary too much in size, the potatoes will cook unevenly.

• Cover the cubed potatoes completely with water or they may dry out. Next, bring them to a gentle boil.

• While many cooks mash their potatoes with milk, others like to use cream. Use whatever you prefer.

• Cooking for someone on a dairy-free diet? Mash the potatoes with unsweetened almond or soy milk, warmed chicken broth or even some of the starchy cooking water.

WINTER BEET SALAD

To save a little time, our Test Kitchen staffers recommend using packaged salad greens in this beautiful recipe. The simple dressing is easy to assemble.
—*Taste of Home* Test Kitchen

PREP: 20 min. • **BAKE:** 1 hour + cooling
MAKES: 4 servings

- 2 medium fresh beets
- 1 pkg. (5 oz.) mixed salad greens
- 2 medium navel oranges, peeled and sliced
- 1 small fennel bulb, halved and thinly sliced
- ¼ cup chopped hazelnuts, toasted

DRESSING
- 3 Tbsp. olive oil
- 2 Tbsp. orange juice
- 1 Tbsp. balsamic vinegar
- 2 tsp. grated orange zest
- ¼ tsp. onion powder

Preheat oven to 425°. Cut slits in beets; place on a baking sheet. Bake until tender, about 1 hour. When cool enough to handle, peel beets and cut into wedges. Divide greens among salad plates; top with beets, oranges, fennel and hazelnuts. Combine the dressing ingredients in a jar with a tight-fitting lid; shake well. Drizzle dressing over the salads.

Note: To toast nuts, bake in a shallow pan in a 350° oven for 5-10 minutes or cook in a skillet over low heat until lightly browned, stirring occasionally.

AUNT MARGARET'S SWEET POTATO CASSEROLE

My great-aunt made an incredible sweet potato casserole for our holiday dinners. I've lightened it up a bit and we love it the same!
—Beth Britton, Fairlawn, OH

PREP: 50 min. • **BAKE:** 50 min.
MAKES: 12 servings

- 3 lbs. sweet potatoes (about 3 large), peeled and cubed

TOPPING
- ¾ cup all-purpose flour
- ¾ cup packed brown sugar
- ¾ cup old-fashioned oats
- ⅛ tsp. salt
- ⅓ cup cold butter, cubed

FILLING
- ½ cup sugar
- ½ cup 2% milk
- 2 large eggs, lightly beaten
- ¼ cup butter
- 1 tsp. vanilla extract
- 2 cups miniature marshmallows

1. Preheat oven to 350°. Place sweet potatoes in a 6-qt. stockpot; add water to cover. Bring to a boil. Reduce heat; cook, uncovered, 10-12 minutes or until tender. Meanwhile, make topping by combining flour, brown sugar, oats and salt; cut in butter until crumbly.

2. Drain potatoes; return to pan. Beat until mashed. Add sugar, milk, eggs, butter and vanilla; beat until combined. Transfer to a broiler-safe 13x9-in. baking dish. Sprinkle topping over potato mixture.

3. Bake casserole, uncovered, until topping is golden brown, 40-45 minutes; let stand 10 minutes. Sprinkle with marshmallows. If desired, broil for 30-45 seconds, 4-5 in. from the heat, or until marshmallows are puffed and golden.

Test Kitchen tip: By adding marshmallows to the casserole right out of the oven, they'll start to melt together and form a silky layer of yumminess.

SAUSAGE-HERB DRESSING

To make time for last-minute holiday essentials, I prep the sausage part of this recipe a day or two ahead, then finish the dressing in my slow cooker on the big day. It has stood the test two years running.

—Judy Batson, Tampa, FL

PREP: 20 min. • **COOK:** 2 hours
MAKES: 10 servings

- 1 lb. bulk sage pork sausage
- 1 medium sweet onion, chopped (about 2 cups)
- 2 celery ribs, chopped
- ¼ cup brewed coffee
- ½ tsp. poultry seasoning
- ½ tsp. dried oregano
- ½ tsp. rubbed sage
- ½ tsp. dried thyme
- ½ tsp. pepper
- 1½ cups chicken or turkey broth
- 1 pkg. (12 oz.) seasoned stuffing cubes (8 cups)
  Chopped fresh parsley

1. In a 6-qt. stockpot, cook and crumble the sausage with sweet onion and celery over medium heat until no longer pink, 5-7 minutes; drain. Stir in the coffee and seasonings; cook for 3 minutes, stirring mixture occasionally.

2. Add broth; bring to a boil. Remove from heat; stir in stuffing cubes. Transfer to a greased 4- or 5-qt. slow cooker.

3. Cook, covered, on low until heated through and edges are lightly browned, 2-2½ hours, stirring once. Sprinkle with chopped parsley.

CORN & ONION SOUFFLE

I changed my dependable cheese souffle recipe to prepare it with fresh corn. If you're souffle-challenged, just remember to hold off on adding the whipped egg whites until right before you slip it in the oven.

—Lily Julow, Lawrenceville, GA

PREP: 25 min. • **BAKE:** 45 min.
MAKES: 10 servings

- 6 large eggs
- 2 Tbsp. plus ½ cup cornmeal, divided
- 2 cups fresh or frozen corn (about 10 oz.), thawed
- 2 cups 2% milk
- 1 Tbsp. sugar
- ¾ cup heavy whipping cream
- ½ cup butter, melted
- 1 Tbsp. canola oil
- 1 cup chopped sweet onion
- 3 oz. cream cheese, softened
- 1 tsp. plus ⅛ tsp. salt, divided
- ½ tsp. freshly ground pepper
- ⅛ tsp. baking soda

1. Separate the eggs; let stand at room temperature 30 minutes. Grease a 2½-qt. souffle dish; dust dish lightly with 2 Tbsp. of the cornmeal.

2. Preheat oven to 350°. Place corn, milk and sugar in a blender; cover and process until smooth. Add the cream and butter; cover and process 15-30 seconds longer.

3. In a large saucepan, heat oil over medium heat. Add onion; cook and stir 4-6 minutes or until tender. Stir in corn mixture, cream cheese, 1 tsp. salt, pepper and the remaining cornmeal until heated through. Remove to a large bowl.

4. Whisk a small amount of hot mixture into the egg yolks; return all to the bowl, whisking constantly.

5. In a large bowl, beat the egg whites with baking soda and the remaining salt on high speed until stiff but not dry. With a rubber spatula, gently stir a fourth of the egg whites into corn mixture. Fold in remaining egg whites. Transfer to prepared dish.

6. Bake 45-50 minutes or until the top is deep golden brown and puffed and center appears set. Serve immediately.

FAST FIX

PARMESAN ROASTED BROCCOLI

Sure, it's simple and healthy—but, oh, is this roasted broccoli delicious! Cutting the stalks into tall trees transforms this ordinary veggie into a standout side dish.

—Holly Sander, Lake Mary, FL

....

TAKES: 30 min. • **MAKES:** 4 servings

- 2   small broccoli crowns (about 8 oz. each)
- 3   Tbsp. olive oil
- ½   tsp. salt
- ½   tsp. pepper
- ¼   tsp. crushed red pepper flakes
- 4   garlic cloves, thinly sliced
- 2   Tbsp. grated Parmesan cheese
- 1   tsp. grated lemon zest

1. Preheat oven to 425°. Cut broccoli crowns into quarters from top to bottom. Drizzle with oil; sprinkle with seasonings. Place in a parchment paper-lined 15x10x1-in. pan.

2. Roast until crisp-tender, 10-12 minutes. Sprinkle with the garlic; roast 5 minutes. Sprinkle with Parmesan cheese; roast until cheese is melted and broccoli stalks are tender, 2-4 minutes more. Sprinkle with lemon zest.

❄ Reader Review

"So, so good! Layer upon layer of my favorite flavors!"

JUSTMBETH TASTEOFHOME.COM

SWISS CORN CASSEROLE

My mom shared this recipe with me back in the '80s, and now it's a holiday mainstay. We freeze locally grown corn during peak season, and I love to use it in this special side.

—Wendy Young, Cordova, MD

PREP: 20 min. • **BAKE:** 35 min. + standing
MAKES: 8 servings

4	large eggs
1	can (12 oz.) evaporated milk
½	tsp. salt
¼	tsp. pepper
4	cups frozen corn (about 20 oz.), thawed
3	cups shredded Swiss cheese, divided
¼	cup chopped onion
3	cups soft bread crumbs
¼	cup butter, melted

1. Preheat oven to 350°. In a large bowl, whisk together first four ingredients; stir in corn, 1½ cups cheese and onion. Transfer to a greased 11x7-in. baking dish.
2. Toss bread crumbs with melted butter; distribute over casserole. Sprinkle with remaining cheese.
3. Bake, uncovered, until golden brown and heated through, 35-45 minutes. Let stand 10 minutes before serving.
Note: To make soft bread crumbs, tear bread into pieces and place in a food processor or blender. Cover and pulse until crumbs form. One slice of bread yields ½-¾ cup crumbs.

BRUSSELS SPROUTS AU GRATIN

In our house, Brussels sprouts have always been popular. When I topped them with a creamy sauce, Swiss cheese and bread crumbs, it became a new dinner tradition.
—Gwen Gregory, Rio Oso, CA

PREP: 30 min. • BAKE: 20 min.
MAKES: 6 servings

- 2   lbs. fresh Brussels sprouts, quartered
- 1   Tbsp. olive oil
- ½   tsp. salt, divided
- ¼   tsp. pepper, divided
- ¾   cup cubed sourdough or French bread
- 1   Tbsp. butter
- 1   Tbsp. minced fresh parsley
- 2   garlic cloves, coarsely chopped
- 1   cup heavy whipping cream
- ⅛   tsp. crushed red pepper flakes
- ⅛   tsp. ground nutmeg
- ½   cup shredded white sharp cheddar or Swiss cheese

1. Preheat oven to 450°. Place Brussels sprouts in a large bowl. Add oil, ¼ tsp. salt and ⅛ tsp. pepper; toss to coat. Transfer to two ungreased 15x10x1-in. baking pans. Roast 8-10 minutes or until lightly browned and crisp-tender. Reduce oven to 400°.
2. Meanwhile, place bread, butter, parsley and garlic in a food processor; pulse until fine crumbs form.
3. Place roasted sprouts in a greased 8-in. square baking dish. In a small bowl, mix cream, pepper flakes, nutmeg, and remaining salt and pepper. Pour over the Brussels sprouts; sprinkle with cheese. Top with crumb mixture. Bake, uncovered, 15-20 minutes or until bubbly and topping is lightly browned.

THYME-ROASTED VEGETABLES

The aroma of roasting vegetables brings everyone to the dinner table. Normally it serves 10, but my husband is known to have more than one serving at a time. It's that good!
—Jasmine Rose, Crystal Lake, IL

PREP: 25 min. • BAKE: 45 min.
MAKES: 10 servings

- 2   lbs. red potatoes, cubed (about 9 cups)
- 3   cups sliced sweet onions (about 1½ large)
- 3   medium carrots, sliced
- ½   lb. medium fresh mushrooms, halved
- 1   large sweet red pepper, cut into 1½-in. pieces
- 1   large sweet yellow pepper, cut into 1½-in. pieces
- 2   Tbsp. butter, melted
- 2   Tbsp. olive oil
- 1   Tbsp. minced fresh thyme or 1 tsp. dried thyme
- 1   tsp. salt
- ¼   tsp. pepper

1. Preheat oven to 400°. In a large bowl, combine vegetables. Add the remaining ingredients; toss to coat.
2. Transfer to a 15x10x1-in. baking pan. Roast 45-50 minutes or until tender, stirring occasionally.

BUTTERNUT SQUASH OVEN RISOTTO

Squash, chili powder and a little beer make my risotto different and delicious. Cooking it in the oven also cuts down on the hands-on time typically spent preparing risotto.
—Katie Ferrier, Houston, TX

PREP: 20 min. • **BAKE:** 30 min.
MAKES: 10 servings

6 cups cubed peeled butternut squash (1-in. cube)
4 Tbsp. olive oil, divided
½ tsp. salt
¼ tsp. pepper
1 carton (32 oz.) chicken broth
1 cup water
1 small onion, chopped
2 cups uncooked arborio rice
2 garlic cloves, minced
1 cup beer
2 Tbsp. butter
½ tsp. chili powder
¼ tsp. ground nutmeg
1 cup grated Parmesan cheese

1. Preheat oven to 375°. Place squash in a greased 15x10x1-in. baking pan. Drizzle with 2 Tbsp. olive oil; sprinkle with salt and pepper and toss to coat. Roast on a lower oven rack for 30-35 minutes or until tender, stirring occasionally.
2. Meanwhile, in a large saucepan, bring broth and water to a simmer; keep hot. In an ovenproof Dutch oven, heat remaining oil over medium heat. Add onion; cook and stir 4-6 minutes or until tender. Add rice and garlic; cook and stir 1-2 minutes longer or until rice is coated.
3. Stir in the beer. Reduce the heat to maintain a simmer; cook and stir until the beer is absorbed. Stir in 4 cups of the hot broth mixture.
4. Place Dutch oven on an oven rack above the squash; bake, covered, 20-25 minutes or until rice is tender but firm to the bite, the risotto is creamy and the liquid is almost absorbed.
5. Remove Dutch oven from oven. Add butter, chili powder, nutmeg and the remaining broth mixture. Stir vigorously until blended and the liquid is almost absorbed. Stir in the roasted squash and cheese. Serve immediately.

FAST FIX
CHARD WITH BACON-CITRUS SAUCE

Chard is often used in Mediterranean cooking. I dress it with orange juice and bacon, and the family gobbles it up.
—Teri Rasey, Cadillac, MI

TAKES: 25 min. • **MAKES:** 6 servings

½ lb. thick-sliced peppered bacon strips
2 lbs. rainbow Swiss chard, chopped
1 cup orange juice
2 Tbsp. butter
4 tsp. grated orange zest
⅛ tsp. salt
⅛ tsp. pepper

1. In a large skillet, cook bacon over medium heat until crisp; drain on paper towels. Discard all but 1 Tbsp. of drippings. Cut bacon into small pieces.
2. Add chard to the remaining drippings; cook and stir just until wilted, 5-6 minutes. Add the remaining ingredients; cook 1-2 minutes, stirring occasionally. Top with bacon.

SWEET ITALIAN HOLIDAY
BREAD, PAGE 157

CHEERY

OVEN-FRESH BREADS

CHRISTMAS STAR TWISTED BREAD

This gorgeous sweet bread swirled with jam may look tricky, but it's not. The best part is opening the oven to find the star-shaped beauty in all its glory.

—Darlene Brenden, Salem, OR

PREP: 45 min. + rising • BAKE: 20 min. + cooling
MAKES: 16 servings

- 1 pkg. (¼ oz.) active dry yeast
- ¼ cup warm water (110° to 115°)
- ¾ cup warm whole milk (110° to 115°)
- 1 large egg
- ¼ cup butter, softened
- ¼ cup granulated sugar
- 1 tsp. salt
- 3¼ to 3¾ cups all-purpose flour
- ¾ cup seedless raspberry jam
- 2 Tbsp. butter, melted
  Confectioners' sugar

1. Dissolve yeast in warm water until foamy. In another bowl, combine milk, egg, butter, sugar and salt; add the yeast mixture and 3 cups flour. Beat on medium speed until smooth, about 1 minute. Stir in enough of the remaining flour to form a soft dough.
2. Turn onto a floured surface; knead until smooth and elastic, 6-8 minutes. Place in a greased bowl, turning once to grease top. Cover and let rise in a warm place until doubled, about 1 hour.
3. Punch down dough. Turn onto a lightly floured surface; divide into four portions. Roll one portion into a 12-in. circle. Place on a greased 14-in. pizza pan. Spread with one-third of the jam to within ½ in. from edge. Repeat twice, layering dough and jam and ending with the final portion of dough.
4. Place a 2½-in. round cutter on top of the dough in center of circle (do not press down). With a sharp knife, make 16 evenly spaced cuts from round cutter to edge of dough, forming a starburst. Remove cutter; grasp two strips and rotate twice outward. Pinch ends together. Repeat with the remaining strips.
5. Cover and let rise until almost doubled, about 30 minutes. Preheat oven to 375°. Bake until golden brown, 18-22 minutes. (Watch bread during final 5 minutes for any dripping.)
6. Remove from oven; brush with melted butter, avoiding areas where jam is visible. Cool completely on a wire rack. Dust with confectioners' sugar.

GINGER-ALMOND PEAR BREAD

We inherited a bountiful pear tree when we moved to our property years ago. The fresh-picked fruit is especially luscious in this moist quick bread spiced with ginger. We love the crunchy, nutty topping.

—Ruth Ealy, Plain City, OH

PREP: 20 min. • BAKE: 50 min. + cooling
MAKES: 1 loaf (16 slices)

- 1½ cups all-purpose flour
- ¾ cup sugar
- 1 tsp. baking powder
- ½ tsp. baking soda
- ½ tsp. salt
- ½ tsp. ground ginger
- ½ tsp. ground cinnamon
- 3 Tbsp. finely chopped crystallized ginger
- 2 large eggs
- ⅓ cup canola oil
- ½ tsp. almond extract
- 2 cups finely chopped peeled ripe pears (about 2 large)
- ½ cup chopped almonds

1. Preheat oven to 350°. In a large bowl, whisk the first seven ingredients. Stir in crystallized ginger. In another bowl, whisk eggs, oil and extract. Add to flour mixture; stir just until moistened. Fold in pears and almonds (batter will be stiff).
2. Transfer to a greased 9x5-in. loaf pan. Bake 50-60 minutes or until a toothpick inserted in center comes out clean. Cool in pan 10 minutes before removing to a wire rack to cool.

SWEET ITALIAN HOLIDAY BREAD

This is authentic *ciambellotto*, a sweet loaf my great-grandmother used to bake in Italy. I use her traditional recipe—the only update I made was to include modern appliances.

—Denise Perrin, Vancouver, WA

PREP: 15 min. • BAKE: 45 min.
MAKES: 1 loaf (20 slices)

- 4 cups all-purpose flour
- 1 cup sugar
- 2 Tbsp. grated orange zest
- 3 tsp. baking powder
- 3 large eggs
- ½ cup 2% milk
- ½ cup olive oil
- 1 large egg yolk
- 1 Tbsp. coarse sugar

1. Preheat oven to 350°. In a large bowl, whisk flour, sugar, orange zest and baking powder. In another bowl, whisk eggs, milk and oil until blended. Add to flour mixture; stir just until moistened.
2. Shape dough into a 6-in. round loaf on a greased baking sheet. Brush top with egg yolk; sprinkle with coarse sugar. Bake 45-50 minutes or until a toothpick inserted in the center comes out clean. Cover top loosely with foil during the last 10 minutes if needed to prevent overbrowning. Remove from pan to a wire rack; serve warm.

❄ Reader Review

"The night before you make this, rub the grated zest into the sugar, then seal it until you're ready to bake. It makes a big difference in the intensity of flavor."

RUSTY TASTEOFHOME.COM

SOFT BUTTERMILK DINNER ROLLS

My warm, buttery dinner rolls are absolutely irresistible. Save time by using a stand mixer for the dough.

—Jennifer Patterson, Shoshone, ID

....

PREP: 40 min. + rising • **BAKE:** 20 min. + cooling
MAKES: 20 servings

1 pkg. (¼ oz.) active dry yeast
¼ cup warm water (110° to 115°)
1 cup plus 2 Tbsp. warm buttermilk (110° to 115°), divided
½ cup plus 1 tsp. softened butter, divided
1 large egg
⅓ cup sugar
1 tsp. salt
4 cups bread flour

1. Dissolve yeast in warm water until foamy. In a large bowl, combine 1 cup buttermilk, ½ cup butter, egg, sugar, salt and yeast mixture, then add 3 cups flour; beat on medium speed until smooth, 1 minute. Add remaining flour, ¼ cup at a time, to form a soft dough.
2. Turn the dough onto a lightly floured surface; knead until smooth and elastic, 6-8 minutes. Place in a greased bowl, turning once to grease the top. Cover and let rise in a warm place until doubled, about 1 hour.
3. Punch down dough. Turn onto a lightly floured surface; divide and shape into 20 balls. Place in a greased 13x9-in. pan. Cover with a kitchen towel; let rise in a warm place until almost doubled, about 45 minutes.
4. Preheat oven to 350°. Brush rolls lightly with remaining buttermilk and butter. Bake until golden brown, 20-25 minutes. Cool in pan 20 minutes. Remove to a wire rack; serve warm.

PARMESAN SESAME CRACKERS

These rustic-looking crackers are crispy, crunchy and topped with cheese and plenty of seeds. Perfect for parties, they have none of the preservatives and additives of many store-bought alternatives.
—Elena Lorga, Helena, MT

PREP: 25 min. • BAKE: 15 min. + cooling
MAKES: 4 dozen

- 2 cups all-purpose flour
- 1/3 cup sesame seeds
- 1/3 cup shredded Parmesan cheese
- 2 Tbsp. poppy seeds
- 1 tsp. baking powder
- 1/2 tsp. salt
- 2/3 cup plus 2 Tbsp. warm water, divided
- 1/3 cup canola oil
- 1 large egg white

TOPPING
- 2 Tbsp. shredded Parmesan cheese
- 1 Tbsp. sesame seeds
- 1 Tbsp. poppy seeds

1. Preheat oven to 400°. In a small bowl, combine the first six ingredients. Gradually add 2/3 cup water and oil, tossing with a fork until dough forms a ball. Turn onto a lightly floured surface; knead 8-10 times.
2. Divide dough in half. Roll each ball directly on a baking sheet coated with cooking spray into a 12x9-in. rectangle. Pierce dough with a fork.
3. Whisk together egg white and remaining water; brush over dough. Combine topping ingredients; sprinkle over tops.
4. Score dough in each pan into 24 pieces. Bake for 15-18 minutes or until golden brown. Immediately cut along the scored lines; cool in pans on wire racks. Store in an airtight container.

PRALINE-TOPPED APPLE BREAD

Apples and candied pecans make this bread so much better than plain coffee cakes.
—Sonja Blow, Nixa, MO

PREP: 30 min. • BAKE: 50 min. + cooling
MAKES: 1 loaf (16 slices)

- 2 cups all-purpose flour
- 2 tsp. baking powder
- 1/2 tsp. baking soda
- 1/2 tsp. salt
- 1 cup sugar
- 1 cup sour cream
- 2 large eggs
- 3 tsp. vanilla extract
- 1 1/2 cups chopped peeled Granny Smith apples
- 1 1/4 cups chopped pecans, toasted, divided
- 1/2 cup butter, cubed
- 1/2 cup packed brown sugar

1. Preheat oven to 350°. In a large bowl, mix the flour, baking powder, baking soda and salt. In another bowl, beat sugar, sour cream, eggs and vanilla until well blended. Stir into flour mixture just until moistened. Fold in apples and 1 cup pecans.
2. Transfer to a greased 9x5-in. loaf pan. Bake 50-55 minutes or until a toothpick inserted in center comes out clean. Cool in pan 10 minutes. Remove to a wire rack to cool completely.
3. In a small saucepan, combine butter and brown sugar. Bring to a boil, stirring constantly to dissolve sugar; boil 1 minute. Spoon over bread. Sprinkle with remaining pecans; let stand until set.
Note: To toast nuts, bake in a shallow pan in a 350° oven for 5-10 minutes or cook in a skillet over low heat until lightly browned, stirring occasionally.

CARAWAY BREAD

Caraway bread is delicious eaten warm from the oven, as a base for sandwiches, alongside soup or as breakfast toast. If you want to experiment, add sliced chives or sunflower seeds, or substitute other herbs for the caraway, such as dried rosemary or thyme.

—Frances Conklin, Cottonwood, ID

PREP: 20 min. + rising • BAKE: 20 min. + cooling
MAKES: 1 loaf (8 wedges)

- 1 pkg. (¼ oz.) active dry yeast
- 1⅓ cups warm water (110° to 115°)
- 2 to 3 tsp. caraway seeds
- 1 tsp. salt
- 1 tsp. honey
- ¾ cup whole wheat flour
- 2½ to 3 cups all-purpose flour
- 2 tsp. cornmeal

1. In a small bowl, dissolve yeast in warm water. In a large bowl, combine caraway seeds, salt, honey, yeast mixture, whole wheat flour and 1½ cups all-purpose flour; beat on medium speed until smooth. Stir in enough of the remaining flour to form a stiff dough (dough will be sticky).
2. Turn dough onto a floured surface; knead 6-8 minutes, until smooth and elastic. Place in a greased bowl, turning once to grease the top. Cover and let rise in a warm place until doubled, about 1 hour.
3. Grease a 15x10x1-in. baking pan; sprinkle with cornmeal. Punch down dough. Turn onto a lightly floured surface. Shape into a round loaf; place on prepared pan. Cover with greased plastic wrap and let rise in a warm place until almost doubled, about 30 minutes. Preheat the oven to 425°.
4. Using a sharp knife, cut a large X in the top of the loaf. Bake on a lower oven rack for 20-25 minutes or until golden brown. Remove from pan to a wire rack to cool.

SAGE FONTINA FOCACCIA

These rustic loaves have plenty of sage flavor—a tasty addition to any special feast.

—Beth Dauenhauer, Pueblo, CO

PREP: 30 min. + rising • BAKE: 10 min.
MAKES: 1 loaf (8 wedges)

- 1¼ tsp. active dry yeast
- ½ cup warm water (110° to 115°)
- ½ tsp. honey
- ¾ to 1 cup all-purpose flour
- ¼ cup whole wheat flour
- 1 Tbsp. olive oil
- 2 tsp. minced fresh sage
- ¼ tsp. salt

TOPPING
- 1½ tsp. olive oil, divided
- 8 fresh sage leaves
- ½ cup shredded fontina cheese

1. In a large bowl, dissolve yeast in warm water. Stir in honey; let stand for 5 minutes. Add ¾ cup all-purpose flour, the whole wheat flour, oil, minced sage and salt. Beat on medium speed for 3 minutes or until smooth. Stir in enough of the remaining flour to form a soft dough (the dough will be sticky).
2. Turn onto a lightly floured surface; knead 6-8 minutes, until smooth and elastic. Place in a large bowl coated with cooking spray, turning once to coat the top. Cover and let rise in a warm place until doubled, about 1 hour.
3. Punch dough down. Cover and let rest for 5 minutes. Shape into an 8-in. circle; place on a baking sheet coated with cooking spray. Cover and let rise until doubled, about 30 minutes. Using the end of a wooden spoon handle, make several ¼-in. indentations in the loaf.
4. For the topping, brush the dough with 1 tsp. oil. Top with sage leaves; brush the leaves with the remaining oil. Sprinkle with cheese. Bake at 400° for 8-10 minutes or until golden brown. Remove to a wire rack. Serve warm.

BRAIDED ORANGE WREATH

All eyes will turn to this gorgeous braid when you set it on the table.

—Shirley Warren, Thiensville, WI

PREP: 40 min. + rising • BAKE: 25 min. + cooling
MAKES: 12 servings

- 4 to 4½ cups all-purpose flour
- ½ cup sugar
- 1 pkg. (¼ oz.) active dry yeast
- 1 tsp. salt
- 1 cup 2% milk
- 3 Tbsp. butter
- 3 large eggs
- 3 Tbsp. orange juice
- 1½ tsp. grated orange zest

GLAZE
- 1½ cups confectioners' sugar
- 2 to 3 Tbsp. orange juice
- ½ tsp. grated orange zest
- ¼ cup dried cranberries

1. In a large bowl, combine 2 cups flour, sugar, yeast and salt. In a small saucepan, heat milk and butter to 120°-130°. Add to the dry ingredients; beat just until moistened. Add eggs, orange juice and zest; beat until blended. Stir in enough of the remaining flour to form a soft dough.
2. Turn onto a floured surface; knead until smooth and elastic, 6-8 minutes. Place in a greased bowl, turning once to grease the top. Cover and let rise in a warm place until doubled, about 1 hour.
3. Punch dough down. Turn onto a lightly floured surface; divide dough into thirds. Shape each into a 30-in. rope. Braid the ropes; shape into a wreath and pinch ends to seal. Place on a greased baking sheet. Cover and let rise in a warm place until doubled, about 30 minutes.
4. Bake at 350° for 25-30 minutes or until golden brown. Remove from pan to a wire rack to cool.
5. In a small bowl, combine confectioners' sugar, orange juice and zest; drizzle over bread. Sprinkle with cranberries.

BANANA EGGNOG BREAD

This special loaf combines two of my favorite winter treats—banana bread and eggnog. Fresh from the oven, a big slice will warm you up from head to toe.

—Kristin Stone, Little Elm, TX

PREP: 20 min. • **BAKE:** 50 min. + cooling
MAKES: 1 loaf (16 slices)

- ½ cup butter, softened
- 1½ cups sugar
- 2 large eggs
- 1 cup mashed ripe bananas (about 2 medium)
- ¼ cup eggnog
- 1 tsp. vanilla extract
- 1¾ cups all-purpose flour
- 1 tsp. baking powder
- ½ tsp. ground nutmeg, divided
- ¼ tsp. salt
- ⅛ tsp. baking soda

1. Preheat oven to 350°. In a large bowl, cream butter and sugar until light and fluffy. Add eggs, one at a time, beating well after each addition. Beat in the bananas, eggnog and vanilla. In another bowl, whisk flour, baking powder, ¼ tsp. nutmeg, salt and baking soda; gradually beat into banana mixture.

2. Transfer to a greased 9x5-in. loaf pan; sprinkle with remaining nutmeg. Bake 50-60 minutes or until a toothpick inserted in center comes out clean. Cool in pan 10 minutes before removing to a wire rack to cool.

Note: This recipe was tested with commercially prepared eggnog.

❄ Holiday Helper

Save money and time by baking several of these festive loaves early in the season. Wrap each well in freezer-proof aluminum foil and store in the freezer for easy last-minute gift giving.

MAKE AHEAD
BEST-EVER CRESCENT ROLLS

My daughter and I have cranked out dozens of homemade crescent rolls. It's a real team effort. I cut the dough into wedges; she rolls.

—Irene Yeh, Mequon, WI

PREP: 40 min. + chilling • **BAKE:** 10 min./batch
MAKES: 32 rolls

- 3¾ to 4¼ cups all-purpose flour
- 2 pkg. (¼ oz. each) active dry yeast
- 1 tsp. salt
- 1 cup whole milk
- ½ cup butter, cubed
- ¼ cup honey
- 3 large egg yolks
- 2 Tbsp. butter, melted

1. Combine 1½ cups flour, yeast and salt. In a small saucepan, heat milk, cubed butter and honey to 120°-130°. Add to the dry ingredients; beat on medium speed for 2 minutes. Add egg yolks; beat on high 2 minutes. Stir in enough remaining flour to form a soft dough (dough will be sticky).

2. Turn onto a floured surface; knead until smooth and elastic, 6-8 minutes. Place in a greased bowl, turning once to grease the top. Cover and let rise until doubled, about 45 minutes.

3. Punch down dough; place in an airtight container. Seal and refrigerate overnight.

4. To bake, turn dough onto a lightly floured surface; divide in half. Roll each portion into a 14-in. circle; cut each circle into 16 wedges. Lightly brush the wedges with melted butter. Roll up each wedge from the wide end, pinching the pointed end to seal. Place 2 in. apart on parchment paper-lined baking sheets, point side down. Cover with lightly greased plastic wrap; let crescents rise in a warm place until doubled, about 45 minutes.

5. Preheat oven to 375°. Bake until golden brown, 9-11 minutes. Remove from pans to wire racks; serve warm.

Note: To make filled crescent rolls, sprinkle dough with filling of choice immediately after brushing with butter; shape and bake as directed.

BACON WALNUT BREAD WITH HONEY BUTTER

Here, my savory loaf filled with bacon bits, walnuts and blue cheese dressing is truly complemented by the sweetness of honey-flavored butter. Cut yourself a thick slice, slather on the butter and enjoy!

—Pam Ivbuls, Elkhorn, NE

PREP: 25 min. • BAKE: 40 min. + cooling
MAKES: 1 loaf (¾ cup butter)

- 2 cups all-purpose flour
- 2 tsp. baking powder
- ½ tsp. baking soda
- ¼ tsp. salt
- ¼ tsp. coarsely ground pepper
- 1 cup half-and-half cream
- ¾ cup refrigerated blue cheese salad dressing
- 2 large eggs
- 1 Tbsp. honey
- ⅔ cup coarsely chopped walnuts
- ½ cup bacon bits

HONEY BUTTER
- ¾ cup butter, softened
- 2 Tbsp. honey

1. Preheat oven to 325°. In a large bowl, whisk the first five ingredients. In another bowl, whisk cream, salad dressing, eggs and honey until blended. Add to the flour mixture; stir just until moistened. Fold in walnuts and bacon bits.
2. Transfer to a greased and floured 9x5-in. loaf pan. Bake 40-50 minutes or until a toothpick inserted in center comes out clean. Cool in pan 10 minutes before removing to wire rack to cool completely.
3. In a small bowl, beat honey butter ingredients. Serve with bread.

MAKE AHEAD

CINNAMON YOGURT TWISTS

I remember the aroma of warm cinnamon twists coming from my mother's kitchen. Now my family enjoys my mom's recipe. I have experimented with it a bit and use yogurt instead of sour cream.
—Kristin Hammill, NY, NY

PREP: 45 min. + chilling • **BAKE:** 15 min.
MAKES: 2 dozen

- 1 pkg. (¼ oz.) active dry yeast
- 1 tsp. salt
- 3¾ to 4 cups all-purpose flour
- 1 cup butter, cubed
- 1 cup plain yogurt
- ¼ cup water
- 2 large eggs
- 1 tsp. vanilla extract
- ¾ cup sugar
- 1 tsp. ground cinnamon

1. In a large bowl, combine yeast, salt and 2½ cups of flour. In a small saucepan, heat the butter, yogurt and water to 120°-130°; add to dry ingredients. Beat on medium speed for 2 minutes.
2. Add the eggs, vanilla and ½ cup of flour; beat 2 minutes longer. Stir in enough of the remaining flour to form a stiff dough. Do not knead. Cover and refrigerate for 2 hours or overnight.
3. Combine sugar and cinnamon; set aside. Punch dough down. On a lightly floured surface, roll dough into a 12x9-in. rectangle. Sprinkle 3 Tbsp. cinnamon sugar over dough; fold into thirds. Give dough a quarter turn and repeat rolling, sugaring and folding three more times.
4. Roll into a 12x6-in rectangle. Cut into twenty-four ½-in.-wide strips; twist. Place on greased baking sheets. Cover and let rise until doubled, about 30 minutes. Bake at 350° for 14-18 minutes or until golden brown. Immediately remove from pans to wire racks to cool.

DRIZZLED BUTTERNUT BREAD

My children love this pretty bread. Squash makes the texture soft and adds a lovely flavor. The loaves are welcome additions to brunch buffets and dinner tables alike.
—Misty Thompson, Gaylesville, AL

PREP: 15 min. • **BAKE:** 55 min. + cooling
MAKES: 2 loaves (12 slices each)

- 1 cup butter, softened
- 1 pkg. (8 oz.) cream cheese, softened
- 2 cups sugar
- 3 large eggs
- 2 cups mashed cooked butternut squash
- 1 tsp. vanilla extract
- 3 cups all-purpose flour
- 1 tsp. baking powder
- 1 tsp. ground cinnamon
- ½ tsp. salt
- ½ tsp. baking soda
- 1 cup chopped walnuts

ICING
- 1 cup confectioners' sugar
- ½ tsp. vanilla extract
- 6 to 8 Tbsp. sweetened condensed milk

1. In a large bowl, cream the butter, cream cheese and sugar until light and fluffy. Add eggs, one at a time, beating well after each addition. Beat in the squash and vanilla. Combine flour, baking powder, cinnamon, salt and baking soda; gradually beat into the creamed mixture. Fold in walnuts.
2. Transfer to two greased 8x4-in. loaf pans. Bake at 350° for 55-65 minutes or until a toothpick inserted in the center comes out clean. Cool for 10 minutes before removing from pans to wire racks to cool completely.
3. In a small bowl, combine confectioners' sugar, vanilla and enough milk to achieve a drizzling consistency. Drizzle over loaves.

BLACK RASPBERRY BUBBLE RING

This ring takes some time to make, but I pull out the recipe any time I want to impress.
—Kila Frank, Reedsville, OH

PREP: 35 min. + rising • **BAKE:** 25 min.
MAKES: 1 loaf (16 wedges)

- 1 pkg. (¼ oz.) active dry yeast
- ¼ cup warm water (110° to 115°)
- 1 cup warm whole milk (110° to 115°)
- ¼ cup plus 2 Tbsp. sugar, divided
- ½ cup butter, melted, divided
- 1 large egg
- 1 tsp. salt
- 4 cups all-purpose flour
- 1 jar (10 oz.) seedless black raspberry preserves

SYRUP
- ⅓ cup corn syrup
- 2 Tbsp. butter, melted
- ½ tsp. vanilla extract

1. In a large bowl, dissolve yeast in warm water. Add the milk, ¼ cup sugar, ¼ cup butter, egg, salt and 3½ cups of the flour. Beat until smooth. Stir in enough of the remaining flour to form a soft dough.
2. Turn onto a floured surface; knead until smooth and elastic, 6-8 minutes. Place in a greased bowl, turning once to grease top. Cover and let rise in a warm place until doubled, about 1¼ hours.
3. Punch dough down. Turn onto a lightly floured surface; divide into 32 pieces. Flatten each into a 3-in. disk. Place about 1 tsp. of preserves on the center of each piece; bring edges together and seal.
4. Place 16 dough balls in a greased 10-in. fluted tube pan. Brush with half of the remaining butter; sprinkle with 1 Tbsp. sugar. Top with remaining balls, butter and sugar. Cover and let rise until doubled, about 35 minutes.
5. Bake at 350° for 25-30 minutes or until golden brown. Combine syrup ingredients; pour over warm bread. Cool for 5 minutes before inverting onto a serving plate.

CRANBERRY QUICK BREAD

My mother loved to make this cranberry bread. I usually stock up on cranberries when they're in season and freeze them so I can make this recipe year-round.

—Karen Czechowicz, Ocala, FL

PREP: 20 min. • **BAKE:** 45 min. + cooling
MAKES: 1 loaf (12 slices)

- 1½ cups all-purpose flour
- ¾ cup sugar
- 1 tsp. baking powder
- ¼ tsp. salt
- ¼ tsp. baking soda
- 1 large egg
- ½ cup orange juice
- 2 Tbsp. butter, melted
- 1 Tbsp. water
- 1½ cups fresh or frozen cranberries, coarsely chopped

1. Preheat oven to 350°. In a large bowl, combine the first five ingredients. In a small bowl, whisk egg, orange juice, butter and water. Stir into the dry ingredients just until moistened. Fold in cranberries.

2. Transfer to an 8x4-in. loaf pan coated with cooking spray and sprinkled with flour. Bake 45-50 minutes or until a toothpick inserted in the center comes out clean. Cool 10 minutes before removing from pan to a wire rack.

❄ Reader Review

"This bread was super easy to make and my family and friends raved about it! They thought for sure I had bought it from a bakery. I will be making this again and again!"

ANNES47 TASTEOFHOME.COM

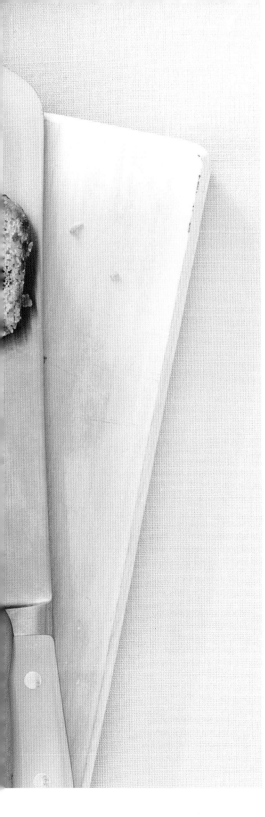

GARLIC-HERB PARMESAN ROLLS

Fresh-baked yeast rolls are always a hit at dinners. I arranged them in a tree shape for the yuletide season, but you can also make them in a 13x9-inch baking pan.
—Lorri Reinhardt, Big Bend, WI

PREP: 20 min. • BAKE: 20 min. + cooling
MAKES: 16 servings

- 1 cup water (70° to 80°)
- 2 Tbsp. butter, softened
- 1 large egg, lightly beaten
- 3 Tbsp. sugar
- 2 tsp. dried minced garlic
- 1 tsp. Italian seasoning
- 1 tsp. salt
- 2¼ cups bread flour
- 1 cup whole wheat flour
- 1 pkg. (¼ oz.) active dry yeast

TOPPING
- 1 Tbsp. butter, melted
- 1 Tbsp. grated Parmesan cheese
- 1 tsp. Italian seasoning
- ½ tsp. coarse salt

1. In bread machine pan, place the first 10 ingredients in order suggested by the manufacturer. Select dough setting (check dough after 5 minutes of mixing and add 1-2 Tbsp. of water or flour if needed).

2. When cycle is completed, turn dough onto a lightly floured surface; divide into 16 balls. Line a baking sheet with foil and grease the foil. Center one roll near the top of the prepared baking sheet. Arrange rolls snugly into four additional rows, adding one more roll for each row, forming a tree.

3. Center the remaining ball under tree for the trunk. Cover and let rise until doubled, about 1 hour.

4. Brush rolls with butter. Combine cheese and Italian seasoning and sprinkle over the rolls. Sprinkle with salt. Bake at 350° for 20-25 minutes or until golden brown. Serve warm.

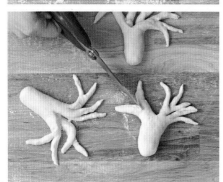

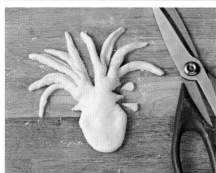

❄ *Holiday Helper*

These adorable Overnight Reindeer Rolls (see recipe at right) make cute additions to holiday bake sales, office potlucks and after-service events at church. While the rolls are buttery, the raisin eyes and cherry noses add just enough sweetness to make these bites a fit with nearly any occasion. The dough needs to sit overnight, so be sure to plan accordingly. Wrapped tightly in plastic wrap, the rolls can be made up to two days ahead of time.

MAKE AHEAD

OVERNIGHT REINDEER ROLLS

Have some family fun baking these reindeer-shaped rolls. Make sure to take pictures of the final product because the cute creations will be gone before you know it!

—Chris O'Connell, San Antonio, TX

PREP: 50 min. + rising • BAKE: 10 min.
MAKES: 3 dozen

- 2 pkg. (¼ oz. each) active dry yeast
- 1½ cups warm water (110° to 115°)
- 2 large eggs
- ½ cup butter, softened
- ½ cup sugar
- 2 tsp. salt
- 5¾ to 6¼ cups all-purpose flour

DECORATIONS
- 1 large egg
- 2 tsp. water
- 36 raisins (about 2 Tbsp.), halved
- 18 red candied cherries, halved

1. In a small bowl, dissolve yeast in warm water. In a large bowl, combine the eggs, butter, sugar, salt, yeast mixture and 3 cups flour; beat on medium speed until smooth. Stir in enough of the remaining flour to form a very soft dough (dough will be sticky). Do not knead. Cover and refrigerate overnight.

2. Turn the dough onto a floured surface; divide and shape into 36 balls. Roll each into a 5-in. log. Cut each log lengthwise halfway down center. Pull the cut sections apart for antlers. Using kitchen shears, snip ½-in. cuts along the outer sides to make antler points. Flatten the uncut half of log for the face.

3. Place 2 in. apart on greased baking sheets. Cover with kitchen towels; let rise in a warm place until doubled, about 30 minutes. Preheat oven to 400°.

4. In a small bowl, whisk egg and water until blended; brush over rolls. Press raisin halves into the dough for eyes; press cherry halves into the dough for noses. Bake rolls for 8-10 minutes or until golden brown. Serve warm.

MAKE AHEAD

CRUSTY HOMEMADE BREAD

Enjoy this lovely loaf as is, or stir in a few faves such as cheese, garlic, herbs or dried fruits. For inspiration, check out the variations on this rustic loaf that follow the recipe.

—Megumi Garcia, Milwaukee, WI

PREP: 20 min. + rising • BAKE: 50 min. + cooling
MAKES: 1 loaf (16 slices)

- 1½ tsp. active dry yeast
- 1¾ cups water (70° to 75°)
- 3½ cups plus 1 Tbsp. all-purpose flour, divided
- 2 tsp. salt
- 1 Tbsp. cornmeal or additional flour

1. In a small bowl, dissolve yeast in water. In a large bowl, mix 3½ cups of flour and the salt. Using a rubber spatula, stir in the yeast mixture to form a soft, sticky dough. Do not knead. Cover and let rise at room temperature 1 hour.

2. Punch down dough. Turn onto a lightly floured surface; pat into a 9-in. square. Fold square into thirds, forming a 9x3-in. rectangle. Fold rectangle into thirds, forming a 3-in. square. Turn dough over; place in a greased bowl. Cover and let rise at room temperature until almost doubled, about 1 hour.

3. Punch down dough and repeat folding process. Return dough to bowl; refrigerate, covered, overnight.

4. Dust the bottom of a disposable foil roasting pan with cornmeal. Turn dough onto a floured surface and knead gently 6-8 times; shape into a 6-in. round loaf. Place in prepared pan; dust top with remaining 1 Tbsp. flour. Cover pan and let rise at room temperature until dough expands to a 7½-in. loaf, about 1¼ hours.

5. Preheat oven to 500°. Using a sharp knife, make a slash (¼ in. deep) across top of loaf. Cover pan tightly with foil. Bake on lowest oven rack for 25 minutes.

6. Reduce oven setting to 450°. Remove foil; bake bread until deep golden brown, 25-30 minutes. Remove loaf to a wire rack to cool.

For Cheddar Cheese Bread: Prepare dough as directed. After refrigerating overnight, knead in 4 oz. diced sharp cheddar cheese before shaping.

For Rustic Cranberry & Orange Bread: Prepare the dough as directed. After refrigerating overnight, knead in 1 cup dried cranberries and 4 tsp. grated orange zest before shaping.

For Garlic & Oregano Bread: Prepare dough as directed. After refrigerating overnight, microwave ½ cup peeled and quartered garlic cloves with ¼ cup milk on high for 45 seconds. Drain garlic, discarding milk; knead garlic and 2 Tbsp. minced fresh oregano into the dough before shaping.

CRANBERRY CHIP MONKEY BREAD

Monkey bread is no stranger at our house, but I wanted a holiday version. This one, featuring cranberries and eggnog, works as both a breakfast treat and dessert knockout.
—Katherine Wollgast, Troy, MO

PREP: 15 min. • **BAKE:** 40 min.
MAKES: 16 servings

- ¾ cup sugar, divided
- 4 tsp. ground cinnamon
- 4 tubes (7½ oz. each) refrigerated buttermilk biscuits
- ½ cup white baking chips
- ½ cup dried cranberries
- ¼ cup chopped walnuts or pecans
- ¼ cup butter, cubed
- ½ cup eggnog

GLAZE
- 1 cup confectioners' sugar
- ½ tsp. rum or vanilla extract
- 2 to 3 Tbsp. eggnog
    Optional toppings: additional dried cranberries, white baking chips and chopped nuts

1. Preheat oven to 350°. In a large bowl, mix ½ cup sugar and cinnamon. Cut each biscuit into quarters; add to the sugar mixture and toss to coat. Arrange half of the biscuits in a greased 10-in. tube pan. Sprinkle with baking chips, cranberries and walnuts. Top with the remaining biscuits.
2. In a microwave, melt butter. Stir in the eggnog and the remaining sugar until blended; pour over biscuits.
3. Bake 40-45 minutes or until golden brown. Cool in pan 5 minutes before inverting onto a serving plate.
4. For glaze, mix the confectioners' sugar, rum extract and enough eggnog to reach a drizzling consistency. Spoon over warm bread. Sprinkle with toppings as desired.
Note: This recipe was tested with commercially prepared eggnog.

GLAZED HOLIDAY BISCUITS

My family likes biscuits for breakfast. One Sunday, I decided to make those golden goodies extra special by adding white chips, dried cranberries and a simple orange glaze.
—Lori Daniels, Beverly, WV

PREP: 30 min. • **BAKE:** 15 min.
MAKES: about 1 dozen

- 2 cups all-purpose flour
- 2 tsp. baking powder
- ½ tsp. salt
- ½ tsp. grated orange zest
- ½ tsp. ground cinnamon
- ¼ cup shortening
- ¼ cup cold butter
- ¾ cup 2% milk
- ¼ cup orange juice
- 1 cup dried cranberries
- ½ cup white baking chips

DRIZZLE
- 1½ cups confectioners' sugar
- 2 Tbsp. orange juice
- ¼ tsp. orange extract

1. In a large bowl, combine the first five ingredients. Cut in shortening and butter until mixture resembles coarse crumbs. Stir in milk and orange juice just until moistened. Stir in cranberries and white baking chips.
2. Turn onto a lightly floured surface; knead gently 8-10 times. Pat or roll dough out to ¾-in. thickness; cut with a floured 2½-in. biscuit cutter.
3. Place 2 in. apart on a greased baking sheet. Bake at 400° for 12-16 minutes or until lightly browned. In a small bowl, combine the confectioners' sugar, orange juice and extract; drizzle over biscuits. Serve warm.

CELERY-ONION POPOVERS

I found this handwritten recipe in a cookbook I received from my mom. With onion and celery, these pleasing popovers taste a little like Thanksgiving stuffing.
—Barbara Carlucci, Orange Park, FL

PREP: 15 min. • BAKE: 40 min.
MAKES: 9 servings

- 2 cups all-purpose flour
- 1 tsp. onion salt
- ⅛ tsp. celery salt
- 4 large eggs
- 2 cups whole milk
- ¼ cup grated onion
- ¼ cup grated celery
- 3 Tbsp. butter, melted

1. In a large bowl, combine the flour, onion salt and celery salt. Combine the eggs, milk, onion, celery and butter; whisk into the dry ingredients just until blended. Grease and flour the bottom and sides of nine popover cups; fill two-thirds full with batter.
2. Bake at 450° for 15 minutes. Reduce heat to 350° (do not open oven door). Bake 25 minutes longer or until deep golden brown (do not underbake). Immediately cut a slit in the top of each popover to allow steam to escape.

DOVE DINNER ROLLS

Fluffy dinner rolls shaped like doves are a sweet nod to the holidays, and they dash away faster than Santa himself.
—Frances Wirtz, West Allis, WI

PREP: 50 min. + rising • BAKE: 10 min.
MAKES: 2 dozen

- 2 cups whole wheat pastry flour
- ½ cup sugar
- 3 pkg. (¼ oz. each) active dry yeast
- 2 tsp. salt
- 1 cup water
- 1 cup 2% milk
- ½ cup butter, cubed
- 1 large egg
- 4 to 4½ cups bread flour

ASSEMBLY
- 48 dried currants
- 24 slivered almonds
- 1 large egg
- 2 Tbsp. 2% milk

1. In a large bowl, mix pastry flour, sugar, yeast and salt. In a small saucepan, heat water, milk and butter to 120°-130°. Add to dry ingredients; beat on medium speed 1 minute. Add egg; beat on high 2 minutes. Stir in enough bread flour to form a soft dough (dough will be sticky).
2. Turn dough onto a floured surface; knead until smooth and elastic, 6-8 minutes. Place in a greased bowl, turning once to grease the top. Cover and let rise in a warm place until doubled, about 45 minutes.
3. Punch down dough. Let stand, covered, for 15 minutes. Turn onto a lightly floured surface; divide and shape into 24 balls. Roll each into a 10-in. rope; tie into a loose knot. Bring one end up and tuck into center of roll to form head. Flatten opposite end; with a sharp knife, cut slits to form tail feathers. Press two currants into head for eyes and one almond for beak. Place 2 in. apart on greased baking sheets.
4. Cover rolls with kitchen towels; let rise in a warm place until doubled in size, about 30 minutes. Preheat oven to 400°.
5. In a small bowl, whisk egg and milk; brush over rolls. Bake 10-12 minutes or until golden brown. Remove from pans to wire racks; serve warm.

ALMOND-FILLED STOLLEN

I've been making this during the holiday season for nearly 50 years. When we flew to Alaska one year to spend Christmas with our daughter's family, I carried my stollen on the plane with me!

—Rachel Seel, Abbotsford, BC

PREP: 1 hour. + rising • **BAKE:** 30 min. + cooling
MAKES: 3 loaves (12 slices each)

- 1¾ cups chopped mixed candied fruit
- ½ cup plus 2 Tbsp. rum, divided
- 2 pkg. (¼ oz. each) active dry yeast
- ½ cup warm water (110° to 115°)
- 1½ cups warm 2% milk (110° to 115°)
- 1¼ cups butter, softened
- ⅔ cup sugar
- 2½ tsp. salt
- 2 tsp. grated lemon zest
- 1 tsp. almond extract
- 7 to 8 cups all-purpose flour
- 4 large eggs
- ⅓ cup slivered almonds
- 1 can (8 oz.) almond paste
- 1 large egg yolk
- 2 tsp. water
- 2 to 2¼ cups confectioners' sugar

1. In a small bowl, combine candied fruit and ½ cup rum; let stand, covered, 1 hour.
2. In a small bowl, dissolve yeast in warm water. In a large bowl, combine milk, butter, sugar, salt, lemon zest, almond extract, remaining rum, yeast mixture and 4 cups of the flour; beat on medium speed until smooth. Cover and let stand in a warm place, about 30 minutes.
3. Beat in the eggs. Stir in enough of the remaining flour to form a soft dough (dough will be sticky). Drain candied fruit, reserving rum for glaze. Reserve ½ cup of candied fruit for the topping. Stir almonds and the remaining candied fruit into dough.
4. Turn the dough onto a floured surface; knead for 6-8 minutes, until smooth and elastic. Place in a greased bowl, turning once to grease the top. Cover bowl and let dough rise in a warm place until doubled, about 1 hour.

5. Punch down dough; divide into three portions. On a greased baking sheet, roll each portion into a 12-in. circle. Crumble one-third of the almond paste over one-half of each circle. Fold dough partially in half, covering filling and placing top layer within 1 in. of bottom edge. Cover with kitchen towels and let rise in a warm place until doubled in size, about 1 hour. Preheat oven to 375°.
6. In a small bowl, whisk the egg yolk and water; brush over loaves. Bake for 30-35 minutes or until golden brown. Cover loosely with foil if tops brown too quickly. Remove from pans to wire racks to cool completely.
7. In a small bowl, mix reserved rum with enough confectioner's sugar to make a thin glaze. Drizzle over stollen. Sprinkle with reserved candied fruit.

174
TASTEOFHOME.COM

PUMPKIN EGGNOG ROLLS

I needed to use up some eggnog, so I swapped it for milk in my sweet roll recipe. What a treat these turned out to be!

—Rebecca Soske, Douglas, WY

....

PREP: 40 min. + rising • **BAKE:** 20 min.
MAKES: 1 dozen

- ½ cup sugar
- 1 pkg. (¼ oz.) active dry yeast
- ½ tsp. salt
- 4½ cups all-purpose flour
- ¾ cup eggnog
- ½ cup butter, cubed
- ¼ cup canned pumpkin
- 2 large eggs

FILLING
- ½ cup sugar
- 1 tsp. ground cardamom
- 1 tsp. ground allspice
- ¼ cup butter, melted

FROSTING
- 2 oz. cream cheese, softened
- 2 Tbsp. eggnog
- 1 Tbsp. canned pumpkin
- ¼ tsp. ground cardamom
- 2 cups confectioners' sugar

1. In a large bowl, mix sugar, yeast, salt and 2 cups flour. In a small saucepan, heat the eggnog, butter and pumpkin to 120°-130°. Add to dry ingredients; beat on medium speed 2 minutes. Add eggs; beat on high 2 minutes. Stir in enough of the remaining flour to form a firm dough.
2. Turn the dough onto a floured surface; knead for 6-8 minutes, until smooth and elastic. Place in a greased bowl, turning once to grease the top. Cover with plastic wrap and let rise in a warm place until doubled, about 1 hour.
3. In a small bowl, mix sugar, cardamom and allspice. Punch dough down. Turn onto a lightly floured surface. Roll into an 18x12-in. rectangle. Brush with butter to within ½ in. of edges; sprinkle with sugar mixture. Roll up jelly-roll style, starting with a long side; pinch seam to seal. Cut into 12 slices.
4. Place in a greased 13x9-in. baking pan, cut side down. Cover with a kitchen towel; let rise in a warm place until doubled, about 45 minutes. Preheat oven to 350°. Bake rolls 20-25 minutes or until golden brown.
5. In a small bowl, beat cream cheese, eggnog, pumpkin and cardamom until blended. Gradually beat in confectioners' sugar; beat until smooth. Spread frosting over the warm rolls.
Note: This recipe was tested with commercially prepared eggnog.

CHIVE & CHEESE BREADSTICKS

With two types of cheese, minced chives and garlic, these tasty twists go above and beyond, making them ideal for special menus.

—Rebekah Beyer, Sabetha, KS

....

PREP: 15 min. + rising • **BAKE:** 15 min.
MAKES: 16 breadsticks

- 1 loaf (1 lb.) frozen bread dough, thawed
- ⅓ cup butter, softened
- 2 Tbsp. minced chives
- 1 garlic clove, minced
- ¾ cup shredded part-skim mozzarella cheese
- ½ cup shredded Parmesan cheese, divided

1. On a lightly floured surface, roll dough into a 12-in. square. In a small bowl, combine butter, chives and garlic; spread over dough. Sprinkle with mozzarella cheese and ¼ cup of Parmesan cheese.
2. Fold dough in half; seal edges. Cut into sixteen ¾-in.-wide strips. Twist each strip 2-3 times; pinch ends.
3. Place breadsticks 2 in. apart in a greased 15x10x1-in. baking pan. Cover and let rise until nearly doubled, about 40 minutes.
4. Preheat oven to 375°. Sprinkle with the remaining Parmesan cheese. Bake for 13-15 minutes or until golden brown.

HOLIDAY HAND TOWELS

These towels are the perfect gift for holiday bakers! For each, start with a clean, ironed white towel. Choose a pattern; choose fabric paint color and spread the paint onto a plastic plate.

For the tree design, place a triangular sponge in the paint, gently patting to ensure coverage. Firmly press sponge onto towel. Repeat to create rows of trees or other patterns as desired.

For the gift box design, cut a smooth kitchen sponge into a square; use narrow masking tape to crisscross the sponge where the ribbon would be. Apply paint to the sponge, then remove the tape and press the sponge onto the towel. Use a triangular sponge to apply paint for the bow.

For the poinsettia design, glue wood diamond shapes in a circle on an acrylic or wood block to create a stamp. Use a foam sponge to apply paint to the diamond shapes, then press the stamp onto the towel.

Let the towels dry completely, then run through the the dryer on the highest setting for 30-40 minutes to heat-set the paint.

ORANGE & SPICE CUTOUT COOKIES, PAGE 178; RED VELVET CRINKLE COOKIES, PAGE 179; CREME DE MENTHE COOKIES, PAGE 181; CREAM CHEESE SPRITZ, PAGE 186; CHOCOLATE-CHERRY THUMBPRINT COOKIES, PAGE 187

DELIGHTFUL

COOKIES
& BARS

RASPBERRY SNOWFLAKE SANDWICH COOKIES

When my son was growing up, I made these cookies with him every Christmas Eve. He loved using the straws to punch out the holes in the snowflakes. Now that he's grown, I make them with my niece.

—Renee Bettich Nelson, Stevensville, MI

PREP: 20 min. + chilling • **BAKE:** 10 min./batch
MAKES: about 1½ dozen

- ½ cup butter, softened
- ¼ cup shortening
- ¾ cup sugar
- 1 large egg
- 1 Tbsp. lemon juice
- 2 cups all-purpose flour
- 1½ tsp. baking powder
- ½ tsp. ground cinnamon
- ¼ tsp. salt
- ¼ tsp. ground nutmeg
- 2 drinking straws (different sizes)
- ½ cup seedless raspberry jam
  Confectioners' sugar

1. In a large bowl, cream butter, shortening and sugar until light and fluffy. Beat in egg and lemon juice. In another bowl, whisk the flour, baking powder, cinnamon, salt and nutmeg; gradually beat into the creamed mixture.
2. Divide dough in half. Shape each into a disk; wrap in plastic. Refrigerate 2 hours or until firm enough to roll.
3. Preheat oven to 375°. On a well-floured surface, roll each portion of dough to ⅛-in. thickness. Cut out with a floured 2½-in. scalloped round cookie cutter. Using straws, cut several holes in half the cutouts, twisting straws to release. Place 2 in. apart on baking sheets.
4. Bake 6-8 minutes or until edges are light brown. Cool on pan slightly. Remove from pans to wire racks to cool completely.
5. Spread about 1 tsp. jam on the bottoms of the solid cookies; top with the cutout cookies. Sprinkle tops of cookies with confectioners' sugar.

ORANGE & SPICE CUTOUT COOKIES

When my mother retired from baking the holiday cookies and passed the mantle on to me, she also passed along this recipe. In time, I will give it to my young niece. Just the smell of these treats takes me back to when I was a little one, just like she is now.

—Lisa Rocco-Price, Bronx, NY

PREP: 45 min. • **BAKE:** 10 min./batch + cooling
MAKES: 3 dozen

- 1 cup butter, softened
- 1½ cups sugar
- 1 large egg
- 2 Tbsp. dark corn syrup
- 4 tsp. grated orange zest
- 3 cups all-purpose flour
- 2 tsp. baking soda
- 2 tsp. ground cinnamon
- ½ tsp. salt
- ½ tsp. ground cloves

ICING
- 4 cups confectioners' sugar
- 3 Tbsp. meringue powder
- 5 to 6 Tbsp. warm water
  Red and green food coloring, optional

1. Preheat oven to 350°. In a large bowl, cream butter and sugar until light and fluffy. Beat in egg, corn syrup and orange zest. In another bowl, whisk flour, baking soda, cinnamon, salt and cloves; gradually beat into the creamed mixture. Divide the dough in half.
2. On a lightly floured surface, roll each portion of dough into a 9-in. square. Cut into 18 rectangles, 3x1½-in. each. Place 2 in. apart on ungreased baking sheets. Bake 10-12 minutes or until edges are light golden. Remove from pans to wire racks to cool completely.
3. For icing, in a large bowl, combine confectioners' sugar, meringue powder and enough water to reach a piping consistency. Beat on high speed with a portable mixer 10-12 minutes or on low with a stand mixer 7-10 minutes or until peaks form. Frost cookies. Using a #3 round tip, pipe designs on cookies. **Note:** If desired, divide the icing into three portions and use red and green food coloring to color two of the portions; use contrasting colors to decorate the cookies.

RED VELVET CRINKLE COOKIES

I was searching for a red velvet crinkle cookie recipe and just couldn't find one, so I decided to create my own. This recipe is special to me because it's totally original and oh so yummy! They are firm but not crunchy on the outside and very tender inside. They have just the perfect red velvet flavor!

—Jane Rundell, Alanson, MI

PREP: 30 min. + chilling
BAKE: 15 min./batch + cooling
MAKES: 3½ dozen

1	cup butter, softened
2½	cups sugar
4	large eggs
2	tsp. white vinegar
2	tsp. red paste food coloring
1	tsp. vanilla extract
4	cups all-purpose flour
½	cup baking cocoa
3	tsp. baking powder
½	tsp. salt
1	cup white baking chips
	Confectioners' sugar

1. In a large bowl, cream butter and sugar until light and fluffy. Beat in eggs, one at a time. Beat in vinegar, food coloring and vanilla. In another bowl, whisk flour, cocoa, baking powder and salt; gradually beat into creamed mixture. Stir in chips. Refrigerate, covered, 1 hour or until firm.

2. Preheat oven to 350°. Shape dough into 1½-in. balls; roll in the confectioners' sugar. Place 2 in. apart on parchment paper-lined baking sheets. Bake 12-15 minutes or until tops are cracked and edges are set. Cool on pans 5 minutes. Remove to wire racks to cool.

CHOCOLATE-CANDY CANE MERINGUE WREATH

These stunning meringues melt in your mouth. Set the minty masterpiece in the center of the table to accent your spread, then enjoy it for dessert later.

—Nicole Tran, Saskatoon, SK

PREP: 40 min. + standing
BAKE: 35 min. + cooling • MAKES: 7 dozen

- 4 large egg whites
- ½ tsp. cream of tartar
- 1 cup sugar
- 2¾ cups miniature semisweet chocolate chips, divided
- ¾ cup finely crushed candy canes or peppermint candies, divided
  Round doily or parchment circle (12 in.)
- 3 tsp. shortening

1. Place egg whites in a large bowl; let stand at room temperature 30 minutes.
2. Preheat oven to 250°. Add cream of tartar to the egg whites; beat on medium speed until soft peaks form. Gradually add sugar, 1 Tbsp. at a time, beating on high after each addition until sugar is dissolved. Continue beating until stiff glossy peaks form. Fold in 1 cup of the chocolate chips and ½ cup of the crushed candies.
3. Drop by rounded teaspoonfuls 1 in. apart onto parchment paper-lined baking sheets. Bake for 35-40 minutes or until firm to the touch. Remove meringues to wire racks to cool completely.
4. Line serving platter with a doily. In a microwave, melt shortening and the remaining chocolate chips. Dip bottoms of cookies into chocolate, allowing excess to drip off. Stack cookies on the prepared platter into a ring to form a wreath. Drizzle remaining melted chocolate over wreath; sprinkle with the remaining candies. Let stand until set, about 30 minutes. Store in an airtight container at room temperature.

CREME DE MENTHE COOKIES

This is my mother's Christmas recipe. She made these every year, and whenever I smell them baking, I think of her.

—Beth Cates, Hampton, TN

PREP: 15 min. + chilling
BAKE: 10 min./batch + cooling
MAKES: about 2 dozen

- ¾ cup margarine, softened
- ½ cup sugar
- 1 large egg
- 2 cups all-purpose flour
- ½ tsp. salt

FILLING/FROSTING
- 2 cups confectioners' sugar
- 4 to 5 Tbsp. creme de menthe
- 1 cup semisweet chocolate chips

1. In a large bowl, cream margarine and sugar until light and fluffy. Beat in egg. In another bowl, whisk flour and salt; gradually beat into the creamed mixture. Divide dough in half. Shape each into a disk; wrap in plastic. Refrigerate 1 hour or until firm enough to roll.
2. Preheat oven to 325°. Roll each portion of dough between two sheets of waxed paper to ¼-in. thickness (dough will be soft). Remove the waxed paper; cut with a floured 2-in. round cookie cutter. Place 2 in. apart on ungreased baking sheets. Bake for 7-8 minutes or until set. Remove from pans to wire racks to cool completely.
3. In a small bowl, mix the confectioners' sugar and enough creme de menthe to reach a spreading consistency. Spread evenly on bottoms of half of the cookies; cover with the remaining cookies. In a microwave, melt chocolate chips; stir until smooth. Frost cookies.

CHURCH WINDOW COOKIES

This is a hit with kids—the little ones just love the colored marshmallows!
—Emmilie Gaston, Wabash, IN

....

PREP: 20 min. + chilling • **MAKES:** 5 dozen

- 2   cups semisweet chocolate chips
- ½   cup butter, cubed
- 1   pkg. (10 oz.) pastel miniature marshmallows
- ½   cup chopped walnuts, toasted
- 2   cups flaked coconut

1. In a large saucepan, melt chocolate chips and butter over low heat; stir until smooth. Cool slightly. Stir in marshmallows and walnuts.

2. Divide mixture into three portions; place each portion on a piece of waxed paper. Using the waxed paper, shape each into a 10-in.-long roll; roll in coconut. Wrap tightly in waxed paper; refrigerate 2 hours or until firm. Cut crosswise into ½-in. slices.

Note: To toast nuts, bake in a shallow pan in a 350° oven for 5-10 minutes or cook in a skillet over low heat until lightly browned, stirring occasionally.

DATE NUT BALLS

A friend gave me this recipe over 30 years ago. It is my husband's favorite treat. I like them with pecans or walnuts, but if you don't like nuts, omit them and increase the Rice Krispies to 3 cups.
—Melinda Lord, Washington, IA

....

PREP: 30 min. • **COOK:** 10 min.
MAKES: about 3½ dozen

- 2   cups Rice Krispies
- 1   cup chopped pistachios or almonds
- ⅓   cup butter, cubed
- 1   pkg. (8 oz.) pitted dates, finely chopped
- 1   cup sugar
- 1   tsp. vanilla extract
      Confectioners' sugar, optional

1. In a large bowl, combine Rice Krispies and pistachios. In a large saucepan, combine butter, dates and sugar. Cook and stir over medium heat until combined.

2. Remove from heat. Stir in vanilla. Pour over the Rice Krispies mixture; stir to coat. When cool enough to handle, press into 1¼-in. balls. Cool. If desired, roll date nut balls in confectioner's sugar. Store in an airtight container at room temperature.

MAKE AHEAD

CITRUS GINGERBREAD COOKIES

Orange and lemon zest give gingerbread a refreshing twist; a honey glaze adds subtle shine and an extra touch of sweetness.

—Monique Hooker, DeSoto, WI

PREP: 40 min. + chilling
BAKE: 10 min./batch + cooling
MAKES: 6 dozen

- ¾ cup sugar
- ½ cup honey
- ½ cup molasses
- ½ cup unsalted butter, cubed
- 1 large egg
- 3½ cups all-purpose flour
- ¼ cup ground almonds
- 2 tsp. baking powder
- 2 tsp. grated lemon zest
- 2 tsp. grated orange zest
- 1 tsp. each ground cardamom, ginger, nutmeg, cinnamon and cloves

GLAZE
- ½ cup honey
- 2 Tbsp. water

1. In a large saucepan, combine sugar, honey and molasses. Bring to a boil; remove from heat. Let stand 20 minutes. Stir in butter; let stand 20 minutes longer, then beat in egg.

2. Whisk flour, almonds, baking powder, zests and spices; gradually beat into sugar mixture. Refrigerate, covered, for 8 hours or overnight.

3. Preheat oven to 375°. On a lightly floured surface, divide dough into three portions. Roll each to ¼ in. thick. Cut with a floured 2-in. cookie cutter. Place 2 in. apart on baking sheets coated with cooking spray.

4. Bake for 7-8 minutes or until lightly browned. Cool on pans 1 minute. Remove to wire racks to cool completely. In a small bowl, mix glaze ingredients; brush over cookies. Let stand until set.

To make ahead: Dough can be made 2 days in advance. Wrap in plastic and place in an airtight container. Store in the refrigerator.

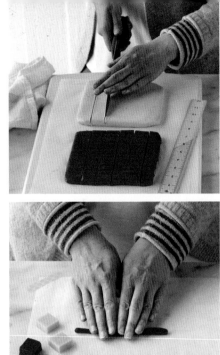

CLASSIC CANDY CANE BUTTER COOKIES

To make cookies that look like candy canes, we color half of the dough in classic red and twist away. They're fun to hang on the side of a coffee mug, or you can devour them all on their own.

—Shannon Roum, Milwaukee, WI

PREP: 45 min. + chilling
BAKE: 10 min./batch + cooling
MAKES: about 3 dozen

- 1 cup butter, softened
- ⅔ cup sugar
- ¼ tsp. salt
- 1 large egg yolk
- 2 tsp. vanilla extract
- 2¼ cups all-purpose flour
  Red paste food coloring

1. In a large bowl, cream butter, sugar and salt until light and fluffy. Beat in egg yolk and vanilla; gradually beat in flour. Divide dough in half; mix food coloring into one half. Roll each dough portion into a 6-in. square. Wrap each in plastic; refrigerate at least 1 hour or overnight.
2. Preheat oven to 350°. Cut each dough into 36 squares. Working with a quarter of the dough at a time, keep remaining dough refrigerated. Roll one piece plain dough into a 6-in. rope; roll one piece red dough into a 6-in. rope. Place ropes side by side. Lift left rope over the right; repeat to form a twist. Repeat with the remaining dough. Curving top of each twist to form hook of cane, place 1 in. apart on parchment paper-lined baking sheets.
3. Bake 7-9 minutes or until set. Cool on pans 3 minutes. Remove to wire racks to cool.

 Holiday Helper

Paste food coloring gives the most vibrant color. Liquid works (just a few drops!), but the color tends to be fainter.

PEANUT BUTTER PIE COOKIES

I love the combination of chocolate and peanut butter, but my favorite—peanut butter pie—is tough to eat on the go. I dreamed up these cookies to get my favorite flavor combo in a bite-sized package. They can be made ahead and taken to any gathering.

—Ashley Moyna, Elkader, IA

PREP: 45 min. • **BAKE:** 10 min. + cooling
MAKES: about 2 dozen

- 3 oz. cream cheese, softened
- ¼ cup confectioners' sugar
- 2 Tbsp. creamy peanut butter
- 1 large egg yolk
- ½ tsp. vanilla extract

COOKIES
- ½ cup butter, softened
- ½ cup packed brown sugar
- 1 large egg white
- 15 Oreo cookies, finely crushed (about 1½ cups)
- 1 cup all-purpose flour
- 1½ tsp. baking powder

TOPPING
- ⅓ cup semisweet chocolate chips, melted
  Confectioners' sugar, optional

1. Preheat oven to 350°. For filling, in a small bowl, beat the first five ingredients until smooth; set aside.
2. For cookies, in a large bowl, cream butter and brown sugar until light and fluffy. Beat in the egg white. In another bowl, mix the crushed cookies, flour and baking powder; gradually beat into creamed mixture.
3. Shape rounded tablespoonfuls of dough into 1½-in. balls; place balls 2 in. apart on ungreased baking sheets. Flatten slightly to ½-in. thickness. With your thumb, press a deep indentation in the center of each, then fill each indentation with 1 rounded teaspoonful of filling.
4. Bake 10-12 minutes or until the filling is almost set. Cool on pan 5 minutes. Remove to wire racks to cool completely.
5. Drizzle cooled cookies generously with melted chocolate. If desired, sprinkle with confectioners' sugar. Refrigerate leftovers.

MAKE AHEAD

CHRISTMAS LIGHTS COOKIES

What better way to brighten chilly winter days than with lightbulb-shaped cookies? My classic dough recipe has been a holiday tradition in our family for years.

—Carolyn Moseley, Dayton, OH

PREP: 45 min. + chilling
BAKE: 10 min./batch + cooling
MAKES: 1½ dozen

- ½ cup butter, softened
- ½ cup sugar
- 1 large egg
- ¾ tsp. vanilla extract
- ¼ tsp. almond extract
- 1¾ cups all-purpose flour
- ½ tsp. ground cinnamon
- ¼ tsp. salt
- ¼ tsp. baking powder

FROSTING
- 5 cups confectioners' sugar
- 1 Tbsp. light corn syrup
- ¾ tsp. vanilla extract
- 5 to 6 Tbsp. water
  Red, blue, green and yellow paste food coloring
  Silver pearl dust

1. In a large bowl, cream the butter and sugar until light and fluffy. Beat in egg and extracts. In another bowl, whisk the flour, cinnamon, salt and baking powder; gradually beat into the creamed mixture. Shape dough into a disk; wrap in plastic. Refrigerate 1 hour or until firm enough to roll.

2. Preheat oven to 350°. On a lightly floured surface, roll dough to ⅛-in. thickness. Cut with a floured 4-in. Christmas light-shaped cookie cutter. Place cookies 1 in. apart on ungreased baking sheets. Bake for 9-11 minutes or until light brown. Remove from pans to wire racks to cool completely.
3. In a small bowl, beat the confectioners' sugar, corn syrup, vanilla and enough water to reach desired consistency. Reserve ⅔ cup frosting for bottom of cookies and reflections. Divide the remaining frosting between four bowls. Tint one red, one blue, one green and one yellow. Frost tops of cookies. Frost the bottoms of the cookies with about half of the reserved frosting; sprinkle with pearl dust. With the remaining white frosting and a #5 round tip, pipe on reflections. Let stand until completely set.
To make ahead: Dough can be made 2 days in advance. Wrap in plastic and place in an airtight container. Store in the refrigerator.

GINGER-CREAM BARS

I rediscovered this nearly forgotten, old-time recipe recently and found it's everyone's favorite. Toddlers have asked for these frosted bars as nursery treats!

—Carol Nagelkirk, Holland, MI

PREP: 20 min. • BAKE: 20 min.
MAKES: 5-6 dozen

- 1 cup butter, softened
- 1 cup granulated sugar
- 2 cups all-purpose flour
- 1 tsp. salt
- 2 tsp. baking soda
- 1 Tbsp. ground cinnamon
- 1 Tbsp. ground cloves
- 1 Tbsp. ground ginger
- 2 large eggs
- ½ cup molasses
- 1 cup hot brewed coffee

FROSTING
- ½ cup butter, softened
- 3 oz. cream cheese, softened
- 2 cups confectioners' sugar
- 2 tsp. vanilla extract
  Chopped nuts, optional

1. Preheat oven to 350°. Cream butter and granulated sugar. Sift together flour, salt, baking soda and spices; add to creamed mixture. Add eggs, one at a time, beating well after each addition, and molasses. Blend in coffee. Spread in a 15x10x1-in. baking pan.
2. Bake 20-25 minutes. Cool. For frosting, cream butter and cream cheese; add confectioners' sugar and vanilla. Spread over bars. If desired, top with nuts.

CREAM CHEESE SPRITZ

A hint of orange and cinnamon highlights these Christmastime classics. I like to add colorful sprinkles before baking them. The recipe is from a booklet that came with a cookie press in the 1950s...and I still have the press!

—Sarah Bedia, Lake Jackson, Texas

PREP: 15 min. • BAKE: 10 min./batch
MAKES: about 6 dozen

- 1 cup shortening
- 3 oz. cream cheese, softened
- 1 cup sugar
- 1 large egg yolk
- 1 tsp. vanilla extract
- 2½ cups all-purpose flour
- ½ tsp. salt
- ¼ tsp. ground cinnamon
- 1 tsp. grated orange zest
  Green food coloring, decorator candies and colored sugar, optional

1. Preheat oven to 350°. Cream shortening, cream cheese and sugar until light and fluffy. Beat in egg yolk and vanilla extract. In another bowl, whisk together flour, salt and cinnamon; gradually add to creamed mixture and mix well. Stir in orange zest. If desired, add food coloring.
2. Using a cookie press fitted with a disk of your choice, press dough 1 in. apart onto ungreased baking sheets. Decorate with candies and colored sugar as desired. Bake cookies until set (do not brown), 9-12 minutes. Remove from pans to wire racks to cool.

CHOCOLATE-CHERRY THUMBPRINT COOKIES

These look so pretty at Christmas on a tea table with other decorated cookies. They taste as good as they look, and they are eaten quickly wherever and whenever I take them. They're also great for Valentine's Day!
—Stephanie Smith, Colorado Springs, CO

....

PREP: 50 min. • **BAKE:** 10 min./batch + cooling
MAKES: 2½ dozen

- ¾ cup butter, softened
- ½ cup sugar
- 1 large egg yolk
- 1 tsp. vanilla extract
- 1½ cups all-purpose flour
- ¼ cup baking cocoa

FILLING
- 1 cup confectioners' sugar
- ¼ cup butter, softened
- 1 Tbsp. maraschino cherry juice

TOPPING
- 30 maraschino cherries, patted dry
- ¼ cup semisweet chocolate chips
- 1½ tsp. shortening

1. Preheat oven to 350°. In a large bowl, cream butter and sugar until light and fluffy. Beat in egg yolk and vanilla. In another bowl, whisk flour and cocoa; gradually beat into creamed mixture.

2. Shape into 1-in. balls; place 2 in. apart on greased baking sheets. Press a deep indentation in center of each with the end of a wooden spoon handle. Bake 7-9 minutes or until firm. Remove to wire racks to cool completely.

3. For the filling, in a small bowl, beat confectioners' sugar, butter and cherry juice. Fill each cookie with ½ tsp. filling. Top each with a cherry. In a microwave, melt chocolate chips and shortening; stir until smooth. Drizzle over cookies. Let stand until set.

ORANGE-NUTELLA COOKIE CUPS

These one-bite delights are easy to put on a platter for an impressive presentation. Trade the raspberries for the fresh fruit of your choice—half a strawberry or a piece of mandarin orange complements the hazelnut chocolate flavor of the Nutella.

—Joanie Fuson, Indianapolis, IN

PREP: 30 min. • BAKE: 10 min./batch + cooling
MAKES: 4 dozen

- 1 tube (16½ oz.) refrigerated sugar cookie dough
- ½ cup all-purpose flour
- 1 Tbsp. grated orange zest
- 1 cup Nutella
- 48 fresh raspberries (about 2 cups)
  Toasted hazelnuts, optional

1. Preheat oven to 350°. In a small bowl, mix cookie dough, flour and orange zest. Shape dough into 1-in. balls; press each ball evenly onto bottom and up the sides of a cup in a greased mini-muffin pan. Bake 10-12 minutes or until light golden brown.
2. Cool in pans for 5 minutes; run a knife around sides of cups. Cool completely before removing from pans. Place 1 tsp. Nutella in the center of each cookie; top with a raspberry. If desired, substitute hazelnuts for the raspberries.

❄ Reader Review

"I never throw away navel or thin-skinned orange peels; I freeze them in plastic bags to use in recipes that call for grated orange peel. The frozen peel grates beautifully and doesn't stick to the grater."

F. VAN BLARCOM LAND O'LAKES, FL

CHOCOLATY S'MORES BARS

One night, my husband had some friends over to play poker and he requested these s'mores bars. They polished off the pan and asked for more! I shared the recipe, and now their families make them, too.

—Rebecca Shipp, Beebe, AR

PREP: 15 min. + cooling • MAKES: 1½ dozen

- ¼ cup butter, cubed
- 1 pkg. (10 oz.) large marshmallows
- 1 pkg. (12 oz.) Golden Grahams cereal
- ⅓ cup milk chocolate chips, melted

1. In a large saucepan, melt butter over low heat. Add marshmallows; cook and stir until blended. Remove from heat. Stir in cereal until coated.
2. Press into a greased 13x9-in. pan using a buttered spatula. Drizzle with melted chocolate. Cool completely before cutting. Store in an airtight container.
Test Kitchen tip: Use a butter wrapper to press the cereal into the pan. For a rich twist on the classic, add ¼ cup of peanut butter to the marshmallows and stir a handful of chopped peanuts into the cereal.

FROSTED CASHEW COOKIES

Merry snacking is guaranteed when you pass out these cashew-packed goodies! I found the recipe years ago in a flyer promoting dairy products. It's been this farm wife's standby ever since.
—June Lindquist, Hammond, WI

PREP: 25 min. • **BAKE:** 10 min./batch
MAKES: about 5 dozen

½ cup butter, softened
1 cup packed brown sugar
1 large egg
½ tsp. vanilla extract
2 cups all-purpose flour
¾ tsp. baking powder
¾ tsp. baking soda
¼ tsp. salt
⅓ cup sour cream
1¾ cups chopped cashews

FROSTING
½ cup butter, cubed
3 Tbsp. half-and-half cream
¼ tsp. vanilla extract
2 cups confectioners' sugar
Cashew halves, optional

1. Preheat oven to 375°. In a bowl, cream butter and brown sugar. Beat in egg and vanilla. Combine the dry ingredients; add alternately with sour cream to the creamed mixture. Stir in the cashews. Drop dough by tablespoonfuls onto greased baking sheets. Bake for 8-10 minutes or until lightly browned. Cool on a wire rack.
2. For frosting, lightly brown butter in a small saucepan. Remove from the heat and cool slightly. Add cream and vanilla. Beat in confectioners' sugar until smooth and thick. Frost cookies; top each with a cashew half if desired.

MAKE AHEAD
BIG & SOFT MOLASSES COOKIES

Some of the best molasses cookies I ever had came from a Mennonite store, and I finally found a recipe that compares. A sprinkling of coarse sugar adds a pretty appearance for special occasions.
—Nancy Foust, Stoneboro, PA

PREP: 45 min. + chilling • **BAKE:** 15 min./batch
MAKES: about 2½ dozen

1 cup butter-flavored shortening
1 cup sugar
2 large eggs
2 cups molasses
1 cup sour cream
½ tsp. vanilla extract
8 cups all-purpose flour
3 tsp. baking soda
1½ tsp. ground cinnamon
1 tsp. ground ginger
½ tsp. salt
½ tsp. ground cloves
½ tsp. ground nutmeg
½ cup coarse sugar

1. In a large bowl, cream shortening and sugar until light and fluffy. Beat in eggs, molasses, sour cream and vanilla extract. In another bowl, whisk flour, baking soda, cinnamon, ginger, salt, cloves and nutmeg; gradually beat into creamed mixture.
2. Divide dough in half. Shape each into a disk; wrap in plastic. Refrigerate 2 hours or until firm enough to roll.
3. Preheat oven to 350°. On a floured surface, roll each portion of dough to ½-in. thickness. Cut with a floured 3-in. round cookie cutter. Place 2 in. apart on parchment paper-lined baking sheets. Sprinkle with sugar. Bake 15-18 minutes or until set. Remove from pans to wire racks to cool.

To make ahead: Dough can be made 2 days in advance. Wrap in plastic and place in an airtight container. Store in refrigerator.
Freeze option: Freeze cookies, layered between waxed paper, in airtight freezer containers. To use, thaw before serving.

COCONUT RUM BALLS

My mom has made rum balls for as long as I can remember. They look beautiful in a dessert buffet and can be easily given as gifts. When I switched the traditional rum to coconut rum and added shredded coconut, I think I made these tasty treats even better!
—Jana Walker, Macomb, MI

PREP: 25 min. + standing
MAKES: about 4½ dozen

- 1 pkg. (12 oz.) vanilla wafers, finely crushed
- 1 cup confectioners' sugar
- 2 Tbsp. baking cocoa
- 1 cup sweetened shredded coconut
- 1 cup chopped pecans
- ½ cup light corn syrup
- ¼ cup coconut rum
  Additional confectioners' sugar

1. Whisk crushed wafers, confectioners' sugar and cocoa. Stir in coconut and pecans. In a separate bowl, whisk corn syrup and rum; stir into wafer mixture. Shape into 1-in. balls; let stand 1 hour.
2. Roll balls in additional confectioners' sugar. Store in an airtight container.

❄ Holiday Helper

To add variety, you can roll these rum balls in granulated sugar, sparkling decorator's sugar or toasted coconut.

MAKE AHEAD

APRICOT-PECAN THUMBPRINT COOKIES

I enjoy experimenting with cake mixes to make new cookie recipes. I love apricot, but feel free to fill the thumbprint in the center of these goodies with any fruit preserve you like.
—Nancy A Johnson, Laverne, OK

PREP: 30 min. • **BAKE:** 15 min./batch + cooling
MAKES: about 7 dozen

- 2 pkg. yellow cake mix (regular size)
- ½ cup all-purpose flour
- 1 cup canola oil
- 6 large eggs, divided use
- 1 tsp. ground cinnamon
- ½ tsp. ground ginger
- 3 Tbsp. water
- 4 cups finely chopped pecans, divided
- ⅔ cup apricot preserves

ICING
- 2 cups confectioners' sugar
- 3 to 5 Tbsp. water

1. Preheat oven to 350°. In a large bowl, beat cake mix, flour, oil, 4 eggs, cinnamon and ginger until well blended.
2. In a shallow bowl, whisk water and the remaining eggs. Place half of the pecans in another shallow bowl. Shape dough into 1-in. balls. Dip in egg mixture, then coat with pecans, adding remaining pecans to bowl as needed. Place cookies 2 in. apart on greased baking sheets.
3. Press a deep indentation in the center of each cookie with the end of a wooden spoon handle. Fill each indentation with preserves. Bake 12-14 minutes or until golden brown. Remove from pans to wire racks to cool completely.
4. In a small bowl, combine confectioners' sugar and enough water to achieve a good drizzling consistency. Drizzle over cookies. Let stand until set.
Freeze option: Freeze drizzled cookies, layered between sheets of waxed paper, in airtight freezer containers. To use, thaw in covered containers.

ALMOND ROCA PINWHEELS

We all love Almond Roca! I crush the candy to use as an ice cream topping, over pudding, and in cakes and cookies. . .and my family expects these pinwheels every Christmas! Use vanilla extract if you don't like rum.

—Nancy Heishman, Las Vegas, NV

PREP: 20 min. + chilling
BAKE: 10 min./batch + cooling
MAKES: about 2½ dozen

- ½ cup butter, softened
- ¾ cup sugar
- 1 large egg
- 1 tsp. rum extract
- 1½ cups all-purpose flour
- ¼ tsp. baking powder
- ¼ tsp. salt
- 6 Almond Roca candies, crushed, or ½ cup brickle toffee bits
- ¼ cup miniature semisweet chocolate chips

1. In a large bowl, cream butter and sugar until light and fluffy. Beat in egg and rum extract. In another bowl, whisk flour, baking powder and salt; gradually beat into the creamed mixture. Shape dough into a disk; wrap in plastic. Refrigerate 1 hour or until firm enough to roll.

2. On a sheet of waxed paper, roll dough into a 10-in. square. In a small bowl, combine crushed candies and chocolate chips; sprinkle over dough to within 1 in. of edges. Using waxed paper, tightly roll dough jelly-roll style, removing the paper as you roll. Wrap in plastic; refrigerate for 1 hour or until firm, up to 24 hours.

3. Preheat oven to 375°. Unwrap dough and cut crosswise into ¼-in. slices. Place slices 2 in. apart on parchment paper-lined baking sheets. Bake for 8-10 minutes or until the edges are light brown. Cool on pans for 2 minutes. Remove to wire racks to cool completely.

POTATO CHIP BANANA BREAD COOKIES

My 5-year-old wanted to bake a cake with potato chips and bananas. I couldn't quite manage that, but I did combine two cookie recipes to create these. Everyone tells me they're addictive!
—Rebecca Emmons, Tulsa, OK

PREP: 25 min. • **BAKE:** 10 min./batch + cooling
MAKES: 4 dozen

- 1   cup butter, softened
- ¾   cup sugar
- ¾   cup packed brown sugar
- 1   cup mashed ripe bananas (about 2 medium)
- 2   large eggs
- 1   tsp. vanilla extract
- 2½   cups all-purpose flour
- 1   tsp. baking soda
- ½   tsp. salt
- 2   cups crushed baked potato chips
- 1   cup butterscotch chips

1. Preheat oven to 350°. In a large bowl, cream butter and sugars until light and fluffy. Beat in bananas, eggs and vanilla. In another bowl, whisk flour, baking soda and salt; gradually beat into the creamed mixture. Fold in the potato chips and butterscotch chips.
2. Drop by heaping tablespoonfuls 2 in. apart onto greased baking sheets. Bake 10-12 minutes or until edges are golden brown. Cool on pans 5 minutes. Remove to wire racks to cool.

RED APPLE BUTTER BARS

Fall means apple-picking time. We love baking these bar treats using apples and apple butter with a crumbly good streusel on top.
—Nancy Foust, Stoneboro, PA

PREP: 40 min. • **BAKE:** 35 min. + cooling
MAKES: 2 dozen

- 3   cups all-purpose flour
- 2   cups quick-cooking oats
- 2   cups packed brown sugar
- 1½   tsp. baking soda
- ¾   tsp. salt
- ¾   tsp. ground cinnamon
- 1½   cups butter, melted
- 2   medium apples, chopped
- 1½   cups apple butter
- 1   cup chopped walnuts

1. Preheat oven to 350°. In a large bowl, combine the first six ingredients; stir in butter. Reserve 1⅓ cups crumb mixture for topping. Press the remaining mixture onto bottom of a greased 13x9-in. baking dish. Bake for 15-20 minutes or until lightly browned. Cool completely on a wire rack.
2. Sprinkle apples over crust; spread with apple butter. Stir walnuts into reserved topping; sprinkle over apple butter. Bake 35-40 minutes or until lightly browned. Cool in pan on a wire rack. Cut into bars.
Note: This recipe was tested with commercially prepared apple butter.

PUMPKIN-GINGERBREAD THUMBPRINT COOKIES

These cookies are the result of an inspiring recipe and an afternoon spent experimenting in the kitchen with my daughters. I took the cookies to a meeting and they were a hit. So yummy with a cup of coffee!
—Jennifer Needham, Woodstock, GA

PREP: 20 min. • **BAKE:** 10 min./batch + cooling
MAKES: about 4½ dozen

- 1   pkg. (14½ oz.) gingerbread cake/cookie mix
- ¼   cup hot water
- 2   Tbsp. unsalted butter, melted
- 1   cup solid-pack pumpkin
- 1   cup all-purpose flour
- 2   to 3 tsp. pumpkin pie spice
- 58   milk chocolate kisses

1. Preheat oven to 375°. In a large bowl, combine cookie mix, hot water and butter. Stir in pumpkin. In a small bowl, whisk flour and pie spice; gradually stir into mixture. Shape dough into 1-in. balls.
2. Place 2 in. apart on ungreased baking sheets. Press a deep indentation in the center of each with your thumb. Bake 6-8 minutes or until set. Immediately press a chocolate kiss into the center of each cookie. Remove from pans to wire racks to cool.

WRAPPED COOKIE CUTTER ORNAMENTS

Cookie cutters make great tree ornaments or gift toppers—especially when you add a dash of color! Choose a cookie cutter, then cut a long length of colored string, yarn or ribbon and roll it into a ball that will fit through the center of the cutter. Use tacky glue to adhere the loose end to the inside of the cutter. Let the glue dry, then wrap the string around the cookie cutter, pulling tightly to smooth out the strands. When the cookie cutter is covered, trim any excess string and glue the end in place. Let dry before hanging.

GINGERBREAD BUDDIES

These cookies were ideal for a winter get-together I hosted. I like to share these crunchy treats on the way home from cutting our fresh Christmas tree.
—Shelly Rynearson, Oconomowoc, WI

PREP: 30 min. + chilling
BAKE: 15 min./batch + cooling
MAKES: 3½ dozen

- 1 cup butter, softened
- 1 cup sugar
- 1 cup molasses
- ¼ cup water
- 5 cups all-purpose flour
- 2½ tsp. ground ginger
- 1½ tsp. baking soda
- 1½ tsp. ground cinnamon
- ½ tsp. ground allspice
- ¼ tsp. salt
  Cinnamon bear-shaped crackers
  Cinnamon Chex
  Frosted bite-sized shredded wheat cereal

FROSTING
- 1¼ cups confectioners' sugar
- 5 tsp. water
- 1 tsp. light corn syrup
- ¼ tsp. vanilla extract
  Paste food coloring
  Assorted candies

1. In a large bowl, cream butter and sugar until light and fluffy. Beat in molasses and water. In another bowl, whisk together flour, ginger, baking soda, cinnamon, allspice and salt; gradually beat into the creamed mixture. Divide dough in half. Shape each into a disk; wrap in plastic. Refrigerate 1 hour or until firm enough to roll.
2. Preheat oven to 350°. On a lightly floured surface, roll each portion of dough to ¼-in. thickness. Cut with a 3½-in. gingerbread man cookie cutter. Place 2 in. apart on ungreased baking sheets. Place a bear-shaped cracker, Cinnamon Chex piece or mini shredded wheat piece in the center of each cookie. Gently fold cookie arms toward cracker or cereal piece; press lightly to adhere.

3. Bake 12-14 minutes or until edges are firm. Cool on pans 2 minutes. Remove to wire racks to cool completely.

4. For frosting, in a small bowl, beat the confectioners' sugar, water, corn syrup and vanilla until smooth. Tint as desired with paste food coloring. Transfer to a resealable plastic bag; cut a very small hole in a corner of bag. Pipe frosting onto cookies. Decorate as desired with candies.

BUTTERSCOTCH WALNUT DROPS

I created this recipe when I had company coming for Christmas and I was fresh out of chocolate chips. The cookies were such a hit with my family that they became a treasured holiday tradition—I've been making the recipe for over 40 years now.

—Jeanne Walker, Oxnard, CA

PREP: 20 min. • BAKE: 15 min./batch
MAKES: about 5 dozen

⅔	cup butter, softened
⅔	cup shortening
1	cup sugar
1	cup packed brown sugar
2	large eggs
2	tsp. vanilla extract
3	cups all-purpose flour
1	tsp. baking soda
¾	tsp. salt
2	cups coarsely chopped walnuts
1	pkg. (10 to 11 oz.) butterscotch chips

1. Preheat oven to 350°. In a large bowl, cream butter, shortening and sugars until light and fluffy. Beat in eggs and vanilla. In another bowl, whisk flour, baking soda and salt; gradually beat into creamed mixture. Stir in walnuts and butterscotch chips.

2. Drop dough by rounded tablespoonfuls 2 in. apart onto ungreased baking sheets. Bake 12-14 minutes or until light brown. Cool on pans 2 minutes. Remove to wire racks to cool.

HAWAIIAN DREAM COOKIES

These cookies are lovely just as they are, but I'll sometimes lightly brush the top cookie with cream, then sprinkle them with a light-colored sanding sugar. This can be done before or after placing the cookie on top of the filling.

—Lorraine Caland, Shuniah, ON

PREP: 15 min. + chilling
BAKE: 15 min./batch + cooling
MAKES: about 2 dozen

⅓	cup shortening
⅓	cup butter, softened
⅔	cup sugar
2	large eggs
1	tsp. vanilla extract
1	tsp. grated lemon zest
2	cups all-purpose flour
1½	tsp. baking powder
¼	tsp. salt

FILLING

¼	cup sugar
1	Tbsp. cornstarch
1	cup undrained crushed pineapple
½	tsp. butter
	Confectioners' sugar

1. In a large bowl, cream the shortening, butter and sugar until light and fluffy. Beat in eggs, vanilla and lemon zest. In another bowl, whisk flour, baking powder and salt; gradually beat into the creamed mixture. Divide dough in half. Shape each into a disk; wrap in plastic. Refrigerate 1 hour.

2. Preheat oven to 350°. On a surface sprinkled with confectioners' sugar, roll the dough to ¼-in. thickness. Cut with a 2-in. round cookie cutter dusted with confectioners' sugar. Using a floured 1-in. star-shaped cookie cutter, cut out centers of half of the cookies; re-roll the scraps as needed. Place solid and window cookies 2 in. apart on greased baking sheets. Repeat with the remaining dough.

3. Bake 12-15 minutes or until edges are brown. Cool on pans 5 minutes. Remove to wire racks to cool completely.

4. For the filling, in a small saucepan, mix sugar and cornstarch. Stir in pineapple. Cook and stir over medium heat until thickened. Stir in butter. Cool completely. Spread filling on bottoms of solid cookies; top with the window cookies. Dust with confectioners' sugar.

CRANBERRY PRETZEL COOKIES

These salty and sweet delights are perfect for cookie exchanges. I use cream cheese to make the cookies extra rich.

—Meg Bagley, Logan, UT

....

PREP: 30 min. • BAKE: 15 min./batch
MAKES: about 3½ dozen

- 1 cup butter, softened
- 1 pkg. (8 oz.) cream cheese, softened
- ¾ cup sugar
- ¾ cup packed brown sugar
- 2 tsp. vanilla extract
- 2¼ cups all-purpose flour
- 1 tsp. baking soda
- ½ tsp. salt
- 2 cups coarsely crushed pretzels (about ½-in. pieces)
- 1 cup dried cranberries
- 1 cup white baking chips

1. Preheat oven to 350°. In a large bowl, cream butter, cream cheese and sugars until light and fluffy. Beat in vanilla. In another bowl, whisk flour, baking soda and salt; gradually beat into the creamed mixture. Stir in pretzels, cranberries and baking chips.
2. Drop dough by rounded tablespoonfuls 2 in. apart onto greased baking sheets. Bake 11-14 minutes or until edges are golden brown. Cool on pans 2 minutes. Remove to wire racks to cool.

❄ Holiday Helper

To crush crackers, candy, nuts or pretzels (as in this recipe) quickly and neatly, use a sturdy plastic liner that comes in a cereal box or a heavy-duty resealable plastic bag. Put your ingredients in the bag and use a rolling pin to do the work; the crumbs will stay nicely contained in the bag. It's easy to select the pieces you want, and then either discard or store the rest.

NEVER-FAIL CUTOUT COOKIES

I've tried many recipes for cutout cookies over the years—this one is foolproof. My daughter and my granddaughter love making these for holidays. Most of all, we enjoy the decorating. You can try almond flavoring or another flavor of choice. This recipe is easily doubled.

—Irene Palm, Mansfield, OH

....

PREP: 45 min. + chilling
BAKE: 10 min./batch + cooling
MAKES: about 5 dozen

- 2 cups butter, softened
- 1 pkg. (8 oz.) cream cheese, softened
- 2 cups granulated sugar
- 2 large egg yolks
- 2 tsp. vanilla extract
- 5 cups all-purpose flour

FROSTING
- 3½ cups confectioners' sugar
- 3 Tbsp. butter, softened
- 1 Tbsp. shortening
- 1 tsp. vanilla extract
- 4 to 5 Tbsp. 2% milk
  Food coloring of choice, optional
  Assorted sprinkles or candies, optional

1. Beat butter, cream cheese and sugar until light and fluffy. Beat in egg yolks and vanilla. Gradually beat in flour. Divide the dough into four portions; shape each into a disk. Wrap in plastic; refrigerate until firm enough to roll, about 30 minutes.
2. Preheat oven to 350°. On a lightly floured surface, roll each portion of dough to ¼-in. thickness. Cut with floured 3-in. holiday-themed cookie cutters. Place 1 in. apart on ungreased baking sheets.
3. Bake until the edges are light golden, 12-14 minutes. Cool on pans 5 minutes. Remove to wire racks to cool completely.
4. For frosting, beat confectioners' sugar, butter, shortening, vanilla and enough milk to reach desired consistency. If desired, tint with food coloring. Spread or pipe over cookies. Decorate as desired.

RASPBERRY COCONUT COOKIES

My mother gave me the recipe for these rich, buttery cookies. Raspberry preserves and a cream filling make them doubly delicious.

—June Brown, Veneta, OR

....

PREP: 20 min. • BAKE: 15 min./batch + cooling
MAKES: 2½ dozen

- ¾ cup butter, softened
- ½ cup sugar
- 1 large egg
- 1 tsp. vanilla extract
- 2 cups all-purpose flour
- ½ cup sweetened shredded coconut
- 1½ tsp. baking powder
- ¼ tsp. salt

FILLING
- ¼ cup butter, softened
- ¾ cup confectioners' sugar
- 2 tsp. 2% milk
- ½ tsp. vanilla extract
- ½ cup raspberry preserves

1. In a large bowl, cream butter and sugar until light and fluffy. Beat in egg and vanilla. Combine the flour, coconut, baking powder and salt; gradually add to the creamed mixture and mix well.
2. Shape into 1-in. balls. Place 1½ in. apart on ungreased baking sheets; flatten with a glass dipped in flour.
3. Bake at 350° for 12-14 minutes or until edges begin to brown. Cool on wire racks.
4. In a small bowl, beat the softened butter, confectioners' sugar, milk and vanilla until smooth. Place ½ tsp. preserves and a scant teaspoonful of filling on the bottoms of half of the cookies; top with remaining cookies. Store, refrigerated, in an airtight container.

CHOCOLATE-DIPPED MERINGUE SANDWICH COOKIES

Oh what fun it is to bite into this delectable combination of chocolate and crunchy meringue! As an alternative to the candy or sugar garnishes, you can use chocolate sprinkles, toasted almonds or toasted sweetened shredded coconut.

—Donna Stelmach, Morristown, NJ

PREP: 1 hour + chilling
BAKE: 40 min./batch + standing
MAKES: 7 dozen

- 4 large egg whites
- 1 cup confectioners' sugar
- ½ cup almond flour
- ⅔ cup sugar

GANACHE

- 6 oz. semisweet chocolate, chopped
- 3 oz. unsweetened chocolate, chopped
- 1¼ cups heavy whipping cream
- 1 Tbsp. light corn syrup

TOPPINGS

- Coarse decorator's sugar, various colors
- Crushed peppermint candies

1. Place egg whites in a large bowl; let stand at room temperature 30 minutes.
2. Preheat oven to 225°. In a small bowl, whisk confectioners' sugar and almond flour until blended. Beat egg whites on medium speed until foamy. Gradually add the sugar, 1 Tbsp. at a time, beating on high after each addition until sugar is dissolved. Continue beating until stiff glossy peaks form. Fold in confectioners' sugar mixture.
3. Cut a small hole in the tip of a pastry bag or in a corner of a food-safe plastic bag; insert a #805 round pastry tip. Fill bag with meringue. Pipe 1-in.-diameter cookies 1 in. apart onto parchment paper-lined baking sheets. Using a finger moistened with water, smooth tops of cookies.
4. Bake 40-45 minutes or until firm to the touch. Turn oven off (do not open oven door); leave cookies in oven for 1 hour. Remove from oven; cool completely on baking sheets.

5. For ganache, place semisweet and unsweetened chocolates in a small bowl. In a small saucepan, combine cream and corn syrup; bring just to a boil. Pour over chocolate; whisk until smooth. Remove 1 cup of the ganache to another bowl and reserve for dipping. Refrigerate the main portion of the ganache 25-30 minutes or until thick enough to pipe; stir occasionally. Let remaining portion stand, covered, at room temperature, stirring occasionally.
6. Cut a small hole in the tip of a pastry bag or in a corner of a food-safe plastic bag; insert a #802 round pastry tip. Fill bag with chilled ganache. Pipe onto bottoms of half of the cookies; cover with the remaining cookies. (Ganache may soften as it warms. If necessary, return ganache to refrigerator until firm enough to pipe.)
7. Place toppings in separate shallow bowls. Dip each sandwich cookie halfway into the room-temperature ganache; allow excess to drip off. (If necessary, warm the ganache in microwave for 10 seconds to thin slightly.) Dip in toppings as desired; place on waxed paper and let stand until set. Store cookies in airtight containers at room temperature.

MAKE AHEAD
HUNGARIAN WALNUT COOKIES

As a child, I always looked forward to eating these goodies at Christmastime. Now I make them for my own family.

—Sharon Kurtz, Emmaus, PA

PREP: 50 min. + chilling
BAKE: 10 min./batch + cooling
MAKES: 4 dozen

- 1 cup butter, softened
- 1 pkg. (8 oz.) cream cheese, softened
- 2½ cups all-purpose flour

FILLING

- 3 large egg whites
- ¾ tsp. vanilla extract
- ⅓ cup sugar
- 3½ cups ground walnuts
- Confectioners' sugar

1. In a large bowl, cream butter and cream cheese until blended. Gradually beat flour into the creamed mixture. Divide dough into three portions. Shape each into a disk; wrap in plastic. Refrigerate 1 hour or until firm enough to roll.
2. Preheat the oven to 375°. For filling, in a small bowl, beat egg whites and vanilla on medium speed until foamy. Gradually add sugar, 1 Tbsp. at a time, beating on medium after each addition until well blended. Stir in walnuts.
3. Generously coat a work surface with confectioners' sugar. Roll one portion of the dough into a 12-in. square about ⅛ in. thick, sprinkling with additional confectioners' sugar as necessary to coat well. Cut into sixteen 3-in. squares.
4. Shape 2 tsp. filling into a small log about 2 in. long. Place diagonally onto a square. Overlap opposite corners of dough over filling; pinch tightly to seal. Place 2 in. apart on greased baking sheets. Repeat with the remaining dough and filling.
5. Bake until bottoms are golden brown, 9-11 minutes. Remove from pans to wire racks to cool completely. Dust with confectioners' sugar.

To make ahead: Dough can be made 2 days in advance. Wrap in plastic and place in an airtight container. Store in the refrigerator.

Freeze option: Freeze cookies in freezer containers. Thaw before serving. If desired, dust with additional confectioners' sugar.

CHERRY PISTACHIO COOKIES

Dried cherries, crunchy nuts, bits of orange, white chocolate—there's a lot to love in these cookies! They're very different from any I've had before.

—Kathy Harding, Richmond, MO

PREP: 25 min. + chilling
BAKE: 10 min./batch + cooling
MAKES: about 3½ dozen

1	cup unsalted butter, softened
1½	cups confectioners' sugar
1	large egg
4	tsp. grated orange zest
2¼	cups all-purpose flour
1	tsp. baking soda
1	tsp. cream of tartar
1½	cups chopped dried cherries or cranberries
½	cup chopped pistachios
8	oz. white baking chocolate, melted

1. In a large bowl, cream the butter and confectioners' sugar until light and fluffy. Beat in egg and orange zest. In another bowl, whisk flour, baking soda and cream of tartar; gradually beat into the creamed mixture. Stir in cherries and pistachios.

2. Divide dough in half; shape each into an 11-in.-long roll. Wrap in plastic; refrigerate at least 2 hours or until firm.

3. Preheat oven to 375°. Unwrap dough and cut crosswise into ½-in. slices. Place 2 in. apart on ungreased baking sheets. Bake 8-10 minutes or until edges are light golden brown. Remove from pans to wire racks to cool completely. Frost cookies with melted white chocolate; let stand until set.

To make ahead: Dough can be made 2 days in advance. Wrap in plastic and place in an airtight container. Store in the refrigerator.

Freeze option: Place the wrapped rolls in an airtight container and freeze. To use, unwrap frozen logs and cut into slices. If necessary, let dough stand for 15 minutes at room temperature before cutting. Bake as directed, increasing time if needed by 1-2 minutes. Frost as directed.

APRICOT-HAZELNUT TRIANGLES

These crispy cookie treats can be changed up. Try different nuts and jams, and use dark or white chocolate depending on the holiday.
—Johnna Johnson, Scottsdale, AZ

PREP: 25 min. • **BAKE:** 30 min. + cooling
MAKES: about 2½ dozen

- ⅓ cup butter, softened
- 1 cup sugar, divided
- 1 large egg
- 1 tsp. vanilla extract
- 1¼ cups all-purpose flour
- ½ tsp. baking powder
- 3 Tbsp. apricot preserves or flavor of your choice
- ⅓ cup butter, melted
- 2 Tbsp. water
- ¾ cup finely chopped hazelnuts or nuts of your choice
- 7 oz. dark chocolate candy coating, melted

1. Preheat the oven to 350°. In a small bowl, cream butter and ½ cup sugar until light and fluffy. Beat in the egg and vanilla extract. In another bowl, whisk the flour and baking powder; gradually beat into creamed mixture.

2. Press dough into a greased 8-in. square baking pan; spread with preserves. In a small bowl, mix melted butter, water and remaining sugar; stir in hazelnuts. Spread over preserves.

3. Bake 30-35 minutes or until edges are golden brown and center is set. Cool for 15 minutes on a wire rack. Cut into sixteen 2-in. squares. Cut squares into triangles. Remove to wire racks to cool completely.

4. Dip one side of each triangle halfway into melted chocolate; allow excess to drip off. Place on waxed paper; let stand until set. Store in an airtight container.

MINCEMEAT COOKIE BARS

My daughter won the grand champion title at the Alaska State Fair with these bars when she was 10 years old! The topping is delicious but a bit crumbly—if you like your cookies with neat edges, freeze before cutting.

—Mary Bohanan, Sparks, NV

PREP: 15 min. • **BAKE:** 30 min. + cooling
MAKES: 3 dozen

- 1 tsp. butter
- 2 cups all-purpose flour
- 1 cup sugar
- ½ tsp. baking soda
- ½ tsp. salt
- ½ cup canola oil
- ¼ cup 2% milk
- 1 jar (28 oz.) prepared mincemeat
- 1 cup chopped pecans

1. Preheat oven to 400°. Line an 8-in. square baking pan with foil; grease foil with butter. In a large bowl, whisk flour, sugar, baking soda and salt. Stir in oil and milk. Reserve 1 cup for topping. Press remaining crumb mixture onto bottom of prepared pan. Spread with mincemeat. Stir pecans into reserved crumb mixture; sprinkle over top. Bake 30-35 minutes or until topping is golden brown.
2. Cool completely in pan on a wire rack. Cut into bars.

MAKE AHEAD
STAINED GLASS CHERRY MACAROONS

Macaroons have been around for ages. I wanted to keep the true cookie but make a neat addition to a family favorite. Be sure the eggs are at room temperature before whisking them.

—Jamie Jones, Madison, GA

PREP: 45 min. • **BAKE:** 15 min./batch
MAKES: about 7 dozen

- 6 large egg whites
- ¾ tsp. vanilla extract
- ½ tsp. salt
- ¾ cup sugar
- 8 cups sweetened shredded coconut (22 oz.)
- ¾ cup finely chopped green candied cherries
- ¾ cup finely chopped red candied cherries
- ⅓ cup all-purpose flour

1. Place egg whites in a large bowl; let stand at room temperature 30 minutes. Preheat oven to 325°. Add vanilla and salt to egg whites; beat on medium speed until foamy. Gradually add sugar, 1 Tbsp. at a time, beating on high after each addition until sugar is dissolved. Continue beating until stiff glossy peaks form. In another bowl, combine coconut, cherries and flour; stir into the egg white mixture.
2. Drop by tablespoonfuls 1 in. apart onto parchment paper-lined baking sheets. Bake 14-16 minutes or until edges are golden. Cool on pans 2 minutes. Remove to wire racks to cool. Store in an airtight container.
Freeze option: Freeze the macaroons, layered between sheets of waxed paper, in freezer containers. To use, thaw in covered containers.

WAFFLE IRON COOKIES

The recipe for these cookies is the easiest to find in my book because it's a beautiful mess. It's covered with fingerprints, flour smudges and memories of more than 30 Christmases! I made these with my daughters, and now I make them with my granddaughters.

—Judy Taylor, Quarryville, PA

PREP: 10 min. • BAKE: 5 min./batch + cooling
MAKES: 32 cookies (8 batches)

½ cup butter, softened
1 cup sugar
2 large eggs
1 tsp. vanilla extract
1½ cups all-purpose flour
1 tsp. baking powder
½ tsp. salt
　　Confectioners' sugar

1. In a large bowl, cream butter and sugar until light and fluffy. Beat in the eggs and vanilla. In another bowl, whisk flour, baking powder and salt; gradually beat into the creamed mixture (mixture will be thick).
2. Working in batches, drop the dough by tablespoonfuls 3-4 in. apart onto a greased, preheated waffle iron. Bake 2-3 minutes or until dark brown.
3. Remove to wire racks to cool completely. Sprinkle with confectioners' sugar.

❄ Holiday Helper

This cookie dough is thicker than a usual waffle batter, and so it's important that you grease the waffle iron to keep the cookies from sticking. You may need to regrease the iron as you cook more batches of cookies.

GRANDMA'S RASPBERRY RUGELACH

I remember sitting down on the couch in my great-grandmother's house with a pad and pen as she told me each ingredient and measurement for her special rugelach. Some of the ingredients are different from the typical version.

—Dalya Rubin, Boca Raton, FL

....

PREP: 45 min. + chilling
BAKE: 25 min./batch + cooling
MAKES: about 5 dozen

1½	cups margarine, softened
⅓	cup sugar
3	tsp. vanilla extract
	Pinch salt
1	cup heavy whipping cream
4	to 4½ cups all-purpose flour
1	cup seedless raspberry jam

OPTIONAL GLAZE

1	cup confectioners' sugar
4	tsp. 2% milk

1. In a large bowl, beat the margarine, sugar, vanilla and salt on medium-low until combined. Slowly beat in whipping cream. Gradually beat in enough flour until dough is no longer sticky. Divide dough into four portions, then flatten into a disk. Wrap in plastic; refrigerate for at least 2 hours or overnight.

2. Preheat the oven to 350°. On a lightly floured surface, roll each portion of dough into a 12-in. circle; spread each circle with ¼ cup of raspberry jam. Cut each circle into 16 wedges.

3. Gently roll up wedges from the wide ends. Place 2 in. apart on parchment-lined baking sheets, point side down. Bake for 25-30 minutes or until light golden, then remove to wire racks to cool.

4. If desired, combine confectioners' sugar and milk until smooth. Drizzle glaze over cooled rugelach.

For Apricot Rugelach: You can substitute apricot filling for the raspberry jam. In a small bowl, combine ½ cup sugar and 1 Tbsp. ground cinnamon. Spread ¼ cup apricot jam over dough; sprinkle with 2 Tbsp. cinnamon sugar, then proceed as directed.

FROSTED TURTLE BROWNIES

Homemade brownies are a sweet addition to any party buffet table or dessert platter—and these brownies, frosted and topped with nuts and caramel, are a step above the ordinary.

—Sherry Miller, Columbia Heights, MN

....

PREP: 20 min. • **BAKE:** 25 min. + chilling
MAKES: 2 dozen

1	cup butter, softened
2	cups sugar
2	tsp. vanilla extract
4	large eggs
1	cup baking cocoa
1	cup all-purpose flour
½	tsp. baking powder
¼	tsp. salt

TOPPING

3	cups confectioners' sugar
¾	cup baking cocoa
½	cup butter, melted
⅓	cup 2% milk
¾	tsp. vanilla extract
1	cup chopped pecans, toasted
12	caramels
1	Tbsp. heavy whipping cream

1. In a large bowl, cream butter and sugar until light and fluffy. Add vanilla extract. Add eggs, one at a time, beating well after each addition. Combine the cocoa, flour, baking powder and salt; gradually add to the butter mixture.

2. Spread into a greased 13x9-in. baking pan. Bake at 350° for 23-28 minutes or until a toothpick inserted in center comes out clean (do not overbake). Cool on a wire rack.

3. In a large bowl, beat the confectioners' sugar, cocoa, butter, milk and vanilla until fluffy. Frost brownies. Sprinkle with pecans. Refrigerate for at least 1 hour.

4. In a microwave, melt caramels with whipping cream; stir until smooth. Drizzle over brownies.

SLICE & BAKE COCONUT SHORTBREAD COOKIES

Light and buttery, these delicate shortbread cookies are melt-in-your-mouth good. The coconut flavor makes them extra special. They were made to nestle beside a teacup.
—Roberta Otto, Duluth, MN

PREP: 15 min. + chilling
BAKE: 20 min./batch + cooling
MAKES: about 4 dozen

- 1 cup butter, softened
- ¾ cup sugar
- 1 tsp. vanilla extract
- 1¾ cups all-purpose flour
- 1 cup sweetened shredded coconut

1. In a large bowl, cream butter and sugar until light and fluffy. Beat in the vanilla. Gradually beat flour into the creamed mixture. Stir in coconut.
2. Using a sheet of waxed paper, shape the dough into a 12x3x1-in. rectangle. Wrap in waxed paper; refrigerate 3 hours or overnight.
3. Preheat oven to 300°. Unwrap dough and cut crosswise into ¼-in. slices. Place 1 in. apart on ungreased baking sheets. Bake 18-20 minutes or until the edges are light golden. Cool on pans 5 minutes. Remove to wire racks to cool.

❄ Holiday Helper

If you prefer a less-sweet cookie, substitute unsweetened coconut for the sweetened shredded coconut called for in the recipe. The result will be less sweet, more crisp—and still delicious!

TOFFEE COFFEE COOKIES

Inspired by my favorite ice cream, I created a cookie with the same great toffee and coffee taste. The toffee bits are a happy surprise.
—Joanne Wright, Niles, MI

PREP: 30 min. • **BAKE:** 20 min./batch
MAKES: 4 dozen

- 3 Tbsp. instant coffee granules
- 1 Tbsp. hot water
- ½ cup butter, softened
- ½ cup shortening
- ¾ cup sugar
- ¾ cup packed brown sugar
- 2 large eggs
- 2 oz. semisweet chocolate, melted
- 1 tsp. vanilla extract
- 3¼ cups all-purpose flour
- 1 tsp. baking soda
- ½ tsp. salt
- 1 cup milk chocolate English toffee bits
- 1 cup 60% cacao bittersweet chocolate baking chips

1. Preheat oven to 350°. In a small bowl, dissolve coffee granules in hot water.
2. In a large bowl, cream butter, shortening and sugars until light and fluffy. Beat in eggs, melted chocolate, vanilla and coffee mixture. In another bowl, whisk the flour, baking soda and salt; gradually beat into creamed mixture. Stir in toffee bits and baking chips.
3. Drop by rounded tablespoonfuls 2 in. apart onto greased baking sheets. Bake 16-18 minutes or until edges are lightly browned. Cool on pans 2 minutes. Remove to wire racks to cool.

WHITE CHOCOLATE MAPLE PECAN MACAROONS

I love macaroons and wanted to give them a different twist—with white chocolate and pecans, two of my favorite ingredients.
—Patricia Harmon, Baden, PA

PREP: 30 min. • **BAKE:** 20 min./batch + cooling
MAKES: 5 dozen

- 2 large egg whites
- ½ cup sugar
- ½ tsp. maple flavoring
- 1⅓ cups flaked coconut
- 1 cup plus 1 pkg. (10 to 12 oz.) white baking chips, divided
- ¾ cup chopped pecans
- 2 tsp. shortening

1. Place egg whites in a large bowl; let stand at room temperature 30 minutes.
2. Preheat oven to 325°. Beat the egg whites on medium speed until foamy. Gradually add sugar, 1 Tbsp. at a time, beating on high after each addition until sugar is dissolved. Beat in maple flavoring. Continue beating until stiff glossy peaks form. Fold in coconut, 1 cup of the baking chips and the pecans.
3. Drop batter by rounded teaspoonfuls 1 in. apart onto parchment paper-lined baking sheets. Bake 18-20 minutes or until firm to the touch. Remove to wire racks to cool completely.
4. In a microwave, melt shortening and the remaining baking chips; stir until smooth. Dip bottoms of macaroons into the melted baking chips, allowing excess to drip off. Place on waxed paper; let stand until set. Store in an airtight container.

HOLIDAY KIPFERL COOKIES

My family has been making classic *kipferl* cookies on the first of December every year since I can remember. During the last two weeks of the month, we make them with the addition of dried cranberries and toasted pecans for Christmas time.

—Brooke Maynard, Poughkeepsie, NY

PREP: 30 min. + chilling
BAKE: 15 min. + cooling • **MAKES:** 4 dozen

- ⅔ cup blanched almonds
- 2 cups all-purpose flour
- ½ cup granulated sugar
- ½ tsp. salt
- ¾ cup plus 2 Tbsp. cold butter, cubed
- 3 large egg yolks
- 2 Tbsp. cold water
- ½ cup chopped pecans, toasted
- ½ cup dried cranberries, chopped
  Confectioners' sugar

1. Pulse almonds in a food processor until finely ground. Add flour, granulated sugar and salt; pulse until combined. Add butter; pulse until the mixture resembles coarse crumbs. In a small bowl, whisk egg yolks and water. Add to almond butter mixture, and pulse until dough forms. Shape dough into a disk; wrap in plastic. Refrigerate until easy to handle, about 1 hour.

2. Preheat oven to 325°. Divide dough into fourths. On a lightly floured surface, roll each portion into an 8-in. circle. Sprinkle with pecans and cranberries; lightly press into dough. Cut each circle into 12 wedges. Roll wedges from the wide end; place point side down 1 in. apart on greased baking sheets. Curve ends to form crescents.

3. Bake for 12-15 minutes, until lightly browned. Carefully roll warm cookies in confectioners' sugar. Cool on wire racks. Sprinkle with additional confectioners' sugar. Store in an airtight container.

Note: To toast nuts, bake in a shallow pan in a 350° oven for 5-10 minutes or cook in a skillet over low heat until lightly browned, stirring occasionally.

RUSTIC NUT BARS

My friends love crunching into the crust, so much like shortbread, and the wildly nutty topping on these chewy, gooey bars.
—Barbara Driscoll, West Allis, WI

....

PREP: 20 min. • **BAKE:** 35 min. + cooling
MAKES: about 3 dozen

- 1 Tbsp. plus ¾ cup cold butter, divided
- 2⅓ cups all-purpose flour
- ½ cup sugar
- ½ tsp. baking powder
- ½ tsp. salt
- 1 large egg, lightly beaten

TOPPING

- ⅔ cup honey
- ½ cup packed brown sugar
- ¼ tsp. salt
- 6 Tbsp. butter, cubed
- 2 Tbsp. heavy whipping cream
- 1 cup chopped hazelnuts, toasted
- 1 cup salted cashews
- 1 cup pistachios
- 1 cup salted roasted almonds

1. Preheat oven to 375°. Line a 13x9-in. baking pan with foil, letting the ends extend over the sides by 1 in. Grease foil with 1 Tbsp. butter.

2. Whisk flour, sugar, baking powder and salt. Cut in remaining butter until mixture resembles coarse crumbs. Stir in egg until blended (mixture will be dry). Press firmly onto bottom of prepared pan.

3. Bake 18-20 minutes or until edges are golden brown. Cool on a wire rack.

4. In a large heavy saucepan, combine honey, brown sugar and salt; bring to a boil over medium heat, stirring frequently to dissolve the sugar. Let boil for 2 minutes without stirring. Stir in butter and cream; return to a boil. Cook and stir 1 minute or until smooth. Remove from heat; stir in nuts. Spread over crust.

5. Bake 15-20 minutes or until topping is bubbly. Cool completely in pan on a wire rack. Lifting with foil, remove from pan. Discard foil; cut into bars.

Note: To toast nuts, bake in a shallow pan in a 350° oven for 5-10 minutes or cook in a skillet over low heat until lightly browned, stirring occasionally.

KIPPLENS

My Great-Aunt Hilda makes these cookies every Christmas, and everybody loves them! Kipplens taste a lot like Mexican wedding cakes, but I like my aunt's version better.

—Susan Bohannon, Kokomo, IN

PREP: 15 min. • **BAKE:** 20 min./batch
MAKES: 12 dozen

- 2   cups butter, softened
- 1   cup sugar
- 2   tsp. vanilla extract
- 5   cups all-purpose flour
- 2   cups chopped pecans
- ¼   tsp. salt
      Confectioners' sugar

1. In a large bowl, cream butter and sugar until light and fluffy; beat in vanilla. Add flour, pecans and salt; mix well. Roll dough into 1-in. balls and place on ungreased baking sheets.
2. Bake at 325° for 17-20 minutes or until lightly browned. Cool the cookies slightly before rolling them in confectioners' sugar.

❄ Reader Review

"My grandmother used to make these all the time when I was a kid! They are so simple to make and the dough can be made and tossed in the fridge for a quick batch later. My husband calls these the Warm Cloud Cookies. Heavenly!"

FLORIDAYSGIRL TASTEOFHOME.COM

MAKE AHEAD
MEXICAN CHOCOLATE SUGAR CRISPS

My grandma loved these so much, she would hide them from my grandpa! I think of her every time I make a batch. If you like Mexican spice, try stirring in a little chili powder.

—Michele Lovio, Thousand Oaks, CA

PREP: 30 min. • **BAKE:** 10 min./batch
MAKES: 4½ dozen

- ¾   cup shortening
- 1¼   cups sugar, divided
- 1   large egg
- ¼   cup light corn syrup
- 2   oz. unsweetened chocolate, melted and cooled
- 1¾   cups all-purpose flour
- 1½   tsp. ground cinnamon
- 1   tsp. baking soda
- ¼   tsp. salt
- 1   cup semisweet chocolate chips

1. Preheat oven to 350°. In a large bowl, cream shortening and 1 cup sugar until fluffy. Beat in egg, corn syrup and melted chocolate. In another bowl, whisk flour, cinnamon, baking soda and salt; gradually beat into creamed mixture. Stir in the chocolate chips.
2. Shape dough into 1-in. balls; roll in the remaining sugar. Place cookies 2 in. apart on ungreased baking sheets (don't flatten). Bake 8-10 minutes or until tops are puffed and cracked. Cool on pans for 2 minutes. Remove to wire racks to cool.
To make ahead: Dough can be made 2 days in advance. Wrap in plastic and place in an airtight container. Store in the refrigerator.
Freeze option: Freeze shaped balls of dough on baking sheets until firm. Transfer to an airtight container; return to freezer. To use, bake cookies as directed.

SNICKERDOODLE BLONDIE BARS

As an alternative to brownies, these bars offer a different take on a classic cookie favorite. When I whipped them up for my boys, I was instantly named the greatest mom!

—Valonda Seward, Coarsegold, CA

PREP: 15 min. • BAKE: 35 min. + cooling
MAKES: 20 bars

- 1 cup butter, softened
- 2 cups packed brown sugar
- 3 tsp. vanilla extract
- 2 large eggs
- 2⅔ cups all-purpose flour
- 2 tsp. baking powder
- 1 tsp. ground cinnamon
- ¼ tsp. ground nutmeg
- ½ tsp. salt

TOPPING

- 1½ tsp. sugar
- ½ tsp. ground cinnamon

1. Preheat oven to 350°. Cream butter and brown sugar until light and fluffy. Beat in vanilla and eggs, one at a time. In another bowl, whisk together flour, baking powder, spices and salt; gradually beat into the creamed mixture. Spread into a greased 9-in. square baking pan.
2. Mix topping ingredients; sprinkle over the top. Bake until set and golden brown, 35-40 minutes. Cool completely in pan on a wire rack. Cut into bars.

❄ Holiday Helper

If you prefer thinner bars, prepare the recipe as directed, but spread the batter in a 13x9-in. greased baking pan instead. Decrease baking time to 25-30 minutes.

MAKE AHEAD
CHOCOLATE-FILLED COOKIES WITH PEPPERMINT FROSTING

Baking is one of the things I enjoy most about Christmas. These special cookies draw you in with candy-topped frosting and seal the deal with a chocolate center.

—Deborah Puette, Lilburn, GA

PREP: 35 min. + chilling
BAKE: 10 min. + cooling
MAKES: about 2 dozen

- ⅔ cup shortening
- 1 cup granulated sugar
- 1 large egg
- 1¾ cups all-purpose flour
- ½ tsp. baking powder
- ½ tsp. baking soda
- ½ tsp. salt
- 2 milk chocolate candy bars (1.55 oz. each)

FROSTING

- 2 cups confectioners' sugar
- 2 Tbsp. unsalted butter, melted
- ¼ tsp. peppermint extract
- 3 to 4 Tbsp. evaporated milk
- 24 miniature candy canes, crushed

1. Cream the shortening and granulated sugar until light and fluffy. Beat in egg. In another bowl, whisk the flour, baking powder, baking soda and salt; gradually beat into the creamed mixture.

2. Divide dough in half. Shape each into a disk and wrap in plastic. Refrigerate until firm enough to roll, about 30 minutes.
3. Preheat oven to 350°. Break each candy bar into 12 pieces. On a lightly floured surface, roll each portion of dough to ⅛-in. thickness. Cut with a floured 2-in. square cookie cutter. Place half of the squares 2 in. apart on ungreased baking sheets. Place a chocolate piece in the center of each square; cover with the remaining squares, pressing edges to seal.
4. Bake until edges are golden brown, 9-11 minutes. Remove from pans to wire racks to cool completely.
5. For frosting, combine confectioners' sugar, butter, extract and enough milk to reach a spreading consistency. Spread over the cookies; sprinkle with crushed candy canes.

To make ahead: Dough can be made 2 days in advance. Wrap in plastic and place in an airtight container. Refrigerate.
Freeze option: Place wrapped dough in an airtight container and freeze. If necessary, let dough stand for 15 minutes at room temperature before cutting. Prepare and bake cookies as directed. Iced cookies can be frozen up to 1 month.

PAINTED TREAT TINS

Paint and embellish old tins to create shiny new containers for cookies, candies and gifts! Set each tin and lid on a disposable paper cup to elevate it while painting and drying. Use spray paint to cover the metal, spraying in light layers until the tin is covered. You can even add stripes if you like; first paint the whole tin the color you want the stripes to be. When the paint is dry, use blue painter's tape to mark out the stripes and apply a second, contrasting color of paint, then remove the tape. Embellish the tins with tags, ribbons or decorative cord—whatever you like!

BLACK WALNUT LAYER
CAKE, PAGE 218

TRULY

HEAVENLY DESSERTS

BLACK WALNUT LAYER CAKE

My sister gave me this recipe years ago, and everyone seems to love it!

—Lynn Glaze, Warren, OH

PREP: 25 min. • **BAKE:** 20 min. + cooling
MAKES: 16 servings

- ½ cup butter, softened
- ½ cup shortening
- 2 cups sugar
- 2 tsp. vanilla extract
- 4 large eggs
- 3¾ cups all-purpose flour
- 2 tsp. baking soda
- ½ tsp. salt
- 1½ cups buttermilk
- 1¼ cups finely chopped black or English walnuts

FROSTING
- ½ cup butter, softened
- 1 pkg. (8 oz.) cream cheese, softened
- 1 tsp. vanilla extract
- 4½ cups confectioners' sugar
- 1 to 3 Tbsp. buttermilk
  Additional black walnuts

1. Preheat oven to 350°. Line the bottoms of three greased 9-in. round baking pans with parchment paper; grease paper.
2. Cream butter, shortening and sugar until light and fluffy. Add vanilla and eggs, one at a time, beating well after each addition. In another bowl, whisk together flour, baking soda and salt; add to creamed mixture alternately with buttermilk, beating after each addition. Fold in walnuts.
3. Transfer to prepared pans. Bake until a toothpick inserted in center comes out clean, 20-25 minutes. Cool in pans 10 minutes before removing to wire racks; remove paper. Cool completely.
4. Beat butter and cream cheese until smooth. Beat in vanilla. Gradually beat in confectioners' sugar and enough of the buttermilk to reach spreading consistency.
5. Spread 1 cup frosting between each layer and 1 cup on top of cake. Spread the remaining frosting in a thin layer over sides of cake. Top with the additional walnuts.

YULETIDE EGGNOG CUPCAKES

If I want a creamier frosting on these, I add more eggnog. The nog lovers in your life won't complain!

—Salina Moore, Woodward, OK

PREP: 30 min. • **BAKE:** 20 min. + cooling
MAKES: 2 dozen

- 4 large eggs, separated
- ⅔ cup butter, softened
- 1½ cups sugar, divided
- 2⅓ cups all-purpose flour
- 3 tsp. baking powder
- ½ tsp. ground nutmeg
- ¼ tsp. salt
- 1 cup eggnog

FROSTING
- 1 pkg. (8 oz.) cream cheese, softened
- ¼ cup butter, softened
- 3¾ cups confectioners' sugar
- 2 Tbsp. eggnog
  Freshly grated or additional ground nutmeg

1. Place egg whites in a large bowl; let stand at room temperature 30 minutes. Preheat oven to 350°. Line 24 muffin cups with paper liners.
2. In a large bowl, cream the butter and 1¼ cups sugar until light and fluffy. Add egg yolks, one at a time, beating well after each addition. In another bowl, whisk flour, baking powder, nutmeg and salt; add to the creamed mixture alternately with eggnog, beating well after each addition.
3. With clean beaters, beat the egg whites on medium speed until soft peaks form. Gradually add remaining sugar, 1 Tbsp. at a time, beating on high after each addition until sugar is dissolved. Continue beating until stiff glossy peaks form. Fold into the cupcake batter.
4. Fill the prepared muffin cups three-fourths full. Bake 18-22 minutes or until a toothpick inserted in center comes out clean. Cool in pans for 10 minutes before removing to wire racks to cool completely.
5. For frosting, in a large bowl, beat cream cheese and butter until blended. Gradually beat in confectioners' sugar and eggnog until smooth. Frost cupcakes. Sprinkle with nutmeg. Refrigerate leftovers.

CRANBERRY-ORANGE CAKE WITH LEMON GLAZE

I used cranberries in some decorations for a wedding, then challenged myself to find a way to use the surplus. This super moist cake was the result! It's even better on the second day.
—S. Jade Klope, Paducah, KY

PREP: 55 min. + cooling
BAKE: 45 min. + cooling • **MAKES:** 12 servings

- 1 pkg. (12 oz.) fresh or frozen cranberries
- 1½ cups sugar
- ½ cup butter, softened
- 1½ cups packed brown sugar
- 3 large eggs
- ⅓ cup unsweetened applesauce
- 1¾ cups all-purpose flour
- 3 tsp. baking powder
- ½ tsp. cream of tartar
- ¼ tsp. salt
- ⅔ cup orange juice

GLAZE

- ⅔ cup confectioners' sugar
- 2 Tbsp. butter, melted
- 4 tsp. lemon juice

1. Preheat oven to 350°. Place cranberries in a 15x10-in. baking pan; sprinkle with sugar. Bake berries until soft and bubbly, 35-45 minutes, stirring occasionally. Cool to room temperature.

2. Grease and flour a 10-in. fluted tube pan. In a bowl, beat butter and brown sugar until crumbly. Add eggs, one at a time, beating well after each addition. Beat in applesauce. In another bowl, whisk flour, baking powder, cream of tartar and salt; add to creamed mixture alternately with orange juice, beating well after each addition. Stir in the cooled cranberries.

3. Transfer batter to the prepared pan. Bake until a toothpick inserted in the center comes out with moist crumbs, 45-55 minutes. Cool in pan 15 minutes before inverting onto a serving plate.

4. Mix confectioners' sugar, butter and lemon juice until smooth. Brush over cake. Cool cake completely. Top with sugared cranberries (recipe at right).

MAKING SUGARED CRANBERRIES

Mix 2 Tbsp. water and 1 Tbsp. egg substitute with 12 oz. fresh cranberries. Place on a baking pan and sprinkle with 1 cup superfine sugar. Transfer to a wire rack; let stand at room temperature until dry, about 2 hours. When sprinkling the sugar on the cranberries, don't worry about completely coating the berries. Allowing the red berry to peek through adds to the festive look.

For another method for sugared cranberries, see the recipe for Amaretto Ricotta Cheesecake, page 238.

ELF CUPCAKES

These rich and buttery vanilla cupcakes make a perfect base for these whimsical elves.
—*Taste of Home* Test Kitchen

PREP: 45 min. • **BAKE:** 15 min. + cooling
MAKES: 22 cupcakes

- ⅔ cup butter, softened
- 1¾ cups sugar
- 1½ tsp. vanilla extract
- 2 large eggs
- 2½ cups all-purpose flour
- 2½ tsp. baking powder
- ½ tsp. salt
- 1¼ cups 2% milk

FROSTING
- ¾ cup butter, softened
- ¾ cup shortening
- 1½ tsp. clear vanilla extract
- 6 cups confectioners' sugar
- 4 to 6 Tbsp. 2% milk

DECORATIONS
- 44 miniature candy canes
  - Pastel miniature marshmallows
  - Candy cane kisses

1. Preheat oven to 350°. Line 22 muffin cups with paper liners. Cream butter and sugar until light and fluffy. Beat in vanilla and eggs, one at a time. In another bowl, whisk together flour, baking powder and salt; add to creamed mixture alternately with milk, beating well.
2. Fill the prepared cups two-thirds full. Bake until a toothpick inserted in center comes out clean, 15-20 minutes. Cool in pans 10 minutes before removing to wire racks to cool completely.
3. Beat butter, shortening and vanilla until blended; gradually beat in confectioners' sugar and enough milk to reach spreading consistency. Spread over cupcakes.
4. Break off curved end of candy canes; use straight portions for legs. Cut pink and green marshmallows diagonally in half and attach to legs for shoes; insert legs into frosting. Cut orange marshmallows diagonally in half for ears. Insert kisses and orange marshmallows for heads.

CARAMEL FLUFF & TOFFEE TRIFLE

The best part of this delicious dessert is you need just five ingredients to put it together.
—Daniel Anderson, Kenosha, WI

PREP: 15 min. + chilling • **MAKES:** 12 servings

- 2 cups heavy whipping cream
- ¾ cup packed brown sugar
- 1 tsp. vanilla extract
- 1 prepared angel food cake (8 to 10 oz.), cut into 1-in. cubes
- 1 cup milk chocolate English toffee bits

1. In a large bowl, beat cream, brown sugar and vanilla just until blended. Refrigerate, covered, for 20 minutes. Beat until stiff peaks form.
2. In a 4-qt. glass bowl, layer one-third of each of the following: cake cubes, whipped cream and toffee bits. Repeat layers twice. Refrigerate until serving.

❄ Holiday Helper

Trifle bowls traditionally have straight, vertical sides, to help with the construction of the dessert, and are made of clear glass, to show off the beautiful layers. A trifle bowl is no single-purpose space hog, though; when you're not serving a trifle, the bowl makes a great container for a decorative centerpiece, and it also makes a beautiful fruit bowl.

MAKE AHEAD

CHOCOLATE HAZELNUT PUDDING TORTE

This recipe is a busy mom's twist on one of my favorite desserts—tiramisu. It's great to make the day before you want to serve it. The hardest thing about this recipe is waiting for it to chill so you can eat it!

—Cheryl Snavely, Hagerstown, MD

PREP: 15 min. + chilling • **MAKES:** 8 servings

- 24 soft ladyfingers
- ½ cup Nutella
- 1½ cups half-and-half cream
- 1 pkg. (3.4 oz.) instant French vanilla pudding mix
- 1 carton (12 oz.) frozen whipped topping, thawed
  Grated or shaved chocolate

1. Arrange 12 ladyfingers in an 11x7-in. dish. Spread with half of the Nutella.
2. In a large bowl, whisk the cream and pudding mix for 2 minutes. Stir in whipped topping. Spread half of the mixture over the Nutella. Top with remaining ladyfingers; spread with the remaining Nutella and top with the remaining pudding mixture. Sprinkle with grated or shaved chocolate. Refrigerate, covered, 8 hours or overnight. Refrigerate leftovers.

MAKE AHEAD

CANDY CANE PIE

When my college roommate first made this pie, I couldn't get enough! The store-bought crust saves time when you're in the midst of the holidays.

—Charlotte Stewart, Mesa, AZ

PREP: 15 min. + chilling • **MAKES:** 8 servings

- 24 large marshmallows
- ½ cup whole milk
- 1 tsp. vanilla extract
- ⅛ tsp. salt
- 6 drops peppermint extract
- 6 drops red food coloring
- 2 Tbsp. plus 1 tsp. crushed peppermint candy, divided
- 1 cup heavy whipping cream, whipped
- 1 chocolate crumb crust (8 in.)

1. In a heavy saucepan, combine the marshmallows and milk. Cook and stir over low heat until marshmallows are melted and mixture is smooth. Remove from heat.
2. Stir in vanilla, salt, peppermint extract and food coloring. Cool 30 minutes, stirring several times. Stir in 2 Tbsp. of the crushed candies; fold in whipped cream.
3. Spoon into crust. Refrigerate, covered, 8 hours or overnight. Just before serving, sprinkle with remaining candy.

SPIKED EGGNOG BREAD PUDDING

With a little imagination, I transformed my family's favorite holiday drink into a delightful dessert. If I have leftover eggnog, I use it here.
—Marie Bruno, Greensboro, GA

PREP: 10 min. + standing • **BAKE:** 40 min.
MAKES: 8 servings

  2 Tbsp. butter, softened
  8 large eggs, lightly beaten
  2 cups eggnog
  ¼ cup sugar
  ¼ cup rum or ½ tsp. rum extract plus
     2 Tbsp. eggnog
  3 Tbsp. butter, melted
1½ tsp. baking powder
  ½ tsp. ground nutmeg, divided
 10 cups cubed day-old egg bread or challah
     (about 12 oz.)
     Sweetened whipped cream, optional

1. Generously grease bottom and sides of an 11x7-in. baking dish with softened butter. In a large bowl, whisk eggs, eggnog, sugar, rum, melted butter, baking powder and ¼ tsp. nutmeg until blended. Stir in bread; let stand 30 minutes. Preheat the oven to 350°.

2. Transfer bread mixture to prepared dish; sprinkle with remaining nutmeg. Bake for 40-45 minutes or until puffed and golden brown and a knife inserted in center comes out clean. Serve warm; if desired, top with whipped cream.

Note: This recipe was tested with commercially prepared eggnog.

LEMONY WALNUT-RAISIN GALETTE

This flaky, buttery pastry dessert has a filling of fruit, walnuts, coconut and cinnamon. There's a lot to love! For even more appeal, dollop sweetened whipped cream on each serving.
—Ellen Kozak, Milwaukee, WI

PREP: 30 min. • **BAKE:** 30 min. + cooling
MAKES: 10 servings

- 1 medium lemon
- 1 cup finely chopped walnuts
- 1 cup raisins
- 1 cup apricot spreadable fruit
- ⅔ cup unsweetened finely shredded coconut
- 2 tsp. ground cinnamon
- 8 sheets phyllo dough (14x9-in. size)
- ⅓ cup butter, melted
  Sweetened whipped cream, optional

1. Preheat oven to 350°. Cut unpeeled lemon into eight wedges; remove seeds. Place wedges in a food processor; process until finely chopped. Transfer to a large bowl; stir in walnuts, raisins, spreadable fruit, coconut and cinnamon.
2. Place one sheet of phyllo dough on a parchment paper-lined baking sheet; brush with butter. Layer with remaining phyllo sheets, brushing each layer. (Keep the remaining phyllo covered with plastic wrap and a damp towel to prevent it from drying out.)
3. Spoon filling onto the center of the phyllo, leaving a 2-in. border on all sides. Fold edges of phyllo over filling, leaving center uncovered. Brush folded edges with butter. Bake 30-35 minutes or until golden brown. Using parchment paper, carefully slide galette onto a wire rack to cool slightly. If desired, serve with whipped cream.
Note: Look for unsweetened coconut in the baking, bulk or health food section.

FLOURLESS CHOCOLATE TORTE

Here's the perfect dessert for chocoholics like me! I bake this melt-in-your-mouth torte all the time for special occasions. For an elegant finish, dust it with confectioners' sugar.
—Kayla Albrecht, Freeport, IL

PREP: 20 min. • **BAKE:** 40 min. + cooling
MAKES: 12 servings

- 5 large eggs, separated
- 12 oz. semisweet chocolate, chopped
- ¾ cup butter, cubed
- ¼ tsp. cream of tartar
- ½ cup sugar
  Confectioners' sugar, optional

1. Place egg whites in a large bowl; let stand at room temperature 30 minutes. Preheat the oven to 350°. In the top of a double boiler or in a metal bowl over barely simmering water, melt the chocolate and butter; stir until smooth. Remove from heat; cool slightly.
2. In another large bowl, beat egg yolks until thick and lemon-colored. Beat in the chocolate mixture. With clean beaters, beat the egg whites and cream of tartar on medium speed until foamy.
3. Gradually add sugar, 1 Tbsp. at a time, beating on high after each addition until sugar is dissolved. Continue beating until stiff glossy peaks form. Fold a fourth of the egg whites into the chocolate mixture, then fold in the remaining whites.
4. Transfer to a greased 9-in. springform pan. Bake for 40-45 minutes or until a toothpick inserted in center comes out with moist crumbs (do not overbake). Cool completely on a wire rack.
5. Loosen sides from pan with a knife. Remove rim from pan. If desired, dust with confectioners' sugar.

SANDY'S CHOCOLATE CAKE

Years ago, I drove several hours to a cake contest, holding my entry on my lap the whole way. It paid off. One bite and you'll see why this velvety beauty won first prize.

—Sandy Johnson, Tioga, PA

PREP: 30 min. • BAKE: 30 min. + cooling
MAKES: 16 servings

- 1 cup butter, softened
- 3 cups packed brown sugar
- 4 large eggs
- 2 tsp. vanilla extract
- 2⅔ cups all-purpose flour
- ¾ cup baking cocoa
- 3 tsp. baking soda
- ½ tsp. salt
- 1⅓ cups sour cream
- 1⅓ cups boiling water

FROSTING
- ½ cup butter, cubed
- 3 oz. unsweetened chocolate, chopped
- 3 oz. semisweet chocolate, chopped
- 5 cups confectioners' sugar
- 1 cup sour cream
- 2 tsp. vanilla extract

1. Preheat oven to 350°. Grease and flour three 9-in. round baking pans.

2. In a large bowl, cream butter and brown sugar until light and fluffy. Add eggs, one at a time, beating well after each addition. Beat in vanilla. In another bowl, whisk flour, cocoa, baking soda and salt; add to the creamed mixture alternately with sour cream, beating well after each addition. Stir in water until blended. Transfer to the prepared pans. Bake until a toothpick comes out clean, 30-35 minutes. Cool in pans 10 minutes; remove to wire racks to cool completely.

3. For the frosting, in a metal bowl over simmering water, melt butter and both chocolates; stir until smooth. Cool slightly.

4. In a large bowl, combine confectioners' sugar, sour cream and vanilla. Add the chocolate mixture; beat until smooth. Spread frosting between layers and over top and sides of cake. Refrigerate leftovers.

❄ Reader Review

"This recipe is amazing and makes a large cake. Very moist and dense. Be prepared and have some cake lovers ready to help eat it! This will forever be my chocolate cake recipe!"

SARAH TASTEOFHOME.COM

CRANBERRY-FILLED ORANGE POUND CAKE

I made this for a holiday dinner with my family. Everyone loved the cran-orange flavor and the sweet glaze. For a fun variation, add ⅔ cup flaked sweetened coconut when adding the orange juice to the batter, and sprinkle the finished cake with toasted coconut.

—Patricia Harmon, Baden, PA

PREP: 25 min. • BAKE: 50 min. + cooling
MAKES: 12 servings

- 1   cup butter, softened
- 1   pkg. (8 oz.) reduced-fat cream cheese
- 2   cups sugar
- 6   large eggs
- 3   Tbsp. orange juice, divided
- 4   tsp. grated orange zest
- 3   cups all-purpose flour
- 1   tsp. baking powder
- ½   tsp. baking soda
- ½   tsp. salt
- 1   can (14 oz.) whole-berry cranberry sauce
- ½   cup dried cherries

GLAZE
- 1   cup confectioners' sugar
- ¼   tsp. grated orange zest
- 4   to 5 tsp. orange juice

1. Preheat oven to 350°. Grease and flour a 10-in. fluted tube pan.
2. In a large bowl, cream the butter, cream cheese and sugar until light and fluffy. Add eggs, one at a time, beating well after each addition. Beat in 2 Tbsp. orange juice and zest. In another bowl, whisk flour, baking powder, baking soda and salt; gradually add to the creamed mixture, beating just until combined.
3. In a small bowl, mix cranberry sauce, dried cherries and remaining orange juice. Spoon two-thirds of batter into prepared pan. Spread with cranberry mixture. Top with remaining batter.
4. Bake 50-60 minutes or until a toothpick inserted in center comes out clean. Loosen sides from pan with a knife. Cool in pan for 10 minutes before removing to a wire rack to cool completely.

5. In a small bowl, mix confectioners' sugar, orange zest and enough orange juice to achieve the desired consistency. Pour the glaze over top of cake, allowing some to flow over sides.

MILE-HIGH CRANBERRY MERINGUE PIE

Your holiday crowd will be blown away when they see this pie with towering meringue on top. Let it sit in your refrigerator for at least four hours for best results.

—Marcia Whitney, Gainesville, FL

PREP: 1 hour • BAKE: 25 min. + chilling
MAKES: 8 servings

- 4   large eggs, separated
      Pastry for single-crust pie (9 in.)
- 4   cups fresh or frozen cranberries, thawed
- 2¼ cups sugar, divided
- ¾   cup water
- 2   Tbsp. all-purpose flour
- ¼   tsp. salt
- 2   Tbsp. butter
- 2   tsp. vanilla extract, divided
- ½   tsp. cream of tartar

1. Preheat oven to 425°. Let egg whites stand 30 minutes at room temperature.
2. On a lightly floured surface, roll dough to a ⅛-in.-thick circle; transfer to a 9-in. pie plate. Trim pastry to ½ in. beyond rim of plate; flute edge. Refrigerate 30 minutes.
3. Line unpricked pastry with a double thickness of foil. Fill with pie weights, dried beans or uncooked rice. Bake on a lower oven rack 15-20 minutes or until edges are light golden brown. Remove foil and weights; bake 3-6 minutes longer or until the bottom is golden brown. Cool on a wire rack. Reduce heat to 325°.
4. In a large saucepan, combine the cranberries, 1½ cups sugar and water. Bring to a boil, stirring to dissolve sugar. Reduce heat to medium; cook, uncovered, 4-6 minutes or until berries stop popping, stirring occasionally. Remove from heat. In a small bowl, whisk yolks, ¼ cup sugar, flour and salt until blended. Gradually whisk in ½ cup of the hot cranberry liquid; return all to saucepan, stirring constantly. Bring to a gentle boil; cook and stir for 2 minutes. Remove from heat; stir in the butter and 1 tsp. vanilla.
5. For meringue, beat the egg whites with cream of tartar and the remaining vanilla on medium speed until foamy. Add the remaining sugar, 1 Tbsp. at a time, beating on high after each addition until sugar is dissolved. Continue beating until stiff glossy peaks form. Transfer hot filling to pastry. Spread meringue evenly over hot filling, sealing to the edge of pastry. Bake for 25-30 minutes or until the meringue is golden brown. Cool 1 hour on a wire rack. Refrigerate at least 4 hours before serving.

Pastry for single-crust pie (9 in.): Combine 1¼ cups all-purpose flour and ¼ tsp. salt; cut in ½ cup cold butter until crumbly. Gradually add 3-5 Tbsp. ice water, tossing with a fork until dough holds together when pressed. Wrap in plastic and refrigerate for 1 hour.

❄ Holiday Helper

To keep meringue from getting beads of moisture on top, try not to make a meringue on a humid day, since the sugar absorbs moisture and excess moisture may cause beading. Also, be certain the sugar is completely dissolved during beating. Rub a small amount between your fingers—if it's grainy, continue to beat.

MAKE AHEAD

CHOCOLATE GINGERBREAD YULE LOG

If you've tasted a yule log sponge cake, you'll love this version with fresh ginger and spices. This holiday stunner can be made ahead.

—Lauren Knoelke, Milwaukee, WI

PREP: 1¼ hours • **BAKE:** 10 min. + cooling
MAKES: 16 servings

- 5 large eggs, separated
- ¾ cup cake flour
- 1 to 1½ tsp. each ground ginger and cinnamon
- ¼ tsp. each ground nutmeg and pepper
- ¼ tsp. salt
- ⅓ cup packed dark brown sugar
- ¼ cup molasses
- 2 Tbsp. canola oil
- 1 Tbsp. grated fresh gingerroot
- ⅛ tsp. cream of tartar
- ¼ cup sugar
  Baking cocoa

FILLING
- 1 carton (8 oz.) mascarpone cheese
- ⅓ cup confectioners' sugar
- 2 Tbsp. heavy whipping cream
- ⅛ tsp. salt
- ⅓ cup crystallized ginger, dried cranberries or miniature semisweet chocolate chips

CHOCOLATE BARK
- 4 to 6 oz. high-quality bittersweet chocolate, melted

BUTTERCREAM
- 2 large egg whites
- ½ cup sugar
- ⅛ tsp. salt
- ¾ cup unsalted butter, softened
- 4 oz. high-quality milk chocolate, melted and cooled

1. Place egg whites in a large bowl; let stand at room temperature 30 minutes. Preheat oven to 350°. Line bottom of a greased 15x10x1-in. baking pan with parchment paper; grease paper. Sift flour, spices and salt together twice.

2. In a large bowl, beat egg yolks until slightly thickened. Gradually add brown sugar, beating on high speed until thick. Beat in molasses, oil and fresh ginger. Fold in flour mixture (batter will be thick).

3. Add cream of tartar to egg whites; with clean beaters, beat on medium until soft peaks form. Gradually add sugar, 1 Tbsp. at a time, beating after each addition until sugar is dissolved. Beat on high until stiff glossy peaks form. Using a large whisk, fold a fourth of the whites into batter, then fold in the remaining whites. Transfer to the prepared pan, spreading evenly.

4. Bake 10-12 minutes or until top springs back when lightly touched. Cool 5 minutes. Invert onto a tea towel dusted with cocoa. Gently peel off the paper. Roll up cake in the towel jelly-roll style. Cool completely on a wire rack.

5. For filling, mix the mascarpone cheese, confectioners' sugar, cream and salt just until blended; stir in ginger. Refrigerate, covered, while preparing chocolate bark and buttercream.

6. For the bark, line the underside of a 15x10x1-in. baking pan with parchment paper. Using an offset spatula, spread melted chocolate in a thin, even layer.

❄ Holiday Helper

Boost the flavor of your filling with dried cranberries, mini chocolate chips or crystallized ginger—or a combination of any or all of them. You'll need about ⅓ cup of added ingredients to balance the frosting.

Refrigerate until set, about 30 minutes.

7. For buttercream, place egg whites, sugar and salt in a heatproof bowl; whisk until blended. Place bowl over simmering water in a large saucepan over medium heat. Whisking constantly, heat until a thermometer reads 160°, 1-2 minutes.

8. Remove from heat. With the whisk attachment of a hand mixer, beat on high speed until stiff glossy peaks form and mixture has cooled, about 5 minutes. Gradually beat in butter, 2-3 Tbsp. at a time, on medium speed until smooth. Beat in the cooled chocolate.

9. To assemble, unroll cake; spread filling over cake to within ¼ in. of edges. Roll up again, without towel; trim ends. Transfer to a platter. Spread buttercream over cake.

10. To add bark, lift chilled chocolate with fingers and break carefully into shards; arrange over the buttercream, overlapping slightly. If the chocolate becomes too soft, return to refrigerator as necessary.

11. Refrigerate cake, loosely covered, until ready to serve. Using a serrated knife, cut cake into slices.

Freeze option: Prepare and decorate cake as directed; freeze 2 hours or until firm. Wrap cake in several layers of plastic. Return to freezer; freeze for up to 1 week. To serve, partially thaw wrapped cake in refrigerator overnight. Carefully remove plastic; let cake stand at room temperature 15-30 minutes before serving.

CRANBERRY APPLE-NUT PIE

Wedges of this tangy Christmas-red pie are a feast for the eyes and the taste buds.
—Peggy Burdick, Burlington, MI

PREP: 20 min. • **BAKE:** 45 min. + cooling
MAKES: 8 servings

- 2 cups fresh or frozen cranberries, chopped
- 1¾ cups sliced peeled tart apples
- ½ cup slivered almonds, toasted
- 1 Tbsp. grated orange zest
- 1¾ cups sugar
- ¼ cup all-purpose flour
- ½ tsp. ground cinnamon
- ½ tsp. ground nutmeg
- ⅛ tsp. salt
  Pastry for double-crust pie (9 in.)
- 2 Tbsp. butter, melted

1. Preheat oven to 400°. Combine the cranberries, apples, almonds and orange zest. In another bowl, mix sugar, flour, cinnamon, nutmeg and salt; add to the fruit mixture and toss gently.

2. On a lightly floured surface, roll one half of dough to a ⅛-in.-thick circle; transfer to a 9-in. pie plate. Trim pastry even with rim. Add filling. Drizzle with butter. Roll the remaining dough to a ⅛-in.-thick circle. Place over filling. Trim, seal and flute edge. Cut slits in top.

3. Bake until crust is golden brown and filling is bubbly, 45-50 minutes. Cool on a wire rack.

Pastry for double-crust pie (9 in.): Combine 2½ cups all-purpose flour and ½ tsp. salt; cut in 1 cup cold butter until crumbly. Gradually add ⅓-⅔ cup ice water, tossing with a fork until dough holds together when pressed. Divide dough in half. Shape each into a disk; wrap in plastic. Refrigerate for 1 hour or overnight.

MERINGUE SNOWBALLS IN CUSTARD

My family has passed down this elegant dessert for generations. It started with my Russian great-grandmother, who traveled to America more than 100 years ago. I love continuing the tradition with her recipe.
—Tonya Burkhard, Palm Coast, FL

PREP: 5 min. • **COOK:** 20 min. + chilling
MAKES: 12 servings

- 4 large egg whites
- 4 large egg yolks plus 2 large eggs
- 1½ cups sugar, divided
- 1 Tbsp. cornstarch
- 6¼ cups whole milk, divided
- 2 tsp. vanilla extract, divided
- ½ tsp. cream of tartar
  Chopped glazed pecans, optional

1. Place egg whites in a large bowl; let stand at room temperature 30 minutes. In a large heavy saucepan, whisk egg yolks, eggs, 1 cup sugar and the cornstarch until blended; stir in 4 cups of milk. Cook over medium-low heat 10-15 minutes or until mixture is just thick enough to coat a metal spoon and a thermometer reads at least 160°. Stir constantly; do not allow mixture to boil. Remove from heat immediately. Strain through a fine-mesh strainer into a large bowl.

2. Place bowl in an ice-water bath. Stir occasionally for 5 minutes. Stir in 1½ tsp. vanilla. Press waxed paper onto surface of custard. Refrigerate until cold, about 1 hour.

3. For snowballs, add cream of tartar to the egg whites; beat on medium speed until foamy. Gradually add the remaining sugar, 1 Tbsp. at a time, beating on high after each addition until sugar is dissolved. Stir in the remaining vanilla. Continue beating until stiff glossy peaks form.

4. In a large heavy skillet, bring remaining milk barely to a simmer over medium-low heat. Working in batches and using two soup spoons, drop meringue by ⅓ cupfuls into milk; poach 4-6 minutes or until firm to the touch, turning once. Using a slotted spoon, remove meringues to paper towels to drain. Repeat with remaining meringue, making a total of 12 snowballs. (Discard the remaining milk.) Serve with custard and, if desired, glazed pecans.

RICH RUM CAKE

We like a touch of rum for the holidays, and this orangey rum cake is decadent alone or with big swoops of whipped cream.
—Nancy Heishman, Las Vegas, NV

PREP: 35 min. • **BAKE:** 25 min. + cooling
MAKES: 12 servings

- 4 large eggs, separated
- 2½ cups confectioners' sugar
- ¾ cup orange juice
- ¼ cup butter, cubed
- ¾ cup rum
- 1 cup all-purpose flour
- 1 tsp. baking powder
- ½ tsp. ground cinnamon
- ¼ tsp. salt
- ¼ tsp. ground nutmeg
- ½ cup packed brown sugar, divided
- 1 tsp. vanilla extract
- ¾ cup butter, melted
  Whipped cream and finely chopped glazed pecans, optional

1. Place egg whites in a large bowl; let stand at room temperature 30 minutes. For sauce, in a saucepan, combine confectioners' sugar, juice and ¼ cup butter; cook and stir over medium-low heat until sugar is dissolved. Remove from heat; stir in rum. Reserve ¾ cup for serving.
2. Preheat oven to 375°. Grease and flour a 10-in. tube pan. Sift flour, baking powder, cinnamon, salt and nutmeg together twice; set aside.
3. In a large bowl, beat the egg whites on medium until soft peaks form. Gradually add ¼ cup brown sugar, 1 Tbsp. at a time, beating on high after each addition until sugar is dissolved. Continue beating until stiff peaks form.
4. In another bowl, beat egg yolks until slightly thickened. Gradually add ¼ cup brown sugar and the vanilla, beating on high speed until thick. Fold a fourth of the egg whites into batter. Alternately fold in the flour mixture and the remaining whites. Fold in melted butter.
5. Transfer to the prepared pan. Bake on lowest oven rack 25-30 minutes or until the top springs back when lightly touched. Immediately poke holes in cake with a fork; slowly pour the remaining sauce over cake, allowing the cake to absorb the sauce. Cool completely in the pan on a wire rack. Invert onto a serving plate. Serve with reserved sauce and, if desired, whipped cream and candied pecans.
Note: To remove cakes easily, use solid shortening to grease plain and fluted tube pans.

TURTLE TART WITH CARAMEL SAUCE

Between the creamy filling, crispy crust and gooey caramel sauce, there's a lot to love about this tart. One of my daughters even asks for this instead of cake on her birthday.
—Leah Davis, Morrow, OH

PREP: 15 min. • **BAKE:** 15 min. + chilling
MAKES: 12 servings

- 2 cups pecan halves, toasted
- ½ cup sugar
- 2 Tbsp. butter, melted

FILLING
- 2 cups semisweet chocolate chips
- 1½ cups heavy whipping cream
- ½ cup finely chopped pecans, toasted

CARAMEL SAUCE
- ½ cup butter, cubed
- 1 cup sugar
- 1 cup heavy whipping cream

1. Preheat oven to 350°. Place pecans and sugar in a food processor; pulse until the pecans are finely ground. Add melted butter; pulse until combined. Press onto bottom and up sides of a 9-in. fluted tart pan with removable bottom. Bake for 12-15 minutes or until golden brown. Cool completely on a wire rack.
2. For the filling, place chocolate chips in a small bowl. In a small saucepan, bring cream just to a boil. Pour over chocolate; stir with a whisk until smooth. Pour into the cooled crust; cool slightly. Refrigerate until slightly set, about 30 minutes.
3. Sprinkle pecans over filling. Refrigerate, covered, until set, about 3 hours.
4. For sauce, in a large heavy saucepan, melt butter over medium heat; stir in sugar until dissolved. Bring to a boil and cook for 10-12 minutes or until deep golden brown, stirring occasionally. Slowly whisk in cream until blended. Remove from heat; cool slightly. Serve with tart.
Note: To toast nuts, bake in a shallow pan in a 350° oven for 5-10 minutes or cook in a skillet over low heat until lightly browned, stirring occasionally.

RUSTIC CRANBERRY TARTS

For holiday gatherings with family and friends, we love a dessert with a splash of red. These beautiful tarts are filled with cranberry and citrus flavor and are easy to make and serve.
—Holly Bauer, West Bend, WI

PREP: 15 min. • **BAKE:** 20 min./batch
MAKES: 2 tarts (6 servings each)

- 1 cup orange marmalade
- ¼ cup sugar
- ¼ cup all-purpose flour
- 4 cups fresh or frozen cranberries, thawed
- 1 pkg. (14.1 oz.) refrigerated pie crust
- 1 large egg white, lightly beaten
- 1 Tbsp. coarse sugar

1. Preheat oven to 425°. In a large bowl, mix marmalade, sugar and flour; stir in cranberries.

2. Unroll one pie crust onto a parchment paper-lined baking sheet. Spoon half of the cranberry mixture over crust to within 2 in. of edge. Fold edge over filling, pleating as you go and leaving a 5-in. opening in the center. Brush folded crust with egg white; sprinkle with half of the coarse sugar.

3. Bake 18-22 minutes or until crust is golden and the filling is bubbly. Repeat with the remaining ingredients. Transfer each tart to a wire rack to cool.

❄ Reader Review

"These tarts are beautiful! Not only did they turn out picture perfect, they were easy to put together and delicious. Note that the tarts are fragile until they are completely cool."

MAMAKNOWSBEST TASTEOFHOME.COM

MERINGUE TORTE WITH PEPPERMINT CREAM

I made this torte to surprise my brother-in-law one Christmas after his mother passed away. A melt-in-your-mouth delight, this was a specialty of hers. He was so touched.

—Christine Venzon, Peoria, IL

PREP: 30 min. • BAKE: 20 min. + cooling
MAKES: 8 servings

- 3 large egg whites
- 1 tsp. water
- 1 tsp. white vinegar
- 1 tsp. vanilla extract
  Dash salt
- 2 drops red food coloring, optional
- 1 cup sugar
- ½ cup semisweet chocolate chips
- 1 tsp. shortening
- 1 cup heavy whipping cream
- ⅔ cup crushed soft peppermint candies
  Chocolate curls
  Additional crushed soft peppermint candies

1. Let the egg whites stand at room temperature 30 minutes. Add water, vinegar, extract, salt and, if desired, food coloring; beat on medium speed until soft peaks form. Gradually beat in the sugar, 1 Tbsp. at a time, on high until stiff glossy peaks form and the sugar is dissolved.
2. Preheat oven to 300°. With a pencil, draw three 8x5-in. rectangles on a sheet of parchment paper. Place paper, pencil marks down, on baking sheets. Spread meringue evenly over parchment, using the rectangles as guides.
3. Bake 20 minutes. Turn oven off but do not open; leave meringues in oven for 1½ hours. Remove from oven; cool on baking sheets. When cooled completely, remove meringues from paper.
4. In a microwave, melt chocolate and shortening; stir until smooth. Spread a third of the chocolate mixture over each meringue. In a large bowl, beat cream until stiff peaks form; fold in crushed peppermint candies.
5. Place a chocolate-covered meringue on a serving plate; top with a third of the peppermint cream. Repeat layers twice. Top with chocolate curls and additional crushed candies.

MAPLE WALNUT CAKE

This cake reminds me of my beloved grandpa, who made delicious maple syrup when I was a child. This cake honors his memory, and has proved to be a favorite with family and friends.

—Lori Fee, Middlesex, NY

PREP: 45 min. • BAKE: 15 min. + cooling
MAKES: 16 servings

- ½ cup unsalted butter, softened
- 1½ cups packed light brown sugar
- 3 large eggs
- 1 tsp. maple flavoring or maple syrup
- 2 cups all-purpose flour
- 1 tsp. baking powder
- 1 tsp. baking soda
- ¼ tsp. salt
- 1 cup buttermilk

CANDIED WALNUTS
- 1 Tbsp. unsalted butter
- 1½ cups coarsely chopped walnuts
- 1 Tbsp. maple syrup
- ¼ tsp. salt

FROSTING
- 2 cups unsalted butter, softened
- 1 tsp. maple flavoring or maple syrup
- ¼ tsp. salt
- 5 cups confectioners' sugar
- ¼ to ½ cup half-and-half cream
- 3 Tbsp. maple syrup, divided

1. Preheat oven to 350°. Line the bottoms of three greased 9-in. round baking pans with parchment paper; grease paper.
2. Cream butter and brown sugar until light and fluffy. Add eggs, one at a time, beating well after each addition. Beat in maple flavoring. In another bowl, whisk together flour, baking powder, baking soda and salt; add to creamed mixture alternately with buttermilk, beating after each addition.
3. Transfer to the prepared pans. Bake until a toothpick inserted in center comes out clean, 11-13 minutes. Cool in pans 10 minutes before removing to wire racks; remove paper. Cool completely.
4. For candied walnuts, in a large skillet, melt butter over medium heat; saute walnuts until toasted, about 5 minutes. Stir in maple syrup and salt; cook and stir 1 minute. Spread onto foil; cool completely.
5. For frosting, beat butter until creamy. Beat in maple flavoring and salt. Gradually beat in confectioners' sugar and enough cream to reach the desired consistency.
6. Place one cake layer on a serving plate; spread with 1 cup of the frosting. Sprinkle with ½ cup candied walnuts and drizzle with 1 Tbsp. maple syrup. Repeat layers.
7. Top with the remaining layer. Frost top and sides of cake. Top with the remaining walnuts and syrup.

❄ Holiday Helper

To frost a cake without getting crumbs in the frosting, be certain your cake is thoroughly cool before frosting it. Then brush off any loose crumbs with a pastry brush. Apply a very thin layer of frosting to "set" the crumbs (don't worry if there are crumbs in this layer). Allow it to dry, then apply a final top coat of frosting.

EGGNOG POUND CAKE

When you're having company, this cake—
served with a custard sauce and a dash of
nutmeg—inspires oohs and aahs!
—Audrey Kaalaas, Kirkland, IL

....

PREP: 15 min. • **BAKE:** 40 min. + cooling
MAKES: 20 servings

1	pkg. yellow cake mix (regular size)
1¼	cups eggnog
3	large eggs
¼	cup butter, softened
2	tsp. ground nutmeg
½	to 1 tsp. vanilla extract

CREAMY CUSTARD SAUCE

¼	cup sugar
1	Tbsp. cornstarch
¼	tsp. salt
1	cup whole milk
1	large egg yolk, beaten
1	tsp. butter
¼	tsp. vanilla extract
½	cup heavy whipping cream, whipped
	Additional nutmeg, optional

1. Preheat oven to 350°. Grease and flour a
10-in. fluted tube can. Combine the first six
ingredients; beat on low speed 30 seconds.
Beat on medium 2 minutes.
2. Transfer batter to prepared pan. Bake
until a toothpick inserted in center comes
out clean, 40-45 minutes. Cool in pan for
10 minutes before removing to a wire rack
to cool completely.
3. For sauce, in a heavy saucepan, mix
sugar, cornstarch and salt. Whisk in milk.
Cook and stir over medium until thickened
and bubbly. Reduce heat to low; cook and
stir 1-2 minutes longer. Remove from heat.
4. In a bowl, whisk a small amount of the
hot mixture into egg yolk; return all to pan,
whisking constantly. Bring to a gentle boil;
cook and stir for 2 minutes. Remove from
heat; stir in the butter and vanilla. Cool
completely. Fold in whipped cream;
refrigerate until cold. Serve sauce with
cake; if desired, sprinkle with nutmeg.
Note: This recipe was tested with
commercially prepared eggnog.

PEPPERMINT CAKE ROLLS

With angel food cake, fudge sauce and peppermints, this cake roll is easy to make and very pretty!

—Suellen Calhoun, Des Moines, IA

....

PREP: 25 min. • **BAKE:** 15 min. + cooling
MAKES: 2 cakes (10 slices each)

- 1 pkg. (16 oz.) angel food cake mix
  Confectioners' sugar
- 1 carton (16 oz.) frozen whipped topping, thawed
- 1½ tsp. peppermint extract
- 1 cup hot fudge ice cream topping
- ½ cup crushed peppermint candies, divided
  Fresh mint leaves, optional

1. Line two greased 15x10x1-in. baking pans with waxed paper. Prepare cake mix according to package directions. Divide evenly into prepared pans; spread evenly.
2. Bake at 350° for 12-15 minutes or until tops spring back when lightly touched. Cool for 5 minutes.
3. Invert each cake onto a kitchen towel dusted with confectioners' sugar. Gently peel off paper. Roll up cake in the towel jelly-roll style, starting with a short side. Cool completely on a wire rack.
4. In a small bowl, mix whipped topping and extract until blended. Unroll cakes; spread each with 1½ cups peppermint mixture to within ½ in. of edges.
5. Cut a small hole in the corner of a food-safe plastic bag; fill with fudge topping. Drizzle each cake with half of the fudge topping; sprinkle with 2 Tbsp. of crushed candies. Roll again, without towel.
6. Transfer cakes to platters. Frost with the remaining peppermint mixture. Just before serving, top with the remaining candies and, if desired, mint leaves.

Freeze option: Omit candy topping and mint leaves. Place frosted cakes in airtight freezer containers; cover and freeze. Remove from freezer 10 minutes before serving. Top with remaining candies and, if desired, mint leaves.

PINEAPPLE & MACADAMIA NUT CAKE

This delicious cake is one of my own invention. It's been a huge hit among family and friends and even inspired fierce bidding at a local charity auction!

—Greta Kirby, Carthage, TN

....

PREP: 20 min. • **BAKE:** 25 min. + cooling
MAKES: 16 servings

- 1 pkg. white or yellow cake mix, regular size
- 1¼ cups unsweetened pineapple juice
- ½ cup canola oil
- 3 large eggs

FILLING
- ¾ cup granulated sugar
- 4 tsp. all-purpose flour
- 2 large egg yolks
- ¼ cup butter, melted
- 1 can (8 oz.) unsweetened crushed pineapple, undrained
- ¼ cup chopped macadamia nuts, toasted

FROSTING
- ½ cup butter, softened
- 4 cups confectioners' sugar
- 2 to 4 Tbsp. 2% milk
  Additional macadamia nuts, optional

1. Preheat oven to 350°. Combine cake mix, pineapple juice, oil and eggs; beat on low speed for 30 seconds. Beat on medium for 2 minutes. Pour into three greased and floured 8-in. round baking pans.
2. Bake until a toothpick inserted in center comes out clean, 25-30 minutes. Cool for 10 minutes before removing from pans to wire racks to cool completely.
3. Combine sugar and flour in a large saucepan. Whisk in egg yolks, butter and pineapple until blended. Bring to a boil over medium heat; cook and stir until thickened and bubbly, about 2 minutes. Remove from heat; cool to room temperature. Reserve ⅓ cup of the pineapple mixture for frosting; stir nuts into remaining pineapple mixture.
4. Place one cake layer on a serving plate; spread with half of the filling. Repeat. Top with remaining cake layer.
5. Cream butter, confectioners' sugar, reserved pineapple mixture and enough milk to reach a spreading consistency. Spread over top and sides of cake. If desired, chop and toast additional nuts; sprinkle on top and around bottom of cake.
Note: To toast nuts, bake in a shallow pan in a 350° oven for 5-10 minutes or cook in a skillet over low heat until lightly browned, stirring occasionally.

TANGERINE TUILES WITH CANDIED CRANBERRIES

Delicate cookie cups create delightful serving bowls for creamy tangerine mousse, and cranberry syrup makes a delectable garnish.
—Jessie Sarrazin, Livingston, MT

....

PREP: 2 hours + standing • **BAKE:** 5 min./batch
MAKES: 16 servings

    1   pkg. (12 oz.) fresh cranberries
 2½   cups sugar, divided
TUILES
    3   large egg whites
  ¾   cup confectioners' sugar
  ½   cup all-purpose flour
    6   Tbsp. butter, melted
  ½   tsp. almond extract
  ¼   tsp. salt
TANGERINE CREAM
    1   carton (8 oz.) Mascarpone cheese
  ¼   cup honey
    1   Tbsp. grated tangerine zest
    2   cups whipped cream
    2   tangerines, peeled, sectioned and chopped

1. Line a 15x10x1-in. baking pan with parchment paper. Place cranberries in pan; sprinkle with 2 cups sugar. Cover and bake at 350° for 1 hour. Cool. Drain, reserving syrup for garnish.
2. Transfer berries to another parchment paper-lined 15x10x1-in. baking pan. Bake at 200° for 1¼-1¾ hours or until almost dry to the touch. Toss with remaining sugar.
3. Using a pencil, draw four 3-in. circles on a sheet of parchment paper. Place paper, pencil mark down, on a baking sheet; set aside.
4. In a large bowl, combine egg whites, confectioners' sugar and flour until blended. Beat in butter, almond extract and salt.
5. Spread 1 Tbsp. batter over each circle. Bake at 350° for 5-7 minutes or until golden around the edges.
6. With a spatula, carefully remove cookies and immediately drape over inverted shot glasses or small juice glasses. When the cookies are cool, transfer to a wire rack. Repeat with remaining batter, forming 16 tuiles.
7. In a small bowl, beat the mascarpone, honey and tangerine zest. Fold in whipped cream and tangerines.
8. To serve, spoon about 3 Tbsp. tangerine cream into each cookie. Garnish with candied cranberries and reserved syrup.
To make ahead: Prepare the tuiles a few days before. Store in an airtight container. Candied cranberries can be made two weeks before serving. Store cranberries in a single layer covered lightly with waxed paper. Cover and refrigerate syrup.

AMARETTO RICOTTA CHEESECAKE

There's a good reason this cherished recipe was handed down to me by a relative. It's a keeper! The amaretto and ricotta make this a truly unique dessert.
—Isabel Neuman, Surprise, AZ

....

PREP: 35 min. + standing
BAKE: 1 hour + chilling • **MAKES:** 16 servings

 2¾   cups whole-milk ricotta cheese
  ⅓   cup cornstarch
  ¼   cup amaretto
    2   pkg. (8 oz. each) cream cheese, softened
 1½   cups sugar
    1   cup sour cream
    5   large eggs, lightly beaten
TOPPING
    1   cup sour cream
    2   Tbsp. sugar
    2   Tbsp. amaretto
GARNISH
    1   Tbsp. light corn syrup
    1   cup fresh cranberries
  ⅓   cup sugar
  ½   cup sliced almonds, toasted

1. Line a strainer or colander with four layers of cheesecloth or one coffee filter; place over a bowl. Place ricotta in the prepared strainer; cover with sides of the cheesecloth. Refrigerate for at least 8 hours or overnight. Remove ricotta from cheesecloth; discard liquid in bowl.
2. Preheat oven to 350°. In a small bowl, mix cornstarch and amaretto. In a large bowl, beat cream cheese, sugar, sour cream and drained ricotta until smooth. Beat in amaretto mixture. Add eggs; beat on low speed just until blended.
3. Pour into a greased 10-in. springform pan. Place on a baking sheet. Bake for 1-1¼ hours or until the center is almost set. Let stand 5 minutes on a wire rack.
4. In a small bowl, mix topping ingredients; spread over top of cheesecake. Bake 5 minutes longer.
5. Cool on a wire rack 10 minutes. Loosen sides from pan with a knife. Cool 1 hour longer. Refrigerate overnight, covering when completely cooled. Remove rim from pan.
6. For the garnish, place corn syrup in a small microwave-safe bowl. Microwave, uncovered, for 10 seconds or until warm. Add cranberries; toss to coat. Place sugar in a small bowl; add cranberries and toss to coat. Place on waxed paper and let stand until set, about 1 hour.
7. Top cheesecake with almonds and sugared cranberries.
Note: To toast nuts, bake in a shallow pan in a 350° oven for 5-10 minutes or cook in a skillet over low heat until lightly browned, stirring occasionally.

❄ *Holiday Helper*

It is best to cut a cheesecake right after you remove it from the refrigerator. Dip a clean knife in a glass of hot water and wipe it dry before cutting. Wipe the knife clean after each cut and dip in warm water again. Remove slices to a serving plate with a pie spatula.

MOCHA BAKED ALASKAS

Make these Baked Alaskas ahead of time—you can torch the completed desserts and freeze them up to 24 hours before serving.

—Kerry Dingwall, Wimington, NC

....

PREP: 30 min. + freezing • **BROIL:** 5 min.
MAKES: 6 servings

- 8 oz. semisweet chocolate, chopped
- 1 cup heavy whipping cream
- 1 loaf (10¾ oz.) frozen pound cake, thawed
- ¼ cup strong brewed coffee
- 3 cups coffee ice cream
- 6 large egg whites
- 1 cup sugar
- ½ tsp. cream of tartar
- 1 tsp. vanilla extract
- ⅛ tsp. salt

1. Place chocolate in a small bowl. In a small saucepan, bring cream just to a boil. Pour over chocolate; whisk until smooth. Refrigerate, stirring occasionally, until completely cooled, about 1 hour.
2. Slice pound cake horizontally into three layers. Cut cake into six 3-in. circles; brush tops with coffee (save remaining cake for another use).
3. Line six jumbo muffin cups with foil liners. Spoon ice cream into each. Spread ganache evenly over ice cream. Top with cake, coffee side down; press gently. Cover and freeze until firm, about 3 hours.
4. In a large heavy saucepan, combine the egg whites, sugar and cream of tartar. With a hand mixer, beat on low speed for 1 minute. Continue beating over low heat until the egg white mixture reaches 160°, about 10 minutes. Transfer to a bowl. Add vanilla and salt; beat until stiff glossy peaks form and sugar is dissolved.
5. Invert layered cakes onto an ungreased foil-lined baking sheet; remove foil liners. Immediately spread meringue over cakes, sealing to cover completely.
6. Heat with a kitchen torch or broil 8 in. from heat for 3-4 minutes or until meringue is lightly browned. Serve immediately.

SOUTHERN BOURBON PECAN PIE

For this bourbon-splashed pie, I added vanilla extract and eliminated the flour from another recipe. We loved the result.

—Paul Falduto, Efland, NC

....

PREP: 15 min. • **BAKE:** 55 min. + cooling
MAKES: 8 servings

- ¼ cup butter, cubed
- 1 cup sugar
- 1 cup dark corn syrup
- 3 large eggs
- ¼ cup bourbon
- 1 tsp. vanilla extract
  Pinch salt
- 1½ cups pecan halves
- 1 frozen deep-dish pie shell (unbaked)

1. Preheat the oven to 325°. In a large saucepan, combine butter, sugar and corn syrup. Cook over medium-low heat until sugar is dissolved; cool slightly. In a large bowl, whisk eggs, bourbon, vanilla and salt; slowly whisk in sugar mixture. Stir in pecans; pour into the pie shell.
2. Place on a baking sheet. Bake for 55-60 minutes or until a knife inserted in center comes out clean. Cool on wire rack.

MULLED WINE-POACHED APPLES

For a satisfying touch of sweetness at the end of a meal, try these ruby red apples. The spices and wine sauce makes them a nice stand-in for heavier desserts.

—*Taste of Home* Test Kitchen

....

PREP: 20 min. • **COOK:** 20 min. + chilling
MAKES: 6 servings

- 1 bottle (750 milliliters) merlot
- ½ cup mulling spices
- 6 medium apples, peeled and cored

1. In a Dutch oven, bring wine and mulling spices to a boil. Reduce heat; carefully add apples. Cover and simmer 15-20 minutes or just until apples are tender, turning once.
2. With a slotted spoon, remove the apples to a large bowl. Bring wine mixture to a boil; cook, uncovered, until the liquid is reduced to about ½ cup. Let cool, then pour over apples; cover and refrigerate for at least 1 hour before serving.

SPECIAL RASPBERRY TORTE

With raspberry preserves, a burst of lemon
and a homemade buttercream frosting, this
berry-topped cake is my mom's favorite.
—Lori Daniels, Beverly, WV

PREP: 45 min. + chilling
BAKE: 20 min. + cooling • MAKES: 12 servings

- 5   large egg whites
- ½   cup butter, softened
- ½   cup shortening
- 2   cups sugar
- 1   tsp. lemon extract
- 3   cups all-purpose flour
- 2   tsp. baking powder
- ½   tsp. baking soda
- ⅛   tsp. salt
- 1½ cups buttermilk

FROSTING
- ¾   cup shortening
- ⅓   cup butter, softened
- 4½ cups confectioners' sugar
- 1½ tsp. lemon extract
- 5   to 6 Tbsp. 2% milk
- 1   jar (10 oz.) seedless raspberry preserves
      Fresh raspberries

1. Place egg whites in a large bowl; let
stand at room temperature 30 minutes.
Preheat oven to 350°. Line bottoms of two
greased 9-in. round baking pans with
parchment paper; grease the paper.

2. In a large bowl, cream butter, shortening
and sugar until light and fluffy. Beat in
lemon extract. In another bowl, whisk flour,
baking powder, baking soda and salt; add
to the creamed mixture alternately with
buttermilk, beating well after each addition.

3. With clean beaters, beat the egg whites
on medium speed until stiff peaks form.
Fold into the batter.

4. Transfer the batter to prepared pans.
Bake 20-25 minutes or until a toothpick
inserted in center comes out clean and the
edges are golden.

5. Cool cakes in pans 10 minutes before
removing to wire racks; remove paper
and cool completely. In a large bowl, beat
shortening and butter until combined.
Beat in confectioner's sugar alternately
with extract and enough milk to reach
a spreading consistency.

6. Using a long serrated knife, cut each
cake horizontally in half. Place one cake
layer on a serving plate; spread with half of
the preserves. Top with another cake layer
and ¾ cup frosting. Place third cake layer
over frosting; spread with the remaining
preserves. Top with remaining cake layer.

7. Frost top and sides of the cake with
1 cup of frosting, forming a crumb coating.
Refrigerate cake until frosting is set, about
30 minutes. Remove from refrigerator and
cover with the remaining frosting. Top with
fresh raspberries.

SUGAR PLUM PHYLLO KRINGLE

Thanks to store-bought phyllo dough, this pastry is easier to make than it looks. Serve it not only for breakfast, but also for dessert with a scoop of ice cream.

—Johnna Johnson, Scottsdale, AZ

PREP: 30 min. • **BAKE:** 20 min. + cooling
MAKES: 6 servings

¾ cup chopped dried apricots
½ cup dried cherries
⅓ cup water
¼ cup sugar
¼ cup raisins
¾ cup chopped walnuts
1 Tbsp. lemon juice
1 pkg. (8 oz.) cream cheese, softened
12 sheets phyllo dough (14x9 in.)
    Butter-flavored cooking spray
    Confectioners' sugar

1. Preheat the oven to 375°. In a large saucepan, bring apricots, cherries, water, sugar and raisins to a boil. Reduce heat; simmer, uncovered, 6-8 minutes or until the liquid is thickened. Stir in walnuts and lemon juice. Remove from heat; cool completely.
2. In a small bowl, beat cream cheese until smooth. Place one sheet of phyllo dough on a work surface; spritz with cooking spray. Layer with the remaining phyllo, spritzing each layer. Spread cream cheese over phyllo to within 2 in. of edges; top with dried fruit mixture. Fold in edges; roll up, starting with a long side.
3. Line a 15x10x1-in. baking pan with parchment paper; place kringle in pan, seam side down. Spritz top with cooking spray. Bake 20-25 minutes or until golden brown. Cool on a wire rack. Sprinkle with confectioners' sugar.

HOLIDAY WHITE FRUITCAKE

Years ago, when I attended a church in Hawaii, a friend gave me this recipe. Now I whip up at least 60 loaves for the holidays!
—Eileen Sokolowski Flatt, Chandler, AZ

....

PREP: 20 min. • **BAKE:** 50 min. + cooling
MAKES: 4 loaves (16 slices each)

- 1 pkg. (8 oz.) chopped mixed candied fruit
- 1¼ cups golden raisins
- 1 cup chopped walnuts, toasted
- 3 cups all-purpose flour, divided
- 2 cups butter, softened
- 2 cups sugar
- 6 large eggs

1. Preheat the oven to 275°. Line the bottoms of four greased 9x5-in. loaf pans with parchment paper; grease the paper.
2. In a small bowl, toss candied fruit, raisins and walnuts with ½ cup flour. In a large bowl, cream butter and sugar until light and fluffy. Add eggs, one at a time, beating well after each addition. Gradually beat in remaining flour. Fold in fruit mixture.
3. Transfer to prepared pans. Bake for 50-60 minutes or until a toothpick inserted in the center comes out clean. Cool in pans for 10 minutes before removing to wire racks to cool.
Note: To toast nuts, bake in a shallow pan in a 350° oven for 5-10 minutes or cook in a skillet over low heat until lightly browned, stirring occasionally.

❄ Reader Review

"Love this recipe! I usually make three loaf pans and two smaller loaf pans out of this recipe. It's the best-tasting fruit cake and it keeps well."

ROSEMARIEP TASTEOFHOME.COM

HOMEMADE PEAR PIE

I entered this pie in a local baking contest and ended up winning! Bartlett pears hold up well when baked, adding a nice layer of texture.
—Darlene Jacobson, Waterford, WI

....

PREP: 40 min. + chilling
BAKE: 45 min. + cooling • **MAKES:** 8 servings

- 2 cups all-purpose flour
- 1 tsp. salt
- ¾ cup shortening
- 6 Tbsp. cold water

FILLING
- 5 cups sliced peeled fresh pears
- 1 Tbsp. lemon juice
- ⅓ cup all-purpose flour
- ½ cup plus 1 Tbsp. sugar, divided
- 1 tsp. ground cinnamon
- 2 Tbsp. butter

1. In a large bowl, mix flour and salt; cut in shortening until crumbly. Gradually add water, tossing with a fork until dough holds together when pressed. Shape into a disk; wrap in plastic. Refrigerate 1 hour.
2. Preheat oven to 425°. In a large bowl, toss pears with lemon juice. In a small bowl, mix flour, ½ cup sugar and cinnamon; add to pear mixture and toss to coat.
3. On a lightly floured surface, roll one half of dough to ⅛ in. thick; transfer to a 9-in. pie plate. Trim pastry even with rim. Add filling; dot with butter.
4. Roll remaining dough to ⅛ in. thick. Place over filling. Trim, seal and flute edge. Cut slits in top. Sprinkle with the remaining sugar. Bake 45-50 minutes or until the crust is golden brown and the filling is bubbly. Cover edge loosely with foil during the last 20 minutes if needed to prevent overbrowning. Cool on a wire rack.

CRANBERRY CAKE WITH CARAMEL SAUCE

This sweet and tangy cake, loaded with bits of cranberries and topped with warm caramel sauce, is even better served with ice cream.

—Darlene Brenden, Salem, OR

PREP: 15 min. • **BAKE:** 30 min. + cooling
MAKES: 15 servings (2 cups sauce)

- 2   cups all-purpose flour
- 1   cup sugar
- 2   tsp. baking powder
- ¼   tsp. salt
- 1   cup heavy whipping cream
- 1   Tbsp. butter, melted
- 2   cups fresh or frozen cranberries, halved

SAUCE
- ½   cup butter, cubed
- 1   cup heavy whipping cream
- ½   cup sugar
- ½   cup packed brown sugar
- 1   tsp. vanilla extract

1. Preheat oven to 350°. Grease a 13x9-in. baking dish.

2. Whisk together flour, sugar, baking powder and salt. Stir in cream and butter just until moistened. Fold in cranberries. Transfer to prepared pan. Bake until golden brown, 30-35 minutes. Cool in pan on a wire rack for 10 minutes.

3. Meanwhile, in a small saucepan, melt butter; stir in cream, sugar and brown sugar. Bring to a boil over medium heat, stirring constantly. Remove from heat; stir in vanilla. Serve with warm cake.

RED VELVET CAKE ROLL WITH WHITE CHOCOLATE FILLING

Get ready for oohs and aahs when you set this on the table! To make it extra festive, dust with confectioners' sugar in a candy cane pattern.

—Tonya Forsyth, Waurika, OK

PREP: 25 min. + chilling
BAKE: 15 min. + cooling • MAKES: 16 servings

- 4 large eggs
- ¾ cup sugar
- 2 Tbsp. buttermilk
- 1 Tbsp. canola oil
- 1 Tbsp. red food coloring
- 1 tsp. white vinegar
- 1 tsp. vanilla extract
- 1 cup all-purpose flour
- ¼ cup baking cocoa
- 1 tsp. baking powder
- ½ tsp. salt

FILLING
- 1 pkg. (8 oz.) cream cheese, softened
- ¼ cup butter, softened
- 1 tsp. vanilla extract
- 1 cup confectioners' sugar
- 5 oz. white baking chocolate, melted
  Additional confectioners' sugar, optional

1. Preheat oven to 350°. Line a greased 15x10x1-in. baking pan with parchment paper; grease paper.

2. In a large bowl, beat eggs on high speed for 3 minutes. Gradually add sugar, beating until thick and lemon-colored. Beat in the buttermilk, oil, food coloring, vinegar and vanilla. In another bowl, whisk flour, cocoa, baking powder and salt; gradually beat into the egg mixture. Beat on high speed for 2 minutes. Transfer to the prepared pan, spreading evenly.

3. Bake 12-15 minutes or until top springs back when lightly touched. Cool 5 minutes. Invert onto a clean tea towel dusted with confectioners' sugar. Gently peel off the paper. Roll up cake in the towel jelly-roll style, starting with a short side. Cool completely on a wire rack.

4. In a large bowl, beat cream cheese, butter and vanilla until blended. Gradually beat in confectioners' sugar and baking chocolate until smooth. Unroll cake; spread filling over cake to within ½ in. of the edges. Roll up again, without towel; trim ends. Place on a platter, seam side down. Refrigerate, covered, for at least 2 hours. If desired, place 1-in. strips of waxed paper across cake roll; dust lightly with additional confectioners' sugar. Carefully remove and discard strips.

❄ Holiday Helper

To give this jelly-roll cake a cleaner look, use a sharp knife to taper the last ½ inch of the cake on each short end before filling. The tapered ends offer a more attractive center, and they will result in a cleaner, more even seam.

APPLE CINNAMON CAKE

This cake is equally good for breakfast or dessert, so be sure to save some for the morning! Easy to make, it's super moist on the inside and has a crispy, cinnamon-rich crunch on the outside.

—Marideane Maxwell, Albany, GA

PREP: 15 min. • BAKE: 40 min. + cooling
MAKES: 12 servings

- 1 pkg. yellow cake mix (regular size)
- 1 can (21 oz.) apple pie filling
- 4 large eggs
- ⅔ cup canola oil
- 6 Tbsp. cinnamon sugar, divided

GLAZE
- 1 cup confectioners' sugar
- ¼ tsp. ground cinnamon
- 1 to 2 Tbsp. water

1. Preheat oven to 350°. Grease and flour a 10-in. fluted tube pan. Combine cake mix, pie filling, eggs and oil; beat on low speed 30 seconds. Beat on medium 2 minutes. Pour half of the batter into prepared pan. Sprinkle with 3 Tbsp. cinnamon sugar. Add the remaining cake mix; top with remaining cinnamon sugar.
2. Bake until a toothpick inserted in the center comes out clean, 40-45 minutes. Cool in the pan for 10 minutes before removing to a wire rack to cool completely. Mix the confectioners' sugar, cinnamon and enough water to reach the desired consistency. Spoon glaze over cake, allowing some to flow over sides.
Note: For easier removal of cakes, use solid shortening to grease plain and fluted tube pans.

FAST FIX
PEPPERMINT LAVA CAKES

These cakes are a showstopper on a plate, with warm chocolate pudding oozing out of the center of tender chocolate cake. Serve with whipped cream or ice cream.

—Carolyn Crotser, Colorado Springs, CO

TAKES: 30 min. • MAKES: 4 servings

- ⅔ cup semisweet chocolate chips
- ½ cup butter, cubed
- 1 cup confectioners' sugar
- 2 large eggs
- 2 large egg yolks
- 1 tsp. peppermint extract
- 6 Tbsp. all-purpose flour
- 2 Tbsp. crushed peppermint candies

1. Preheat oven to 425°. In a microwave-safe bowl, melt chocolate chips and butter for 30 seconds; stir until smooth. Whisk in confectioners' sugar, eggs, egg yolks and extract until blended. Fold in flour.
2. Transfer to four generously greased 4-oz. ramekins. Bake on a baking sheet until a thermometer reads 160° and edges of cakes are set, 14-16 minutes.
3. Remove from oven; let stand 5 minutes. Run a knife around sides of ramekins; invert onto dessert plates. Sprinkle with crushed candies. Serve immediately.
Note: You may substitute ¾ tsp. orange extract and 1½ tsp. orange zest mixed with 1 Tbsp. coarse sugar for the peppermint extract and peppermint candies.

EGGNOG BREAD PUDDING WITH CRANBERRIES

My parents love this bread pudding loaded with cranberries and pecans—and it uses up leftover dinner rolls. For eggnog lovers, it makes a divine dessert.

—Emily Hobbs, Springfield, MO

....

PREP: 15 min. + standing • **BAKE:** 35 min.
MAKES: 9 servings

- 4   large eggs
- 2   cups eggnog
- 6   cups cubed soft dinner rolls
- ¾   cup finely chopped glazed pecans
- ½   cup dried cranberries

1. Preheat oven to 375°. In a large bowl, whisk eggs and eggnog until blended. Stir in cubed rolls, pecans and cranberries; let stand for about 15 minutes or until the bread is softened.
2. Transfer to a greased 8-in. square baking dish. Bake 35-40 minutes or until puffed, golden and a knife inserted in the center comes out clean. Serve warm.

MAKE AHEAD
CREAMY HAZELNUT PIE

I've always been a huge fan of peanut butter. Then I tried Nutella—and I was hooked! I even changed one of my favorite pie recipes by adding that ingredient.

—Lisa Varner, El Paso, TX

....

PREP: 10 min. + chilling • **MAKES:** 8 servings

- 1   pkg. (8 oz.) cream cheese, softened
- 1   cup confectioners' sugar
- 1¼ cups Nutella, divided
- 1   carton (8 oz.) frozen whipped topping, thawed
- 1   chocolate crumb crust (9 in.)

1. In a large bowl, beat cream cheese, confectioners' sugar and 1 cup Nutella until smooth. Fold in whipped topping. Spread evenly into crust.
2. Warm the remaining Nutella in the microwave for 15-20 seconds; drizzle over the pie. Refrigerate at least 4 hours or overnight.

MAKE AHEAD
LEMON SNOWBALL

For a special occasion like a church supper, I make this beautiful dessert. Lemon and coconut go wonderfully together—and the finished cake just looks like Christmas!

—Lucy Rickers, Bonsall, CA

....

PREP: 25 min. + chilling • **MAKES:** 20 servings

- 2   envelopes unflavored gelatin
- ¼   cup cold water
- 1   cup boiling water
- 1   cup granulated sugar
- 1   can (12 oz.) frozen orange juice concentrate, thawed
- 2   Tbsp. grated lemon zest
- 2   Tbsp. lemon juice
      Dash salt
- 3   cups heavy whipping cream, divided
- 1   prepared angel food cake (8 to 10 oz.), cubed
- ¼   cup confectioners' sugar
- ½   cup sweetened shredded coconut

1. Sprinkle gelatin over cold water. Let stand 5 minutes. Add boiling water; stir until gelatin is dissolved. Add the next five ingredients; mix well. Refrigerate, stirring occasionally, until the mixture begins to thicken, about 25 minutes.
2. In another bowl, beat 2 cups cream until stiff peaks form; fold into the lemon mixture. Line a 12-cup bowl with plastic wrap. Layer with 1 cup each lemon filling and cake cubes. Repeat layers five times; top with remaining filling. Refrigerate, covered, 6 hours or up to 2 days.
3. To serve, invert the bowl onto a large serving platter. Remove plastic wrap. Beat confectioners' sugar and remaining cream until stiff peaks form; spread over cake. Sprinkle with coconut.

HOMEMADE PEANUT
BUTTER CUPS, PAGE 265

CANDY &

CONFECTION
SAMPLER

FAMILY-FAVORITE CINNAMON CANDY

I have fond memories of standing at my grandmother's stove with my mom and my aunts, helping to make this cherished recipe. Now I share the tradition with my own kids.
—Wendy Hagan, Oak Grove, LA

PREP: 10 min. • COOK: 40 min. + cooling
MAKES: 3½ lbs.

- 1 Tbsp. butter
- 3¾ cups sugar
- 1¼ cups light corn syrup
- 1 cup water
- 3 pkg. (6 oz. each) Red Hots
- ¼ cup confectioners' sugar

1. Grease two 15x10x1-in. pans with the butter.
2. In a large heavy saucepan, combine the sugar, corn syrup and water. Bring to a boil over medium heat, stirring constantly to dissolve sugar. Add Red Hots; return to a boil, stirring carefully until Red Hots are melted, about 10 minutes. (Mixture will be very hot; wear an oven mitt while stirring to prevent burns.) Cook, without stirring, until a candy thermometer reads 300° (hard-crack stage).
3. Remove from heat. Immediately divide mixture between the prepared pans; cool completely, about 1 hour.
4. Break the candy into pieces. Place confectioners' sugar in a large resealable bag. In batches, add candy and toss to coat lightly.
Note: We recommend testing your candy thermometer before each use by bringing water to a boil; the thermometer should read 212°. Adjust the recipe temperature up or down based on your test.

WHITE CANDY BARK

I use walnuts from our tree to make this quick and easy recipe, but you can use whatever fruits or nuts are on hand. Pecans always work well, and dried cherries are an easy swap for the cranberries.
—Marcia Snyder, Grand Junction, CO

PREP: 20 min. + chilling • MAKES: 2 lbs.

- 1 Tbsp. butter, melted
- 2 pkg. (10 to 12 oz. each) white baking chips
- 1½ cups walnut halves
- 1 cup dried cranberries
- ¼ tsp. ground nutmeg

Line a 15x10x1-in. baking pan with foil. Brush with butter. Microwave white chips on high until melted; stir until smooth. Stir in walnuts, cranberries and nutmeg. Spread into prepared pan. Chill until firm. Break into pieces.

CREAMY ORANGE CARAMELS

Each Christmas I teach myself a new candy recipe. Last year I started with my caramel recipe and added a splash of orange extract for fun. The results were delicious!

—Shelly L Bevington, Hermiston, OR

PREP: 10 min. • **COOK:** 30 min.+ standing
MAKES: about 2½ lbs. (80 pieces)

- 1 tsp. plus 1 cup butter, divided
- 2 cups sugar
- 1 cup light corn syrup
- 1 can (14 oz.) sweetened condensed milk
- 1 tsp. orange extract
- 1 tsp. vanilla extract

1. Line an 11x7-in. dish with foil; grease foil with 1 tsp. butter.
2. In a large heavy saucepan, combine the sugar, corn syrup and remaining butter. Bring to a boil over medium heat, stirring constantly. Reduce heat to medium-low; boil gently, without stirring, for 4 minutes.
3. Remove from the heat; gradually stir in the condensed milk. Cook and stir until a candy thermometer reads 244° (firm-ball stage). Remove from the heat; stir in extracts. Immediately pour into prepared dish (do not scrape saucepan). Let stand until firm.
4. Using foil, lift out candy; remove foil. Using a buttered knife, cut caramel into 1x¾-in. pieces. Wrap individually in waxed paper; twist ends.
Note: We recommend you test your candy thermometer before each use by bringing water to a boil; the thermometer should read 212°. Adjust your recipe temperature up or down based on your test.

❋ Holiday Helper

Be sure to store your homemade candy so it stays fresh longer. Stored in an airtight container in a cool dry place, most candy will keep for 2 to 3 weeks. Fudge and caramels can be wrapped tightly and frozen for up to 1 year. To prevent candies from exchanging flavors, store different types in separate containers, using waxed paper between layers. Keep hard candy and soft candy in different containers; moisture from soft candy will cause hard candy to become sticky.

FAST FIX

CHEWY CARAMEL-COATED POPCORN

When I was a kid, my mom often made this recipe. I've adapted it to make a more chewy, gooey version. I get requests to make this for every event that I host. Packed into pretty decorative bags, it makes a welcome holiday gift for co-workers.

—Shannon Dobos, Calgary, AB

TAKES: 25 min. • **MAKES:** about 6 qt.

1½ cups butter, cubed
2⅔ cups packed light brown sugar
1 cup golden syrup
1 tsp. vanilla extract
24 cups popped popcorn

1. Line two 15x10x1-in. pans with parchment paper. In a large heavy saucepan, melt butter over medium-high heat. Add brown sugar and syrup, stirring to dissolve the brown sugar. Bring to a full rolling boil. Boil and stir 1 minute. Remove from heat and quickly stir in vanilla.
2. Pour the caramel mixture over popcorn; stir lightly to coat. Using a rubber spatula, press the popcorn into prepared pans. Cool. Pull caramel popcorn into pieces. Store in airtight containers.
Note: This recipe was tested with Lyles Golden Syrup.

QUICK & EASY GUMDROPS

These homemade candies are sweet little gummy bites that are softer than the store-bought varieties.

—Leah Rekau, Milwaukee, WI

PREP: 25 min. + chilling
MAKES: 1 lb. (64 pieces)

3 envelopes unflavored gelatin
½ cup plus ¾ cup water, divided
1½ cups sugar
¼ to ½ tsp. raspberry extract
    Red food coloring
    Additional sugar

1. In a small bowl, sprinkle gelatin over ½ cup water; let stand for 5 minutes. In a small saucepan, bring sugar and the remaining water to a boil over medium heat, stirring constantly. Add gelatin and reduce heat. Simmer 5 minutes, stirring frequently. Remove from heat; stir in extract and food coloring as desired.

2. Pour into a greased 8-in. square pan. Refrigerate, covered, 3 hours or until firm.

3. Loosen edges of candy from pan with a knife; turn onto a sugared work surface. Cut into 1-in squares; roll each square in sugar. Let stand, uncovered, at room temperature 3-4 hours or until all sides are dry; turn every hour. Store between layers of waxed paper in an airtight container in the refrigerator.

Note: For lemon gumdrops, use lemon extract and yellow food coloring. For orange gumdrops, use orange extract, yellow food coloring and a drop of red food coloring.

CHERRY DIVINITY

This light and airy confection is a treat any time of year, and especially brightens up dessert platters for Christmas and Valentine's Day. Replace the cherry gelatin with any flavor to suit your taste.

—Crystal Ralph-Haughn, Bartlesville, OK

PREP: 35 min. • **COOK:** 25 min. + standing
MAKES: 5 dozen

- 2 large egg whites
- 3 cups sugar
- ¾ cup water
- ¾ cup light corn syrup
- 1 pkg. (3 oz.) cherry gelatin
- 1 cup chopped walnuts

1. Place egg whites in the bowl of a large stand mixer; let stand at room temperature for 30 minutes. Line three 15x10x1-in. baking pans with waxed paper.

2. In a heavy saucepan, combine sugar, water and corn syrup; cook and stir until the sugar is dissolved and the mixture comes to a boil. Cook over medium heat, without stirring, until a candy thermometer reads 250° (hard-ball stage).

3. Just before the temperature is reached, beat egg whites until foamy. Gradually beat in gelatin. Beat until stiff peaks form. With mixer running on high speed, carefully pour hot syrup in a slow, steady stream into the bowl. Beat just until candy loses its gloss and holds its shape, about 5 minutes. Immediately stir in walnuts.

4. Quickly drop candy by tablespoonfuls onto prepared pans. Let stand at room temperature overnight or until pieces are dry to the touch. Store in airtight containers at room temperature.

Note: We recommend testing your candy thermometer before each use by bringing water to a boil; the thermometer should read 212°. Adjust the recipe temperature up or down based on your test.

CARAMEL PRETZEL BITES

I created this recipe for a twist on pretzel logs dipped in caramel, chocolate and nuts—similar to a version from a popular candy store. These homemade treats are simply delightful.

—Michilene Klaver, Grand Rapids, MI

PREP: 45 min. + cooling • **MAKES:** 6 dozen

- 2 tsp. butter, softened
- 4 cups pretzel sticks
- 2½ cups pecan halves, toasted
- 2¼ cups packed brown sugar
- 1 cup butter, cubed
- 1 cup corn syrup
- 1 can (14 oz.) sweetened condensed milk
- ⅛ tsp. salt
- 1 tsp. vanilla extract
- 1 pkg. (11½ oz.) milk chocolate chips
- 1 Tbsp. plus 1 tsp. shortening, divided
- ⅓ cup white baking chips

1. Line a 13x9-in. pan with foil; grease foil with softened butter. Spread pretzels and pecans on bottom of prepared pan.

2. In a large heavy saucepan, combine brown sugar, cubed butter, corn syrup, milk and salt; cook and stir over medium heat until a candy thermometer reads 240° (soft-ball stage). Remove from heat. Stir in vanilla. Pour over pretzel mixture.

3. In a microwave, melt chocolate chips and 1 Tbsp. shortening; stir until smooth. Spread over caramel layer. In microwave, melt white baking chips and remaining shortening; stir until smooth. Drizzle over top. Let stand until set.

4. Using the foil, lift the candy out of the pan; remove foil. Using a buttered knife, cut candy into bite-sized pieces.

3 EASY WAYS TO MELT CHOCOLATE

Our Test Kitchen uses a handful of different techniques to melt chocolate for recipes. Here are three of our favorites!

The Microwave Method

Chop chocolate into small pieces and place in microwave-safe bowl. Microwave at 70% power for 1 minute. Remove from microwave and stir. Continue to microwave in 30-second increments, stirring frequently, until the chocolate has fully melted. Because microwave ovens behave differently, it's easy to overcook chocolate, so keep an eye on your chocolate.

The Double Boiler Method

Place chopped chocolate in the top of a double boiler over barely simmering water. Stir gently and frequently until the chocolate has completely melted. Use a heat-safe rubber spatula to scrape the sides of the bowl as you stir. If you don't have a double boiler, use a metal bowl over a saucepan; just make sure the bottom of the bowl doesn't touch the water in the pan.

The Water Bath Method

Fill a slow cooker one-third full of hot water. Set the heat to high, leaving the lid off. Place wide-mouth mason jars filled with chopped chocolate pieces into the water. Take extra care to keep water from getting inside the jars—no seized chocolate, please! Step away for 30 minutes or so, leaving the lid off, and you'll return to beautifully melted chocolate that's ready to drizzle.

CHEWY SALTED PEANUT BARS

My family has been making this recipe for generations. Whenever we get together, someone always brings these peanuty bars.

—Ann Marie Heinz, Sturgeon Bay, WI

PREP: 10 min. • **BAKE:** 20 min. + cooling
MAKES: 2 dozen

- 1½ cups all-purpose flour
- ¾ cup packed brown sugar
- ½ cup cold butter, cubed
- 2 cups lightly salted dry roasted peanuts
- 1 cup butterscotch chips
- ½ cup light corn syrup
- 2 Tbsp. butter

1. Preheat oven to 350°. Line a 13x9-in. baking pan with foil, letting ends extend up sides; grease foil. In a small bowl, mix flour and brown sugar; cut in butter until crumbly. Press into prepared pan. Bake 8-10 minutes or until lightly browned. Sprinkle peanuts over crust.
2. In a small saucepan, melt butterscotch chips, corn syrup and butter over medium heat; stir until smooth. Drizzle over the peanuts. Bake 6-8 minutes longer or until bubbly. Cool completely in pan on a wire rack. Lifting with foil, remove from pan. Cut into bars.

❄ Reader Review

"These bars were so easy to make, the kids could help! We used honey roasted peanuts and added chocolate chips because, well, chocolate. We've eaten half the pan already!"

JSTOWELLSUPERMOM TASTEOFHOME.COM

MAKE AHEAD
ANISE GUMDROPS

With their bright color and frosty sugared look, these homemade gumdrops are irresistible. They are delicately soft, with a tongue-tingling anise flavor.

—Richard Bunt, Painted Post, NY

PREP: 25 min. + standing • **MAKES:** 1 lb.

- 4 envelopes unflavored gelatin
- 1¼ cups water, divided
- 2 cups sugar
- ½ tsp. anise extract
- 4 drops each pink and red food coloring
  Additional sugar

1. In a small bowl, sprinkle the gelatin over ½ cup water; let stand 5 minutes. In a small saucepan, bring sugar and remaining water to a boil over medium heat, stirring constantly. Reduce heat; simmer, uncovered, 5 minutes. Remove from heat. Stir in gelatin mixture until the gelatin is completely dissolved. Stir in extract.
2. Divide mixture between two small bowls; tint one pink and the other red with food coloring. Transfer to two greased 8x4-in. loaf pans. Refrigerate 30 minutes or until candy is firm.
3. Loosen sides from pan with a knife; turn onto a sugared board. Cut into ½-in. cubes; roll in additional sugar. Let stand, uncovered, at room temperature 3-4 hours or until all sides are dry, turning every hour.
Note: Store candy in a covered container. Refrigerate for up to two weeks.
Freeze option: Freeze candy in an airtight container. To use, thaw, loosely covered, before serving.

CHRISTMAS CRUNCH CANDY

Treat family and friends to a yummy brittle for the holidays. With cashews and Rice Krispies cereal, it's loaded with crunchy goodness.

—Amanda McLemore, Maryville, TN

PREP: 10 min. • **COOK:** 25 min. + cooling
MAKES: about 1½ lbs.

- 1 tsp. butter, softened
- 2 cups sugar
- ⅔ cup light corn syrup
- ½ cup water
- 3 Tbsp. butter, cubed
- 2 cups Rice Krispies
- 1 cup salted cashews
- 1½ tsp. baking soda
- 1 tsp. vanilla extract

1. Line a 15x10x1-in. baking pan with foil. Grease foil with 1 tsp. butter.

2. In a large heavy saucepan, combine sugar, corn syrup and water; bring to a boil over medium heat, stirring constantly. Cook and stir over medium heat until a candy thermometer reads 240° (soft-ball stage). Stir in butter; cook without stirring until the mixture reaches 300° (hard-crack stage), brushing down the sides of the pan with a pastry brush dipped in water as needed.

3. Remove from heat. Stir in the cereal, cashews, baking soda and vanilla. Quickly pour mixture into the prepared pan. Using a buttered metal spatula, spread to ¼-in. thickness. Let cool completely; break into pieces. Store in an airtight container up to 1 month.

MAKE AHEAD

WHITE CHOCOLATE MAPLE BACON FUDGE

Bored with the same old fudge? Prepare it with white chips, add maple flavoring and load it up with bacon. Then be prepared to share the recipe!

—Mindie Hilton, Susanville, CA

....

PREP: 10 min. + chilling • **MAKES:** about 2½ lbs.

- 1 tsp. plus ¼ cup butter, cubed, divided
- 10 slices ready-to-serve fully cooked bacon
- 2 pkg. (10 to 12 oz. each) white baking chips
- 1 can (14 oz.) sweetened condensed milk
- ¾ tsp. maple flavoring

1. Line a 9-in. square pan with foil; grease the foil with 1 tsp. butter. Heat bacon according to package directions; crumble and set aside.

2. In a large microwave-safe bowl, combine baking chips, condensed milk, flavoring and remaining butter. Microwave on high for 1 minute; stir until smooth. (If chips aren't completely melted, microwave in 10- to 20-second intervals until melted; stir until smooth.) Stir in the bacon; pour into the prepared pan. Refrigerate, covered, for 2 hours or until firm.

3. Using foil, lift fudge out of the pan. Remove foil; cut fudge into 1-in. squares. Store fudge, layered between waxed paper, in an airtight container in the refrigerator. Serve at room temperature.

Freeze option: Wrap fudge in waxed paper, then in foil. Place in freezer containers and freeze. To thaw, bring wrapped fudge to room temperature.

FESTIVE HOLIDAY FRUITCAKE BARK

Every year I make brandy-soaked dried fruit for my fruitcake, but I always make too much. When I tried turning the extras into candy, the result was a sweet and colorful bark just for grown-ups.

—Susan Bickta, Kutztown, PA

PREP: 25 min. + standing • **MAKES:** 2 lbs.

- ⅔ cup chopped mixed candied fruit
- 2 Tbsp. brandy
- ½ cup walnut pieces, toasted, divided
- 20 oz. white candy coating, coarsely chopped
- ⅔ cup miniature marshmallows
- 10 shortbread cookies, coarsely chopped

1. In a small bowl, combine candied fruit and brandy. Refrigerate, covered, 2 hours, stirring occasionally.

2. Line a 15x10x1-in. baking pan with waxed paper. Reserve 2 Tbsp. candied fruit and 2 Tbsp. walnuts for topping. In a microwave-safe bowl, melt the candy coating; stir until smooth. Stir in the marshmallows, cookie pieces and the remaining fruit and walnuts.

3. Spread into prepared pan (pan will not be full). Sprinkle with the reserved fruit and walnuts; press into candy coating. Let stand until set. Break or cut bark into pieces. Store in an airtight container.

HOMEMADE PEANUT BUTTER CUPS

I choose pretty mini muffin liners and colored sprinkles to coordinate with whatever holiday we're celebrating. These irresistible candies with gooey peanut butter centers are so easy to make!

—LaVonne Hegland, St. Michael, MN

PREP: 20 min. + chilling • **MAKES:** 3 dozen

- 1 cup creamy peanut butter, divided
- ½ cup confectioners' sugar
- 4½ tsp. butter, softened
- ½ tsp. salt
- 2 cups semisweet chocolate chips
- 4 milk chocolate candy bars (1.55 oz. each), coarsely chopped
  Colored sprinkles, optional

1. Combine ½ cup peanut butter, confectioners' sugar, butter and salt until smooth.

2. In a microwave, melt chocolate chips, candy bars and the remaining peanut butter; stir until smooth.

3. Drop teaspoonfuls of the chocolate mixture into paper-lined miniature muffin cups. Drop a scant teaspoonful of the peanut butter mixture into each cup; top with another teaspoonful of the chocolate mixture. If desired, decorate with sprinkles. Refrigerate until set. Store in an airtight container.

❄ Holiday Helper

It is important to chop chocolate before you melt it. Chopping ensures more even melting, since chocolate may burn before large pieces melt.

EASY PEANUT BUTTER TRUFFLES

During the Christmas season, I decided to make a peanut butter and honey fudge. My husband is a huge peanut butter fan and grew up where honey was a household staple. This pairing goes so well together.
—Tami Kuehl, Loup City, NE

PREP: 20 min. • COOK: 10 min. + chilling
MAKES: 64 truffles

- 1 tsp. plus ¼ cup butter, divided
- ¼ cup honey
- 2 cups creamy peanut butter
- 1¼ cups confectioners' sugar
- 1 tsp. vanilla extract
- 1½ cups finely chopped honey-roasted peanuts or miniature semisweet chocolate chips

1. Line an 8-in. square pan with foil; grease foil with 1 tsp. butter.
2. In a small saucepan, combine honey and the remaining butter over medium heat; cook and stir until blended. Stir in peanut butter until smooth. Remove from heat; whisk in confectioners' sugar and vanilla. Spread into the prepared pan. Refrigerate, covered, 2 hours or until firm.
3. Place peanuts in a shallow bowl. Using foil, lift candy out of pan. Remove foil; cut candy into 64 squares. Shape squares into balls; roll in peanuts. Store between layers of waxed paper in an airtight container in the refrigerator.
Note: Reduced-fat peanut butter is not recommended for this recipe.

CHOCOLATE, PEANUT & PRETZEL TOFFEE CRISPS

These crisps are the ultimate combination of salty and sweet. Make the recipe the way it's written or sprinkle on any personal favorites.
—Jennifer Butka, Livonia, MI

PREP: 25 min. • BAKE: 10 min. + chilling
MAKES: 2½ lbs.

- 40 saltines
- ¾ cup butter, cubed
- ¾ cup packed brown sugar
- 1 tsp. vanilla extract
- 2 cups semisweet chocolate chips
- 1 cup cocktail peanuts
- 1 cup broken pretzel sticks
- ¾ cup M&M's minis

1. Preheat oven to 350°. Line a 15x10x1-in. baking pan with foil; grease foil. Arrange saltines in a single layer on foil.
2. In a large heavy saucepan, melt butter over medium heat. Stir in brown sugar. Bring to a boil; cook and stir 2-3 minutes or until sugar is dissolved. Remove from heat; stir in vanilla. Spread evenly over crackers.
3. Bake for 8-10 minutes or until bubbly. Immediately sprinkle with chocolate chips. Allow chips to soften for 2 minutes, then spread over top. Sprinkle with peanuts, pretzels and M&M's minis; shake pan to settle toppings into chocolate. Cool.
4. Refrigerate, uncovered, for 1 hour or until set. Break into pieces. Store in an airtight container.

SNOWMAN JAR

Transform a plain mason jar into a frosty friend filled with snowy white cookies or candies.

Coat the lid and outside band of a large canning jar with black spray paint. Let dry.

Place the jar upside down on a piece of black craft foam; trace around the mouth of the jar. Draw a second circle 1 in. larger around the traced circle. Cut along the outside circle, then cut along the inner circle to form a ring.

Wrap a long fabric strip around the mouth of the jar, and cross the ends to make a scarf. Wrap a small fabric strip around the point where the ends cross; glue the small strip at the back.

Glue three black buttons down the front of the jar. Let dry.

Slip the foam ring over the mouth of the jar. Fill the jar with goodies and replace the lid—a perfect treat for someone sweet!

AUNT ROSE'S FANTASTIC BUTTER TOFFEE

Even though I don't live in the countryside, I love everything about it—especially good old-fashioned home cooking! This toffee is that kind of treat.
—Kathy Dorman, Snover, MI

PREP: 25 min. • **COOK:** 15 min.
MAKES: about 2 lbs

- 2 cups unblanched whole almonds
- 11 oz. milk chocolate, chopped, divided
- 1 cup butter, cubed
- 1 cup sugar
- 3 Tbsp. cold water

1. Preheat oven to 350°. In a shallow baking pan, toast almonds until golden brown, 5-10 minutes, stirring occasionally. Cool. Pulse chocolate in a food processor until finely ground (do not overprocess); transfer to a bowl. Pulse the almonds in food processor until coarsely chopped. Sprinkle 1 cup almonds over bottom of a greased 15x10x1-in. pan. Sprinkle with 1 cup chocolate.

2. In a heavy saucepan, combine butter, sugar and water. Cook over medium heat until a candy thermometer reads 290° (soft-crack stage), stirring occasionally.

3. Immediately pour mixture over the almonds and chocolate in pan. Sprinkle with the remaining chocolate and almonds. Refrigerate until set; break into pieces.

Note: We recommend testing your candy thermometer before each use by bringing water to a boil; the thermometer should read 212°. Adjust the recipe temperature up or down based on your test.

MAKE AHEAD

MARTHA WASHINGTON CANDY

Passed down by my grandmother and mother, this recipe is a beloved family tradition. Each grandchild and great-grandchild gets a turn stirring the candy mixture!
—Cindi Boger, Ardmore, AL

PREP: 45 min. + chilling
MAKES: about 8½ dozen

- 1 cup butter, softened
- 4 cups confectioners' sugar
- 1 can (14 oz.) sweetened condensed milk
- 1 tsp. vanilla extract
- 3 cups sweetened shredded coconut
- 2 cups chopped pecans, toasted
- 6 cups (36 oz.) semisweet chocolate chips
- ¼ cup shortening

1. In a large bowl, beat the butter, confectioners' sugar, condensed milk and vanilla until blended. Stir in coconut and pecans. Divide the dough in half; refrigerate, covered, 1 hour.

2. Working with half the dough at a time, shape into 1-in. balls; place on waxed paper-lined baking sheets. Refrigerate 30 minutes longer.

3. In the top of a double boiler or a metal bowl over barely simmering water, melt chocolate chips and shortening; stir until smooth. Dip balls in melted chocolate; allow excess to drip off. Return to waxed paper. Refrigerate until set. Store in an airtight container in the refrigerator.

Freeze option: Freeze candy, layered between pieces of waxed paper, in freezer containers. To use, thaw in refrigerator 2 hours before serving.

Holiday Helper

Dipping candies and confections in chocolate doesn't have to be messy work—all you need are a fork and a knife and you can keep your fingers clean! Drop each candy center in the melted chocolate, then scoop it out with a fork, holding it over the bowl to catch the drips. Use a knife to roll the coated candy off the fork and onto waxed paper to set.

MAKE AHEAD

TOFFEE CHEESECAKE POPS

Goodbye, sticky fingers! Everyone adores food on a stick, and these cute pops combine that novelty with the fabulous flavors of cheesecake and toffee.

—Lauralee Englehart, Fredericton, NB

PREP: 55 min. + freezing
BAKE: 40 min. + chilling
MAKES: about 6½ dozen

3	pkg. (8 oz. each) cream cheese, softened
¾	cup sugar
3	tsp. vanilla extract
3	large eggs, lightly beaten
2	pkg. (8 oz. each) brickle toffee bits, divided
80	lollipop sticks (4 in. long)
1¾	lbs. dark chocolate candy coating, melted

1. Preheat oven to 350°. Coat the bottom and sides of a 9-in. springform pan with cooking spray.

2. In a large bowl, beat cream cheese and sugar until smooth. Beat in vanilla until blended. Add eggs; beat on low speed just until blended. Fold in one package of toffee bits. Pour into the prepared pan; place on a baking sheet. Bake for 40-45 minutes or until the center is almost set. Cool on a wire rack for 10 minutes. Loosen sides from pan with a knife. Cool 1 hour longer. Refrigerate overnight, covering when completely cooled.

3. Shape cheesecake mixture into eighty 1-in. balls (about 1 Tbsp. each); insert a lollipop stick in each. Place on waxed paper-lined baking sheets. Freeze for 1 hour or until firm.

4. Place the remaining bag of toffee bits in a small bowl. Dip pops in melted candy coating; allow excess to drip off. Dip tops in the toffee bits. Place on waxed paper-lined baking sheets; let stand until set. Store in airtight containers in the refrigerator.

LEMON CREAM BONBONS

These bonbons with a hint of lemon are lovely for any special occasion. They're in such high demand with my family that I now keep them on hand all year-round.

—Ann Barber, Creola, OH

PREP: 30 min. + freezing
MAKES: about 4 dozen

- 2 pkg. (8 oz. each) cream cheese, softened
- 2 Tbsp. grated lemon zest
- 3 Tbsp. lemon juice
- 1 tsp. lemon extract
- 1 cup confectioners' sugar
- 1 lb. dark chocolate candy coating, melted
- 4 oz. white candy coating, melted

1. In a large bowl, beat the cream cheese, lemon zest, juice and extract. Gradually beat in confectioners' sugar. Cover and freeze for 2 hours.

2. Using a small ice cream scoop, drop mixture by 1-in. balls onto waxed paper-lined baking sheets. Cover and freeze for 1 hour.

3. Working with a few frozen balls at a time, dip into melted chocolate; allow excess to drip off. Place on waxed paper-lined baking sheets. Let stand until set.

4. Spoon the melted candy coating into a heavy-duty resealable plastic bag. Cut a small hole in the corner of the bag; drizzle the coating over candies. Store in the refrigerator; remove just before serving.

RASPBERRY-MOCHA CHOCOLATE BARK

Give classic candy bark a bit of coffee-shop sophistication with crushed chocolate-covered espresso beans. Swirls of raspberry preserves and white baking chips make it even more special.

—Aysha Schurman, Ammon, ID

PREP: 10 min. + chilling • MAKES: 1 lb.

- 1¼ cups white baking chips
- 1 tsp. shortening, divided
- ¼ cup seedless raspberry preserves
- 4 Tbsp. finely crushed chocolate-covered espresso beans, divided
- 1 cup plus 2 Tbsp. dark chocolate chips, divided

1. Line a 9-in. square pan with foil; set aside. In a microwave, melt white baking chips and ½ tsp. shortening; stir until smooth. Spread into prepared pan.

2. Microwave the raspberry preserves in 10- to 20-second intervals until melted; stir until smooth. Drop teaspoonfuls of preserves over top of pan. Cut through the layer with a knife to swirl. Sprinkle with 2 Tbsp. espresso beans. Refrigerate for 10 minutes or until firm.

3. In a microwave, melt 1 cup dark chocolate chips and the remaining shortening; stir until smooth. Spread over the white chocolate layer. Finely chop the remaining dark chocolate chips. Sprinkle chips and the remaining espresso beans over the top. Refrigerate until firm. Break into pieces. Store in an airtight container.

PRETTY PACKAGING IDEAS

Often the most priceless Christmas gifts are your own homemade treats —even better when you present them in seasonal tins or a pretty package. Looking for suggestions?

- Craft stores sell holiday themed papier-mache boxes perfect for gift giving. Stack star-shaped sugar cookies in a star-shaped box lined with waxed paper.

- Look for decorative tins, plates and candy dishes throughout the year at stores, rummage sales and after-Christmas sales. Keep them on hand for last-minute gifts.

- Stack cookies or candies in a wide-mouth canning jar, cover the lid with fabric and screw on the band. (You may want to include the recipe!)

- Wash empty potato chip cans, coffee tins or shortening cans, and decorate the outside with wrapping paper or contact paper, and attach a bow to the lid.

- Wrap sweets in plastic wrap, set a bow on top and tuck the package inside a coffee mug or teacup.

❄ Holiday Helper

If you're melting large batches of chocolate for dipping candy, you can use a slow cooker. Place the chopped chocolate directly in the slow cooker, set the heat to high, cover and cook for 1 hour. Reduce heat to low and continue cooking, covered, for an additional hour or until completely melted, stirring every 15 minutes. The slow cooker will keep the chocolate warm and liquid until you've finished dipping all your candies. (For other methods for melting chocolate, see page 259.)

SALTED PEANUT ROLLS

A Christmas gift of homemade candy is always a hit with sweet tooths! I dip these peanut rolls in chocolate, but they're yummy plain, too.
—Elizabeth Hokanson, Arborg, MB

PREP: 1 hour + freezing
MAKES: about 5 dozen

- 1 jar (7 oz.) marshmallow creme
- 2 to 2¼ cups confectioners' sugar, divided
- 1 pkg. (14 oz.) caramels
- 2 Tbsp. water
- 4 cups salted peanuts, chopped
- 2 cups semisweet chocolate chips
- 2 tsp. shortening

1. Line two 15x10x1-in. pans with waxed paper. In a large bowl, beat marshmallow creme and 1 cup confectioners' sugar until blended. Knead in enough of the remaining confectioners' sugar until the mixture is smooth and easy to handle.
2. Divide mixture into four portions. Roll each portion into ½-in.-thick logs. Cut each log crosswise into 1½-in. pieces; place on one prepared pan. Freeze 15 minutes or until firm. Meanwhile, heat caramels and water over low heat until melted, stirring occasionally. Working with one-fourth of the logs at a time, dip in melted caramel, then roll in peanuts. Place on remaining prepared pan. Repeat with the remaining logs. Freeze coated logs until set.
3. In the top of a double boiler or in a metal bowl over barely simmering water, melt chocolate chips and shortening; stir until smooth. Dip bottom of rolls into the melted chocolate; allow excess to drip off. Return to prepared pans. Refrigerate until set. Store between layers of waxed paper in airtight containers at room temperature.

SPICED ALMOND BRITTLE

I like sending homemade goodies to family and friends. When I couldn't decide between brittle and spiced nuts, I combined the two into one tasty bite.
—Leslie Dixon, Boise, ID

PREP: 15 min. • **COOK:** 15 min. + cooling
MAKES: 1¼ lbs.

- 1 cup sugar
- ½ cup light corn syrup
- ¼ cup water
- ¼ tsp. salt
- 1½ cups unblanched almonds
- 2 Tbsp. butter
- ½ tsp. pumpkin pie spice
- ¼ tsp. cayenne pepper
- ¼ tsp. dried rosemary, crushed
- ⅛ tsp. ground nutmeg
- 1 tsp. baking soda

1. Line a 15x10x1-in. pan with parchment paper. (Do not spray or grease.)
2. In a large heavy saucepan, combine sugar, water, corn syrup and salt. Bring to a boil, stirring constantly to dissolve sugar. Using a pastry brush dipped in water, wash down the sides of the pan to eliminate sugar crystals. Cook, without stirring, over medium heat until a candy thermometer reads 260° (hard-ball stage).
3. Stir in almonds, butter and seasonings; cook, stirring frequently, until a candy thermometer reads 300° (hard-crack stage), about 8 minutes longer.
4. Remove from heat; stir in baking soda. (Mixture will foam.) Immediately pour onto the prepared pan, spreading as thin as possible. Cool completely.
5. Break brittle into pieces. Store between layers of waxed paper in airtight containers.

CREAMY CARAMELS,
PAGE 279

HOMEMADE

GIFTS FROM
THE KITCHEN

GINGERBREAD-SPICED SYRUP

Here's a wonderful treat for the season. Stir a tablespoon into coffee, tea or cider; drizzle it over pancakes, hot cereal or yogurt; or use it as a glaze for chicken or pork chops.
—Darlene Brenden, Salem, OR

PREP: 20 min. • COOK: 30 min. + cooling
MAKES: 2 cups

2 cinnamon sticks (3 in.), broken into pieces
16 whole cloves
3 Tbsp. coarsely chopped fresh gingerroot
1 tsp. whole allspice
1 tsp. whole peppercorns
2 cups sugar
2 cups water
2 Tbsp. honey
1 tsp. ground nutmeg

1. Place the first five ingredients on a double thickness of cheesecloth; bring up corners of cloth and tie with string to form a bag.
2. In a large saucepan, combine the sugar, water, honey, nutmeg and spice bag; bring to a boil. Reduce heat; simmer, uncovered, for 30-45 minutes or until syrup reaches the desired consistency.
3. Remove from the heat; cool to room temperature. Discard spice bag; transfer syrup to airtight containers. Store in the refrigerator for up to 1 month.

FAST FIX

BUFFALO WING MUNCH MIX

I jazz up party mix with spicy hot and cool ranch flavors. Serve this mix tableside with hot wings and celery sticks.

—Keri Thompson, Pleasant Hill, IA

TAKES: 20 min. • **MAKES:** 3 qt.

- 4 cups Corn Chex
- 4 cups Wheat Chex
- 2 cups cheddar-flavored snack crackers
- 2 cups potato sticks
- 6 Tbsp. butter, melted
- 2 Tbsp. hot pepper sauce
- 1 Tbsp. Worcestershire sauce
- 1 envelope ranch salad dressing mix
- ⅛ tsp. cayenne pepper

1. In a large bowl, combine the cereals, crackers and potato sticks. Combine the butter, pepper sauce and Worcestershire sauce. Drizzle over cereal mixture and toss to coat. Sprinkle with salad dressing mix and cayenne; toss to coat.

2. Microwave half of mixture on high for 2 minutes, stirring once. Spread onto waxed paper to cool. Repeat. Store in an airtight container.

❄ Reader Review

"This is my favorite game-day snack mix! So easy and delicious!"

ANGEL182009 TASTEOFHOME.COM

Recipe for . . . . spice
1 tsp. . . . . 3 tbsp wa . . .
3/4 . . . . . . vinegar
. . . . ple syrup
. . . c. . . . ple syrup

FRENCH MUSTARD

Have grill masters on your Christmas list? Consider giving them a special homemade mustard flavored with maple syrup, allspice and turmeric. Everyone just loves it.

—Lorraine Caland, Shuniah, ON

PREP: 15 min. • COOK: 30 min. + chilling
MAKES: 1 cup

- 1 tsp. whole allspice
- ¾ cup plus 3 Tbsp. water, divided
- ½ cup white vinegar
- ¼ cup maple syrup
- 1 Tbsp. all-purpose flour
- 1 Tbsp. cornstarch
- 2 tsp. ground mustard
- 1 tsp. ground turmeric
- ¾ tsp. salt

1. Place allspice on a double thickness of cheesecloth. Gather the corners of the cloth to enclose seasonings; tie securely with string. In a small bowl, mix ¾ cup water, vinegar and maple syrup until blended. In a small saucepan, mix flour, cornstarch, mustard, turmeric, salt and remaining water until smooth. Gradually whisk in vinegar mixture. Add spice bag; bring to a boil. Reduce heat and simmer, uncovered, for 25-30 minutes or until thickened, stirring occasionally.
2. Discard spice bag. Transfer to a covered container; cool slightly. Refrigerate until cold. Store in refrigerator for up to 1 month.

❄ Holiday Helper

Ground mustard is also called dry mustard or ground mustard seed. There are three types of mustard seeds—white/yellow, brown and black. Of the dry mustards available in the United States, English dry mustard uses mostly yellow seeds with some brown; Chinese dry mustard uses brown and black seeds and is spicier.

CREAMY CARAMELS

I discovered this recipe in a local newspaper years ago and have made these soft caramels ever since. I make them for Christmas, picnics and charity auctions—they're so much better and butterier than store-bought.

—Marcie Wolfe, Williamsburg, VA

PREP: 10 min. • COOK: 30 min. + cooling
MAKES: 2½ lbs.

- 1 tsp. plus 1 cup butter, divided
- 1 cup sugar
- 1 cup dark corn syrup
- 1 can (14 oz.) sweetened condensed milk
- 1 tsp. vanilla extract

1. Line an 8-in. square pan with foil; grease the foil with 1 tsp. butter and set aside.
2. In a large heavy saucepan, combine sugar, corn syrup and remaining butter; bring to a boil over medium heat, stirring constantly. Boil slowly for 4 minutes without stirring.
3. Remove from heat; stir in milk. Reduce heat to medium-low and cook until a candy thermometer reads 238° (soft-ball stage), stirring constantly. Remove from the heat; stir in vanilla.
4. Pour into prepared pan (do not scrape saucepan). Cool. Using foil, lift candy out of pan. Discard foil; cut candy into 1-in. squares. Wrap individually in waxed paper; twist ends.
Note: We recommend that you test your candy thermometer before each use by bringing water to a boil; the thermometer should read 212°. Adjust temperature for recipe up or down based on the test.

FAST FIX

HERBED NUT MIX

If you've ever mixed in fresh herbs with a batch of toasted nuts, then you know what a fantastic gift this treat can be. Plus you can make it in advance and store it in the refrigerator.

—Sonya Labbe, West Hollywood, CA

TAKES: 20 min. • MAKES: 2 cups

- 1 Tbsp. butter
- 1 Tbsp. brown sugar
- 1½ tsp. minced fresh rosemary
- 1½ tsp. minced fresh thyme
- 1 cup salted cashews
- ½ cup pecan halves
- ½ cup whole almonds

1. Preheat oven to 350°. Line a 15x10x1-in. baking pan with foil; grease foil. In a small saucepan, melt butter over medium heat. Stir in brown sugar, rosemary and thyme. Add nuts; toss to coat. Spread mixture into the prepared pan. Bake 10-12 minutes or until toasted.
2. Immediately transfer to waxed paper; cool completely. Store the mixture in an airtight container.
Note: This mix may be frozen for up to 3 months.

MAPLE PEANUT MIX

Maple syrup and butter combine to coat a combination of nuts, pretzels, dried cranberries and chocolate chips. I like adding some crushed red pepper flakes for a bit of heat.

—Sharlene Heatwole, McDowell, VA

....

PREP: 15 min. • **BAKE:** 15 min. + standing
MAKES: 10 cups

- 1   cup maple syrup
- 2   Tbsp. butter, melted
- 6   cups unsalted peanuts
- 1   to 1½ tsp. crushed red pepper flakes, optional
- 2   cups pretzel sticks
- 1   cup dried cranberries
- 1   cup milk chocolate chips

1. Line a 15x10x1-in. baking pan with foil; grease foil and set aside. In a large bowl, combine syrup and butter. Stir in peanuts and, if desired, pepper flakes. Spread into prepared pan. Bake at 350° for 15 minutes or until bubbly, stirring occasionally.
2. Transfer to a large bowl; stir in pretzels and cranberries. Spread the mixture onto waxed paper; sprinkle with chips. Let stand until dry. Store in an airtight container.

AMARETTO-PEACH PRESERVES

Chock-full of peaches, raisins and pecans, this lovely conserve enhances ordinary toast.

—Redawna Kalynchuk, Barrhead, AB

....

PREP: 1¼ hours • **PROCESS:** 5 min.
MAKES: 5 half-pints

- 1   cup golden raisins
- ¾   cup boiling water
- 2   lbs. peaches, peeled and chopped
- 4   tsp. grated orange zest
- ⅓   cup orange juice
- 2   Tbsp. lemon juice
- 3   cups sugar
- ½   cup chopped pecans
- 3   Tbsp. amaretto

1. Place raisins in a small bowl. Cover with boiling water; let stand 5 minutes. Place raisins with liquid in a large saucepan. Add peaches and orange zest. Bring to a boil. Reduce heat; cover and simmer for 10-15 minutes or until peaches are tender.
2. Stir in orange and lemon juices; return to a boil. Add sugar. Cook, uncovered, over medium heat for 25-30 minutes or until thickened, stirring occasionally. Add the pecans; cook 5 minutes longer. Remove from heat; stir in amaretto.
3. Carefully ladle hot mixture into five hot sterilized half-pint jars. Remove air bubbles and adjust headspace, if necessary, by adding hot mixture. Wipe rims. Center lids on jars; screw on bands until fingertip tight.
4. Place jars into canner with simmering water, ensuring that they are completely covered with water. Bring to a boil; process for 5 minutes. Remove jars and cool.
Note: The processing time listed here is for altitudes of 1,000 feet or less. Add 1 minute to the processing time for each 1,000 feet of additional altitude.

MAKE AHEAD
ORANGE-ALMOND CHOCLAVA

A twist on classic baklava, this recipe adds semisweet chocolate to the nut filling and drizzles even more on top.

—Nella Parker, Hersey, MI

....

PREP: 1 hour • **BAKE:** 50 min. + chilling
MAKES: about 6 dozen

- 1   lb. slivered almonds
- 1   cup semisweet chocolate chips
- ¾   cup sugar
- 2   Tbsp. grated orange zest
- 1½ cups butter, melted
- 1   pkg. (16 oz., 14x9-in. sheets) frozen phyllo dough, thawed

SYRUP
- 1¼ cups orange juice
- ¾   cup sugar
- ½   cup honey
- 2   Tbsp. lemon juice

DRIZZLE
- 2   oz. semisweet chocolate, chopped
- 3   Tbsp. water

1. Preheat oven to 325°. Pulse almonds and chocolate chips in a food processor until finely chopped. In a bowl, combine almond mixture, sugar and orange zest. Brush a 15x10x1-in. baking pan with some of the butter.
2. Layer 10 sheets of phyllo in prepared pan; brush each with melted butter. Keep the remaining phyllo covered with plastic wrap and a damp towel to prevent it from drying out. Sprinkle with a third of the almond mixture. Repeat layers twice. Top with remaining phyllo sheets; brush each with butter. Cut into 1-in. diamonds. Bake 50-60 minutes or until golden brown.
3. In a medium saucepan, combine the syrup ingredients; bring to a boil. Reduce heat; simmer, uncovered, 20 minutes. In another heavy saucepan, heat chocolate and water over very low heat until melted and smooth; stir constantly. Pour syrup over warm baklava; drizzle with chocolate mixture. Cool completely in pan on a wire rack. Refrigerate, covered, overnight.

ALMOND TEA BREAD

My aunt brought her tea bread recipe with her from Scotland, and a fresh-baked loaf has become a family mainstay during the holidays. Each slice is loaded with red cherries.

—Kathleen Showers, Briggsdale, CO

PREP: 15 min. • BAKE: 1¼ hours + cooling
MAKES: 2 loaves (16 slices each)

- 1 can (8 oz.) almond paste
- ¼ cup butter, softened
- 1 cup sugar
- 3 large eggs
- 1½ cups fresh pitted cherries or blueberries
- 3 cups all-purpose flour, divided
- 4 tsp. baking powder
- ½ tsp. salt
- ¾ cup whole milk

1. In a large bowl, combine the almond paste and butter; beat until well blended. Gradually add sugar, beating until light and fluffy. Add eggs, one at a time, beating well after each addition. In a small bowl, gently toss cherries and 1 Tbsp. flour. Set aside.
2. Combine the baking powder, salt and remaining flour; add to creamed mixture alternately with milk, beating well after each addition.
3. Spoon a sixth of the batter into each of two greased and floured 8x4-in. loaf pans; sprinkle layers with half of the fruit. Cover with another layer of batter and sprinkle with remaining fruit. Top with remaining batter; smooth with a spatula.
4. Bake at 350° for 1¼ hours or until a toothpick inserted in the center comes out clean. Cool for 10 minutes before removing from pans to wire racks to cool.

CARROT CAKE JAM

For a change of pace from berry jams, try this distinctive option. Spread on a bagel with cream cheese, it tastes almost as good as real carrot cake!

—Rachelle Stratton, Rock Springs, WY

PREP: 45 min. • **PROCESS:** 5 min.
MAKES: 8 half-pints

- 1 can (20 oz.) unsweetened crushed pineapple, undrained
- 1½ cups shredded carrots
- 1½ cups chopped peeled ripe pears
- 3 Tbsp. lemon juice
- 1 tsp. ground cinnamon
- ¼ tsp. ground cloves
- ¼ tsp. ground nutmeg
- 1 pkg. (1¾ oz.) powdered fruit pectin
- 6½ cups sugar

1. Place the first seven ingredients in a large saucepan; bring to a boil. Reduce heat; simmer, covered, until the pears are tender, 15-20 minutes, stirring occasionally. Stir in pectin. Bring to a full rolling boil over high heat, stirring constantly. Stir in sugar; return to a full rolling boil. Boil and stir for 1 minute.

2. Remove from heat; skim off foam. Ladle the hot mixture into eight hot sterilized half-pint jars, leaving ¼-in. headspace. Remove the air bubbles and adjust the headspace, if necessary, by adding hot mixture. Wipe rims. Center lids on jars; screw on bands until fingertip tight.

3. Place jars into canner with simmering water, ensuring that they are completely covered with water. Bring to a boil; process for 5 minutes. Remove jars and cool.

Note: The processing time listed here is for altitudes of 1,000 feet or less. Add 1 minute to the processing time for each 1,000 feet of additional altitude.

SAND ART BROWNIES

A jar of this attractive layered mix produces a yummy batch of fudgy brownies dressed up with chocolate chips and M&M's. If you need a gift for a neighbor or teacher, this is a delicious option.

—Joan Hohwald, Lodi, NY

PREP: 15 min. • **BAKE:** 30 min. + cooling
MAKES: 1 batch (4 cups mix); 16 servings

    1   cup plus 2 Tbsp. all-purpose flour
    ½   tsp. salt
    ½   tsp. baking powder
    ⅓   cup baking cocoa
    ⅔   cup sugar
    ⅔   cup packed brown sugar
    ½   cup semisweet chocolate chips
    ½   cup milk chocolate M&M's
ADDITIONAL INGREDIENTS
    3   large eggs
    ⅔   cup vegetable oil
    1   tsp. vanilla extract

1. Combine flour, salt and baking powder. In a 1-qt. glass container, layer the flour mixture, baking cocoa, sugar, brown sugar, chocolate chips and M&M's, packing well between each layer. Cover and store in a cool, dry place up to 6 months.
2. To prepare brownies: Preheat the oven to 350°. Beat eggs, oil and vanilla. Stir in the brownie mix. Pour into a greased 8-in. square baking dish. Bake until center is set, 26-28 minutes (do not overbake). Cool on a wire rack.

❄ Holiday Helper

When giving a brownie mix as a gift, attach a tag listing the additional ingredients needed and the instructions for making the brownies.

SANTA CLAUS SUGAR COOKIES

My mom taught me how to make these Santa cookies. Use a skewer to make a hole at the top of each cut-out cookie before baking, then hang them on the tree when they're done!

—Ann Bush, Colorado City, CO

PREP: 45 min. + chilling
BAKE: 10 min./batch + cooling
MAKES: about 4 dozen

    1   cup unsalted butter
    1½   cups sugar
    2   large eggs
    1   tsp. vanilla extract
    3½   cups all-purpose flour
    1   tsp. baking soda
    1   tsp. cream of tartar
    ½   tsp. ground nutmeg
    ¼   tsp. salt
FROSTING
    ¾   cup unsalted butter, softened
    6   Tbsp. 2% milk
    2¼   tsp. vanilla extract
    ¼   tsp. salt
    6¾   cups confectioners' sugar
         Decorations: red colored sugar, miniature
            semisweet chocolate chips and Red Hots

1. In a large bowl, cream butter and sugar until light and fluffy. Beat in the eggs and vanilla. In another bowl, whisk flour, baking soda, cream of tartar, nutmeg and salt; gradually beat into creamed mixture.
2. Divide dough in half. Shape each into a disk; wrap in plastic. Refrigerate 1 hour or until firm enough to roll.
3. Preheat oven to 375°. On a lightly floured surface, roll each portion of dough to ¼-in. thickness. Cut with a floured 3-in. Santa-shaped cookie cutter. Place 2 in. apart on greased baking sheets.
4. Bake 8-10 minutes or until light brown. Remove from pans to wire racks to cool completely.
5. For frosting, in a large bowl, beat butter until creamy. Beat in milk, vanilla and salt. Gradually beat in confectioners' sugar until smooth. Pipe onto cookies and decorate as desired.

MAKE AHEAD

CRANBERRY ORANGE VINEGAR

I make an assortment of vinegars, and this is a favorite. The longer the fruits sit in the vinegar, the more intensely flavored it becomes.
—Kathy Rairigh, Milford, IN

PREP: 10 min. + standing • **MAKES:** 6 cups

- 6 cups white wine vinegar
- 1 pkg. (12 oz.) fresh or frozen cranberries, chopped
- 3 medium oranges, sectioned and chopped

1. In a large saucepan, heat vinegar to just below the boiling point. In a large bowl, lightly mash the cranberries and oranges; add heated vinegar. Cover and let stand in a cool dark place for 10 days.

2. Strain mixture through a cheesecloth and discard pulp. Pour into sterilized jars or decorative bottles. Seal tightly. Store in a cool, dark place.

CHUNKY FRUIT & NUT RELISH

I tuck a glass jar of this condiment into holiday baskets. It's delicious with ham or poultry.
—Donna Brockett, Kingfisher, OK

PREP: 5 min. • **COOK:** 10 min. + chilling
MAKES: 6 cups

- 2 pkg. (12 oz. each) fresh or frozen cranberries
- 1½ cups sugar
- 1 cup orange juice
- 1 can (15¼ oz.) sliced peaches, drained and cut up
- 1 cup chopped pecans
- ¾ cup pineapple tidbits
- ½ cup golden raisins

1. In a large saucepan, bring cranberries, sugar and orange juice to a boil, stirring occasionally. Reduce heat; simmer, uncovered, 8-10 minutes or until the cranberries pop.

2. Remove from heat; stir in the peaches, pecans, pineapple and raisins. Cool. Cover and refrigerate at least 3 hours.

SPLIT PEA SOUP MIX

My mother sent me some of this pretty blend along with the recipe. This hearty soup is thick with lentils, barley and peas, and chicken is a nice change from the usual ham.

—Susan Ruckert, Tangent, OR

PREP: 10 min. • **COOK:** 1¼ hours
MAKES: 13 batches; 4 servings (4 cups) per batch

- 1 pkg. (16 oz.) dried green split peas
- 1 pkg. (16 oz.) dried yellow split peas
- 1 pkg. (16 oz.) dried lentils, rinsed
- 1 pkg. (16 oz.) medium pearl barley
- 1 pkg. (12 oz.) alphabet pasta
- 1 jar (½ oz.) dried celery flakes
- ½ cup dried parsley flakes

ADDITIONAL INGREDIENTS
- 4 cups chicken broth
- ¼ tsp. pepper
- 1 cup cubed cooked chicken, optional

1. Combine the first seven ingredients. Transfer to airtight containers, or divide equally among 13 plastic bags. Store in a cool, dry place for up to 1 year.
2. To prepare soup: In a large saucepan, combine 1 cup soup mix with broth, pepper and, if desired, cubed chicken. Bring to a boil. Reduce heat; simmer, covered, until peas and lentils are tender, 1-1¼ hours.

❄ Holiday Helper

To give this soup mix as a gift, pair it with an oversize mug for a teacher, a set of pretty bowls for a friend or a saucepan and cooking utensils for a young adult in their first apartment.

MAKE AHEAD
ROSEMARY-LEMON SEA SALT

Making flavored sea salt is so easy. Mix in grated lemon zest and minced rosemary for a delicious way to enhance chicken, fish and salads.

—Shelley Holman, Scottsdale, AZ

PREP: 5 min. + standing • **MAKES:** about ⅔ cup

- ½ cup sea salt, fine grind
- 1 Tbsp. grated lemon or orange zest
- 1 tsp. minced fresh rosemary or thyme

In a small bowl, combine all ingredients. Spread onto a parchment paper-lined pan. Let stand overnight. Store in an airtight container in a cool, dry place for up to 3 months.

FAST FIX
SWEET & SALTY POPCORN

There's nothing like making memories with grandkids in the kitchen and seeing their excited, happy faces while they help.

—Diane Smith, Pine Mountain, GA

TAKES: 25 min. • **MAKES:** 4 qt.

- 10 cups popped popcorn
- 1 cup broken miniature pretzels
- 1 cup candies of your choice, such as Almond Joy pieces or milk chocolate M&M's
- 1 cup chopped dried pineapple
- 10 oz. white candy coating, coarsely chopped

1. In a large bowl, combine popcorn, pretzels, candies and pineapple. In the microwave, melt candy coating; stir until smooth. Pour over popcorn mixture; toss to coat.
2. Immediately spread onto waxed paper; let stand until set. Break into pieces. Store in airtight containers.

MAKE AHEAD
ALMOND COCONUT KRINGLES

My mom was known for her kringle. She made it from memory and when she passed away, we didn't have the recipe! We found her original starting recipe, and I adjusted the filling ingredients until it came out just right. Try this tender, flaky pastry with its almond and coconut filling, and you'll be hooked!

—Deborah Richmond, Trabuco Canyon, CA

PREP: 1 hour + chilling
BAKE: 25 min. + cooling
MAKES: 4 kringles (9 slices each)

- 2 cups all-purpose flour
- 1 cup cold butter, cubed
- 1 cup sour cream

FILLING
- 1¼ cups butter, softened
- 1 cup packed brown sugar
- 3 cups sliced almonds, toasted
- 1½ cups sweetened shredded coconut, toasted

GLAZE
- 1 cup confectioners' sugar
- 1 Tbsp. butter, softened
- 1 tsp. vanilla extract
- 4 to 6 tsp. 2% milk

1. Place flour in a large bowl; cut in butter until crumbly. Stir in sour cream. Wrap in plastic. Refrigerate overnight.
2. Preheat oven to 375°. In a small bowl, cream butter and brown sugar until light and fluffy. Stir in almonds and coconut.
3. Divide dough into four portions. On a lightly floured surface, roll one portion into a 12x10-in. rectangle. (Keep remaining dough refrigerated until ready to use.) Spread 1 cup filling lengthwise down the center. Fold in sides of pastry to meet in the center; pinch seam to seal. Repeat with remaining dough and filling. Transfer to two ungreased baking sheets. Bake for 23-27 minutes or until lightly browned. Remove to wire racks to cool completely.
4. Meanwhile, combine the confectioners' sugar, butter, vanilla and enough milk to achieve the desired consistency; drizzle over pastries.

CHRISTMAS JAM

A few years ago, I hit upon the idea of presenting family and friends with baskets of homemade jam as gifts. With cherries, cinnamon and cloves, this smells and tastes like Christmas!

—Marilyn Reineman, Stockton, CA

PREP: 40 min. • **PROCESS:** 5 min./batch
MAKES: 12 half-pints

- 3 pkg. (12 oz. each) frozen pitted dark sweet cherries, thawed and coarsely chopped
- 2 cans (8 oz. each) unsweetened crushed pineapple, drained
- 1 pkg. (12 oz.) frozen unsweetened raspberries, thawed
- 9 cups sugar
- ¼ cup lemon juice
- ¼ cup orange juice
- ¼ tsp. ground cinnamon
- ¼ tsp. ground cloves
- ¼ tsp. butter
- 2 pouches (3 oz. each) liquid fruit pectin

1. In a Dutch oven, combine cherries, pineapple and raspberries. Stir in the sugar, juices, cinnamon, cloves and butter. Bring to a full rolling boil over high heat, stirring constantly. Stir in pectin. Continue to boil 1 minute, stirring constantly.
2. Remove from heat; skim off foam. Ladle hot mixture into 12 hot sterilized half-pint jars, leaving ¼-in. headspace. Remove air bubbles and adjust headspace, if necessary, by adding hot mixture. Wipe rims. Center lids on jars; screw on bands until fingertip tight.
3. Place jars into canner with simmering water, ensuring that they are completely covered with water. Bring to a boil; process for 5 minutes. Remove jars and cool.
Note: The processing time listed here is for altitudes of 1,000 feet or less. Add 1 minute to the processing time for each 1,000 feet of additional altitude.

TRIPLE CHOCOLATE COOKIE MIX

Everyone likes a good old-fashioned cookie mix—and this one is especially popular with chocoholics! Tie the preparation and baking directions to the jar with a colorful ribbon.
—Patricia Swart, Galloway, NJ

PREP: 30 min. • **BAKE:** 15 min./batch
MAKES: 1 batch (about 5 cups mix);
5 dozen cookies

2¼ cups all-purpose flour, divided
1 tsp. baking powder
½ tsp. salt
½ tsp. baking soda
½ cup baking cocoa
1 cup packed brown sugar
½ cup sugar
¾ cup semisweet chocolate chips
¾ cup white baking chips

ADDITIONAL INGREDIENTS
¾ cup butter, melted and cooled
3 large eggs
3 tsp. vanilla extract

1. In a small bowl, whisk 1¼ cups flour, baking powder, salt and baking soda. In another bowl, whisk cocoa and the remaining flour. In an airtight 5-cup or larger container, layer half of flour mixture and half of cocoa mixture; repeat. Layer the sugars and chips in the order listed. Cover and store in a cool, dry place for up to 3 months.
2. To prepare cookies: Preheat oven to 350°. In a large bowl, beat butter, eggs and vanilla until well blended. Add cookie mix; mix well.
3. Drop dough by tablespoonfuls 2 in. apart onto ungreased baking sheets. Bake for 12-14 minutes or until firm. Remove from pans to wire racks to cool. Store cookies in an airtight container.

KUMQUAT MARMALADE

I didn't even know what a kumquat was until my husband and I discovered them in southern Florida...now I love using them for marmalade! I always get carried away making it and am happy to share.
—Faye Robinson, Pensacola, FL

PREP: 50 min. • **PROCESS:** 10 min.
MAKES: 7 half-pints

- 1¾ lbs. kumquats
- 1 cup water
- 1 pkg. (1¾ oz.) powdered fruit pectin
- 6½ cups sugar

1. Rinse kumquats; cut in half and remove seeds. Place in a food processor; process until coarsely chopped.
2. In a Dutch oven, combine kumquats and water. Stir in pectin. Bring to a full rolling boil over high heat, stirring constantly. Stir in sugar; return to a full rolling boil. Boil and stir 1 minute.
3. Remove from heat; skim off foam. Ladle the hot mixture into seven hot half-pint jars, leaving ¼-in. headspace. Remove air bubbles and adjust headspace, if necessary, by adding hot mixture. Wipe rims. Center lids on jars; screw on bands until fingertip tight.
4. Place jars into canner with simmering water, ensuring that they are completely covered with water. Bring to a boil; process for 10 minutes. Remove jars and cool.
Note: The processing time listed here is for altitudes of 1,000 feet or less. Add 1 minute to the processing time for each 1,000 feet of additional altitude.

❄ Holiday Helper

Kumquats are small citrus fruits with a very thick, dense skin. Unlike other citrus fruits, the skin of a kumquat is sweet and highly edible; often, it's sweeter than the flesh!

CRANBERRY-NUT GRANOLA

I take care of my fitness buffs with a powerhouse snack of crunchy granola loaded with oats, nuts and fruity goodness.
—Melanie Schreiner, Liverpool, NY

PREP: 25 min. • **BAKE:** 20 min. + cooling
MAKES: 18 cups

- 8 cups old-fashioned oats
- 1½ cups toasted wheat germ
- 1½ cups oat bran
- 1 cup sunflower kernels
- 1 cup coarsely chopped almonds
- 1 cup coarsely chopped pecans
- 1 cup coarsely chopped walnuts
- ¾ cup canola oil
- ½ cup packed brown sugar
- ½ cup honey
- ¼ cup maple syrup
- 3 tsp. ground cinnamon
- 1½ tsp. salt
- 3 tsp. vanilla extract
- 2 cups dried cranberries
- ½ cup sweetened shredded coconut

1. In a large bowl, combine the first seven ingredients. In a small saucepan, combine the oil, brown sugar, honey, maple syrup, cinnamon and salt. Cook and stir over medium heat until the brown sugar is dissolved. Remove from heat; stir in vanilla. Pour over the oat mixture; stir to coat.
2. Transfer to two parchment paper-lined 15x10x1-in. baking pans. Bake at 325° for 20-25 minutes or until crisp, stirring once. Cool completely on a wire rack. Stir in the cranberries and coconut. Store granola in an airtight container.

MAKE AHEAD
APPLE BRANDY

I spend a lot of time developing recipes for the many fruits and vegetables we grow on our farm. In this creation, brandy is enhanced with apples and spices for a delightful drink.
—Deanna Seippel, Lancaster, WI

PREP: 35 min. + standing • **MAKES:** 2 qt.

- 4 cups sugar
- 2 cups water
- 4 lbs. apples, sliced
- 1 liter brandy
- 3 whole cloves
- 1 cinnamon stick (3 in.)
  Additional whole cloves and cinnamon sticks

1. Combine sugar and water in a large saucepan. Bring to a boil; cook and stir until sugar is dissolved. Remove from heat.
2. Place apples in a large glass or plastic container; add the sugar mixture, brandy, cloves and cinnamon stick. Cover and let stand at room temperature for at least two weeks, stirring once a week.
3. Strain brandy mixture; discard apples and spices. Pour into glass bottles. Place additional three cloves and one cinnamon stick in each bottle.

HOMEMADE SPICY HOT SAUCE

I created this spicy recipe one day using what I had available from my garden—hot peppers, carrots, onions and garlic. The carrots made this recipe stand out.

—Carolyn Wheel, Fairfax, VT

....

PREP: 45 min. • PROCESS: 10 min.
MAKES: 5 half-pints

- 20 habanero peppers (4½ oz.)
- 5 serrano peppers (2½ oz.)
- 15 dried arbol chiles
- 2 large carrots (5½ oz.), peeled, halved lengthwise and quartered
- 1 large sweet onion (15 oz.), cut into eight wedges
- 8 garlic cloves, halved
- 1 cup water
- ¾ cup white vinegar (minimum 5% acetic acid)
- ½ cup fresh lime juice
- 3 tsp. salt
- 1 tsp. coarsely ground pepper

1. Cut habanero and serrano peppers in half; discard stems and seeds. In a bowl, combine arbol chiles and enough boiling water to cover. Let stand, covered, for 10 minutes, then drain.
2. Meanwhile, in a well-ventilated area, fill a 6-qt. stockpot three-quarters full with water; bring to a boil. Add carrots, onion and garlic. Return to a boil; cook until soft, 20-22 minutes. Remove with a slotted spoon to a bowl. Add peppers to stockpot; return to a boil. Boil 1 minute; drain. Place water, vinegar, lime juice, salt and pepper in a blender. Add vegetables; cover and process until smooth. Return to stockpot; bring to a boil.
3. Carefully ladle the mixture into five hot half-pint jars, leaving ½-in. headspace. Remove air bubbles and adjust headspace, if necessary, by adding hot mixture. Wipe rims. Center lids on jars; screw on bands until fingertip tight.
4. Place jars into canner with simmering water, ensuring that they are completely covered with water. Bring to a boil; process for 10 minutes. Remove jars and cool.
Note: Wear disposable gloves when cutting hot peppers; the oils can burn skin. Avoid touching your face.

CINNAMON SUGAR CRACKLE COOKIES

Gift boxes filled with my crackle cookies are a tradition during the holiday season. Christmas wouldn't be the same without them!

—Sarah Miller, Wauconda, WA

....

PREP: 20 min. • BAKE: 10 min./batch + cooling
MAKES: about 6 dozen

- 1 cup shortening
- 1¾ cups sugar, divided
- 2 large eggs
- 2¾ cups all-purpose flour
- 2 tsp. cream of tartar
- 1 tsp. baking soda
- ½ tsp. salt
- 4 tsp. ground cinnamon

1. Preheat oven to 400°. In a large bowl, cream shortening and 1½ cups sugar until light and fluffy. Beat in eggs. In another bowl, whisk flour, cream of tartar, baking soda and salt; gradually beat into the creamed mixture.
2. In a small bowl, mix cinnamon and remaining sugar. Shape dough into 1-in. balls; roll in cinnamon sugar. Place 2 in. apart on ungreased baking sheets.
3. Bake 8-10 minutes or until golden brown. Cool 2 minutes before removing to wire racks to cool.

FAST FIX

HOMEMADE CAJUN SEASONING

We in Louisiana love seasoned foods. I use this in gravy, over meats and with salads. It makes an excellent gift for teachers. Many have asked for the recipe.

—Onietta Loewer, Branch, LA

TAKES: 5 min. • **MAKES:** about 3½ cups

- 1 carton (26 oz.) salt
- 2 containers (1 oz. each) cayenne pepper
- ⅓ cup pepper
- ⅓ cup chili powder
- 3 Tbsp. garlic powder

Combine all ingredients; store in airtight containers. Use to season pork, chicken, seafood, steaks or vegetables.

MAKE A GIFT MIX COMBO

Looking for a new way to package gift mixes? Check out transparent ornaments at your local craft store. Load up one or more with a selection of mixes and present them as a set!

WILD RICE STUFFED
SQUASH, PAGE 296

BONUS

THANKSGIVING GATHERING

FAST FIX

APPLE-GOUDA PIGS IN A BLANKET

For special occasions, I used to make beef and cheddar pigs in a blanket, but now I like apple and Gouda for an even better flavor celebration.

—Megan Weiss, Menomonie, WI

TAKES: 30 min. • **MAKES:** 2 dozen

1 tube (8 oz.) refrigerated crescent rolls
1 small apple, peeled and cut into 24 thin slices
6 thin slices Gouda cheese, quartered
24 miniature smoked sausages
Honey mustard salad dressing, optional

1. Preheat oven to 375°. Unroll crescent dough and separate into 8 triangles; cut each lengthwise into 3 thin triangles. On the wide end of each triangle, place 1 slice of apple, 1 folded piece of cheese and 1 sausage; roll up tightly.
2. Place 1 in. apart on parchment paper-lined baking sheets, point side down. Bake until golden brown, 10-12 minutes. If desired, serve with dressing.

WILD RICE STUFFED SQUASH

I made this recipe when we invited both families to celebrate our first Thanksgiving in our new home. There were 37 of us, and everyone who tried this dish raved about it.

—Robin Thompson, Roseville, CA

PREP: 45 min. • **BAKE:** 50 min.
MAKES: 8 servings

4 medium acorn squash (about 22 oz. each)
3 Tbsp. olive oil, divided
1 pkg. (6 oz.) long grain and wild rice mix
2⅓ cups vegetable or chicken broth
1 tsp. rubbed sage
1 tsp. dried thyme
2 celery ribs, chopped
1 medium onion, chopped
¾ cup dried cranberries
½ cup coarsely chopped pecan halves, toasted
2 Tbsp. minced fresh parsley

1. Preheat oven to 400°. Cut the squash crosswise in half; remove and discard the seeds. Cut a thin slice from bottom of each squash half to allow them to lie flat. Place on baking sheets, hollow side up; brush tops with 2 Tbsp. olive oil. Bake until almost tender, 30-35 minutes.
2. In a large saucepan, combine rice with contents of seasoning mix, the broth, sage and thyme. Bring to a boil. Reduce heat; simmer, covered, until rice is tender and liquid is almost absorbed, 23-25 minutes. Meanwhile, in a large skillet, saute celery and onion in the remaining oil until tender. Stir in cranberries, pecans and parsley. Remove from heat. Stir in the rice mixture.
3. Fill each squash half with about ½ cup rice mixture. Return to oven, uncovered, until rice is heated through and the squash is tender, 12-15 minutes.

CREAMY PARMESAN SPINACH BAKE

This creamy, comforting side dish wonderfully rounds out Thanksgiving dinner. Just a little of this rich casserole goes a long way.

—Jennifer Bley, Austin, TX

PREP: 35 min. • **BAKE:** 20 min.
MAKES: 12 servings

3 pkg. (9 oz. each) fresh baby spinach
1 small red onion, chopped
1 Tbsp. butter
1 pkg. (8 oz.) cream cheese, cubed
1 cup sour cream
½ cup half-and-half cream
⅓ cup plus 3 Tbsp. grated Parmesan cheese, divided
3 garlic cloves, minced
⅛ tsp. pepper
2 cans (14 oz. each) water-packed artichoke hearts, rinsed, drained and chopped
1 Tbsp. snipped fresh dill
¼ tsp. seasoned salt
8 butter-flavored crackers, coarsely crushed

1. Preheat oven to 350°. Place half of the spinach in a steamer basket; place in a large saucepan over 1 in. of water. Bring to a boil; cover and steam for 3-4 minutes or just until wilted. Transfer to a large bowl. Repeat with remaining spinach; set aside.
2. In a large saucepan, saute onion in butter until tender. Reduce heat to low; stir in cream cheese, sour cream, half-and-half, ⅓ cup Parmesan cheese, the garlic and pepper. Cook and stir until the cream cheese is melted. Stir in artichokes, dill, seasoned salt and spinach.
3. Transfer to an ungreased 2-qt. baking dish. Sprinkle with cracker crumbs and the remaining Parmesan cheese. Bake, uncovered, for 20-25 minutes or until edges are bubbly.

SPICED SWEET POTATO SOUP

Sweet potatoes that simmer in a pot with ginger, cinnamon and curry make a cheerful soup that warms our spirits.
—Lisa Speer, Palm Beach, FL

PREP: 20 min. • **COOK:** 6 hours
MAKES: 12 servings (2¼ qt.)

- 2 lbs. sweet potatoes (about 4 medium), peeled and chopped
- 1 large sweet onion, finely chopped
- 1 medium sweet red pepper, finely chopped
- 1½ tsp. curry powder
- 1 tsp. sea salt
- ½ tsp. ground cinnamon
- ¼ tsp. ground ginger
- ¼ tsp. ground allspice
- ¼ tsp. grated lemon zest
- ⅛ tsp. coarsely ground pepper
- 6 cups reduced-sodium chicken broth
  Salted pumpkin seeds or pepitas, optional

1. In a 5-qt. slow cooker, combine the first 11 ingredients. Cook, covered, on low for 6-8 hours or until vegetables are tender.
2. Puree soup using an immersion blender. Or cool soup slightly and puree in batches in a blender; return to slow cooker and heat through. If desired, top servings with the pumpkin seeds.

❄ Reader Review

"This soup is lovely...so very creamy! We like a lot of spice, so we grated about 3 inches of fresh ginger and added it with 4 large grated carrots. Fantastic recipe!"

LAURA TASTEOFHOME.COM

EASY YEAST ROLLS

If you've never made homemade yeast bread, this simple dough is the perfect place to start. You can easily cut the recipe in half. These tender dinner rolls disappear in no time!

—Wilma Harter, Witten, SD

....

PREP: 45 min. + rising • **BAKE:** 15 min.
MAKES: 4 dozen

  2   pkg. (¼ oz. each) active dry yeast
  2   cups warm water (110° to 115°)
  ½   cup sugar
  1   large egg
  ¼   cup canola oil
  2   tsp. salt
  6   to 6½ cups all-purpose flour

1. In a small bowl, dissolve yeast in warm water. In a large bowl, combine sugar, egg, oil, salt, yeast mixture and 4 cups of flour; beat on medium speed until smooth. Stir in enough of the remaining flour to form a stiff dough.

2. Turn the dough onto a floured surface; knead until smooth and elastic, about 6-8 minutes. Place in a greased bowl, turning once to grease the top. Cover with plastic wrap and let rise in a warm place until doubled, about 1 hour.

3. Punch down dough. Turn onto a lightly floured surface; divide into 4 portions. Divide and shape each portion into 12 balls. Roll each ball into an 8-in. rope; tie into a loose knot. Tuck ends under. Place 2 in. apart on greased baking sheets. Cover with kitchen towels; let rise in a warm place until doubled, about 30 minutes. Preheat oven to 350°.

4. Bake 15-20 minutes or until golden brown. Remove from pans to wire racks.

FAST FIX

POMEGRANATE-HAZELNUT ROASTED BRUSSELS SPROUTS

I converted many people to Brussels sprouts with this recipe! The richness of the hazelnuts and the sweetness of pomegranate and orange elevate the sprouts to a new level.

—Melanie Stevenson, Reading, PA

....

TAKES: 25 min. • **MAKES:** 8 servings

  2   lbs. fresh Brussels sprouts, trimmed and
      halved
  ¼   cup olive oil
1½   tsp. kosher salt
  1   tsp. coarsely ground pepper
  6   Tbsp. butter, cubed
  ⅔   cup chopped hazelnuts, toasted
  1   Tbsp. grated orange peel
  ½   cup pomegranate seeds

1. Preheat oven to 400°. Place Brussels sprouts in a foil-lined 15x10x1-in. baking pan. Drizzle with oil; sprinkle with salt and pepper. Toss to coat. Roast 15-20 minutes or until tender, stirring occasionally. Remove from oven.

2. Meanwhile, in a small heavy saucepan, melt butter over medium heat. Heat for 5-7 minutes or until golden brown, stirring constantly. Remove from heat; drizzle over the Brussels sprouts. Add hazelnuts and orange peel; gently toss to coat. Transfer to a serving bowl. Just before serving, sprinkle with pomegranate seeds.

ROASTED VEGETABLES WITH SAGE

When I can't decide what veggie to serve, I just roast a bunch. That's how we boost veggie love at our house.

—Betty Fulks, Onia, AR

PREP: 20 min. • BAKE: 35 min.
MAKES: 8 servings

- 5   cups cubed peeled butternut squash
- ½ lb. fingerling potatoes (about 2 cups)
- 1   cup fresh Brussels sprouts, halved
- 1   cup fresh baby carrots
- 3   Tbsp. butter
- 1   Tbsp. minced fresh sage or 1 tsp. dried sage leaves
- 1   garlic clove, minced
- ½ tsp. salt

1. Preheat oven to 425°. Place vegetables in a large bowl. In a microwave, melt butter; stir in the remaining ingredients. Add to vegetables and toss to coat.
2. Transfer to a greased 15x10x1-in. baking pan. Roast 35-45 minutes or until tender, stirring occasionally.

❄ Reader Review

"Our family loved this wonderful mixture of vegetables with sage butter. The recipe may say it serves 8, but after my husband and one son went back for seconds, there was nary a scrap of it left!"

LSHAW@SCSK12.ORG TASTEOFHOME.COM

BEST-EVER STUFFED MUSHROOMS

Every Christmas Eve, I bring out a platter of my fresh-from-the-oven mushrooms. If you want a change, try fixing the sausage filling all by itself—it's good spread on baguette slices and crackers.

—Debby Beard, Eagle, CO

PREP: 20 min. • **BAKE:** 15 min.
MAKES: 2½ dozen

- 1   lb. bulk pork sausage
- ¼   cup finely chopped onion
- 1   garlic clove, minced
- 1   pkg. (8 oz.) reduced-fat cream cheese
- ¼   cup shredded Parmesan cheese
- ⅓   cup seasoned bread crumbs
- 3   tsp. dried basil
- 1½ tsp. dried parsley flakes
- 30 large fresh mushrooms (about 1½ lbs.), stems removed
- 3   Tbsp. butter, melted

1. Preheat oven to 400°. In a large skillet, cook the sausage, onion and garlic over medium heat 6-8 minutes or until sausage is no longer pink and the onion is tender, breaking up sausage into crumbles; drain. Add cream cheese and Parmesan cheese; cook and stir until melted. Stir in the bread crumbs, basil and parsley.
2. Meanwhile, place mushroom caps in a greased 15x10x1-in. baking pan, stem side up. Brush with butter. Spoon the sausage mixture into the mushroom caps. Bake, uncovered, for 12-15 minutes or until the mushrooms are tender.

CRANBERRY-PECAN BRIE CUPS

These appetizer cups are custom-made for entertaining since you can make them ahead of time and refrigerate until you're ready to pop them in the oven. You can serve them hot right out of the oven or at room temperature—whatever works best.

—Trisha Kruse, Eagle, ID

PREP: 25 min. • **BAKE:** 10 min. • **MAKES:** 2 dozen

- 24 wonton wrappers
     Cooking spray
- 1   cup whole-berry cranberry sauce
- ¼   cup orange marmalade
- ¼   cup honey
- 2   Tbsp. brandy
- ½   tsp. ground ginger
- ½   tsp. apple pie spice
- ½   lb. Brie cheese (rind removed), cut into 24 pieces
- ½   cup chopped pecans

1. Preheat oven to 350°. Press wonton wrappers into miniature muffin cups coated with cooking spray. Spritz wrappers with cooking spray. Bake 6-8 minutes or until edges begin to brown.
2. Meanwhile, in a small saucepan, combine cranberry sauce, marmalade, honey, brandy and spices; heat through over medium heat, stirring frequently. Remove from heat.
3. Divide cheese among wonton cups; top with cranberry mixture. Sprinkle with pecans. Bake 8-10 minutes or until heated through and wrappers are golden brown.

LEMON & THYME ROASTED CHICKEN

Lemon and thyme go together beautifully, so I decided to roast a chicken with that combo. The seasoning is simple, and the meat comes out moist and tender.

—Pam Nelson, Beaverton, OR

....

PREP: 25 min. • **BAKE:** 1½ hours + standing
MAKES: 6 servings

- 1 Tbsp. minced fresh thyme or 1 tsp. dried thyme
- 1 tsp. sea salt
- ¼ tsp. garlic powder
- ¼ tsp. coarsely ground pepper
- 1 roasting chicken (5 to 6 lbs.)
- 1 medium lemon, halved
- ¼ large sweet onion
- ¼ cup fresh thyme sprigs
- 6 garlic cloves, peeled
  Lemon wedges

1. Preheat oven to 350°. Mix the minced thyme, salt, garlic powder and pepper. Place the chicken on a rack in a shallow roasting pan, breast side up. Tuck wings under chicken; tie drumsticks together. Squeeze the juice from the lemon halves over the chicken; sprinkle top with the thyme mixture.
2. Loosely stuff chicken with the squeezed lemon halves, onion, thyme sprigs and garlic. Roast for 1½ to 2 hours or until a thermometer inserted in the thickest part of a thigh reads 170°-175°. (Cover chicken loosely with foil if it browns too quickly.)
3. Remove chicken from oven; tent with foil. Let stand 15 minutes before carving. Serve with lemon wedges.

ROASTED ORANGE TURKEY

I like to bake my turkey a little differently every year, so I came up with an orange mixture to rub under the skin. It gives the meat a delicate citrus flavor that seems to taste even better the next day.

—Brenda Brooks, Bowie, MD

PREP: 20 min. • **BAKE:** 3 hours + standing
MAKES: 12 servings

- 1 turkey (12 to 14 lbs.)
- ½ cup butter, softened
- ½ cup packed brown sugar
- ¼ cup grated orange peel
- ½ tsp. ground ginger
- 1 large navel orange, quartered
- 1 large apple, quartered
- 1 small onion, quartered
- 1 cup unsweetened apple juice
- ½ cup orange juice

1. Preheat oven to 325°. Place turkey on a rack in a shallow roasting pan, breast side up. In a small bowl, combine butter, brown sugar, orange peel and ginger. With your fingers, carefully loosen skin from turkey breast; rub some of the butter mixture under skin. Secure skin to the underside of the breast with toothpicks.
2. Rub the remaining butter mixture inside the turkey cavity; fill with orange, apple and onion. Tuck the wings under the turkey; tie the drumsticks together. Carefully pour juices over the turkey.
3. Bake, uncovered, for 3-3¾ hours or until a thermometer inserted in thickest part of thigh reads 170°-175°, basting turkey occasionally with pan drippings. Cover loosely with foil if turkey browns too quickly.
4. Cover and let stand 20 minutes before carving. Discard fruit and onion from cavity. Skim fat and thicken pan juices if desired.

SAUSAGE BREAD DRESSING

My husband and father go crazy for this dressing. Leftovers are rare, but they freeze quite well. To save time, chop the veggies and prepare (but don't bake) the dressing up to two days ahead of time and refrigerate. Add a little baking time since it will be cold.

—Bette Votral, Bethlehem, PA

PREP: 30 min. • **BAKE:** 40 min.
MAKES: about 12 cups

- 4 cups seasoned stuffing cubes
- 1 cup corn bread stuffing mix (about 3 oz.)
- ½ lb. bulk Italian sausage
- 1 large onion, chopped
- 3 Tbsp. butter
- 1 large tart apple, peeled and chopped
- 1⅓ cups sliced fresh shiitake mushrooms (about 4 oz.)
- 1¼ cups sliced fresh mushrooms (about 4 oz.)
- 1 celery rib, chopped
- ½ cup minced fresh parsley
- 1 Tbsp. fresh sage or 1 tsp. dried sage leaves
- ⅛ tsp. salt
- ⅛ tsp. pepper
- 1 can (14½ oz.) chicken broth
- 1 cup pecan halves

1. Preheat oven to 325°. In a large bowl, combine stuffing cubes and stuffing mix.
2. In a large skillet, cook sausage and onion over medium heat for 4-6 minutes or until the sausage is no longer pink, breaking up sausage into crumbles. Remove from pan with a slotted spoon and add to the stuffing mixture.
3. Add butter to the same pan. Add apple, mushrooms and celery; cook and stir over medium-high heat until mushrooms are tender. Stir in the parsley, sage, salt and pepper. Stir into the stuffing mixture. Stir in broth and pecans.
4. Transfer to a greased 3-qt. baking dish. Bake, covered, 30 minutes. Uncover; bake 10 minutes longer or until lightly browned.

GIBLET TURKEY GRAVY

Gravy enhanced with giblets is traditional in our house. Try this hearty gravy with sage and a dash of wine; I think you'll love it, too.

—Jeff Locke, Arma, KS

TAKES: 25 min.
MAKES: 16 servings

- ¼ cup cornstarch
- 4 cups chicken stock, divided
- 1 Tbsp. butter
- 1 Tbsp. olive oil
  Giblets from 1 turkey, finely chopped
- ½ cup dry white wine or additional chicken stock
- 2 Tbsp. minced fresh sage or 2 tsp. dried sage leaves
- ¼ tsp. salt
- ¼ tsp. pepper

1. In a small bowl, mix cornstarch and ½ cup of stock until smooth. In a large saucepan, heat the butter and oil over medium-high heat. Add giblets; cook and stir 5-8 minutes or until browned.
2. Add wine and sage to pan; cook for 3-5 minutes, stirring to loosen browned bits from pan. Add the remaining stock; bring to a boil. Stir in the cornstarch mixture; return to a boil. Reduce heat; simmer 3-5 minutes or until thickened to desired consistency, stirring occasionally. Stir in salt and pepper.

CHEDDAR CORN BISCUITS

Everyone asks for my biscuits with cheddar and corn, especially when I serve soup. Leftovers are great with butter and jam!

—Susan Braun, Swift Current, SK

PREP: 20 min. • **BAKE:** 20 min.
MAKES: 16 biscuits

- 4¼ cups all-purpose flour
- 2 Tbsp. baking powder
- 1 tsp. ground mustard
- ¾ tsp. salt
- ¾ cup cold butter, cubed
- 1 can (14¾ oz.) cream-style corn
- 1½ cups shredded cheddar cheese
- 2 large eggs, lightly beaten
- 2 Tbsp. 2% milk

1. Preheat oven to 425°. In a large bowl, whisk flour, baking powder, mustard and salt. Cut in butter until mixture resembles coarse crumbs. Add corn, cheese and eggs; stir just until moistened.
2. Turn onto a lightly floured surface; knead gently 8-10 times. Pat or roll dough to 1-in. thickness; cut with a floured 2½-in. biscuit cutter. Place 2 in. apart on ungreased baking sheets; brush with milk. Bake 18-22 minutes or until golden brown. Serve warm.

FAST FIX

CHIVE BUTTERED CARROTS

It's nice to have a reliable side dish like this that pairs well with any entree. A friend shared the recipe with me several years ago, and now I use it all the time.

—Opal Snell, Jamestown, OH

TAKES: 25 min. • **MAKES:** 8 servings

- 2½ lbs. carrots, diagonally sliced ½ in. thick
- 6 Tbsp. butter, cubed
- ¼ to ½ tsp. seasoned salt
- ¼ tsp. pepper
- 1 to 2 Tbsp. minced fresh chives

1. Place 1 in. of water and carrots in a large saucepan; bring to a boil. Cook, covered, for 3-4 minutes or until crisp-tender. Drain well.
2. In a large skillet, heat butter over medium-high heat. Add the carrots, seasoned salt and pepper; cook and stir for 1-2 minutes or until the carrots are tender. Sprinkle with chives.

FAST FIX

BUTTERMILK SMASHED POTATOES

Our family loves this luscious and decadent recipe with buttermilk, potatoes and butter Serve with your favorite toppings and indulge or skip the sour cream and bacon!

—Marla Clark, Albuquerque, NM

TAKES: 30 min. • **MAKES:** 8 servings

- 4 lbs. Yukon Gold potatoes, peeled and cubed (about 8 cups)
- ½ cup butter, softened
- 1¼ tsp. salt
- ¼ tsp. pepper
- ¾ to 1 cup buttermilk
  Optional toppings: crumbled cooked bacon, sour cream and thinly sliced green onions

1. Place potatoes in a 6-qt. stockpot; add water to cover. Bring to a boil. Reduce heat; cook, uncovered, 10-15 minutes or until potatoes are tender.
2. Drain; return to pan. Mash potatoes, gradually adding butter, salt, pepper and enough buttermilk to reach the desired consistency. Serve potatoes with toppings as desired.

❄ Holiday Helper

To help alleviate the last-minute rush when cooking for a crowd at the holidays, you can prepare mashed potatoes in advance. Mash them 1-2 hours ahead of time, and then put them in a slow cooker on low. They'll stay piping hot until serving time.

DIJON SCALLOPED POTATOES

My family loves cheesy potatoes. I was so happy to find this recipe using both sweet potatoes and russet potatoes for something a little different.

—Carolyn Putnam, Norwalk, OH

PREP: 25 min. • **BAKE:** 50 min. + standing
MAKES: 8 servings

- ⅔ cup chopped onion
- 2 tsp. canola oil
- 1 can (14½ oz.) chicken broth
- 6 oz. cream cheese, cubed
- 1 Tbsp. Dijon mustard
- 3 medium russet potatoes, peeled and thinly sliced
- 2 medium sweet potatoes, peeled and thinly sliced
- 1½ to 2 cups crushed butter-flavored crackers
- 3 Tbsp. grated Parmesan cheese
- 2 Tbsp. butter, melted
- 2 tsp. minced fresh parsley

1. Preheat oven to 350°. In a Dutch oven, saute onion in oil until tender. Reduce heat to medium; stir in broth, cream cheese and mustard until blended. Remove from heat. Stir in potatoes.
2. Transfer to a 13x9-in. baking dish coated with cooking spray. In a small bowl, combine crushed crackers, Parmesan cheese and butter; sprinkle over the top.
3. Bake, uncovered, 50-60 minutes or until potatoes are tender. Sprinkle with parsley. Let stand 10 minutes before serving.

BOURBON CHOCOLATE PECAN PIE

When my fiance first made this for me, I declared it to be the best pie ever! Creamy chocolate combines with crunchy nuts in a sensuous filling.

—Tanya Taylor, Cary, NC

PREP: 25 min. + chilling
BAKE: 55 min. • MAKES: 8 servings

1¼ cups all-purpose flour
1 Tbsp. sugar
½ tsp. salt
½ cup cold butter
3 to 5 Tbsp. ice water
FILLING
3 large eggs
1 cup packed dark brown sugar
½ cup light corn syrup
½ cup dark corn syrup
¼ cup bourbon
2 Tbsp. butter, melted
½ tsp. salt
1½ cups pecan halves, divided
¾ cup 60% cacao bittersweet chocolate baking chips, divided

1. Combine flour, sugar and salt; cut in butter until crumbly. Gradually add water, tossing with a fork until the dough holds together when pressed. Flatten into a disk. Wrap in plastic; refrigerate until easy to handle, about 1 hour.

2. Preheat oven to 325°. On a floured surface, roll dough to a ⅛-in.-thick circle; transfer to a 9-in. pie plate. Trim dough to ½ in. beyond rim of plate; flute edge.

3. Beat the first seven filling ingredients until blended. Stir in 1 cup pecans and ½ cup chocolate chips. Pour the filling into crust; sprinkle with the remaining pecans and chocolate chips. Bake until crust is golden brown and filling is puffed, 50-60 minutes. Cool completely on a wire rack.

GRANDMA'S CRANBERRY STUFF

What tastes better than the classic combination of turkey and cranberry on Thanksgiving Day? My grandmother's recipe makes the best cranberry sauce to share with your family and friends this holiday.

—Catherine Cassidy, Milwaukee, WI

TAKES: 10 min. • **MAKES:** 3 cups

- 1 medium navel orange
- 1 pkg. (12 oz.) fresh or frozen cranberries, thawed
- 1 cup sugar
- 1 cup chopped walnuts, toasted

Cut the unpeeled orange into wedges, removing any seeds, and place in a food processor. Add cranberries and sugar; pulse until chopped. Add walnuts; pulse just until combined.

Note: To toast nuts, bake in a shallow pan in a 350° oven for 5-10 minutes or cook in a skillet over low heat until lightly browned, stirring occasionally.

❄ Holiday Helper

Leftover cranberry sauce can be safely stored in the refrigerator for 5-7 days. If you're looking for ways to use cranberry sauce after Thanksgiving, try stirring a few tablespoons into hot, cooked oatmeal; or use it to fill apples before baking them—the blend of flavors is delicious!

TWICE-BAKED POTATOES SUPREME

When hosting all our nearby relatives for the holidays, I want to make the meal memorable. One way I do that is with my twice-baked potatoes with a touch of cayenne and topped with Parmesan.

—Ruth Andrewson, Leavenworth, WA

PREP: 15 min. • **BAKE:** 1 hour 20 min.
MAKES: 12 servings

8	large baking potatoes
¼	cup butter, softened
½	tsp. salt
½	tsp. garlic powder
½	tsp. dried oregano
¼	tsp. cayenne pepper
⅛	tsp. celery salt
⅓	to ½ cup whole milk
	Grated Parmesan cheese
	Paprika, optional

1. Preheat oven to 400°. Pierce potatoes with a fork. Bake for 60-70 minutes or until tender. Cut potatoes in half lengthwise; scoop out the pulp, leaving a thin shell. Set 12 shell halves aside (discard the remaining shells or save for another use).
2. Lower oven setting to 350°. In a large bowl, mash pulp; add butter, salt, garlic powder, oregano, cayenne, celery salt and enough milk to reach desired consistency. Pipe or spoon mixture into the shells; place in 2 greased 13x9-in. baking pans. Sprinkle with Parmesan cheese and, if desired, paprika. Bake potatoes, uncovered, for 20-25 minutes or until heated through.

DRIED CHERRY & SAUSAGE DRESSING

Apples and dried cherries add a sweet-tart flavor to my homemade stuffing. It makes a holiday dinner to remember.

—Connie Boll, Chilton, WI

PREP: 40 min. • **BAKE:** 45 min.
MAKES: 20 servings

1	loaf (1 lb.) unsliced Italian bread
¼	cup cherry juice blend or unsweetened apple juice
1	cup dried cherries
1	lb. bulk Italian sausage
2	celery ribs, chopped
1	medium onion, chopped
2	medium Granny Smith apples, chopped
½	cup chopped fresh parsley
½	cup butter, melted
1	tsp. Italian seasoning
1	tsp. fennel seed
1	tsp. rubbed sage
½	tsp. salt
¼	tsp. pepper
2	large eggs
2	cups chicken stock

1. Preheat oven to 375°. Cut bread into 1-in. cubes; transfer to two 15x10x1-in. baking pans. Bake for 10-15 minutes or until toasted. Cool slightly. In a small saucepan, bring juice to a boil. Stir in cherries. Remove from heat; let stand 10 minutes. Drain.
2. Meanwhile, in a large skillet, cook sausage, celery and onion over medium heat for 8-10 minutes or until the sausage is no longer pink and the vegetables are tender, breaking up sausage into crumbles; drain. Transfer to a large bowl; stir in apples, parsley, butter, seasonings, bread cubes and drained cherries. In a small bowl, whisk eggs and stock; pour over bread mixture and toss to coat.
3. Transfer to a greased 13x9-in. baking dish (dish will be full). Bake, covered, 30 minutes. Uncover and bake 15-20 minutes longer or until golden brown.

PEAR CIDER

A wonderful alternative to traditional apple cider, our perfectly spiced, pear-flavored beverage will warm you from head to toe.
—*Taste of Home* Test Kitchen

PREP: 5 min. • **COOK:** 3 hours
MAKES: 20 servings

- 12 cups unsweetened apple juice
- 4 cups pear nectar
- 8 cinnamon sticks (3 in.)
- 1 Tbsp. whole allspice
- 1 Tbsp. whole cloves

1. In a 6-qt. slow cooker, combine juice and nectar. Place the cinnamon sticks, allspice and cloves on a double thickness of cheesecloth; bring up the corners of the cloth and tie with string to form a bag. Place in slow cooker.
2. Cover and cook on low for 3-4 hours or until heated through. Discard spice bag. Serve warm cider in mugs.

MUSHROOM & WILD RICE SOUP

You can tell how much I adore mushrooms by looking at this recipe, which uses four different kinds. The wild rice mix makes it very easy to put this special soup together.
—Mary McVey, Colfax, NC

PREP: 25 min. + standing • **COOK:** 45 min
MAKES: 12 servings (2¼ qt.)

- 2½ cups water
- 1 oz. dried porcini mushrooms
- 1 oz. dried shiitake mushrooms
- 3 Tbsp. butter
- 1 small onion, finely chopped
- ½ lb. sliced fresh mushrooms
- ½ lb. sliced baby portobello mushrooms
- 3 garlic cloves, minced
- 4 cups chicken broth
- 1 pkg. (6 oz.) long grain and wild rice mix
- ½ tsp. salt
- ¼ tsp. white pepper
- ½ cup cold water
- 4 tsp. cornstarch
- 1 cup heavy whipping cream

1. In a small saucepan, bring water to a boil; add dried mushrooms. Remove from the heat; let stand 25-30 minutes or until mushrooms are softened.
2. Using a slotted spoon, remove the mushrooms; rinse. Trim and discard stems from the shiitake mushrooms. Chop mushrooms. Strain soaking liquid through a fine-mesh strainer. Reserve mushrooms and soaking liquid.
3. In a Dutch oven, heat the butter over medium-high heat. Add onion; cook and stir until tender. Add the fresh and baby portobello mushrooms; cook and stir until tender. Add garlic; cook 1 minute longer.
4. Stir in broth, rice mix with contents of seasoning packet, the reserved dried mushrooms and soaking liquid, salt and pepper. Bring to a boil. Reduce heat; simmer, covered, 20-25 minutes or until rice is tender. In a small bowl, mix water and cornstarch until smooth; stir into soup. Bring to a boil; cook and stir 2 minutes or until thickened. Stir in cream; heat through.

COLLARD GREENS & BEANS

I didn't eat southern-style collard greens until a friend gave me a recipe that had bacon along with pinto beans. Now I'm delighted to make greens.
—April Burroughs, Vilonia, AR

PREP: 20 min. • **COOK:** 55 min.
MAKES: 8 servings

- 2 lbs. collard greens
- 3 bacon strips, chopped
- 1 small red onion, chopped
- 2 garlic cloves, minced
- 2½ cups water
- 2 Tbsp. brown sugar
- 1 Tbsp. cider vinegar
- ¾ tsp. salt
- ½ tsp. pepper
- 1 can (15 oz.) pinto beans, rinsed and drained

1. Remove and discard center ribs and stems from collard greens. Cut leaves into 1-in. pieces. In a Dutch oven, cook bacon over medium heat until crisp, stirring occasionally.
2. Add onion and garlic to the bacon and drippings; cook and stir 2 minutes. Add collard greens; cook and stir until they begin to wilt. Stir in water, brown sugar, vinegar, salt and pepper. Bring to a boil. Reduce heat; simmer, covered, for 55-65 minutes or until greens are tender, adding beans during the last 15 minutes.

❄ Holiday Helper

Collard greens, like kale, have a thick center rib that should be removed before cooking. When choosing collards, look for firm, deep green leaves. To store, wrap them in paper towels and place them in a plastic bag in the refrigerator; they'll keep for up to five days.

SOUR CREAM PUMPKIN PIE

This is traditional pumpkin pie—with a twist! I like the zesty orange taste of the sour cream topping paired with the pumpkin custard. When I serve this pie, there's never any left, so you might want to make two!

—Joan Bingham, Cornwall, VT

PREP: 15 min. • **BAKE:** 45 min. + cooling
MAKES: 8 servings

      Pastry for single-crust pie (9 in.)
  2 large eggs
  1 can (15 oz.) solid-pack pumpkin
  1 can (14 oz.) sweetened condensed milk
2½ tsp. grated orange peel, divided
  2 tsp. pumpkin pie spice
  ½ tsp. salt
1¼ cups sour cream
  2 Tbsp. sugar
  2 tsp. thawed orange juice concentrate

1. Preheat oven to 425°. On a lightly floured surface, roll pie dough to a ⅛-in.-thick circle; transfer to a 9-in. pie plate. Trim crust to ½ in. beyond rim of plate; flute edge. Refrigerate while preparing filling.
2. In a large bowl, whisk eggs, pumpkin, milk, 2 tsp. orange peel, pie spice and salt until well blended. Pour into crust. Bake on a lower oven rack 15 minutes. Reduce the oven setting to 350°; bake 25-30 minutes longer or until a knife inserted in the center comes out clean.
3. In a small bowl, mix the sour cream, sugar, orange juice concentrate and the remaining orange peel; spread evenly over the filling. Bake 5 minutes longer or until set. Cool on a wire rack; serve or refrigerate within 2 hours.
Pastry for single-crust pie (9 in.): Combine 1¼ cups all-purpose flour and ¼ tsp. salt; cut in ½ cup cold butter until crumbly. Gradually add 3-5 Tbsp. ice water, tossing with a fork until the dough holds together when pressed. Wrap in plastic wrap and refrigerate 1 hour.

WHITE CHOCOLATE CRANBERRY ALMOND TART

This tart of white chocolate and cranberries is my signature holiday dessert. I also make it for local coffee houses and restaurants—it's the sweet treat they request most often.

—Trisha Kruse, Eagle, ID

PREP: 55 min. • BAKE: 20 min. + chilling
MAKES: 12 servings

- ½ cup slivered almonds, toasted
- 3 Tbsp. sugar
- 1⅔ cups all-purpose flour
- ¼ tsp. salt
- ¼ cup butter, melted
- ¼ cup heavy whipping cream
- ⅔ cup white baking chips

FILLING
- 2 cups fresh or frozen cranberries
- 1 cup sugar
- ½ cup dried cranberries
- ⅓ cup orange juice
- 2 Tbsp. butter

TOPPING
- ⅔ cup white baking chips
- 2 tsp. shortening
- ⅓ cup slivered almonds, toasted

1. Preheat oven to 375°. Place almonds and sugar in a food processor; pulse until almonds are ground. Add flour and salt; pulse until blended. Transfer mixture to a small bowl; stir in melted butter and cream. Press onto the bottom and up sides of an ungreased 9-in. fluted tart pan with removable bottom.

2. Bake 15-18 minutes or until lightly browned. Remove from oven; sprinkle baking chips evenly over bottom. Cool on a wire rack.

3. In a saucepan, combine the filling ingredients; bring to a boil. Reduce heat, simmer, uncovered, 10-15 minutes or until slightly thickened, stirring occasionally. Pour over the baking chips.

4. Bake 20-25 minutes or until the filling is bubbly and crust is golden brown. Cool on a wire rack. Refrigerate 2 hours or until cold.

5. In a microwave, melt the baking chips and shortening; stir until smooth. Drizzle over tart. Sprinkle with almonds.

Note: To toast nuts, bake in a shallow pan in a 350° oven for 5-10 minutes or cook in a skillet over low heat until lightly browned, stirring occasionally.

SPOON BREAD

Enjoy an easy and convenient take on this southern specialty by using the slow cooker. It's an excellent side dish for Thanksgiving, Easter or any special feast.

—*Taste of Home* Test Kitchen

PREP: 20 min. • COOK: 4 hours
MAKES: 8 servings

- 1 pkg. (8 oz.) cream cheese, softened
- 2 Tbsp. sugar
- 2 large eggs, beaten
- 1 cup 2% milk
- 2 Tbsp. butter, melted
- ½ tsp. salt
- ¼ tsp. cayenne pepper
- ⅛ tsp. pepper
- 2 cups frozen corn
- 1 can (14¾ oz.) cream-style corn
- 1 cup yellow cornmeal
- 1 cup shredded Monterey Jack cheese
- 3 green onions, thinly sliced
  Coarsely ground pepper and thinly sliced green onions, optional

1. In a large bowl, beat cream cheese and sugar until smooth. Gradually beat in eggs. Beat in the milk, butter, salt, cayenne and pepper until blended. Stir in the remaining ingredients.

2. Pour into a greased 3-qt. slow cooker. Cover and cook on low for 4-5 hours or until a toothpick inserted in the center comes out clean. If desired, top with additional pepper and green onions.

PLACE OF GRACE UTENSIL HOLDERS

Set out these simple paper utensil holders with a pencil or pen at each place setting so that your guests can reflect on the year's blessings.

Fold one end of a piece of 8½ x 11-in. decorative paper up about 5 in. so that the short end of the fold is on top. Measure 2¼ in. in from each side; mark lightly with pencil. Fold flaps back at measured marks, making a 4-in.-wide front pocket. Overlap the flaps at back and secure with tape or a sticker.

Use letter stamps and an ink pad— or your best penmanship—to write "Count Your Blessings" near the top edge of the pocket. Add numerals to form a list. Using a ruler as guide, make dotted lines next to each numeral with a fine-tip marker. If desired, stamp a holiday-themed decoration near the bottom of the pocket.

RECIPE INDEX

C

DIXON PUBLIC LIBRARY
DIXON ILLINOIS

RECIPE & CRAFT INDEX